D0215548

Introduction to Population Biology

How do plant and animal populations change genetically to evolve and adapt to their local environments? How do populations grow and interact with one another through competition and predation? How does behaviour influence ecology and evolution? *Introduction to Population Biology* covers all these areas and more. Taking a quantitative and Darwinian perspective, the basic theory of population processes is developed using mathematical models. To allow students of biology, ecology and evolution to gain a real understanding of the subject, key features include:

- step-by-step instructions for spreadsheet simulations of many basic equations to explore the outcomes or predictions of models
- worked examples showing how the equations are applied to biological questions
- problem sets together with detailed solutions to help the reader test their understanding
- real-life examples to help the reader relate the theory to the natural world.

DICK NEAL is Professor of Biology at the University of Saskatchewan. His main interests are in population ecology, particularly relating to the breeding biology of small mammals and the ecological impacts of mining. He has taught ecology to undergraduate students for many years, and enjoys helping students to integrate their knowledge of different areas and to be critical in their thinking.

Introduction to Population Biology

Dick Neal

University of Saskatchewan

PUBLISHED BY THE PRESS SYNDICATE OF THE UNIVERSITY OF CAMBRIDGE
The Pitt Building, Trumpington Street, Cambridge, United Kingdom

CAMBRIDGE UNIVERSITY PRESS
The Edinburgh Building, Cambridge, CB2 2RU, UK
40 West 20th Street, New York, NY 10011–4211, USA
477 Williamstown Road, Port Melbourne, VIC 3207, Australia
Ruiz de Alarcón 13, 28014 Madrid, Spain
Dock House, The Waterfront, Cape Town 8001, South Africa

http://www.cambridge.org

© Dick Neal 2004

First published 2004

Printed in the United Kingdom at the University Press, Cambridge

Typefaces Swift 9.5/12.25 pt. and GillSans   *System* LaTeX 2_ε [TB]

A catalogue record for this book is available from the British Library

Library of Congress Cataloguing in Publication data

ISBN 0 521 82537 7 hardback
ISBN 0 521 53223 X paperback

Contents

Preface

This introduction to population biology is based on a 13-week course I have taught at the University of Saskatchewan since 1979. When I developed the course I was inspired by Wilson and Bossert's 1971 book, *A Primer of Population Biology*, by Emlen's 1973 book, *Ecology: An Evolutionary Approach* and by Wilson's 1975 book, *Sociobiology*. It was a revelation to me how these three books used an evolutionary perspective to synthesize such areas as population ecology, population genetics and behavioural ecology, because I had been educated in a tradition where such subjects were taught separately.

Over the past decade I became increasingly frustrated in my attempts to find an appropriate text for my course. There are many superb texts available: encyclopedic texts on either ecology or evolution; more specific texts dealing with population ecology or population genetics or behaviour; and a few texts that cover two of these more specific areas, but to cover the breadth of material I teach would require using parts of two or three of these books. What is disappointing, however, is the lack of any evolutionary perspective in most of the ecology books. This is surprising given that Darwin used various principles of population biology to develop his theory of natural selection: the potential for geometric growth of population numbers, and the limitation of resources that leads to a struggle for existence through the effects of competition, disease, and predation. Thus, most students of ecology and population biology would have little reason to agree with Theodosius Dobzhansky's famous statement 'Nothing in biology makes sense except in the light of evolution.'

The purpose of this book

This book aims to give students a solid introduction to Darwin's theory of natural selection, and then use this as an underlying theme to introduce the basic principles of population ecology, population genetics and some aspects of behavioural ecology. The book is suitable for second- or third-year university students seeking a broad introduction to population biology. It is expected that students will have a background in general biology, Mendelian genetics, algebra and calculus, although the latter is not essential.

The book treats the subject in a quantitative way, developing various mathematical models in a step-by-step manner, and showing how they apply to the real world. This is done in a variety of ways. First, spreadsheet simulations are developed for most of the basic equations so that students can explore the outcomes or predictions of the various models and see how they may change when the variables are altered. Detailed instructions are provided so that students can construct these spreadsheet simulations themselves, using either Quattro

Pro or Excel spreadsheet programs. Second, there are many worked examples in the text to show how the equations are applied to biological questions, and students can test their understanding of this by answering the problems that are provided at the end of many chapters. Detailed solutions of these problems are provided at the end of the book. Third, the analysis of the mathematical models through the use of simulation studies or the solving of simple problems allows us to develop a set of general predictions, conclusions, or principles. Finally, a series of empirical examples are examined to illustrate how well the various principles apply to world around us.

The content of this book

Part I (Chapters 1–3) covers Darwin's theories of evolution, including a biographical sketch outlining the experiences that led to his questioning of the fixity of species, a review of his great synthesis *The Origin of Species*, and finally a more detailed examination of the theory of natural selection.

Part II (Chapters 4 and 5) covers the mathematical models of exponential and logistic growth. These two models occur in various modified forms in models of selection (Chapter 10) and interspecific competition (Chapter 17), and have great heuristic value. They are also highly relevant to Darwin's theory of natural selection in relation to the consequences of overproduction of offspring and the struggle for existence through intraspecific competition.

Part III (Chapters 6–13) covers classical population genetics, mainly for single gene loci with two alleles, but also for polygenic systems (quantitative inheritance). This section makes a quantitative assessment of how mutation, migration, chance and selection effect changes in allelic frequencies to determine whether there is support for Darwin's assertion that natural selection is the main factor guiding evolution.

Part IV (Chapters 14–16) returns to the topic of population growth and examines the effects of age on the basic demographic parameters of birth and death, and then develops both age-structured and state-structured population growth models. This section concludes by giving a brief overview of the evolution of the life-history characteristics of organisms.

Part V (Chapters 17–20) covers the interaction between species and the social behaviour of animals. First, interspecific competition is reviewed, including two-species Lotka–Volterra models both with and without a removal factor operating. The implications of competition and predation on the species composition of communities are also assessed. Then a few predator–prey models are examined, followed by a review of the various ways by which prey reduce the risk of being eaten. The genetic basis of behaviour is briefly examined, followed by a consideration of altruistic acts between relatives and ritualized contests or fighting, two types of behaviour that seem contrary to

Darwin's theory of natural selection. Altruism is explained in terms of inclusive fitness, or kin selection, and ritualized contests are explained by using game theory, which considers the optimum behaviour of an individual in relation to what all the other individuals in the population are doing. Finally, the book concludes with a brief introduction to sexual selection and mating systems in animals.

There is sufficient content to cover a one-semester course on population biology, and I suspect that most students will find it difficult to cover every aspect of the book in that time. Consequently, instructors will be able to pick and choose to some extent, concentrating on some topics and either omitting or briefly reviewing others according to their particular interests and objectives. I hope you will find this book to be a useful introduction to population biology. Colour versions of the photographs in the text and copies of the various spreadsheet programs may be obtained from the following website: http://arts.usask.ca/population/.

Acknowledgements

First and foremost I wish to thank my wife, Jenny, for her help, support and encouragement throughout the development of this book. She read the first crude draft and gave invaluable advice about how it could be improved. Her ability to counter my amazing ability to procrastinate during the revision and publication process really helped to bring this book to fruition.

This book was drafted during an administrative leave from the University of Saskatchewan, and I wish to thank the University for its generous support. I spent most of my leave at the University of Natal, Durban, South Africa. I sincerely thank Professor John Cooke, and the faculty, staff and students in the School of Life and Environmental Science who showed so much interest in my work, and freely gave ideas and help in so many ways. They made my time there both enjoyable and intellectually stimulating.

I also wish to thank my colleagues in the Department of Biology at the University of Saskatchewan who have made it a pleasure to study biology. So many have contributed to this book that it is dangerous to single anyone out. However, I would be remiss not to acknowledge Bill Maher and the late Jan Smith, who helped to mould my approach to population biology during many evenings of animated discussion, and Scott Halpin who has taught the laboratory component of my population biology course for many years and has helped me to better understand the problems that students have with the subject.

I am greatly indebted to those who have given permission to use certain figures in the text: Mr D. W. Miller (Fig. 1.1); Dr Robert Selander (Fig. 7.6 and Table 7.2); Dr Lawrence Cook (Fig. 11.2); Dr Bill Murdoch (Fig. 18.9); Vanessa Bourhis (Fig. 18.12); and Dr Dick Alexander (Fig. 20.6). The various publishers of other figures are acknowledged in the figure legends.

Dennis Dyck and Lianne and Stephen McLeod provided considerable technical help with many of the figures. My students have detected various typographical errors and ambiguities in an earlier version of this text, as well as incorrect answers to some of the problems. I am indebted to Seth Reice who read the complete manuscript and made many constructive suggestions for improvement. Finally, I am particularly grateful to Dr Tracey Sanderson, Commissioning Editor for Biological Sciences, Cambridge University Press, whose support, advice and guidance have been invaluable.

Part I

Evolution by natural selection

Population biology has its roots in many different areas: in taxonomy, in studies of the geographical distribution of organisms, in natural history studies of the habits and interactions between organisms and their environment, in studies of how the characteristics of organisms are inherited from one generation to the next, and in theories which consider how different types of organisms are related by descent. Charles Darwin made a synthesis of these areas in his 1859 book, *The Origin of Species by Means of Natural Selection*, and this provides us with a convenient starting-point for our introduction to population biology.

The theory of evolution by means of natural selection is the most important theory in biology, but with some notable exceptions one would not realize this after reading many of texts in the area of population biology. Thus, it is no accident that we begin this book with an evolutionary bias.

The purpose of the following three chapters is to provide a historical perspective, and also an understanding of the philosophical content, of Charles Darwin's theory of evolution through the process of natural selection. It is important to understand this Darwinian perspective of biology, because it provides a loose framework for the remainder of this book. In the first chapter we will examine some of the early experiences of Darwin, which may have led him to conclude that organisms evolve and are related by descent. In the second chapter we examine his book *The Origin of Species* in more detail to see how he structured his argument for his two theories of evolution: that all organisms are related by descent, and that the main mechanism for this evolutionary change is the process of natural selection. In the third chapter we will examine the theory of natural selection in more detail in an attempt to explain why so many people have had difficulty with the theory since it was first proposed by Darwin more than a century ago.

Chapter 1

Darwin concludes that organisms evolve

Prior to the time of Charles Darwin, there were many fine natural history studies that shed some light on the areas of population ecology and animal behaviour. Studies on population genetics were largely related to the breeding of domesticated animals and plants. Although considerable success had been made in breeding new varieties of many species, how the characteristics of organisms were inherited remained a mystery. Carl Linnaeus had developed the binomial classification system during the previous century and collectors were roaming the globe finding ever more species and plotting the distributions of many species. The astonishing variety of organisms was becoming more and more apparent. There had also been speculation about the evolution of organisms, in fact Charles Darwin's paternal grandfather, Erasmus Darwin, had written on the subject in his book *Zoonomia*, but undoubtedly the most famous theory on this subject was that of Jean Baptiste de Lamarck in 1801. However, these evolutionary ideas had little scientific credence at the time when Charles Darwin was receiving his education. So we may ask: what led Charles Darwin to conclude that organisms had evolved from a common ancestor?

1.1 Charles Darwin: some important early influences (1809–31)

Charles, born in 1809, was the fifth of six children of the physician Robert Darwin and his wife Susannah. When Susannah died in 1817 the household was ruled by the triumvirate of Charles' older sisters, whilst his father was a domineering presence who had little sympathy with the antics of a small boy. One can only imagine what it was like for Charles. After the trauma of his mother's death her name was not even allowed to be mentioned in the household; he had three older sisters who zealously provided him with moral guidance; and over all he had the overwhelming presence of his father who had strong opinions about what Charles should be doing with his life. He escaped by collecting things like minerals, shells and bird's eggs. At least he was praised for this type of endeavour.

As Charles grew older he became close to his elder brother Ras (Erasmus). They overlapped for a period at Shrewsbury School where they were provided with a classical, but somewhat dull, education. The two brothers set up a chemistry lab in the garden shed and had a grand time creating explosions and dreadful smells, in the manner of so many small boys. By the time he was 15 he had taken up shooting and revelled in hunting birds. Charles loved the outdoor life but was not doing well in his school work. His father worried about his lack of ambition and decided that Charles should join his brother, Ras, to study medicine at Edinburgh University. This maintained a family tradition because both Charles's father and grandfather had studied to be physicians at Edinburgh.

Prior to his going it appeared that he had an aptitude for medicine. Charles accompanied his father on his visits to patients throughout the district during the summer of 1825 and by all accounts did well. He kept records, administered prescriptions, and even had a few patients of his own, all under the approving and watchful eye of his father. All seemed to bode well. There would be another generation of physicians in the family.

Charles was to spend two years (1825–7) in Edinburgh. When he joined his brother there, at the tender age of 16, they dutifully went to classes and studied together. However, his interest in medicine slowly withered. Although his chemistry professor, Thomas Hope, was lively and interesting, he found his medical professors to be incredibly dull. His anatomy professor, Alexander Munro III, was rumoured to even use his grandfather's lecture notes on occasion! If true, it would mean that Charles literally heard some of the same material as his own grandfather, another Erasmus Darwin. Charles detested the practical side of anatomy where human cadavers were slowly dissected week by week. However, the final straw was his horror of surgical operations that were performed on patients at a time when there were no general anaesthetics. They were bloody, ghastly affairs, carried on at the utmost speed to shorten the period of pain for the patient. He witnessed two operations, and fled during the second one never to return to an operating theatre. He was just too queasy at the sight of blood to become a physician.

Although Darwin lacked the motivation, and the stomach, to apply himself to the drudgery of learning medicine, he revelled in his natural history pursuits. He and his brother went for walks along the seashore collecting marine invertebrates, and Charles even learned how to do taxidermy from a freed South American slave. However, when his brother left to study anatomy in London at the end of the first year Charles essentially stopped studying medicine and began to study natural history in earnest. The academic year of 1826–7 saw some important developments in his education.

He joined the Plinian Society which was dominated by freethinking students who insisted that all science, biology included, was governed by physical laws, not supernatural forces. There were numerous debates between them and the more orthodox Christians, and so Darwin became familiar with the arguments for and against natural philosophy. The Plinians also did rambles along the shores of the Firth of Forth, and so Darwin had numerous colleagues with whom he could share his interest in natural history.

The most important influence on Darwin, however, was his mentor, Dr Robert Grant, who was an expert on sponges (Porifera). Grant was a radical freethinker and a convinced evolutionist. On their walks along the seashore collecting marine life they discussed the evolutionary ideas of Lamarck and Erasmus Darwin. More particularly, Grant introduced Charles to a more scientific approach to the study of natural history and how it could be used to investigate evolutionary questions. Grant collected and kept alive many curious marine invertebrates, including sponges, sea-mats (phylum Bryozoa) and sea-pens (phylum Cnidaria). He was particularly interested in their eggs and larvae and their microscopic structure. He was able to show that sponges had characteristics common to both plants and animals and so could be near the root of the animal and plant kingdoms. With Darwin's help, he also showed that many different phyla possessed similar free-swimming ciliated larvae, which suggested links between the different groups. Grant was convinced that all organisms were related by descent and his comparative studies of lowly invertebrates showed possible links between the various phyla and kingdoms. Darwin did not appear to be impressed by Grant's conclusions but one wonders how this experience may have influenced his later thinking about evolution. Darwin made a few discoveries of his own that were referred to by Grant in his work, but it is clear that he was a little disenchanted by Grant stealing his observations. Darwin, however, was to form a habit of working closely with senior scientists and learning the art of scientific investigation.

Finally, another important influence on Darwin during his studies at Edinburgh was the natural history course given by the Regius Professor of Natural History, Robert Jameson, who had founded the Plinian Society in 1823. The course dealt with the emerging science of geology, and how to interpret the various rock strata. Jameson believed, and taught, that the various rock strata had been precipitated from the ocean, but Darwin had already been taught that the rocks had been crystallized from molten magma by his chemistry professor, Thomas Hope. Darwin believed Hope's views rather than Jameson's, because Jameson was a very boring lecturer. However, Jameson taught the practical side of geology well, showing his students the various minerals in the museum and taking them on field trips to see the various rock strata in situ. Darwin learned the sequence of rock strata and how to recognize them. The course helped to broaden Darwin's viewpoint on natural history but he found the subject of geology so boring that he never wanted to study it again.

When he left Edinburgh in April of his second year, it was clear that his medical studies were at an end. He made a trip to France with some of his Plinian Society friends, with his sister Caroline to keep him out of mischief, all paid for by his father, of course. Then it was off to Shropshire in England to hobnob with the local squires and plan for the autumn shoot which would start 1 September. His father's patience was finally wearing thin. When Charles returned to Shrewsbury to face the music, his father angrily told him 'You care for nothing but shooting, dogs, and rat-catching, and you will be a disgrace to you and your family'![1] Charles was suitably chastened and humbled.

One can sympathize with his father's concern. Charles seemed to have little ambition other than natural history, and indulging in hunting and shooting. His father certainly didn't want a son who was dependent on him for his livelihood. What possible career could there be? Once again his father would dictate Charles's future, deciding that he would become a vicar in the Church of England. In many respects this was a sensible decision because vicars with interests in natural history and shooting were common. But first there were two hurdles to overcome. Charles was not particularly religious and neither was he a hypocrite, so he had to persuade himself that he could believe in the doctrines of the Anglican Church. He was able to do this after reading, among others, the Reverend Sumner's book, *The Evidences of Christianity*. Secondly, he had to brush up his Greek and Latin because he had forgotten most of what he had learned at Shrewsbury School. His father hired a tutor to help with this task and this delayed his departure to Christ's College, Cambridge until the start of 1828, where he would read for a B.A. in Natural Theology. He would be at Cambridge for much of the next four years (1828–31).

He nearly failed again. As usual he started with good intentions, but the subject matter he had to learn in order to become a parson wasn't exactly riveting compared to natural history. At that time the nation was being swept by a passion for collecting beetles and Darwin joined in the fad in earnest. He avidly collected beetles, when he should have been studying, and during his time at Cambridge built up a very fine collection. He even hired locals to collect for him until he discovered them selling the rarer specimens to a fellow student first, presumably for a better price! There was also a technical and academic side to this hobby. Beetles had to be identified, and their habits known if one was to build a superior collection. When the books failed him, he could ask other beetle fanatics at the university. He took up with his cousin William Darwin Fox, another beetle enthusiast, who introduced him to the Friday night discussions at the home of the Reverend John Stevens Henslow, professor of botany, where undergraduates and professors would mingle. There he met some of the great scientists of the day, such as Adam Sedgwick, professor of geology, and William Whewell, the new professor of mineralogy.

---

[1] Some biographies indicate that this comment was made at the end of Charles's schooling at Shrewsbury; before going to study medicine in Edinburgh rather than after.

Unfortunately, his initial efforts at studying for his degree didn't last and he started to miss lectures again and slowly drifted away from Henslow's discussion group. His lack of direction, similar to his history at Edinburgh, was all too evident. By the middle of his second year at Cambridge his tutor warned him that he was not prepared for his preliminary exam, which was scheduled for March of 1830. Darwin was depressed and probably afraid of what his father would say if he failed again. He began to apply himself to his studies in a more disciplined way in the autumn of 1829. He was fortunate in that the curriculum was not particularly onerous, and so a few months of cramming and hard work could make up for 18 months of idleness. His strategy worked and to his great relief he succeeded in passing his preliminary exam.

It was during this period that he rekindled his association with Professor Henslow. Before long, the two of them could be seen walking together discussing a wide range of topics. Darwin became entranced by botany, not just the collecting and identification of plants around Cambridge but also looking at their pollen under the microscope. Thus, Darwin was getting excellent training in yet another branch of natural history. His new found enthusiasm for botany did not divert Darwin from his studies for his degree. He stayed in Cambridge over Christmas cramming for his finals and he duly passed them in January 1831, ranking tenth out of the 178 who passed. He finally had a B.A. degree but had to remain in Cambridge until June to attain his residency requirement for the degree.

It was time to prepare himself for ordination and a country parish, but he seemed to be in no hurry. He continued to collect beetles and also to botanize with Henslow. He also continued with his studies, but now out of self-interest rather than simply trying to pass exams. Darwin had been impressed by William Paley's works on *The Principles of Moral and Political Philosophy* and *A View of the Evidences of Christianity*, which were required material for his degree; now he read the last of the famous archdeacon's trilogy, *Natural Theology*, which argued that we live in a world designed by God. To Darwin, Paley's logic seemed irrefutable. He was later to change his mind on this matter (see Chapter 3).

Two other works fired Darwin's zeal for scientific study. The first was on the philosophy of science by Sir William Herschel, who had discovered the planet Uranus. To Darwin it seemed as if the explanatory powers of the scientific method were limitless if applied in the proper manner, and built on the work of earlier scientists. The second was the seven-volume work of Alexander von Humboldt's account of his travels to South America. Darwin was fascinated by his observations on natural history, particularly his description of the forests and volcanic cones of Tenerife in the Canary Islands. Why not make an expedition there? He persuaded Henslow and three others that they should go for a month the following year, and even obtained the permission to go from his father, as well as the all-important financial backing. This development was to lead to a final, and crucial influence on his intellectual development at Cambridge.

An expedition to Tenerife would require a geologist and Darwin was given this task. He needed to develop his skills in that area and so was directed to take Adam Sedgwick's course. Sedgwick was a much better lecturer than Jameson in Edinburgh and Darwin became an ardent disciple of the subject. Later, that summer, Sedgwick took Darwin on a field trip to north Wales where he learned the art of interpreting the earth's crust from one of the foremost masters of the craft. They spent a week together until Darwin felt confident that he could interpret all that the Canary Islands had to offer. They went their separate ways and Darwin arrived home in Shrewsbury on 29 August to find a letter from Henslow.

Henslow had been asked to recommend a young gentleman, interested in science and natural history, to act as a companion for Captain Robert Fitzroy of HMS *Beagle*. Fitzroy was going to make a voyage to survey the coast of South America that would last for some years. Henslow considered Darwin to be just the man for the (unpaid) job, and pointed out to Darwin that the voyage would provide ample opportunity to conduct natural history studies. The ship was due to leave in four weeks. Charles was jubilant; this was much better than a month-long trip to Tenerife. His enthusiasm was not shared by his family and his father responded with a resounding 'No'. The good doctor had several reasons for his decision. It seemed rather dubious having an invitation like this so late in the day; presumably others had been offered the position and had turned it down; he feared that his son would never settle down to a steady life afterwards and the trip might ruin his reputation as a clergyman; and yet again he was changing his profession, when it was time for him to settle down and earn his own living. His father's decision came as a heavy blow, but Charles could hardly ignore his father's opinion because he would have to rely on his father to pay for his expenses on the voyage. He went to visit his uncle Jos Wedgwood[2] who, when he learned of the invitation, favoured the voyage and persuaded Charles's father to change his mind.

Darwin went to visit Fitzroy in London. It was an important meeting for both young men (Charles was 22 and Fitzroy 26 years of age) because they would be spending some years in close company on the ship. Social conventions dictated that a ship's captain could not fraternize with his crew and so Fitzroy would be almost entirely dependent on Charles for social discourse. Fortunately, the two warmed to each other and it was agreed that Darwin would join the ship.

The next few months were a whirlwind of activity for Charles as he prepared for the voyage. He accumulated the necessary materials and equipment to collect rocks, minerals, fossils, and all manner of animals and plants. He also acquired several books to help him identify and interpret what he would see. One of these was the first volume of *Principles of Geology* by Charles Lyell (the other two volumes were sent to him during the voyage). The book discussed how to interpret the

---

[2] The brother of Robert Darwin's deceased wife, Susannah.

earth's crust and was to have a major impact on Darwin's views. Before dealing with Darwin's experiences on the *Beagle* we will examine this last influence on his intellectual development.

1.2 The earth's crust: uniformitarian and catastrophist theories

As people began to examine the rocks which make up the earth's crust, they were faced by a gigantic puzzle. Some of the rock strata had clearly been laid down by sedimentary processes because one could see the fossil remains of organisms embedded in them, while others were of volcanic origin. As time went on it was recognized that there was some regularity in the sequence of sedimentary rocks over large areas, and there was speculation that the same sequence of rocks existed throughout the world. The puzzle was complex because at any locality there was only part of the sequence of strata and so to determine the whole sequence one had to combine the sequences from different localities. This was difficult for two reasons. First, in many cases certain strata appeared to be missing from a sequence, so that the sequence of strata might be A B D F in one locality, A C D in another, B C E F in a third, and so on. What was the correct sequence? This could only be discovered when the sequences of rocks from many localities were compared and an explanation could be provided to account for the missing strata. Second, as rocks were examined more closely more strata were recognized, and so areas had to be restudied to see if the newly discovered stratum was present or not. Each rock stratum was characterized by different fossilized plants and animals. In many cases, these fossils represented entire faunas and floras that were no longer living; several mass extinctions seemed to have occurred.

We can gain some appreciation of the complexity of the puzzle by examining a modern interpretation of some aspects of the geology of the south-western United States where a considerable thickness of the earth's crust has been exposed (Fig. 1.1). It may be seen that the top of the sequence of sedimentary rocks in the Grand Canyon overlaps the bottom of the exposed sequence of rocks in Zion Canyon, and similarly the top of the sequence of rocks at Zion Canyon overlaps the bottom of the exposed sequence of rocks in the Bryce Canyon area. In this case it is relatively simple to combine the sequence of rocks from the three areas into the overall correct sequence, but imagine how difficult it would be to do this where only two or three strata were exposed in each locality and if some of the strata were missing. Together the three areas form an exposed sequence approximately 2.1 km in depth: 1500 m at the Grand Canyon and approximately 300 m at each of the other two localities.

This impressive slice of the earth's history does not provide a complete record of the sequence of sedimentary rocks on earth. There are

Fig. 1.1 Geology of Bryce Canyon, Zion Canyon and Grand Canyon, USA, showing the sequence of rock strata and their relationship to the major geological eras. (Modified from Wise (1998) with permission.)

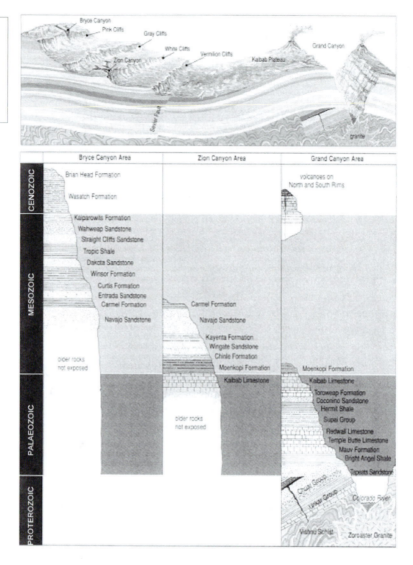

gaps in the sequence, called unconformities, where strata are missing. For example, if we consider the Palaeozoic rocks at the Grand Canyon, the first three strata (Tapeats Sandstone, Bright Angel Shale and the Mauv Formation) form a continuous series of deposits corresponding to the Cambrian period. Between this sequence and the Redwall Limestone, which corresponds to the Mississippian (Carboniferous) period, there is a huge gap in the record corresponding to rocks of the Ordovician, Silurian and Devonian periods (we will consider the Temple Butte Limestone in a moment). This unconformity covers a time span of approximately 145 million years, and Strahler (1987) explains how this may have occurred. We can imagine that during the Cambrian period the area lay under a shallow sea and the Tapeats Sandstone, Bright Angel Shale and Mauv Formation were deposited one after the other. Perhaps there were some younger deposits on top of the Mauv Formation, but we will never know. At some point during the following 145 million years the shallow marine area was uplifted and the surface rocks were eroded away down to the Mauv Formation. The area then subsided and during the Mississippian (Carboniferous) period the Redwall Limestone was deposited. The history of events was undoubtedly more complicated than this because in some areas of the Grand Canyon there are pockets of Temple Butte Limestone sandwiched between the Mauv Formation and the Redwall Limestone. Temple Butte Limestone was laid down during the Devonian period. This means that during the missing 145 million year sequence of strata there were at least two cycles of uplifting and erosion, between which there was a period of subsidence when deposition occurred.

Interpreting the history of the earth by looking at the sequence of rocks was obviously no simple matter, particularly at first. During the eighteenth century two theories were developed to account for the fossil record in the sedimentary rocks. Each theory had a very different view of the earth's history.

The uniformitarian theory was originally proposed by James Hutton (1726–97). This viewed the earth as a steady-state system. Events in the past were the same as those occurring in the present day; fossils were laid down as sediments slowly accumulated in areas of deposition, and exposed sediments were subjected to erosion. There was an endless cycle of subsidence and sedimentation, followed by uplifting and erosion. Organisms became extinct and were replaced, but how they were replaced and how these new species originated was never made clear. There was no progression in the fossil record, indeed at some time in the future one could envision the return of the dinosaurs and other extinct organisms. The earth was extremely old, and in Hutton's view there was no beginning (of time) and there would be no end.

In France, Georges Cuvier (1769–1832), developed the catastrophist theory after he examined the rocks in the Paris basin. He considered that the various fossils in the different rock strata were records of catastrophic events, such as wide-scale floods, which had occurred several times during the earth's history. He considered that the sedimentary rocks were laid down intermittently as a result of cataclysmic forces, rather than continuously. He observed a progression in the fossil record, in the sense that the fossils in the shallower, more recent, deposits were more similar to present-day animals and plants than the fossils in deeper deposits. In his view the world was not very old. Cuvier scrupulously avoided mixing science with his religious views and so it is rather unfortunate that his theory eventually became associated with supernatural forces.

Cuvier's work was translated into English by Robert Jameson, Darwin's geology professor at Edinburgh, who put a theological slant on the catastrophist theory. Fossils were the result of a series of catastrophes sent by God, who then replaced the extinct organisms with new species. This revised form of Cuvier's theory was particularly popular in England when Darwin was receiving his university education. Some geologists, the Reverend William Buckland of Oxford University

Table 1.1	Some components of uniformitarian and catastrophist views at the time of Darwin	
Phenomenon or process	Uniformitarian view	Catastrophist view
1. Age of earth	Extremely old; measured in millions of years.	Not very old; measured in thousands of years.
2. Geological processes of rock formation	The causes of volcanic action, uplifting, erosion, subsidence, and sedimentation operate at all times with the same intensity as at present.	Different causes operated in the early history of the earth. Irregular, cataclysmic events laid down rocks. Now little change is occurring.
3. Directional change in fossil records?	Rejected; the world in a steady state, but there may be cyclical changes over time.	Yes; progressive change with recent fossils more like living forms than older fossils.
4. Theological aspects	(a) Naturalistic; life may have been created by God, but now changes always a result of secondary causes. Or (b) Mainly naturalistic; but there may be occasional divine intervention.	Always allows for direct divine intervention.

Source: After Mayr (1982).

among them, argued that the geological history of the earth was entirely consistent with the biblical stories of Creation and Noah's Flood. Lyell's book, which reargued the uniformitarian theory, would have a major influence on Charles Darwin. Lyell believed that the earth was very old, but not timeless as Hutton had envisioned. One could estimate its age by determining sedimentation rates and then measuring the depth of the various strata of sedimentary rocks. He considered the replacement of extinct species with new species the 'mystery of mysteries', and he probably believed in divine intervention to explain this process, although he never made this clear. Some of the general beliefs of the two camps at the time of Darwin are outlined in Table 1.1.

Darwin liked Lyell's arguments, but he did not accept them uncritically. In time he was persuaded to accept the uniformitarian views about the age of the earth, and that natural causes could account for changes in the earth's surface (Component 2 of Table 1.1). He was particularly attracted to the idea that small, imperceptible changes could accumulate over vast periods of time to create major changes. However, he accepted the catastrophist view of progressive change in the fossil record rather than a steady-state earth (Component 3 of Table 1.1). Perhaps more importantly Darwin was beginning to think about the history of life on earth and developing a worldwide view, which was to have important ramifications as he travelled and made observations around the globe.

1.3 | The voyage of the *Beagle* (1831–6)

We have seen that Darwin had the natural inclination as well as the training to be a superb natural historian, having been mentored by some gifted professors in the areas of marine invertebrates, botany and geology. He had also been exposed to evolutionary ideas, but we should remember he had trained to be an Anglican vicar and so was a person of rather orthodox views who was concerned about what other people thought of him. As Darwin prepared himself for the voyage, he was filled with nervous apprehension. After two false starts, the *Beagle* finally left Plymouth on 27 December 1831 on a voyage that would last almost five years (Fig. 1.2).

Darwin soon discovered he was a wretched sailor and felt home-sick and depressed. Not a very auspicious beginning! The *Beagle* sailed to South America by way of the Canary Islands and the Cape Verde Islands. In order to land on Tenerife in the Canary Islands, the ship would need to be quarantined because of the cholera outbreak in Britain. Fitzroy refused to wait and Darwin was bitterly disappointed at missing one of the objects of his desires. His disappointment evaporated when they landed on St Jago in the Cape Verde Islands. He saw lush tropical vegetation for the first time and was overwhelmed, although the island mainly consisted of arid volcanic terrain. Everywhere he went, he took careful notes which showed he had a good eye for detail. In particular, he noticed a white band of compressed seashells and coral running for miles through the rocks about 10 m above sea-level. Obviously, it had once been under water but was now raised above the sea. It was not distorted and so it did not seem to

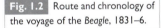

Fig. 1.2 Route and chronology of the voyage of the *Beagle*, 1831–6.

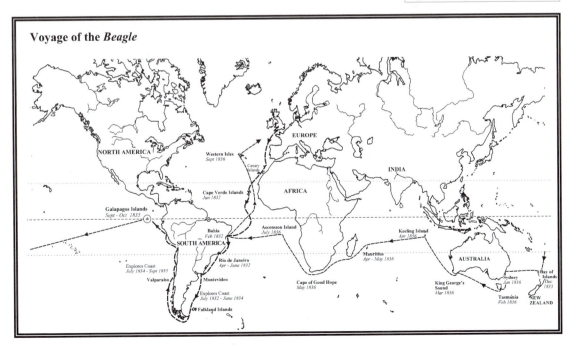

Voyage of the *Beagle*

Western Isles
Sept 1836

EUROPE

NORTH AMERICA

Canary Islands

INDIA

Cape Verde Islands
Jan 1832

AFRICA

Galapagos Islands
Sept - Oct 1835

Ascension Island
July 1836

Bahia
Feb 1832

SOUTH AMERICA

Mauritius
Apr - May 1836

AUSTRALIA

Explores Coast
July 1834 - Sept 1835

Rio de Janeiro
Apr - June 1832

Keeling Island
Apr 1836

Sydney
Jan 1836

Bay of Islands
Dec 1835

Valparaiso

Montevideo

Cape of Good Hope
May 1836

King George's Sound
Mar 1836

Explores Coast
July 1832 - June 1834

Tasmania
Feb 1836

NEW ZEALAND

Falkland Islands

him that it represented a violent, cataclysmic upheaval. Rather it appeared to conform with the uniformitarian view of gradual uplifting, as proposed by Lyell whose book he had been reading on the voyage. This viewpoint of small movements in the earth's crust slowly accumulating to produce mammoth changes would be used by Darwin to interpret the geology of all of the areas he visited. He had begun to be converted to the uniformitarian view.

As they sailed on to South America, he settled more and more into the ship's routine. He read and studied, he collected whenever he had an opportunity, he carefully labelled all he collected, and he made copious notes on all he observed. He wrote to friends and relatives, particularly Professor Henslow and his sister Caroline. He got on well with Fitzroy and the rest of the ship's crew. Because he was the captain's companion, any of Darwin's wishes were attended to by the rest of the crew, which was a great help as he carried out his scientific work. He also hired one of the ship's crew, Syms Covington, to be his servant, secretary and natural-history assistant during the voyage. To begin with he was treated in a stiff, formal manner by the sailors, but eventually Fitzroy gave him the nickname 'Philos', short for the ship's philosopher, and this light-hearted greeting was used by everyone.

They reached Bahia, now called Salvador, in north-eastern Brazil on 28 February 1832, and Fitzroy and his crew would spend the next 42 months carefully charting the coastline of the southern half of the continent. Tedious business, but it allowed Darwin to collect specimens at various landings along the coast and he also made more extensive inland journeys into Uruguay, Argentina and Chile. In fact, Darwin was to spend much more time ashore than on the ship during the nearly five years of the voyage. Overall he spent 39 months on land and only 18 months at sea. While ashore he worked like a man possessed; he had to make his observations and collections quickly because he was seldom sure when the *Beagle* would move on. The intensive fieldwork on land was complemented by periods on the ship where he could review his work and carefully annotate and pack his collections of plants, animals, fossils and rocks, before planning his next adventure ashore.

He made a number of significant observations during this phase of the journey. He marvelled at the wonderful adaptations of plants and animals to different environments in different parts of the continent. He must have wondered if this was evidence of a beneficent creator as Paley had so eloquently argued in his books. He also collected a number of fossils and noted that the more recent ones found in shallow deposits, like the giant sloth, *Megatherium*, and the giant armadillo, *Glyptodon*, were more similar to the present-day fauna than were older fossils found in the deeper deposits. He also continued to interpret the geology of the various areas from a uniformitarian viewpoint. He was to have some first-hand experience of continental uplifting while he was in Chile. On reaching the town of Valdivia he experienced a severe earthquake and was surprised at its intensity. The inhabitants

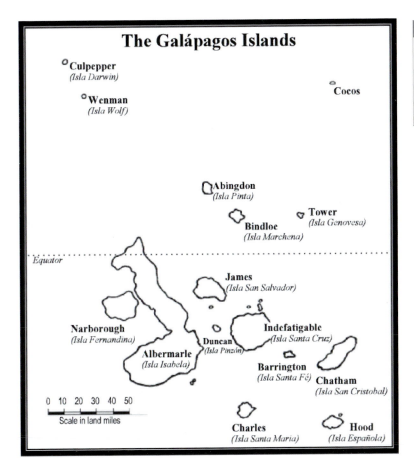

The Galápagos Islands

Culpepper
(Isla Darwin)

Cocos

Wenman
(Isla Wolf)

Abingdon
(Isla Pinta)

Tower
(Isla Genovesa)

Bindloe
(Isla Marchena)

Equator

James
(Isla San Salvador)

Narborough
(Isla Fernandina)

Indefatigable
(Isla Santa Cruz)

Duncan
(Isla Pinzón)

Albermarle
(Isla Isabela)

Barrington
(Isla Santa Fé)

Chatham
(Isla San Cristobal)

0 10 20 30 40 50
Scale in land miles

Charles
(Isla Santa Maria)

Hood
(Isla Española)

Fig. 1.3 Darwin visited Chatham, Charles, Abermarle and James Islands of the Galápagos archipelago during a five-week period in 1835. The present-day names of the islands are shown in italics.

told him it was as severe as the one of 1822, and it was clear that earthquakes were common in the area. They sailed 320 km north to the city of Concepción which was close to the centre of the seismic activity and which had been virtually destroyed. There he noticed that the main beach had been raised above the previous sea level, and Fitzroy measured this gain in elevation at eight feet (2.44 m). Later Darwin observed deposits of seashells, some of which were still coloured, at heights up to 100 m or so above sea level. To Darwin the reason was obvious: a series of earthquakes over a long period of time had combined to elevate the land, increment by increment, on a continental scale. He was observing that the earth was not static and that the effects of several relatively small changes could combine to produce a major change.

The *Beagle* finally left the shores of South America on 6 September 1835 bound for the Galápagos Islands, where Darwin was to have the key experience that would make him question the doctrine of the fixity of species. He only recognized the experience in retrospect, and he almost bungled the opportunity he was given. The Galápagos were a group of 15 or so islands of volcanic origin, straddling the equator, approximately 950 km off the west coast of South America (Fig. 1.3). Darwin was looking forward to the change in scenery and examining the animals and plants of the archipelago because he knew that the islands were populated by a rich variety of species found nowhere else. He had read in Lyell's second volume of his book about the problem of explaining the origins of island species. Lyell postulated two theories: they could immigrate from nearby mainland areas, or they could be unique species created by God. It would seem that the second explanation was the most likely for the Galápagos because they were so isolated.

They reached the islands on the 15 September and over the next five weeks Darwin visited and made collections on four of them. They reached Chatham Island first and the black volcanic terrain reminded him of the industrialized Midlands of England. The strangest animals were the black, seagoing iguanas which he discovered ate only seaweed. They were 60–90 cm long, and scuttled among the black larval rocks along the shore like giant rats. Darwin did not realize they were unique to the Galápagos because museum specimens in England had been mistakenly labelled as from South America. He was astonished at the tameness of the animals; they were totally unafraid of humans and could be collected with ease. He noted that the mockingbirds were similar to the Chilean species except that they had a different song. The ship's crew brought 18 giant tortoises aboard for fresh meat and then they sailed on to Charles Island where there was a penal colony run by an English acting-governor, Nicholas Lawson. He told them the giant tortoises had different-shaped shells on each of the islands, but this information made no impression on Darwin because he believed the tortoises had been imported from the Indian Ocean by buccaneers. He did notice that the mockingbirds were different from those on Chatham Island and from this point on he kept these birds separated by island in his collection, although at the time he did not consider the variation to be of great significance. He assumed that there was little variation from island to island because they were mostly in sight of one another. Consequently, he was much more casual with the other plants and animals he collected and rarely bothered indicating which island he collected them from. They went on to Albermarle, the largest island of the archipelago, where he saw the brightly coloured land iguanas which, like the sea iguanas, were also vegetarian. The mockingbirds were similar to those he had collected on Chatham Island, but when he moved to James Island they were different again and so there were two or three varieties.

Darwin had great difficulty with many of the smaller birds that are now known as Darwin's finches. The plumage was similar in many of them and they fed in large irregular flocks. He tentatively identified them on the basis of their beaks. He called some 'Grosbeaks', others 'Fringilla' (true finches), the cactus-eaters he called 'Icterus' (a family which includes orioles and blackbirds), and he even identified one as a wren. He realized he was totally confused by these birds and that they would require a more expert ornithologist than he to sort them out.

The *Beagle* finally left the Galápagos and sailed on to Tahiti, then New Zealand, Australia, through the Indian Ocean to the Cape of Good

Hope in South Africa. England was getting ever closer and Darwin was anxious to be home. With the help of his servant, Covington, he began to organize his field notes, his catalogues of specimens, his geological and zoological logbooks, and his diary as the *Beagle* sailed on across the Atlantic. As he listed the mockingbirds from the Galápagos he considered afresh the implications of having different types on different islands, and he wrote these prophetic words in his private notebook, in July of 1836:

> When I recollect, the fact that from the form of the body, shape of scales & general size, the Spaniards can at once pronounce, from which Island any tortoise may have been brought. When I see these islands in sight of each other, & possessed of but a scanty stock of animals, tenanted by these birds, but slightly differing in structure & filling the same place in Nature, I must suspect they are only varieties. The only fact of a similar kind of which I am aware, is the constant asserted difference – between the wolf-like Fox of East and West Falkland Islds. – If there is the slightest foundation for these remarks the zoology of the Archipelagoes – will be well worth examining; for such facts would undermine the stability of Species.

Darwin was beginning to have vague doubts about the fixity of species. It didn't seem logical that God would create different types of similar animals on islands so close together, it would seem more likely that a species had diverged in its characteristics on different islands. Perhaps species could change their characteristics, but he kept these thoughts to himself. It would take longer than expected to reach England because after leaving Ascension Island Fitzroy steered back to Bahia in South America to check his longitude measurements, to the dismay of everyone else on board. Fortunately all was well, the chronometers had kept the correct time for the perfectionist Fitzroy, and almost two months after leaving Bahia they anchored off Falmouth on 2 October 1836. The voyage of a lifetime was finally over.

1.4 | Island biogeography provides the key (1836–7)

Darwin began a whirlwind of activity on his return; he literally had thousands of specimens to be identified by experts as well as his account of his travels to be written up and included with Fitzroy's narrative. He met Charles Lyell who was delighted to have a convert to his uniformitarian view. Darwin became more and more active in scientific circles, and it was clear that he could more than hold his own in this heady atmosphere.

The greatest impact on his thinking, however, was made by John Gould at the British Museum who identified his birds during January and February of 1837. Darwin was astonished by what Gould told him. The mockingbirds from the Galápagos represented three distinct species, each on a separate island, and the birds that Darwin had tentatively identified as Grosbeaks, finches, icterids and a wren, was in fact a unique group of finches represented by 13 different species. Gould told him that he thought that different species occurred on different islands, but could not be sure because they were inadequately labelled. Fortunately, Darwin was able to obtain other specimens from his servant, Covington, and from Captain Fitzroy, and Gould was able to partially reconstruct the island localities of all but two of the species. The distribution of finches seemed complicated and confusing, although there was an indication that some species were confined to individual islands. In fact, more than a century would pass before their distribution and taxonomy would be resolved (Lack 1947). Nevertheless, Darwin's prophetic words came back to haunt him, but what he had speculated as varieties were in fact distinct species. In addition, the mockingbirds and finches had relatives living in South America which was the obvious source of colonization. Darwin speculated that if certain ancestral species had somehow reached the archipelago perhaps they had changed and diverged on the different islands.

Darwin was to start his 'Transmutation' notebooks immediately. He was convinced that the characteristics of species were not fixed but could change. Perhaps he could solve Lyell's 'mystery of mysteries' of how extinct species could have been replaced by new species in a natural way, rather than by divine intervention. His research into evolution had begun.

Chapter 2

Darwin's theories of evolution

Darwin began his 'Transmutation' notebooks in the spring of 1837 primarily because of John Gould's taxonomic findings on the birds of the Galápagos Islands. The fact that there were different closely related species of mockingbirds on different islands seemed at odds with the explanation that all species had been created by God (see Chapter 1). Why would a deity create different species, living much the same sort of lifestyle, on islands that were within sight of one another? To Darwin it seemed much more logical that one or more ancestral species had migrated to the islands from South America (where related species were known to occur), and that subsequently they had diverged to form different species on different islands. If that is what had happened on relatively young volcanic islands, imagine how much divergence would be possible worldwide over a much longer geological time period. This transmutation of species would also explain some of the observations he had made in South America. For example, he had found fossils of the giant sloth and the giant armadillo in shallow deposits which indicated that they had become extinct relatively recently. They were also very similar in body form to the present-day species. Perhaps the giant forms had given rise to the smaller species before their demise, or the larger and smaller species had diverged from a common ancestor and the giant forms had lost in the competitive struggle for survival. In this way, Darwin freely speculated about various possibilities, and then began to collect facts that would support one possibility or another.

Darwin realized that he would have to amass a considerable body of evidence to support his speculation that organisms could evolve. From his discussions with Lyell and others of the scientific establishment he knew that evolution was not a respectable idea. He was not inclined to ruffle feathers and was concerned about what other scientists thought of him, so he kept his new-found speculations to himself. It was only much later that he reluctantly revealed his theories to a few close friends.

He began to ask some fundamental questions and, as a result, developed two basic theories on evolution.[1] First, Darwin considered how many times life had been created or had come into being. He theorized that life had only been created once and so all organisms were related by descent. Perhaps this was a legacy from his discussions with Robert Grant in his Edinburgh days, or perhaps for simplicity's sake he wished to consider divine intervention as little as possible. In any case, he began to collect and synthesize all sorts of facts that would support or falsify this theory. These included information on geology and the fossil record, the geographical distribution of organisms, and the comparative morphology, anatomy and embryology of organisms.

It was one thing to provide evidence for relationships between organisms that were consistent, or consilient, with the theory that all organisms are related by descent, but what was the mechanism for transmutation of species? Darwin was convinced that the mechanism involved selection because plant and animal breeders were able to change the characteristics of domesticated species by means of artificial selection. The question for him was how selection could operate in nature, or how natural selection could operate in an analogous way to artificial selection. Darwin's second theory was the theory of natural selection, and he considered this to be his greatest intellectual achievement.

It would take Darwin about five years to accumulate the necessary facts, synthesize them, make logical inferences with respect to evolution and sketch out his two theories. For various reasons he was extremely reluctant to publish his work. Before considering why this was so, we will examine how he structured his arguments in his book, *The Origin of Species*.

2.1 Darwin's evolutionary theories: *The Origin of Species* (1859)

Darwin's two evolutionary theories are integrated in his book in a way that makes it easy for the reader to slip from one theory to the other without realizing it. In general terms, the first part of the book deals with the theory of natural selection (see Fig. 2.1), and the second part of the book with the theory that all organisms are related by descent (see Fig. 2.2). There is substantial material relating to both theories in chapters four to eight.

2.1.1 Are the characteristics of species fixed?

Darwin began his argument for evolution by considering whether it was possible for a species to change from one form to another. In

---

[1] Ernst Mayr (1982, 1997), considers that Darwin had five independent theories relating to evolution. In addition to the two theories described in this chapter Mayr would add the theories that organisms evolve, that evolution is gradual, and that speciation or divergence between groups is a population phenomenon.

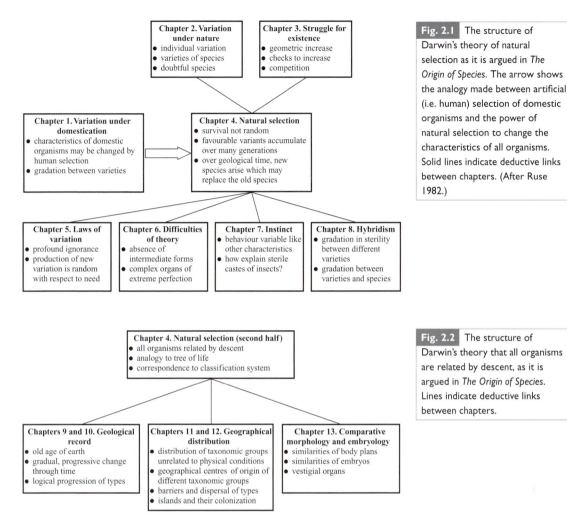

Fig. 2.1 The structure of Darwin's theory of natural selection as it is argued in *The Origin of Species*. The arrow shows the analogy made between artificial (i.e. human) selection of domestic organisms and the power of natural selection to change the characteristics of all organisms. Solid lines indicate deductive links between chapters. (After Ruse 1982.)

Fig. 2.2 The structure of Darwin's theory that all organisms are related by descent, as it is argued in *The Origin of Species*. Lines indicate deductive links between chapters.

effect he was questioning two basic ideas of the doctrine of special creation: that the characteristics of species are fixed, and that different species are always distinct from one another. He did this by looking at the variation of both domesticated and natural species in the first two chapters of his book (Fig. 2.1).

He noted that the individuals of a species are not identical, but vary in their characteristics such that no two individuals are the same. Breeders have produced different breeds or varieties through artificial selection in many domesticated species, and the variation between breeds may be enormous. Darwin was particularly interested in pigeons and described an astonishing diversity between such breeds as the English carrier, short-faced tumbler, runt, pouter, Jacobin, trumpeter and fantail. The differences between these breeds were so great that they would probably be classified as different species, or perhaps even genera, if they were wild animals. However, they have all descended from the rock-pigeon (*Columba livia*) and can interbreed with one another and so they belong to the same species. Similar observations can be made in relation to dogs (*Canis familiaris*), where differences in morphology and behaviour between such breeds as the chihuahua, dachshund, bulldog, Great Dane and St Bernard are very striking. Finally, we can observe extraordinary variation between the cabbage, cauliflower, broccoli, kale, Brussels sprouts and kohlrabi, which have all been produced by artificial selection from the common wild mustard (*Brassica oleracea*). These examples of variation of domesticated species show that differences between varieties of the same species are frequently greater than the differences between many species. Thus, living species are defined on the basis of their reproductive isolation from one another, rather than on the degree of morphological differences.

Much of this variation is heritable (i.e. has a genetic basis), at least in part. Darwin also noted that new variation is continuously being created, because new types (or sports) are produced every generation, and so we should not be surprised that even the oldest domesticated species, like wheat, are still capable of yielding new varieties. Plant and animal breeders have produced an amazing range of varieties of plants and animals, and all characters seem capable of being changed by selection.

The individuals of wild species also vary from one another. Many species have well-differentiated varieties which may represent geographical races or may occur in different habitats within the same geographical area. However, even today there are many cases where we are uncertain as to whether a type represents a variety or a true species (i.e. are reproductively isolated from other types). For example, some plants might be classified as distinct species by one authority, but be classified as varieties within a common species by another authority. By way of example, Darwin considered the difficulty of determining the taxonomic status of the primrose (*Primula veris*) and the cowslip (*P. elatior*) in more detail. These plants differ in appearance and flavour, emit a different odour, flower at slightly different periods, have different geographical ranges, and can only be crossed with much difficulty. However, there are many intermediate forms between the two plants that are not hybrids. One could argue that they represent two distinct species, because of their differences and the difficulty of getting them to interbreed. However, one could also argue that they merely represent varieties of a single species because there are intermediate forms that represent a breeding connection between them. Darwin argued that there is not always a simple distinction between varieties and species. In his opinion, the distinction would be especially difficult if an ancestral species was in the process of splitting into two or more species and the process was incomplete.

From his discussion of variation, Darwin concluded that the characteristics of species are not fixed and could be changed by selection. He argued that it was possible for a species to change from one form to another, or divide into two or more daughter species, over the course of many thousands of generations. His next task was to explain how selection could occur in nature so that there was a mechanism for these evolutionary changes.

2.1.2   Darwin's theory of natural selection

From his first two chapters, Darwin observed two main facts: (1) that individuals within a population and a species varied in their characteristics, and (2) much of the variation was heritable (i.e. has a genetic basis). He went on to discuss competition between individuals and species in a process he termed the 'struggle for existence'. We can note that his views in this respect had been greatly influenced by the essay of Thomas Malthus (1826). Darwin noted three additional facts: (3) all species have the ability to produce more offspring than are required merely to replace the number of parents, and so populations have the power to increase their numbers geometrically or exponentially; (4) the resources required to sustain organisms are finite, and they stay relatively constant (i.e. relative to the organism's ability to increase) and so there is a limited potential for growth; and (5) populations display stability in size, relative to what is possible given their power to increase. From these last three facts, he could infer or deduce that as there are more individuals produced than can be supported by the available resources then there must be a fierce 'struggle for existence'. Put simply, only some of the offspring can survive to reproduce.

Darwin combined his inference about the struggle for existence with the first two facts on variation and argued that survival was not random with respect to variation. Some variants are better able to survive and produce more offspring than others. As a consequence, the favoured variants accumulate at the expense of less favoured variants through the process of natural selection, generation after generation, and the characteristics of the population may therefore slowly change over time.

We can see that Darwin's theory of natural selection was similar to his uniformitarian views of the earth's history (see Chapter 1), because small incremental changes slowly accumulate over vast geological time spans to produce large changes ultimately. He argued that eventually the changes in characteristics could be such that a species might be transformed into a new species, or a species might be divided to form two or more daughter species. This would explain how species are replaced by others in the geological record.

Darwin provided various examples of how natural selection could act to modify the characteristics of a species. He observed, for example, that certain plants excrete a sweet juice from certain glands located in different parts of the plant, perhaps to eliminate something injurious from their sap. This juice is very attractive to certain insects. He then supposed that this sweet juice or nectar might be secreted from the inner bases of the petals of a flower. Insects seeking this nectar as a source of food would get dusted with pollen and would then transport the pollen from one flower to another, promoting cross-fertilization between different individuals of the same species. Darwin argued that flowers that had their stamens and pistils so placed to favour an increased transportation of pollen from one flower to another would be favoured by natural selection. Likewise, insects whose body size, and curvature and length of proboscis provided improved access to the sources of nectar would also be favoured by natural selection. In this manner, the characteristics of the insect and flower might coevolve so that the two species become adapted in a remarkable way to each other. Coevolution is possible in this case because the advantages to the two species are mutual. Darwin noted that natural selection cannot modify the structure of one species for the good of another species unless there is some advantage to the first species.

Darwin also argued that natural selection would not act on all the individuals of a species in the same way. For example, a predator might eat different prey in different habitats or in different regions of its geographical range, and be modified accordingly. He reported that there were two forms of the wolf inhabiting the Catskill Mountains in the United States, one with a light greyhound-like form that hunted deer, and the other with a more bulky build with shorter legs that attacked sheep. Whatever the truth of this matter, it was plausible to argue that selection is unlikely to mould the characteristics of a species in the same way throughout the range of a species, and that as a consequence there would be geographical races or varieties in many cases. This led to the topic of divergence of form and the possibility that different species might be related by descent.

2.1.3 Darwin's theory that all organisms are related by descent

Natural selection causes populations of individuals to become better suited to their local environments. This will lead to local varieties or races within a species because the environment is not uniform throughout a species' range. Consequently, these local varieties might diverge in their characteristics such that each is more suited, or adapted, to different conditions. Darwin viewed these varieties as species in the process of formation, or as incipient species. Not all varieties will become new species, but there is potential for different varieties to diverge sufficiently from each other and from their common parent to become distinct species.

Darwin illustrated this using an abstract example in the form of a diagram (Fig. 2.3), which is the only illustration in his book. He considered the fate of 11 species (A–L) of a genus over the course of a long period of time, which he divided into 14 equal periods (I–XIV). The variation in form of the different types is represented by the divergence of the dotted lines. First, he imagined that each time period represented 1000 generations. We see that after the first 1000 generations, species A has produced two fairly well marked varieties, a^1 and m^1. These two varieties have diverged only slightly from their common parent (A), and each variety is itself variable. Over the next 1000 generations the two varieties continue to diverge due to selection, variety a^1 changing to a^2 and variety m^1 producing two varieties, namely m^2 and s^2. In this way we can trace the history of daughter varieties over time. We can see that species A gives rise to three distinct varieties (a^{10}, f^{10} and m^{10}) after ten such time periods

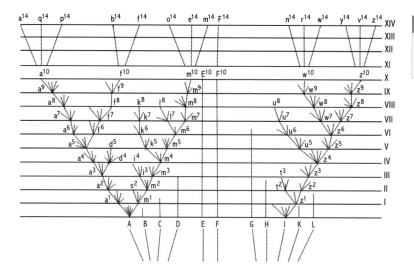

Fig. 2.3 Darwin's diagram representing the descent of species A–L over 14 time periods (I–XIV). (From *The Origin of Species*.)

or 10 000 generations, and eventually after 14 time periods there are eight distinct varieties that have been formed. Similarly we see that species I eventually gives rise to six different varieties.

The divergence of the different varieties from one another and from their parent species may be of sufficient magnitude that some of them attain the rank of species. Darwin reasoned that if this did not happen during the course of 14 000 generations, one only had to suppose that each time period was longer, say 10 000 or 100 000 generations, to increase the likelihood of speciation. Darwin went on to make two important remarks about this formation of distinct varieties and species that we have just outlined.

First, he recognized that the process did not have to proceed as regularly as is shown in the diagram, as divergence or modification of form does not necessarily occur over time. For example, we can see that species F persists unchanged throughout the 14 time periods. Thus, although time is required for divergence or modification of form to occur through the action of natural selection, the mere passage of time does not imply that change will occur.

Second, the multiplication of varieties and species from some ancestral forms means that other varieties and species become extinct, because he did not observe an overall increase in diversity over time. Darwin viewed this in terms of the overall struggle for existence, where the better-adapted varieties and species out-compete and cause the extinction of the less-adapted forms. For example if we refer back to Fig. 2.3, we can envisage that the m-line of varieties of species A slowly wins in the struggle for existence against species B, C and D and cause their extinction.

If we return to the issue of the relationship between species and consider the eight species that are descendants of species A over the course of many thousands of generations, we can see from Fig. 2.3 that some species are more closely related than others. The three species marked a^{14}, q^{14} and p^{14} have descended from a^{10} and so are more closely related to each other than they are to species b^{14} and f^{14}, which have descended from f^{10}. These five species have a^5 as a common descendant and are more distantly related to the remaining three species (o^{14}, e^{14} and m^{14}). If the divergence between these three groups of species is sufficiently great, they might be placed in different genera, or the first two groups might be placed in one genus and the third group in another genus. One can extend this argument to have different genera diverging to form new families, families being modified to form new orders, orders being modified to form new classes, and so on. In this way Darwin showed that the classification system could be interpreted as reflecting the different levels of relationship, so that as one proceeds from phyla to classes, from classes to orders, from orders to families, from families to genera, and from genera to species the individuals in these taxonomic groupings become progressively more closely related.

Only in the summary of chapter four does Darwin state explicitly that all organisms are related by descent, implying that life originated only once, and makes his famous analogy to a tree of life to represent the diversity of all living things. He pointed out that the structure of the tree corresponded to the classification system of Linnaeus. Thus, the smallest end twigs corresponded to species, which then joined to form larger twigs corresponding to genera; these linked to form small branches corresponding to families; and so on through orders, classes and phyla, the latter of which corresponded to some of the major branches. Finally, the animal and plant kingdoms formed the main trunks which joined toward their base. If one looks at the tree as a whole, one would see many dead branches and twigs, which represent the extinct lines. The whole tree could be related to the geological timescale if the highest parts corresponded to present-day organisms, and as you went down the tree you descended to older and older periods until reaching the oldest original organism at the bottom.

2.1.4 The logical consequences of Darwin's theories

In the first four chapters of his book Darwin argued that species could evolve or change over time; he theorized that the main mechanism for this change was the process of natural selection; and finally he theorized that all species were related by descent. Darwin then proceeded to consider the various deductions or logical consequences of his two theories in the remaining nine chapters (Figs. 2.1 and 2.2).

In chapter five of *The Origin of Species*, Darwin considered the genetic basis of his theory of natural selection and had to admit profound ignorance on the subject. He was so confused on this matter that in later editions of his book he introduced a fatal flaw in his theory by proposing blending inheritance.[2] This is incompatible with the

---

[2] Blending inheritance assumes that hereditary substances from the parents merge in the offspring, and if the parents are different the offspring will be intermediate for that trait.

theory of natural selection as some critics were quick to point out. The following example should make this clear. Imagine a light-coloured insect that relies on its camouflage to escape predation. All is well until the general colour of the environment becomes darkened as a result of industrial pollution. At this point it would be advantageous for the insect to be darker in colour. From time to time darker individuals would arise through the process of mutation, but if there is blending inheritance the offspring would be intermediate in colour and the dark colour would tend to be diluted in succeeding generations because most of the population is light. With this type of inheritance, the population can only change to a darker colour through repeated mutations of dark forms. Therefore it is mutation that is directing the evolutionary process, not natural selection which merely acts as the executioner of lightest-coloured individuals. We can see that for natural selection to direct the evolutionary process it is important that new variants are inherited in a discrete way, rather than blending with the existing variants. Thus, in our example, the gene coding for light body colour must remain distinct from the gene coding for the new variant of dark body colour. This is known as particulate inheritance. This issue was not solved until Mendel's work was rediscovered at the turn of the century, and even then its relevance to Darwin's theory would not be generally understood and accepted until much later. Darwin was clear on one fact, however, that the production of new variants was random with respect to need, i.e. mutation is not preferentially inclined toward adaptation. The importance of this observation will be made clear in the next chapter.

Darwin went on to consider certain difficulties with both of his theories (*The Origin of Species*, chapter six). The first concerned the absence of intermediate forms. If populations gradually changed over time, where were the intermediate forms? Darwin explained that they would have been eliminated by the better-adapted forms, but if this is the case, why don't we see all of the intermediate forms in the fossil record? Darwin argued that the absence of most transitional forms from the geological record was because it was so incomplete. He was to expound upon this issue at great length in chapters nine and ten of his book, explaining that the fossil record only included a minute fraction of all of the organisms that had once lived and that we had only looked at a small fraction of that record at relatively few localities around the world. Therefore, the absence of certain types from the fossil record proved very little.

A second difficulty concerned the evolution of organs of extreme perfection like the eye. Darwin freely confessed that it seemed absurd that the human eye, with all its contrivances for adjusting the focus to different distances, for admitting different amounts of light, and for the correction of spherical and chromatic aberration, could have been formed by natural selection. We should remember that every one of the intermediate steps in its development would need to be better adapted than the preceding step, otherwise the new variants would not accumulate by natural selection. Nevertheless, Darwin reasoned that the eye could have been formed by natural selection because numerous transitional forms of the eye are found in other organisms, and these types of eyes seem to function appropriately for each type of animal.

Behaviour or instinct was shown in chapter seven to be variable, just like any other characteristic of the organism, and so was subject to natural selection. Darwin described a few examples of how complex behaviours could have developed, or evolved, by this process. However, there was one particular difficulty to explain, the evolution of sterile castes in the social insects. How can sterile individuals be selected for if they do not leave any descendants? Darwin was not certain, but pointed out that selection occurred at the family or group level as well as the level of the individual, and perhaps the group was better off with sterile workers. He was on the right track, but this particular problem would not be solved until the 1950s (see Chapter 19).

Finally, in chapter eight, Darwin considered the logical consequences of producing new species by natural selection. The process is a gradual one and so one should not expect a clear distinction between varieties that can interbreed, and species that cannot interbreed. Darwin was able to show that there was a complete gradient in fertility (or sterility), between populations that could interbreed totally and those populations that could not interbreed at all. This gradation between varieties and species is precisely what one would expect if species evolved through natural selection, but it is difficult to see how it could be accounted for by special creation.

It may be seen that Darwin's consideration of the theory of natural selection in the first eight chapters was not superficial. He had a very clear picture of its logical constructs, and the necessary consequences or deductions that could be made from the theory.

Darwin then considered the various facts that were consistent with his theories that new species arise through the process of natural selection and that all organisms are related by descent (Fig. 2.2). Obviously, the process occurs extremely slowly and so the earth must be extremely old, in contrast to the biblical interpretation. By examining the geological record (chapters nine and ten) Darwin showed that sedimentary rocks containing fossils had an accumulated depth of a few kilometres (see Fig. 1.1). From what was known about sedimentation rates, and the erosion rates of exposed strata, he calculated that the history of life on earth must span hundreds of millions of years, which is sufficiently long for the process of natural selection to create the known variety of life. Although he was in error on some details, Darwin was correct in his overall interpretation. He showed that there was a progressive change in the fossil record, with recent fossils being more like present-day forms than the older, deeper, fossils. Thus, there was a succession of new species and also a logical progression in the fossil record. For example, the sequence of fish, amphibians, reptiles and mammals is logical, but a sequence of reptiles, fish, mammals and amphibians is not logical. He observed that transitional forms were frequently absent, owing to the fragmentary and incomplete nature of the fossil record, but many links could be found and in some cases they had led to a revision of the classification of some groups. For example, Cuvier had ranked the ruminants (even-toed mammals that chew cud which included sheep, giraffes, deer and camels) and pachyderms (thick-skinned nonruminant mammals which included elephant, rhinoceros and pigs) as the two most distinct orders of mammals. However, Owen was able to show from the fossil record that there were numerous intermediate forms between pigs and camels, and so placed the pigs in a suborder with the ruminants.

Chapters eleven and twelve of *The Origin of Species* considered the geographical distribution of organisms. If species were related by descent, then closely related groups should be in geographical proximity to one another. Darwin showed that the present distribution of organisms was more related to geography than to the physical conditions where they occur. If one compares the faunas and floras of Australia, Africa and South America at the same latitudes, where the physical conditions are similar, we see that they are completely different even though they show the same sort of adaptation to their local environments. For example, if we consider succulent plants, the South American cacti and the African euphorbia are quite distinct taxonomically but they are superficially very similar in general form. Similarly, the marsupials (i.e. mammals whose young complete their development in the mother's pouch or marsupium) of Australia have radiated to fill many of the same ecological niches as the eutherians (i.e. placental mammals) in Africa and South America. The opossum marsupials of South America are also quite distinct from the numerous types of marsupials in Australia. It is as if there are centres of creation of various groups so that organisms are most closely related to those living on the same continent. These facts are consistent with the theory of common ancestry.

Darwin also showed that the distribution of species was frequently affected by barriers to dispersal, so that different species often occurred on either side of major rivers, mountain ranges and deserts, even where the physical conditions were similar. A particularly striking example is provided by the marine faunas living on either side of the isthmus of Panama. They are only separated by a few miles and yet they are quite distinct from each another, with those on the eastern side of the isthmus being most closely related to Atlantic faunas and those on the western side being most closely related to Pacific faunas, even though the physical conditions that they experience are virtually identical. Again this makes little sense in terms of special creation, but is consistent with the theory of common ancestry.

Finally, the distribution of organisms on islands was also instructive. Remember that Darwin had been led to question the fixity of species because of his experience on the Galápagos Islands. He noted that the closest relatives of an island's inhabitants occurred on the mainland upwind and upcurrent of the prevailing winds and water currents. It seemed logical to suppose that the inhabitants had originally been transported by natural means from the mainland to the islands, and that they had subsequently diverged in their characteristics. However, organisms vary in their ability to migrate and so we find that more distant islands are frequently deficient in certain types of organisms. Darwin noted that amphibians are absent naturally from all oceanic islands even though they are present on the mainland, probably because their eggs are killed by sea water, but that they had been successfully introduced by humans into Madeira, the Azores and Mauritius. Similarly, terrestrial mammals are absent from oceanic islands which are more than 500 km from a continent or large continental island, unless they have been introduced by humans. However, bats are found throughout the oceanic islands because of their greater powers of dispersal through flight. In conclusion, Darwin observed that closely related species were in close geographical proximity to each other and that discontinuities of distribution corresponded to barriers to dispersal. The facts were in accordance with the theory that all organisms were related by descent.

Finally, in chapter thirteen, Darwin considered the internal structure and embryonic development of animals and showed that there were many facts consistent with the theory of common ancestry. In related groups of animals, one would expect a similarity of body plans, with certain structures being modified for different purposes. The classic example is the forelimbs of vertebrates which have been modified for flying, swimming, running, digging, grasping, and so on. The general structure is the same in all cases, and Darwin interpreted this as revealing a common ancestry. Similarly, the embryos of different vertebrates tend to be similar early in life because they are related, and divergence of body form occurs during development, e.g. humans have gill slits and a post-anal tail during development. This makes no sense in terms of special creation but is consistent with the theory that we have descended or evolved from a fish-like ancestor. Likewise, rudimentary or vestigial organs may reveal ancestry and common descent. The rudimentary hind legs of whales and snakes link them to four-legged vertebrates, and the appendix in humans is a rudimentary form of the caecum which is common in other mammals.

Today we could considerably update and amplify on the facts Darwin presented to support his theories. Some of the gaps in the fossil record have been filled, though many still remain; the movement of huge landmasses through continental drift has explained many of the anomalies in the geographical distribution of organisms; we know considerably more about population genetics; and studies of comparative biochemistry are also consistent with the view that all organisms are related by descent.

Darwin concluded his book with a summarizing chapter which briefly reviewed his arguments. Toward the end of the chapter is a single sentence which reads 'Light will be thrown on the origin of man and his history.' So in this quiet way, he let it be known that humans are not excluded from his theories of evolution. Finally, he ends with the eloquent statement:

There is a grandeur in this view of life, with its several powers, having been originally breathed into a few forms or into one; and that, whilst this planet has gone cycling on according to the fixed law of gravity, from so simple a beginning endless forms most beautiful and most wonderful have been, and are being, evolved.

2.2 Darwin's hesitation to publish, and the reaction to his theories

One can see from our synopsis of Darwin's book that he had developed a very mature pair of theories. Why was he so reluctant to publish? He wrote an initial sketch in 1842 and revised this into a 230-page essay on evolution in 1844. Neither was published, although he gave his wife money and instructions to publish his 1844 essay in the event of his death, and so he clearly understood the scientific importance of his work. Soon after writing this essay he made the acquaintance of Joseph Hooker who was to become the Director of Kew Gardens. For some reason Darwin felt he could reveal to Hooker that he believed in the transmutation of organisms, and added that 'It's like confessing a murder.' He was only half talking in jest and was obviously horrified at the probable reaction of the scientific establishment to his ideas. In all likelihood, it was the philosophical content of his theory of natural selection that he was concerned about. In any case, Darwin kept his views to himself and a few good friends like Joseph Hooker.

For eight years he worked on the taxonomy of barnacles while his friends urged him to publish his book on evolution. Darwin was not tempted because he had seen the reaction to an anonymous book, written by Robert Chambers (of encyclopaedia fame), called the *Vestiges of the Natural History of Creation* which argued for evolution. Although it was a popular book and sold well, scientists wrote scathing critiques, much of it justified because there was a lot of poor science in the book, but it was obvious that they had little sympathy with the idea of transmutation of species. Eventually, Darwin started work in 1856 on an enormous book on evolution which would take many years to complete. He was obviously in no hurry and felt confident that he would not be scooped, in spite of the comments of his learned friends. You can imagine his horror and despair in 1858 when he received a copy of a manuscript from Alfred Wallace, who was working in the East Indies, on a theory of natural selection to account for changes in species. Wallace's theory was identical in concept to Darwin's but not as well developed. Wallace asked Darwin for his comments and to forward it for publication if Darwin considered it suitable. Darwin was in a quandary; Wallace's paper should be published but Darwin was very unhappy that he would not have the honour of being the first to propose the theory of natural selection. Lyell and Hooker persuaded Darwin to submit his own paper on natural selection along with Wallace's manuscript and so both papers were presented at the same time to the Linnean Society. There were all the makings of a scientific scandal, but Wallace, to his credit, acknowledged Darwin's precedence and also realized that Darwin had a much better understanding of the entire subject.

Now Darwin could no longer afford to take his time in publishing his theories and he worked frantically to publish his work in the following year (1859). The book was titled *The Origin of Species by Means of Natural Selection, or the Preservation of Favoured Races in the Struggle for Life* and was an abstract of a much longer book that he had been working on for some years, and could be read and understood by any educated person. The response of the scientific community was generally favourable. People were convinced that evolution had occurred, but there was little acceptance of his mechanism of natural selection. Even his most ardent supporters like Thomas Huxley deserted him on this point. Indeed, it would take almost 100 years for most biologists to accept the theory of natural selection, and it is still a contentious theory for some people. We will examine why this should be so in the next chapter.

Chapter 3

Understanding natural selection

The theory of natural selection is deceptively simple. We have seen in Chapter 2 that Darwin formulated the theory as a sequence of facts and logical deductions or inferences arising from these facts:

1. Individuals in a population vary in their characteristics, and these variations[1] are heritable (i.e. genetically based) at least in part.
2. New variation is created generation after generation.
3. Parents produce on average more offspring than are needed to replace them, and so populations have the potential to increase exponentially. Resources are finite and so will be insufficient to sustain all offspring in the long term.
4. As a consequence, there will be a struggle for existence, and only a fraction (often a very small fraction) of the offspring will survive to reproduce.
5. Survival is not random with respect to variation, and some variations will be better able to survive and will produce more offspring than others. This results in the accumulation of favourable variations at the expense of variations that are less favoured, generation after generation. The characteristics of the population slowly change over time (i.e. evolve).
6. Given sufficient time, the accumulated change will be large, and over vast geological time periods could account for the production of all species from a single ancestor.

We will be examining many of these statements in more detail throughout this book. In this chapter we will amplify these six simple statements in order to discuss some of the popular misconceptions about the process of natural selection. In addition, we also need to clarify the philosophical content of the theory.

---

[1] Darwin used the term 'variation' or 'variations' to describe the different forms of a particular characteristic or trait as well as individuals in the population. He did not use the term 'variety' to describe these individual differences because this term was used to describe the differences between different populations or races of a species.

3.1 | Some philosophical considerations

Darwin defined the favourableness of a particular variant in terms of its relative growth rate in the population, with favoured forms being better able to leave more descendants than forms that are less favoured (see statement 5 above). Note the phrase 'better able to', which indicates a probability rather than a certainty to the process. An individual with a favoured variation is not guaranteed to survive and produce more viable offspring than those with less favourable variations, it merely has a better chance of doing so. Thus, selection is stochastic[2] not deterministic, and this is why the eminent philosopher of Darwin's time, John Herschel, did not like the theory of natural selection and called it 'the law of higgledy-piggledy'. Many people still have difficulty comprehending this stochastic nature of natural selection, but, given enough chances, i.e. if the superior variant is produced repeatedly over many generations, the result is inevitable, the superior trait will increase in frequency in the population at the expense of less favoured traits.

Natural selection involves a statistical bias in the relative rates of survival from one generation to the next of alternative forms of the same characteristic or trait. By necessity, the selected entity must also have a high degree of permanence and a low rate of endogenous change (i.e. a low mutation rate) relative to the bias in survival (Williams 1966). This is important because if the character being selected is highly unstable over time, natural selection would be ineffective. In addition, the selected variation must be genetically transmitted from one generation to the next.

Natural selection, then, necessitates that selected variants have a high degree of permanence and be genetically transmitted between generations via the germ line. These fundamental requirements have important implications about how selection operates on populations and at what level (gene, individual or group). In most sexually reproducing populations, natural selection cannot select for a specific overall genotype or phenotype because an individual's genotype and phenotype are unique (see section 7.5). Simply put, an individual cannot be selected for because when it dies its genotype and phenotype is lost and will not be recreated exactly ever again. Thus, individuals in their entirety are not selected for or against in sexually reproducing populations, but certain traits are. The same is not true in asexually reproducing populations because the variation introduced by mutation is not amplified through the process of sexual recombination. In these populations it is more likely that a specific overall genotype or

---

[2] A stochastic process is one where there are chance effects. For example, if I have equal numbers of black and white balls in a bag and take out four balls at random I may pick anywhere from 0 to 4 black balls on any one occasion. However, if I repeat the process a large number of times, overall I will pick equal numbers of the two types (see Chapter 8).

phenotype can be selected. In all populations, however, the gene or genes that help control the various traits are replicated and transmitted from one generation to the next, and are reasonably permanent because mutation rates are low (see Chapter 7). For these reasons some Darwinians consider that selection operates at the level of the gene rather than the individual, although other Darwinians strenuously object to this view because selection involves the differential survival of individuals bearing different variations of traits. To some extent the argument is one of semantics and in most cases the outcomes of these two levels of selection are identical. However, the evolution of altruistic behaviour is best explained if we consider selection at the level of the gene (see section 19.2). For example, an individual may risk its life to protect the offspring of another family member. Such behaviour reduces the fitness of that individual and so one would expect it to be selected against if selection occurs at the level of the individual. However, a gene that promotes such behaviour could be favoured if more copies of the gene are likely to be saved in the offspring than are likely to be lost by the individual risking its life. The argument is complex because it involves the genetic relatedness of the individuals, and for this reason it is often called kin selection, but in essence we can explain this type of altruistic behaviour by examining the relative growth rates of genes in the population rather than the relative number of descendants of the individual risking its life.

What about selection at the group level, where there is differential survival of whole groups or populations which differ in their characteristics? Individual selection is normally stronger than group selection because individuals die faster than groups. Consequently, if a trait is favourable at both the individual and population levels there is usually no need to invoke group selection arguments for its evolution. Group selection, however, has been proposed to explain the evolution of traits where the evolutionary interests of the individual and group do not necessarily coincide. For example, in the early 1960s the British ecologist V. C. Wynne-Edwards proposed that many animals limit their production of offspring and self-regulate their populations so as not to overeat their food supply, and Konrad Lorenz and others proposed that animals with lethal weaponry limit their aggressive behaviour for the good of the species when fighting for mates. We will consider this last example in more detail in Chapter 19 (section 19.2.3) and here will simply consider Wynne-Edwards's group selection argument. He proposed that populations that self-regulate their density to remain in balance with the available resources survive, whereas those populations where there is overproduction of offspring over exploit their resources and die out. This is an anti-Darwinian argument or theory, so let us consider the fate of populations that follow the rules of group selection. Such populations are powerless to prevent the invasion of individuals that follow Darwinian rules. Such individuals could be introduced by either mutation or immigration, and they would overproduce their offspring. As a result, they would reap the benefits by increasing in frequency by leaving more descendants, but the costs would be borne by the whole group or population. It would only be a matter of time before the whole population obeyed Darwinian rules of overproduction. Group selection could occur if the species were subdivided into many small populations of closely related individuals, within which Darwinian mutations would be very rare, but the populations would also need to be totally isolated from each other to prevent the spread by migration of any Darwinian mutation that might arise. Most species don't have their populations structured in this way, and so most group selection arguments have been discredited and are generally no longer in vogue. This is not to say that group selection is impossible. The conditions for its occurrence (loosely described above) have been formulated mathematically by Hamilton (1975), and it has been plausibly proposed that group selection might explain the reduction of virulence toward their hosts by some endoparasites and pathogens (Frank 1996). This is a complex topic and a full discussion of this subject is beyond the scope of this book.

To return to our discussion of natural selection, newly created variation must be random with respect to need, i.e. not preferentially inclined toward adaptation. If new variation were usually advantageous, it would be mutation that was being creative rather than natural selection. The latter would merely remove those who didn't vary in the appropriate way. We will return to this matter again in Chapter 7. Evolution may be regarded as a mixture of chance (in the creation of new variants) and necessity (in the working of selection where inferior variants are slowly weeded out).

Natural selection, then, operates by sifting and sorting these random variations or mutations, so that over the course of long periods of time large changes may become evident through the accumulation of a series of small changes generation after generation. Large changes, however, are not inevitable, as Darwin noted (see section 2.1.3), because some forms stay remarkably constant over time, but if change occurs it is relatively slow and cumulative. This is what is meant by the term *gradualism*, to distinguish it from another possible way of evolution where completely new forms are created in a single step by macromutations. With the exception of polyploidy, we do not believe that new species or complex new structures are created in a single step, but if they were it would be mutation that is the creative force, not natural selection, which would merely serve to eliminate the inferior type. Thus, the formation of new species and complex new structures by natural selection is truly a creative process because they are gradually formed in a step-by-step manner. However, the selected variation must be of immediate advantage to the individual, it will not be selected because it may be of some advantage in the future. In creating complex forms or structures, each step along the way must have a selective advantage over the previous step. Thus, natural selection has no final purpose in mind.

We can summarize the philosophical content of the theory of natural selection as follows:

1. Evolution has no purpose. It is simply the struggle of individuals in populations to survive and to increase the representation of their genes in the next generation.
2. Evolution has no direction. It does not lead inevitably to higher things. In particular, the goal of evolution is not to produce humans. Organisms become better adapted to their local environment, and that is all.
3. Natural selection is materialistic. Evolution does not require the action of a deity, and there is no scientific evidence for God. The remarkable adaptations and structures of organisms have not been designed by a creator but have been formed in an entirely mechanistic manner.

The opposition of the church to this philosophy was understandable. The controversy was bitter and vitriolic at times because philosophical differences arouse greater passions than scientific or theoretical differences. Darwin's two theories were completely at odds with the general belief in Victorian England in the literal truth of the Bible, that the universe had been created and designed by God for humankind. The controversy continues to this day, with most of the criticism being directed towards the theory of natural selection rather than the idea of evolution.

We will now examine various questions, criticisms and misconceptions about natural selection. It is important that we ask such questions, and deal with the criticisms, otherwise we run the risk of the theory becoming a dogma. I should make two things clear, however, about the discussion in the remainder of this chapter. First, it is not intended as an attack on religion. I know that many students think that there is a conflict between Darwinian evolution and their religious belief, but this should not be the case. I profess to be a Christian, but my religious belief is a spiritual matter and not subject to scientific study, whereas my scientific training leads me to conclude that evolution is the only possible explanation for the observed diversity of life.

Second, the following discussion is not designed to persuade ardent antievolutionists and creationists to abandon their beliefs because, like most of us who hold strong convictions about one thing or another, they appear to be immune to rational argument. Rather it is intended to help open-minded students answer some of the common arguments against evolution. Further details may be found in Futuyma (1982), Strahler (1987) and Rennie (2002).

3.2 | Is natural selection a valid scientific theory?

It has been claimed that natural selection is a tautology, i.e. a circular argument of the form: 'Evolution is the survival of the fittest; the fittest are those that survive.' However, as Naylor and Handford (1985) and others have pointed out the logical argument of natural selection is anything but circular. As indicated at the beginning of this chapter, the argument for natural selection takes the form: a statement of facts regarding the variability of populations, a statement of facts regarding population growth and the resources necessary to sustain this growth potential, followed by logical inferences or deductions based on these facts. If either the facts or the inferences are incorrect, then the theory is false.

In a similar vein, it has also been claimed that the theory of natural selection is unscientific because it cannot be disproved, and in the words of one critic 'can explain everything, and therefore, nothing'. The scientific method relies on the ability to test, and potentially falsify, the constructs and predictions of theory. In the case of natural selection there are numerous ways in which the theory can be, and has been, tested. We can see if the basic constructs of the theory are true. Do populations vary in their characteristics and does this variation have a genetic basis, at least in part? Is new variation created every generation by copying errors in the duplication of DNA in the germ cell line? Is this new variation random with respect to need, i.e. is not preferentially inclined toward adaptation? Do populations have the potential to increase exponentially? None of these statements has to be true, but repeated observation has shown that they are, and so in this respect the theory of natural selection has passed repeated testing.

There are other consequences of the theory that can also be tested. For example, we saw in the last chapter (section 2.1.4) that natural selection cannot work if there is blending inheritance, as proposed by Darwin, but requires particulate inheritance (i.e. the genetic coding for particular attributes remain discrete). The type of inheritance was shown to be particulate in 1865 by Gregor Mendel but it was not until the turn of the century that his work was rediscovered.

Another consequence of evolution by natural selection is that it requires a very old earth in order for there to be sufficient time to create the diversity of life. In 1862, the physicist William Thomson (later Lord Kelvin) theorized that the earth had started as a molten mass and had been cooling ever since. He calculated that the age of the earth was probably 98 million years, and the absolute range of possible ages was between 25 and 400 million years. This was a serious blow to Darwinian evolution, and Thomson was quick to point it out. At the turn of the century, however, it was the eminent physicist who was proved to be wrong when it was discovered that radioactive materials produce heat when they decay. This discovery drastically lengthened the estimates of the age of the earth. Today, it is believed that the earth is approximately four and one-half billion years old (i.e. 4.5×10^9 years), and so there has been sufficient time for evolution to have occurred by natural selection. In any case, the point has been made. We can test the theory of natural selection in many ways and so it is a valid scientific theory.

3.3 | The argument from design

Many people, whether religious or not, believe that we are part of some grand design or purpose. Such an idea is very understandable because it is very comforting to believe that somewhere there is some-one in control, and for many people it gives their lives a sense of meaning. I suspect most of us harbour such thoughts to some extent. Darwin certainly did, but he was clear that his theory could not be interpreted in this way.

The argument from design is frequently associated with the the-ologian William Paley, whose 1802 book, *Natural Theology, or Evidences of the Existence and Attributes of the Deity Collected from the Appearances of Nature*, had so impressed Darwin by its logic during his time at Cambridge. Paley begins his argument with the following famous anecdote. Suppose one was crossing a heath and kicked against a stone and asked how it came to be there. One might answer that it might always have been there, but if one had kicked against a watch it would be foolish to answer the same question in the same way because the watch obviously had a maker that had designed it to measure time. Paley extended this logic to the works of nature and concluded that there are many natural contrivances which have been designed, eyes for seeing, wings for flying, and so on. So he argued:

> There cannot be design without a designer; contrivance, without a
> contriver; order without choice; arrangement, without anything capable
> of arranging; subserviency and relation to a purpose, without that
> which could intend a purpose; means suitable to an end, and executing
> their office in accomplishing that end, without the end ever having
> been contemplated, or the means accommodating to it. Arrangement,
> disposition of parts, subserviency of means to an end, relation of
> instruments to a use, imply the presence of intelligence and mind.

Paley concluded that one can see that the works of nature have been designed and, therefore, there must be a deity who has designed the world for humans. His argument was enormously influential on the church and British society and inspired the writing of some beau-tiful hymns. If we consider some of the stanzas of 'All things bright and beautiful', written by Cecil Frances Alexander (1823–95) the general sentiment is eloquently expressed.

> All things bright and beautiful,
> all creatures great and small,
> all things wise and wonderful,
> the Lord God made them all.

> Each little flower that opens,
> each little bird that sings,
> he made their glowing colours,
> he made their tiny wings.

And in verse 7:

> He gave us eyes to see them,
> and lips that we might tell
> how great is God almighty,
> who has made all things well.

It is comforting to think that we are surrounded by the works of God, who has designed things for us: animals and plants for us to eat, provide material for our clothing, housing and medicinal needs; beautiful, sweet-scented flowers for our enjoyment; singing birds; and a whole world of fascinating organisms that inspire us with their wonderful adaptations to one way of life or another. There are, however, some theological puzzles in this view of the world. Just the other day at church I was listening to the minister talk to the children about God's world. He talked of pretty flowers and beautiful birds, and other animals and plants that provide our daily needs. 'It is easy to understand why God created them,' he said, and the children agreed. 'But why did God create mosquitos?' This question simply resulted in puzzled frowns, and the minister and the children could find no answer. The minister told the children to ask their Sunday School teacher to see if they could provide any answer. Well, I was teaching them that day and I wish that I could relate how I gave an inspired answer, involving Darwinian evolution suitable for six- and seven-year-old children. The reality is that I hoped they would forget to ask, but of course they didn't! I simply told them that mosquitos don't make much sense from a human point of view, but from the viewpoint of a mosquito, humans make a lot of sense as a source of food. The children seemed unimpressed by my argument.

Without meaning to, my minister touched the Achilles heel of Paley's argument from design. If one accepts that an omnipotent deity has created the world in which we live to every last detail, then one must question the goodness of the creator. Thousands of babies are born each year with severe birth defects. Is this 'good' design? Let us consider one such genetic disease to make our point. The sickle-cell trait confers an advantage to individuals heterozygous for the trait because it confers a resistance to malaria, a highly adaptive characteristic in regions of the world where malaria is endemic. However, it condemns a large proportion of those individuals who are homozygous for the trait to an early death from complications arising from the distortion of the red blood cells. If we were designing a way to protect people from malaria, would we consider it morally justified protecting a proportion of the population at the expense of another portion of the population? I do not think so. We can, however, explain the evolution of the sickle-cell trait by means of natural selection, because that process is blind to the morality of conferring an increased fitness to one portion of the population at the expense of another portion.

Similarly, although we may be impressed with the apparent design of some organs, like the eye, other features of our anatomy leave much to be desired. Our lungs branch off from our alimentary canal and, as a result, it is common for people to choke to death when some particle of food blocks the trachea. Surely, it would be much better to have our breathing apparatus and alimentary canal totally separate from one another from a design point of view. The poor design is easily explained by evolution, because we are betrayed by our ancestry. Lungs evolved as outgrowths from the gut in certain fish, which swallowed air to provide additional oxygen to what could be supplied by the gills, enabling them to survive in stagnant water. There was no need for a rapid ventilation mechanism for the lungs in these fish because their oxygen requirements were less than ours, and so the problem of blocking the passage to the lungs was not so critical.

Darwin was to answer Paley's logic in his 1862 book, *On the Various Contrivances by which British and Foreign Orchids Are Fertilized by Insects*. The word 'contrivances' in the title was no accident: Darwin showed that orchids use all sorts of devices (contrivances) to encourage fertilization by insects. There seems to be no overall plan; there just seems to be a series of *ad hoc* solutions to ensure fertilization. This is what we might expect from natural selection as by chance one mechanism or another is used to promote fertilization by insects.

Michael Ghiselin (1969) has shown that the argument from design is a fallacy owing to a confusion of the words 'purpose' and 'function'. He provides an amusing example to show the absurdity of the logic. Imagine two gentlemen playing Russian roulette with a revolver with one bullet in the cylinder. They take turns spinning the cylinder, pointing the gun at their head, and pulling the trigger, until one is dead and the other can claim the prize. Now the revolver has a particular function in this game. It also has a particular purpose, but this has little to do with what the gun was originally designed for, i.e. its original purpose. But imagine a naive observer interpreting this differently. The revolver clearly has a purpose to decide a game of chance, and is obviously beautifully 'designed' for the game. The observer concludes that revolvers were designed to play games of Russian roulette. The logic may seem impeccable but we know the conclusion is incorrect. In fact, the revolver is simply functioning to help decide a game of chance. We could have used the gun for other functions, not intended in the original design, such as using the handle to crack open nuts or to knock a nail into a wall. The problem, then, is when we use the word 'purpose' we automatically tend to link it with the word 'design', which implies a designer or somebody who had that purpose in mind, whereas when we use the word 'function' we don't.

So beware of confusing the two words when dealing with the natural world. We may think that an organ has a particular purpose; for example, the purpose of eyes is to see. This implies that they were designed with this purpose in mind, presumably by God. If this were so, we might expect some unity of design. However, if we look at the variety of light sensing structures, including eyes, in the animal kingdom we see a vast array of types ranging from simple light spots that can detect light, to complex structures that can form an image (Dawkins 1996). It appears that different opportunities have been seized by different groups in a random way, just as we would predict from evolution by natural selection. Far better, then, to think of eyes having a particular function, rather than purpose.

3.4 | Explaining the seemingly impossible

Critics of the theory of evolution by means of natural selection frequently make comments like 'it is impossible for the human eye to have evolved by chance', or 'for hummingbirds to have evolved by chance would be just as likely as for a chimpanzee to type the complete works of Shakespeare', or 'it is just as likely that a hurricane driving through a junkyard would assemble a Boeing 747 by chance'. How do we answer this type of criticism?

What the critics mean by evolution by chance is not clear. On the one hand, our understanding of natural selection is that it is a chance affair as to what opportunities, in the form of new variants, arise and are utilized during evolution. On the other hand, however, selection itself is anything but random because the favoured variants must be better adapted than other forms. The main confusion of this type of criticism, however, is that it implies that complex structures or organisms arise in a single step. It envisions that in one generation there is no eye and in the next a fully functional eye, or that a new type of bird like the hummingbird arises in one generation. Of course we do not believe this. Natural selection operates on a series of very small changes and slowly accumulates their effects generation after generation. The eye or hummingbird was created slowly over many thousands of generations.

The power of cumulative selection is astonishing. Richard Dawkins in his 1986 book, *The Blind Watchmaker*, has a marvellous illustration of the difference between single step, and cumulative selection. He looked at the probability of typing the works of Shakespeare at random. To make the problem more manageable he selected a single sentence – METHINKS IT IS LIKE A WEASEL – from an exchange between Hamlet and Polonius in the play *Hamlet*. Now Dawkins didn't have a tame chimpanzee to type at random and so used his 11-month-old daughter instead. Not surprisingly, she failed to type the sentence correctly. We can calculate her chance of typing the sentence correctly by choosing letters at random. Again, to simplify the problem we will imagine a keyboard of only 27 characters: 26 letters of the alphabet and a space. The chance of typing the first letter correctly is one in 27, and the chance of typing the first two letters correctly is $(1/27) \times (1/27)$ or one in 729. The chance of typing all 28 characters in the sentence correctly (a space is a character) is $(1/27)^{28}$ or approximately one in 10 000 000 000 000 000 000 000 000 000 000 000 000 000, which, as we all know, is one in ten thousand million million million

million million million! Obviously, the chance of typing this single sentence by randomly selecting characters from the keyboard is so low as to be practically impossible, and we should remember that the real chance is much lower than this because most keyboards have more than 100 characters, not 27. If we programmed a super fast computer to type 28 characters at random, it would still take an astronomical number of years to type this one sentence correctly. So it is effectively impossible to type at random the complete works of Shakespeare. The critics are correct.

Now instead of single step selection, let us see the effects of cumulative selection. We program a computer to select a sequence of 28 characters at random (only allowing the 26 letters of the alphabet or a space to be selected). The first sequence is almost certainly a meaningless jumble of letters and spaces. The computer is then programmed to 'breed' from this sequence by duplicating the sequence generation after generation, but with a certain chance error (we can call it mutation) in the copying of each character. The computer selects by keeping the correct letters or spaces as they occur at random, and so they progressively accumulate, generation after generation, until the correct sequence is reached.

You can play this game, or a slight variation of it, by logging on to the Populus program.[3] Then you select Games and Woozleology (instructions on how to use the program is provided when you log on to the program). Instead of the sentence used by Dawkins, the programmers have used METHINKS IT IS A WOOZLE. When I ran the game, I obtained the following sequence:

Generation		
	1	G ZFJZF YGJRQXVKZS IVINPGDJ
	4	CDHVKJKZ BEDASRFOOM AMJSBU D
	8	OHHFQTKC QLIGS RLKE ACXITHMJ
	17	GOHYHNKS XGUGS LIKE ALTOA QQ
	41	IUNLINKS EMSLS LIKE A LOVZQA
	80	YUTPINKS IT YS LIKE A WOQZPJ
	125	METHINKS IT IS LIKE A WOOZLE

I didn't have a single correct character in the first try, but generation after generation the correct characters accumulate and one sees the correct phrase being evolved in a sequential way. It took about one-tenth of a second in this case, which tells a great deal about the evolution of faster computers because it took Dawkins's computer about 11 seconds to evolve the sentence in just 43 generations.

We see that what is effectively impossible to create in a single step is very feasible with cumulative selection. In some respects this simple game mimics the process of natural selection but, as the critics will be quick to point out, in other ways it doesn't. For one thing, evolution does not have a long-term goal or target, as we have in this example, and in addition it is difficult to visualize the significance

---

[3] You may download Populus 3.4 from the Internet by accessing www.cbs.umn.edu/software/populus.html.

Fig. 3.1 The 'leaf' in the centre of the collection of dead leaves is a grasshopper. (Photograph by the author.)

of the intermediate steps. Remember that each step on the path to a complex structure must have a selective advantage over the previous step, and so we really do need to answer questions of the sort 'What good is half an eye?'

Let us consider the evolution of natural things that we consider to be perfect, or nearly so. We will look at four examples and show that the approach to solving the riddle of perfection is similar in each case. The first example considers one of the many cases of mimicry. I was walking in a National Park in Zimbabwe, looking for signs of small mammals, when I noticed a set of insect footprints leading to what I thought was a dead leaf. As I stooped to turn over the leaf to see what was hiding underneath I realized that the leaf was, in fact, a grasshopper (Fig. 3.1). One can see that it has a spectacular resemblance to certain fallen leaves. It would be a keen-eyed insectivore that spotted this potential prey item, and it is obvious that the camouflage is highly adaptive for survival. Not only does this insect mimic fallen leaves almost to perfection, it also times its life cycle so that the adult appears at the beginning of the dry season when a fallen leaf doesn't appear out of place.

If we only looked at this single insect we might consider its mimicry to be miraculous, but if we examine a wide range of grasshoppers we would find a wide range of 'attempts' at camouflage, some good and others much less impressive. Two further examples are provided (Figs. 3.2 and 3.3). In fact, even a modest degree of camouflage provides some protection from being eaten. Perhaps in the evolutionary history of our mimicker of dead leaves it began by being brown in colour. Slowly the shade of colouring was selected to match the colour of certain common dead leaves. The shape of the body and legs was slowly modified to resemble the twisted shape of the leaf, and so on. Little by little the perfectness of the resemblance could be improved, and each step would provide the owner with just a little more protection from predators than its relatives and so it would be selected by natural selection.

Fig. 3.2 This dead grasshopper was so well camouflaged that after placing it on the lawn I could not find it in order to take its photograph. I had to wait until a trail of ants led me to it, but not before they had consumed part of the body. (Photograph by the author.)

Fig. 3.3 A more conventional and to most people a less spectacularly camouflaged grasshopper. Nevertheless, on an appropriate background this too is extremely difficult to see. (Photograph by the author.)

Our next example is to explain how our eyes could have evolved. For many people it is incomprehensible how such a complex organ could have evolved little by little. They cannot imagine how less-than-perfect eyes can have any adaptive or selective value. However, if we look at the range of light-detecting organs in molluscs, a phylum which has a wide array of such structures, we can obtain some clues as to the probable evolutionary path in developing such a complex structure (Fig. 3.4). Some of the simplest structures are innervated pigment cells called light spots that can detect light (Fig. 3.4a). The light spot functions to tell the animal if it is light or dark and the animal can adjust its activities to the general pattern of light. This may be all that is required in a sessile, filter-feeding species. One possible next step is to have an invagination or infolding of the pigment cells (Fig. 3.4b) which may provide some protection to the light-detecting

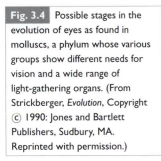

Fig. 3.4 Possible stages in the evolution of eyes as found in molluscs, a phylum whose various groups show different needs for vision and a wide range of light-gathering organs. (From Strickberger, *Evolution*, Copyright © 1990: Jones and Bartlett Publishers, Sudbury, MA. Reprinted with permission.)

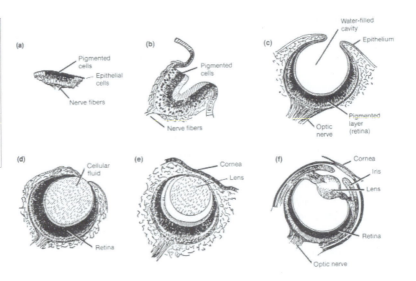

structure. This change also improves light detection in two ways. First, the cells are more concentrated and so there is a better ability to detect variation in light intensity, and second, there is some ability to detect the direction of light because light rays coming from one side will stimulate cells on the opposite side of the invagination. Animals with this type of 'eye' may be more mobile and can move appropriately in relation to changes in light intensity. As the invagination and number of light-sensitive cells increases the eye can begin to function more and more efficiently as a pinhole camera in which images are formed on the pigmented layer (Fig. 3.4c). A fairly sophisticated eye of this type is found in *Nautilus* and allows the animal to search actively for food. The next logical step is where the water-filled cavity is replaced by a transparent cellular fluid to protect the pigmented layer, or retina, from injury (Fig. 3.4d). There is a further development along this line in other molluscs, in which the eye is covered by a layer of transparent skin, providing further protection, and some of the cellular fluid hardens into a primitive convex lens which improves the focusing of light on the retina (Fig. 3.4e). Finally, the complex eye, which is found in squids and octopus, is similar in structure to ours in that there is a cornea, an adjustable iris to vary the amount of light entering the eye, and a lens to focus the light on the retina (Fig 3.4f). These animals are predators and their eyes enable them to locate their prey. What is clear from this series of eyes in the molluscs is that there is a logical sequence of functional eyes from the more simple to the complex. The eyes function in rather different ways, and as they become more complex allow the development of an active way of life.

It is likely that the evolution of the vertebrate eye followed a similar path to what I have described for the molluscs. The evolution of eyes is a complex subject. They have evolved independently no fewer than 40 times, and probably more than 60 times, and there are many different types. An interesting account of the different types of eyes and the way in which they probably evolved is given in Dawkins' 1996 book, *Climbing Mount Improbable*.

Our last two examples look at the molecular level of organization. Michael Behé (1996) has revived the argument from design in his book *Darwin's Black Box*. Behé agrees that arguments for the evolution of complex structures like the eye, in the manner I have just described, are plausible when considered at that level of organization, but he believes that these arguments fail when one considers these structures at the molecular level of organization. Behé's argument is simple. First, there are many biochemical pathways and molecular structures that are irreducibly complex, such that if a part of them were missing they would be non-functional. Second, their complexity cannot be evolved by combining different parts from various areas in the cell because the different parts wouldn't fit together properly, the intermediate steps of doing this wouldn't function, and so they could not be selected for by natural selection. Behé's concludes that these irreducibly complex structures and pathways must have been created by an intelligent designer, presumably God. Behé's arguments have been refuted in detail by Kenneth Miller (1999), and I will briefly use just two of Miller's arguments here.

First, are the biochemical pathways and molecular structures of cells irreducibly complex as Behé claims? Consider Behé's example of the microtubule structure of cilia. If we examine a cross section of a cilium we see an outer ring of 9 doublet microtubules around a central core of 2 single microtubules. Behé implies that this 9 + 2 arrangement of microtubules is universal in eukaryotes, and that this arrangement is necessary for them to function, i.e. they are irreducibly complex. However, as Miller (1999) points out, this arrangement of microtubules is not universal and many other arrangements occur, among them a 9 + 0 arrangement in the sperm of the eel (*Anguilla*), a 6 + 0 arrangement in the protozoan *Lecudina tuzetae* and a 3 + 0 arrangement in another protozoan, *Diplauxis hatti*. All of these arrangements of microtubules are functional, and one can readily imagine the level of complexity of microtubule arrangement being increased in a step-by-step manner through evolution. Clearly, the 9 + 2 arrangement of microtubules in cilia is not irreducibly complex, and Miller (1999) goes on to consider examples of biochemical pathways that are also not irreducibly complex as claimed by Behé.

Second, is it possible to evolve a complex system by combining different parts from different sources? Consider the lac-operon system that regulates the use of lactose sugar as an energy source in cells (Fig. 3.5). To simplify matters I will only consider the operation of the system in the absence of glucose. When there is no lactose, a repressor gene (*lacI*) produces a repressor protein that binds with the operator (O) and prevents transcription of the three structural genes (*lacZ*, *lacY* and *lacA*). When lactose is available, some will leak into the cell, although the cell membrane is largely impermeable to lactose. Some of the lactose molecules are converted to allolactose by the enzyme β-galactosidase (apparently there is some residual activity

Fig. 3.5 The utilization of lactose as controlled by the lac-operon (simplified). The sequence of genes in the operon are the promoter (P) to the regulatory gene (*lacI*) followed by its terminator (t), and the promoter (P) and operator (O) of the three structural genes, *lacZ*, *lacY* and *lacA*, followed by their terminator (t). For explanation of the system see text.

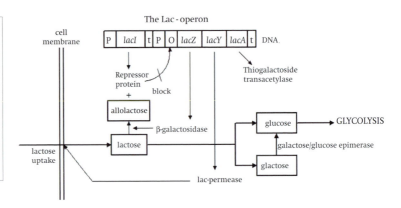

The Lac-operon

of the *lacZ* gene even when the structural genes are switched off) and the allolactose molecules combine with the repressor proteins and modify their shape so that they can no longer bind with the operator. This effectively switches on the gene and three enzymes are produced: *lacY* produces lac-permease which brings lactose into the cell from outside, *lacZ* produces β-galactosidase which hydrolyses this lactose into glucose and galactose (and the latter is converted into glucose by another enzyme from a different gene), and *lacA* produces another enzyme whose function is not clear. If the concentration of lactose falls again, the repressor protein molecules are not blocked and so the gene is switched off. This provides us with an example of a biochemical pathway that is sufficiently complex to see if it could evolve through natural selection. The essential elements are: (1) a system to switch the gene on or off in relation to the concentration of lactose, (2) the production of an enzyme to convert lactose into glucose and galactose, and (3) the production of another enzyme to make the cell membrane permeable to lactose.

Barry Hall (1983) performed a series of experiments on the bacterium *Escherichia coli* to see whether this organism could replace the lac-operon system if it were disabled. He did this by deleting the *lacZ* gene so that no lactose could be utilized by the cell, and then provided lactose as an energy source. At first the cultures couldn't utilize lactose, but before long mutant strains appeared that could utilize the lactose. How was this possible? Studies showed that a single point mutation was occurring in the β-galactosidase gene (*ebgA*) located in the evolved β-galactosidase (ebg) operon, which is not related to the lac-operon. The normal, wild-type β-galactosidase from this gene cannot hydrolyse lactose, but the mutation allowed it to do so. In most cases the mutated gene was always active, but in some of the bacteria a mutation in the regulatory gene (*ebgR*) regulated the activity of the *ebgA* gene according to the concentration of lactose. Thus, some bacteria evolved a system that incorporates the first two essential elements of the lac-operon in another gene.

This all seems perfect, but the bacteria cannot utilize the lactose unless it can enter the cell. To this point Hall had been inducing the production of lac-permease artificially to bring the lactose into the cell. However, some of the cells that had evolved to utilize both lactose and lactulose (another β-galactoside sugar), as a result of a second point mutation in the *ebgA* gene, produced a form of β-galactosidase that naturally converted some of the lactose to allolactose, and this switched on the lac-operon to produce lac-permease in the normal way. Thus, the last essential element of the lactose utilizing system has been partially developed.

What this set of experiments demonstrates is that it is possible to evolve complex systems by the accumulation through natural selection of random mutations. Moreover, we see the modified lac-operon and the mutated ebg-operon interacting to form a system that has all the essential elements of a highly regulated system to utilize lactose as an energy source. The evidence does not support Behé's assertion that this is impossible.

This brings me to the final point I wish to make. We have seen that one frequently obtains clues as to how perfect, or nearly perfect, structures have evolved when one makes a comparative survey of these structures in other groups of organisms. Dawkins in his 1996 book makes a powerful metaphor for what confronts the person who wonders how such exquisitely adapted organ systems and organisms might have been created, and that is Mount Improbable. We reach the base of the mountain and are confronted by enormously high, sheer cliffs, and our object (the eye, or whatever else we wonder about) is at the top. Some travellers stay at the base of the cliffs, staring at the lofty object, and conclude that it is impossible to reach such heights without divine intervention, because they believe that the structure must be formed in a single step. Others question how such complex things could have developed, but by searching further find on the other side of the mountain gentle sloping paths that can be travelled step by step until the summit is reached. No divine intervention is necessary. There are other peaks on Mount Improbable where it is possible to find intermediate types, or totally different types, of the structure we are interested in. The organisms on these peaks usually cannot cross from one peak to another, only the traveller, diligently making a map of the whole mountain, can show the most likely paths these organisms have followed in their evolutionary history.

We will explore this Darwinian view of life in the rest of this book as we consider the way populations grow, either in isolation or in the presence of other populations, as we examine basic population genetics, and finally when we consider certain aspects of animal behaviour.

Part II

Simple population growth models and their simulation

This part of the book provides an introduction to some simple mathematical models that describe the growth of populations, and Quattro Pro and Excel spreadsheet programs are used to simulate these populations. The emphasis is on making a quantitative assessment of the consequences of Darwin's 'overproduction of offspring' and some aspects of 'the struggle for existence'.

Two basic types of population growth models are described. First, the consequences of Darwin's 'overproduction' of organisms are considered in Chapter 4, and described in mathematical terms using the geometric and exponential growth models. These models assume that there are no limits to the numbers of organisms and show that all populations growing in this manner will soon exhaust the earth's resources. Second, in Chapter 5 we look at one aspect of Darwin's 'struggle for existence', intraspecific competition, which occurs when a population grows in an environment of finite size. This form of growth is described using the logistic, or sigmoid, growth model, which has some rather restrictive assumptions. This basic model is then modified to assess the effects of time lags and environmental variation on the form of population growth. The models are applied to laboratory and field data show how they relate to reality.

Many population phenomena can be described by recurrence equations, which can be used repeatedly to describe a population through a series of generations. For example, the number of individuals in the present generation is related in some way to the number in the previous generation, which in turn is related to the number in the generation before that, and so on. Thus, once we know how the state of one generation is related to the next, we can use a single equation repeatedly to estimate the state of a series of generations, providing the relationship does not change. Spreadsheet programs, like Quattro

Pro or Excel, are ideal for simulating simple population phenomena because the cells of spreadsheets can be linked to each other in much the same way that the states of different generations are linked. This will be demonstrated as the various growth models are simulated using either Quattro Pro or Excel. It is important that you try the simulations yourself, because you will learn some very basic skills that should be useful to you for a variety of purposes.

Chapter 4

Density-independent growth and overproduction

Darwin noted that on average parents produce more offspring during their lifetime than are needed to replace themselves, and so populations have the potential to increase in number. This fact is one of the cornerstones of his theory of natural selection and we can ask why organisms should have this characteristic? Why should there be an overproduction of offspring? Perhaps the easiest way to answer this question is to consider the fate of populations which do not have this characteristic. Obviously, if individuals cannot fully replace themselves, the population will decline to zero and be eliminated. Populations adopting an exact replacement strategy suffer the same fate, because there is always a chance that some individuals will die before they reproduce and so these populations will decline to extinction as their reproductive base shrinks. Thus, although natural selection can select for any reproductive rate, providing that rate leaves the most descendants, only those populations where there is an overproduction of offspring survive over the long term, the others are eliminated.

We can conclude that overproduction is one of the necessary conditions for the long-term survival of populations, allowing them to compensate for pre-reproductive losses and to recover from reductions in population size. We can make similar arguments for the long-term survival of variation in the population. There must be overproduction of copies of specific variants if they are to survive and not be eliminated from the population, and we should bear these facts in mind when we consider the production of new variation by mutation in Chapter 7 and the selection of different variants in Chapters 10 to 12.

Thus, organisms produce more offspring than are required to replace themselves, and as a consequence populations have the potential to increase in numbers. In this chapter we will look at two simple models of population growth in which the rate of growth remains constant, in order to understand the consequences of this type of growth.

4.1 | Introducing density-independent growth

In our mathematical models, population size is denoted by the symbol N and we use subscripts to indicate the size of the population at different times. So N_t is the size of the population at time t, N_1 and N_2 the sizes of the population at times 1 and 2, and so on. By convention we use N_0 (i.e. size of the population at time 0) to indicate the starting time of population growth. We also use the symbols Δ and δ to denote changes in population size.

The units of time, t, will vary according to the type of organism we are studying. For rapidly growing populations like bacteria, t may be in minutes; whereas for many trees and vertebrates, t may be measured in years. We use the symbols Δ and δ to denote intervals of time.

Most of us recognize that the series 1, 2, 4, 8, 16, 32, 64, etc., forms an exponential or geometric series. What is the difference in these two terms? Exponential growth is where the population is measured at any point in time, whereas geometric growth is where the population is measured at fixed discrete time intervals. Thus, they amount to the same thing, the only difference being whether we measure time continuously or at discrete intervals.

4.2 | Growth at discrete time intervals: geometric growth

A population may change in size over a discrete time interval as a result of four factors: birth, death, immigration and emigration. If we simplify things by considering a closed population where there is no immigration or emigration we can see that the change in population size over a time interval ($\Delta N/\Delta t$) is equal to the number of births (B) less the number of deaths (D) during that same time interval, as shown in the following expression:

$$\frac{\Delta N}{\Delta t} = B - D \qquad \text{(Exp. 4.1)}$$

The change in population size as well as the number of births (B) and deaths (D) are related to the size of the population, N, and the rates per capita (i.e. rates per individual) are determined by dividing through by the population size, N, at the start of Δt to obtain the following:

$$\frac{(\Delta N/\Delta t)}{N} = \frac{B}{N} - \frac{D}{N} \qquad \text{(Exp. 4.2)}$$

However, the birth rate (B/N) minus the death rate (D/N) is equal to the per capita, or per individual, rate of increase, R_m, and so Exp. 4.2 can be rewritten as:

$$\frac{(\Delta N/\Delta t)}{N} = R_\mathrm{m} \qquad \text{(Exp. 4.3)}$$

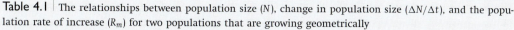

Table 4.1 The relationships between population size (N), change in population size ($\Delta N/\Delta t$), and the population rate of increase (R_m) for two populations that are growing geometrically

	Population A: multiplication rate, λ, $= 2$			Population B: multiplication rate, λ, $= 3$		
Time (t)	N	$\Delta N/\Delta t$	$(\Delta N/\Delta t)/N = R_m$	N	$\Delta N/\Delta t$	$(\Delta N/\Delta t)/N = R_m$
0	1	$2-1=1$	$1/1=1$	1	$3-1=2$	$2/1=2$
1	2	$4-2=2$	$2/2=1$	3	$9-3=6$	$6/3=2$
2	4	$8-4=4$	$4/4=1$	9	$27-9=18$	$18-9=2$
3	8	$16-8=8$	$8-8=1$	27	$81-27=54$	$54-27=2$
4	16	etc.	etc.	81	etc.	etc.

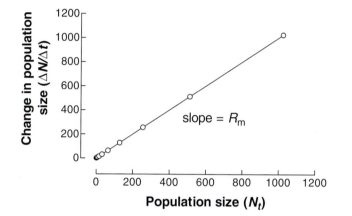

slope = R_m

Fig. 4.1 To show that the change in population size over a fixed time interval ($\Delta N/\Delta t$) is linearly related to population size (N) as described by Eqn 4.1. The slope of the relationship equals the rate of increase, R_m. Data as in Fig. 4.2.

This can be rearranged to form our first equation:

$$\frac{\Delta N}{\Delta t} = R_m N \qquad \text{(Eqn 4.1)}$$

This equation shows that the change in population size is directly proportional to population size, provided the growth rate per capita, R_m, remains constant (Fig. 4.1). We will use this equation in section 4.4 as a basis for the development of the exponential growth model. Meanwhile, we can show that the mathematical relationship described by Eqn 4.1 is correct by looking at two geometric series in Table 4.1, where the population either doubles or triples each time period.

Let us now develop an equation to predict the future size of the population. Population size after one time step will equal the original population size plus the change in number, which is expressed mathematically by the following expression:

$$N_1 = N_0 + \frac{\Delta N}{\Delta t} \qquad \text{(Exp. 4.4)}$$

Substituting Eqn 4.1 for $\Delta N/\Delta t$ and setting $N = N_0$, Exp. 4.4 is modified to:

$$N_1 = N_0 + R_m N_0 \qquad \text{(Exp. 4.5)}$$

This reduces to:

$$N_1 = N_0(1 + R_m) \qquad \text{(Exp. 4.6)}$$

The multiplication rate, λ, from one time period to the next is N_1/N_0, and therefore

$$N_1 = N_0\lambda \qquad \text{(Exp. 4.7)}$$

A comparison of Exps. 4.6 and 4.7 reveals that

$$\lambda = 1 + R_m \qquad \text{(Exp. 4.8)}$$

Thus, the multiplication rate, λ, can be considered to be made up of two parts: the value 1 representing the population size at the start of the time interval, and the value of the rate of increase per capita (or individual), R_m, over the time interval, Δt. We can see that this relationship is consistent if we look at the values of λ and R_m in Table 4.1. If the birth rate exceeds the death rate, then $R_m > 0$ and $\lambda > 1$ and the population will increase in size; if the birth and death rates are equal, then $R_m = 0$ and $\lambda = 1$ and the population will stay the same size; and if the death rate exceeds the birth rate, then $R_m < 0$ (i.e. it will be negative) and $\lambda < 1$ and the population will decrease in size.

From Exp. 4.7 we see that the population size after two time steps is

$$N_2 = N_1\lambda \qquad \text{(Exp. 4.9)}$$

and substituting Exp. 4.7 for N_1 in Exp. 4.9 yields:

$$N_2 = N_0\lambda\lambda = N_0\lambda^2 \qquad \text{(Exp. 4.10)}$$

We can do this for successive time steps to show that the general case is provided by the following equation:

$$N_t = N_0\lambda^t \qquad \text{(Eqn 4.2)}$$

The size of the population at fixed intervals of time can now be predicted (Fig. 4.2) provided we know the starting number, N_0, and there is a constant multiplication rate, λ, during each time interval, Δt.

Fig. 4.2 Geometric growth over 10 discrete time steps, starting with a population size of 1 and a multiplication rate (λ) of 2 each time step.

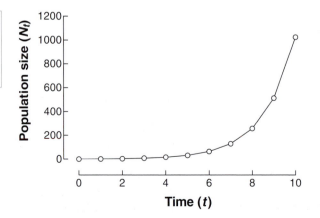

The time intervals, Δt, may be arbitrarily defined (one week, 10 days, 20 minutes, etc.), or may correspond to the natural generation time of the organism.

Many students will have found this section on the geometric growth model to be rather unsatisfying. You may follow the logic of the algebraic proofs, but at the end it all seems so abstract. What does it all mean, what should one remember, and how can one apply the model? To help answer these questions, we will now consider two examples of the use of the model.

Example 4.1 *A bacterial population has a doubling time of 20 minutes (has a λ of 2). Starting with a population of 10 bacteria, what would be the potential population size after 12 hours?*

We can use Eqn 4.2 to solve this problem, where $N_0 = 10$, $\lambda = 2$ and $t = 3 \times 12 = 36$ (there are three 20-minute periods per hour). Thus, $N_t = 10 \times 2^{36} = 687\,194\,767\,360$.

Example 4.2 *An insect population is observed to increase from 6 to 15 individuals over a two-week period. What will be the population size after 10 weeks (from time 0) if the multiplication rate stays the same?*

First, we determine the value of the multiplication rate (λ) which is equal to $15/6 = 2.5$ for a period of two weeks. Then we calculate the number of time intervals, t, which is equal to $10/2 = 5$ (the number of two-week periods in 10 weeks). Finally, we use Eqn 4.2, setting $N_0 = 6$, and solve for N_t. Thus, $N_t = 6 \times 2.5^5 = 585.9$, or 586 individuals.

4.3 | Simulating geometric growth

We can simulate the form of population growth we have just described using a spreadsheet program. This achieves two things: it enables us to use the various equations and graph the results quickly so that we have a visual representation of the various relationships, and it also introduces us to the power of using spreadsheets to simulate all sorts of population models. It is important that you do these simulations yourself, not just read about them in this book. The instructions provided (see Appendix 4.1 at the end of this chapter) are suitable for users of either Quattro Pro or Excel, but other spreadsheet programs follow a similar logic.

Our simulation of geometric growth produces two graphs (Figs. 4.1 and 4.2) which show the form of the relationships of Eqns 4.1 and 4.2, respectively. If we look at the form of growth over time it looks as if the population is growing at a faster and faster rate (Fig. 4.2) even though the growth rate remains constant. This is because the change in population size is linearly related to population size (Fig. 4.1), and so as the population grows larger in size, the increase in size grows proportionately. We will return to this point later.

The model of geometric growth that we have just described and simulated has one quirk. The value of the multiplication rate (λ) is linked to the discrete time step, Δt, and if we change the value of Δt we cannot change the value of λ by simple scaling. For example, imagine we studied a bacterial population at 20-minute intervals and determined that the population was doubling each time step, i.e. $\lambda = 2$. If we wished to model the population at 10-minute intervals, λ would not equal 1 (i.e. half of 2) because this would indicate that the population is not growing at all. The method of converting λ from one time interval to another is developed in the next section at the end of the exponential growth model.

4.4 | Continuous growth through time: exponential growth

If we make the time intervals infinitesimally small in our discrete growth model, Eqn 4.1 is modified to the following differential equation:

$$\frac{\delta N}{\delta t} = r_{\mathrm{m}} N \qquad \text{(Eqn 4.3)}$$

The expression $\delta N / \delta t$ represents the change in population size at an instant of time, and is the tangent to the population growth curve at population size N. The slope of the tangent is r_{m}, which is the instantaneous rate of increase, sometimes called the intrinsic rate of natural increase or the Malthusian parameter after Thomas Malthus. The value of r_{m} is equal to the instantaneous birth rate minus the instantaneous death rate, i.e. $r_{\mathrm{m}} = b - d$. The value of R_{m} in our discrete growth model converges to the value of r_{m} as we make the time steps, Δt, smaller and smaller. Thus, r_{m} is the growth rate per capita, just like R_{m}, only the time scale is different.

To predict population size at any time t, i.e. N_t, we integrate Eqn 4.3 following the rules of calculus. This is a trivial exercise for anyone familiar with the rules of integral calculus, but is unintelligible for those who are not. Do not worry if you don't know calculus. All we are doing by integrating an equation is to add up all of the small changes within defined limits. In this case we add up the infinitesimally small changes in population size from time 0 (our starting time) to time t. When this is done, the integral form is:

$$N_t = N_0 e^{r_{\mathrm{m}} t} \qquad \text{(Eqn 4.4)}$$

This equation is the same as the formula for compound interest, where N_0 is the principle sum invested, r_{m} is the rate of interest, and N_t is the balance after time t. We can also note that Eqn 4.4 is similar in form to Eqn 4.2 ($N_t = N_0 \lambda^t$), and describes the same form of growth that is illustrated in Fig. 4.2. A comparison of Eqns 4.2 and 4.4 reveals that

$$e^{r_{\mathrm{m}}} = \lambda \qquad \text{(Eqn 4.5)}$$

and taking the logarithm of both sides of this equation gives:

$$r_{\mathrm{m}} = \ln \lambda \qquad \text{(Eqn 4.6)}$$

The value of r_m can be easily scaled from one set of time units to another. For example, if the value of r_m is 0.1 per day, then the r_m value per week is $0.1 \times 7 = 0.7$. In order to convert the multiplication rate, λ, from one timescale to another, however, one must first calculate the r_m value equivalent to λ, make the conversion, and then convert the new r_m value back to the new λ using Eqn 4.5. Thus, if λ per week is 2 and we wish to know the λ per day, we first calculate r_m per week ($= \ln 2 = 0.6931$), then divide this by 7 to obtain r_m per day ($0.6931/7 = 0.0990$), and finally convert this value back to λ per-day ($e^{0.099} = 1.104$). Ecologists tend to use r_m rather than λ, because it is very easy to compare the growth rates of different species that have been measured using different time scales. Population geneticists, however, use λ in their models because they are usually considering the growth of genotypes on a per-generation basis.

Finally, we will derive one last pair of equations. If we take the logarithm of both sides of Eqns 4.4 and 4.2, we obtain the following:

$$\ln(N_t) = \ln(N_0) + r_m t \qquad \text{(Eqn 4.7)}$$
$$\ln(N_t) = \ln(N_0) + \ln(\lambda)t \qquad \text{(Eqn 4.8)}$$

These two equations are equivalent. They show that the logarithm of population size changes linearly through time if the populations are growing exponentially or geometrically. Thus, we can see if a population is growing exponentially by plotting the logarithm of population size over time. If it conforms to a straight line the population is growing exponentially and the intrinsic rate of increase, r_m, is given by the slope of the graph (Fig. 4.3).

Let us consider two more examples to show how to apply the exponential growth equations.

Example 4.3 *A certain species of rat breeds continuously and has an estimated rate of natural increase (r_m) of 0.0143 per day. A small number invade a garbage dump where living conditions are ideal. How long will it take the population to double in size?*

First, rearrange Eqn 4.4 ($N_t = N_0 e^{r_m t}$) to $N_t / N_0 = e^{r_m t}$. If the population doubles in size, $N_t/N_0 = 2$. Taking the logarithm of both sides

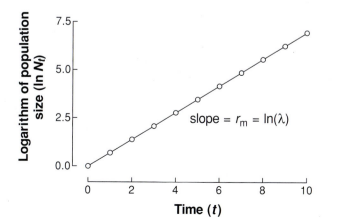

slope $= r_m = \ln(\lambda)$

Fig. 4.3 Exponential and geometric growth of a population plotted on logarithmic scale using the same values as in Fig. 4.2.

of the rearranged equation we have ln 2 = 0.6931 = 0.0143 × t, and so t = 48.47 or approximately 48 days.

Example 4.4 *A continuously growing population was observed to double in size every three days. Calculate the multiplication rate (λ) per day and per week.*

The λ per three days = 2. To calculate the λ at other timescales use Eqns 4.5 and 4.6. From Eqn 4.6 we see that r_m per three days = ln(2) = 0.6931, and so the r_m per day = 0.6931/3 = 0.2310, and the r_m per week is 7 × 0.2310 = 1.6173. Then use Eqn 4.5 to calculate the λ per day = $e^{0.2310}$ = 1.26, and the λ per week = $e^{1.6173}$ = 5.04.

4.5 | Simulating exponential growth

We will now continue with our simulation exercise (see Appendix 4.2 at the end of this chapter) to include the continuous time model. When you do this, you will see that the plot of Eqn 4.7 (and it would be the same for Eqn 4.8) conforms to Fig. 4.3. In addition, we can show that the geometric growth model is a special case of the exponential growth model.

4.6 | The population bomb

Populations can increase to astounding numbers when there are no limits on growth (i.e. growth continues at an exponential rate). We often talk of the population bomb because the process of exponential or geometric population growth resembles that of an atomic bomb, in which an atom splits and the fragments go on to split more atoms leading to a chain reaction and an explosion. The explosion in numbers of organisms takes place more slowly than an atomic explosion but the result is just as inevitable. A few examples will make this clear.

Our spreadsheet simulations show that a single individual will give rise to 1024 individuals after 10 generations of doubling. After another 10 generations the population will be 1 048 576 individuals (2^{20}), and half of this total will have been added in the last generation. Bacteria, such as *E. coli*, can divide (double) every 20 minutes and so a population can potentially double 72 times a day. Thus, a single individual can potentially increase to approximately 4.722 thousand million million million individuals during the course of one day!

I was reading in a local paper that the female housefly (*Musca domestica*) can lay 75–150 eggs at a time, and lays up to 800 in its month-long life. The eggs hatch into maggots within a day and the larvae reach their full size in about five days. They pupate for a few days, and when they emerge they begin mating almost immediately. Their generation time is about two weeks, and so the offspring of a female

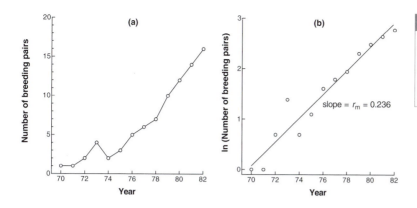

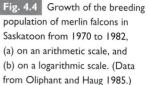

Fig. 4.4 Growth of the breeding population of merlin falcons in Saskatoon from 1970 to 1982, (a) on an arithmetic scale, and (b) on a logarithmic scale. (Data from Oliphant and Haug 1985.)

are producing their own offspring before the female's reproductive life is over. There will be about seven generations of flies during a typical summer in Canada. We can estimate the potential production of a pair of flies, one male and one female, during a summer. We set λ as 400, assuming a 50:50 sex ratio (a female will give rise to 400 female offspring), t is 7, and N_0 is 2. Using Eqn 4.2, the estimated population size at the end of the summer is 3 276 800 000 000 000 000, or approximately 3.28 million million million flies.

Some populations increase much more slowly. For example, Charles Darwin calculated that a pair of elephants would take approximately 750 years to produce a population of 19 million. We can go on making such calculations, some more impressive than others, and they may be useful if we wish to sell disinfectant, fly swatters or elephant traps. The point is, however, that unlimited growth is not sustainable, and we will look at the limits to growth in a preliminary way in the next chapter. For now we will look at some examples of exponential growth that have been observed in nature.

4.7 | Examples of exponential growth

In the city where I live (Saskatoon, Saskatchewan), there was a dramatic increase in the breeding population of the merlin falcon (*Falco columbarius*) throughout the 1970s and early 1980s. This increase has been documented by Oliphant and Haug (1985). The arithmetic plot of the numbers of breeding pairs from 1970 to 1982 appears not to have a smooth exponential growth form (Fig. 4.4a), but a logarithmic plot of the numbers reveals that growth was approximately exponential during this time period (Fig. 4.4b). Note that by exponential growth we mean that the growth rate is approximately constant. The average intrinsic rate of natural increase, r_m, over the 13-year period was 0.236, giving an average yearly multiplication rate (e^r) of 1.266, or an average increase of almost 27% per year.

Several factors have combined to make this population increase possible. The prairie–parkland area of Canada has few suitable

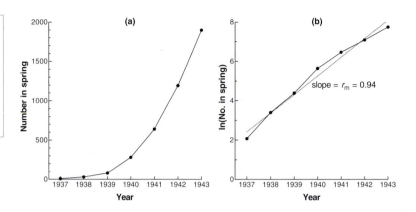

Fig. 4.5 Growth of a pheasant population on Protection Island from 1937 to 1943, (a) plotted on an arithmetic scale, and (b) on a logarithmic scale. The latter is compared to an exponential series (straight dotted line). (Data from Lack 1967.)

nesting habitats for merlins, but Saskatoon is located on the South Saskatchewan River where merlins occur naturally. The urban population was probably started from this source. Merlins do not build their own nests but take over old nests of American crow (*Corvus brachyrhynchos*) or black-billed magpie (*Pica pica*). In Saskatoon these birds nest almost exclusively in large mature spruce trees that are older than 30 years. Thus, the seeds of the merlin invasion were set decades before 1970. Merlins thrive in the urban habitat because there is a large urban prey population of house sparrows (*Passer domesticus*). Once merlins established themselves in the city it is believed that the majority of new nests were established by birds fledged from city nests because the immigration of new birds from surrounding areas was limited. However, only the older parts of the city have mature spruce trees suitable for nesting. All of the nests found during the study period were located within a core area of 35 km² in the city, which in the early 1980s had a total area of 122 km². One can predict that as spruces begin to mature in newer neighbourhoods, and these areas are invaded by crows and magpies, then the merlin population will expand into these areas.

A second example is provided by a population of pheasants (*Phasianus colchicus*) that were introduced onto Protection Island off the coast of Washington State (Lack 1967). The population was a closed one because the island was too far from the mainland for pheasants to fly in or out. Eight pheasants were introduced in 1937 and by the spring of 1943 the population had increased to nearly 2000 birds, aided by the fact that there was abundant food on the island, and there were no bird predators. An arithmetic plot of population size appears to resemble an exponential growth series (Fig. 4.5a), and one can estimate the average intrinsic rate of increase from 1937 to 1943 from the logarithmic plot of the numbers (Fig. 4.5b). A careful examination of the logarithmic plot (Fig. 4.5b) suggests that there is a curvilinear relationship through time (the dashed line) and that the growth rate was gradually declining over time, possibly as a response to declining food resources. Unfortunately, we will never know for certain because the experiment was abruptly terminated when the

United States Army set up a training camp on the island and shot all the pheasants.

There are undoubtedly many other examples of populations showing approximately exponential forms of growth for a period, particularly for introduced species that have been spectacularly successful in their new home. One can think of the prickly pear cactus (*Opuntia*) introduced into Australia, South Africa and the Hawaiian Islands, the rabbit (*Oryctolagus*) introduced to Australia, and the many species of fish that have been introduced to provide freshwater fishing throughout the world. In most of these cases there are inadequate records to document the precise growth forms of the various introductions.

4.8 | Problems

To check your understanding of this chapter, try the following problems. A summary of equations is provided in Box 4.1, and the answers to the problems may be found in the 'Solutions to problems' section at the end of the book.

1. A moth has an annual life cycle. One population was observed to increase from 5000 to 6000 individuals in one year. Predict the size of the population after three years (from the starting population of 5000), assuming no change in the rate of growth.
2. The human population increased from approximately 600 million to 900 million between AD 1700 and 1800. Calculate the value of r_m and λ per year assuming exponential growth.
3. A small population of kudu (*Tragelaphus strepsiceros*), introduced into a reserve area which is being rehabilitated for wildlife, is observed to increase 15% on average every year. Approximately how many years will it take for the population to double in size?
4. The value of r_m for a rat population is 0.14 per week. Starting with a population of 24 rats, what will be the approximate population size after 65 days assuming exponential growth?

Box 4.1 | Summary of equations

Discrete (geometric) growth model

$$\frac{\Delta N}{\Delta t} = R_m N \qquad \text{(Eqn 4.1)}$$

$$N_t = N_0 \lambda^t \qquad \text{(Eqn 4.2)}$$

$$\ln(N_t) = \ln(N_0) + \ln(\lambda)t \qquad \text{(Eqn 4.8)}$$

$$R_m = \frac{B}{N} - \frac{D}{N} \qquad \text{(Exp. 4.3)}$$

$$R_m = \lambda - 1 \qquad \text{(Exp. 4.9)}$$

Continuous time (exponential) growth model

$$\frac{\delta N}{\delta t} = r_m N \qquad \text{(Eqn 4.3)}$$

$$N_t = N_0 e^{r_m t} \qquad \text{(Eqn 4.4)}$$

$$\ln(N_t) = \ln(N_0) + r_m t \qquad \text{(Eqn 4.7)}$$

$$r_m = b - d$$

$$e^{r_m} = \lambda \qquad \text{(Eqn 4.5)}$$

$$r_m = \ln(\lambda) \qquad \text{(Eqn 4.6)}$$

Note that the per capita (i.e. per individual) rate of increase (R_m) is measured over the entire duration of the time step Δt, whereas the intrinsic rate of increase (r_m) is the per capita rate of increase measured over an infinitesimally small time step. In both cases they equal the per capita births less the per capita deaths, but they relate to different time frames.

In some texts, the multiplication rate (λ) is given the symbol R, so be careful when you compare equations from different sources.

5. A population increases fivefold over a four-week period. What is the value of λ per day assuming exponential growth?
6. It is estimated that by 1959 the world's human population was 2 907 000 000 with an overall birth rate of 36 per 1000 people per year and a death rate of 19 per 1000 people per year. What was the expected increase in population size in 1959?
7. In 1959 the human population of the world increased by approximately 50 million from 2 907 000 000. (a) Calculate the value of r_m per year to four decimal places, assuming exponential growth; and (b) if the average death rate was 19 per thousand people per year, what was the average birth rate in 1959.

Appendix 4.1 Simulation of geometric growth

Open Quattro Pro or Excel. The spreadsheet consists of a table with the columns labelled A, B, C, etc. and the rows numbered sequentially. We use the system as a programmable calculator which stores and displays the results in tabular and graphic forms. Do the following steps:

1. To give our simulation a title, type **Simulation of Geometric and Exponential Population Growth** in the A1 cell of the spreadsheet.
2. Type **Multiplication rate (lambda)** = in A3 and enter the value **2** in D3.
3. Type **Geometric Growth Model** in B6
4. Enter the various column headings for our model in rows 8 and 9 of columns A–D, as shown in the diagram below. Adjust the column width to accommodate the text and centre the text in the cell to enhance its presentation. This is done by clicking the appropriate

buttons on the toolbar in Quattro Pro or by clicking format in Excel.

	A	B	C	D
8	Time	Popn size	Change	$(N_{t+1} - N_t)/N_t$
9	(t)	N_t	$(N_{t+1} - N_t)$	Rm

5. To keep track of time enter **0** (zero) in A10 (our starting time); then type = **A10+1** in A11 and then copy A11 to cells A12 to A21. This creates a sequence of numbers from 0 to 11 in column A. We have created a simple formula, to add 1 to the value of the preceding cell in the column and enter the sum in the current cell. Note that when we copied the formula to succeeding cells in the column the spreadsheet program automatically adjusted our formula, from A10 + 1 in cell A11 to A11 + 1 in the A12 cell, and so on.

6. To calculate population size first enter **one** in cell B10 (our starting number N_0; then type = **B$10*$D$3ˆ A11** in B11 and copy B11 to cells B12 to B21. The formula in cell B11 represents Eqn 4.2. $B$10 is the value of N_0 and we use the $ sign before the column and row values to stop the spreadsheet from adjusting these values when we copy the cell to other cells. Similarly we fix the value of λ (lambda) using the term $D$3 (which should equal 2 if we did step 2 correctly), but the value of the power t in the equation is denoted by ˆ A11 because this needs to adjust through time. If we have done step 6 correctly, you should see the familiar geometric series 1, 2, 4, 8, 16, . . . , 2048 in column B. Our equation or formula is correct.

7. To calculate $\Delta N/\Delta t$ type = **B11 ‒ B10** in C10 and then copy C10 to cells C11 to C20 (not C21). You will see the same sequence of numbers as in column B. Don't worry about this because the numbers will vary when we change the value of λ in cell D3.

8. Calculate R_m in column D by typing = **C10/B10** in cell D10 and copying D10 to cells D11 to D20. We should see the value 1 throughout the column if we have done everything correctly. Note that this calculation uses a simple rearrangement of Eqn 4.1.

9. To graph the results of our simulation click onto the histogram button on the power bar and move the cursor down and insert the chart below the tabulated results of the spreadsheet by left clicking the mouse. In Quattro Pro, a clear rectangle will appear and another row will appear on the toolbar. Look for the row of histogram buttons on the row below the one you have just used. Find the one which indicates it is to add or revise cells to be plotted and click on that. You can now create a graph by inserting the correct series to be plotted. In Excel, ChartWizard will appear and you will follow the steps as outlined in 10.

10. First graph population size through time, as predicted by Eqn 4.2. In Quattro Pro, type **A10 . . A20** for the *x*-axis, type **B10 . . B20** in the 1st: series, then click OK. Title the graph **Geometric growth**, label the *x*-axis **Time (t)** and the *y*-axis **Popn. Size (N_t)**. When you click OK the graph will be complete and should look something like Fig. 4.2. In Excel, move your cursor to outline cells A10 to B20 and follow the instructions as outlined in step 10, only using the titles as indicated for Quattro Pro in step 11. Your graph should resemble Fig. 4.2.

11. Next graph the relationship between the change in population size ($\Delta N / \Delta t$) and population size (N), as predicted by Eqn 4.1, by following step 9 again. In Quattro Pro, type **B10 . . B20** for the *x*-axis but don't press Enter. Instead, move the cursor to the 1st: series and type **C10 . . C20**, then click OK. A graph will appear. Now find the button to add titles and click on that. Label your graph by typing **Change in N vs. N** in the Title box, **Popn. Size (N)** in the *x*-axis box, and **Change in N** in the *y*-axis box. When you click OK the graph will be complete and should be similar to Fig. 4.1. In Excel, move your cursor to outline cells B10 to C20 and enter this series in step 1 of ChartWizard; in step 2 click on XY Scatter; in step 3 select format 2; ignore step 4; and in step 5 add the titles as outlined for Quattro Pro above. The final graph should resemble Fig. 4.1. The slope of the relationship is R_m, the value of which is indicated in column D of the spreadsheet.

12. Our simulation model of geometric growth is complete. Now change the value of λ and see that the spreadsheet automatically recalculates the values of the dependent variables and plots the new values on the two graphs. Set in cell D3 equal to 1.5 and note that the population grows more slowly than when λ equalled 2, and that $R_m = 0.5$. If $\lambda = 0.9$ we see that the population declines in a geometric fashion and now R_m equals -0.1, because the death rate exceeds the birth rate. Note that the forms of the relationships remain constant even though the values of the variables N_t, R_m and so on change as λ changes. You may see that λ always equals $1 + R_m$, as shown in Exp. 4.9, or to express this another way $R_m = \lambda - 1$.

13. Save your spreadsheet, because we will use it again later.

Appendix 4.2 Simulation of exponential growth

1. Open your simulation program for geometric growth.
2. Add the various headings by typing **Exponential Growth Model** in F6, **Popn. Size** in F8, $N_t = N_0 e^{rt}$ in F9, and $\ln(N_t)$ in G9.
3. Type $r_m =$ in F3 and then enter the formula $= \ln(\$D\$3)$ in G3. If the value of λ in cell D3 is 2, then r_m should equal 0.693147 in cell G3.

4. To calculate population size in column F input the same starting value as for geometric growth in F10, i.e. = **$B$10**. Then enter the formula equivalent to $N_t = N_0 e^{r_m t}$ in F11, which is =**$F$10*EXP($G$3*A11)**, and copy F11 to cells F12 to F20. The exponential series in column F is identical to the geometric series in column B and so there is no need to graph this simulation.

5. To calculate the logarithmic values of N_t in column G enter the formula = **ln(F10)** in G10 and then copy this to cells G11 to G20.

6. Now create a graph of $\ln(N_t)$ over time to simulate Eqn 4.7. You may need to refresh your memory of how to do this by looking over steps 9 and 10 in the simulation of geometric growth. Your chart should use cells A10 .. A20 in the x-axis, and cells G10 .. G20 in the y-axis. Your graph should be similar to Fig. 4.3 and you can see that the logarithm of population size changes linearly over time.

7. Finally, we can explore the relationship between the discrete time model of geometric growth and the continuous time model of exponential growth. In some respects they give identical results, but if we set λ equal to 2 we can see that the value of R_m equals 1 whereas the value of r_m equals 0.6931. This is because R_m is the growth rate over a discrete time period whereas r_m is an instantaneous rate. If we reduce the time steps to shorter and shorter intervals, r_m converges to the value of r_m. We can simulate this by progressively reducing the value of λ in cell D3. Various values are shown below and they indicate that the discrete time model is a special case of the continuous time model.

λ	r_m	R_m	r_m/R_m
1.500	0.40547	0.500	0.8109
1.100	0.09531	0.100	0.9531
1.010	0.00995	0.010	0.9950
1.001	0.00100	0.001	1.0000

8. Save your program and exit Quattro Pro or Excel.

Chapter 5

Density-dependent growth, and the logistic growth model

Organisms have a phenomenal potential for increase in numbers when there are no limits to growth. We may enjoy calculating this potential, but don't worry that if we leave the house for a few days we will return to find bacteria many metres deep over the kitchen counters, or if we lock up our summer cabin and inadvertently enclose a female housefly that we will return next spring to find trillions of her offspring buzzing about the place. We recognize that there are insufficient resources to sustain such growth because we live in a finite world, and although we see many instances of population increase we know that there are limits to the size they may eventually reach.

This chapter will focus on developing models which describe how population growth may be influenced by population density through the effects of intraspecific competition for resources. As populations increase in density, the resources needed to sustain them become limiting. For example, barnacles may cover the entire surface of a rock until there is no more space available for further growth of the population. Similarly, cavity nesting birds may have the size of the breeding population limited by the availability of suitable holes in trees. The basic premise of our models is that the realized growth rate will decline as population density increases.

5.1 | Logistic growth model

The logistic growth model modifies the exponential growth equation $\delta N/\delta t = r_m N$ by making the growth rate per capita, r, a function of density, $f(N)$. Thus:

$$\frac{\delta N}{\delta t} = rN \tag{Exp. 5.1}$$

And

$$r = f(N) \tag{Exp. 5.2}$$

To determine the form of this function we assume that there are sufficient resources to sustain a stable population density of K individuals, called the *carrying capacity* of the population. The maximum growth rate per capita is equal to r_m, which is the growth rate when there are no effects of density (i.e. growth is exponential). When all individuals are identical, each individual uses $1/K$ of the resources and reduces the maximum growth rate, r_m, by $1/K$. Thus, N individuals reduce r_m by N/K. This relationship is expressed in the following way:

$$r = r_m \left(1 - \frac{N}{K} \right) \qquad \text{(Eqn 5.1)}$$

This equation shows that the growth rate per capita, r, is dependent on the population density (N). In populations where there is a large carrying capacity (K) and N is small, r approximates r_m, its value when there are no density-dependent effects. As the population density (N) increases to the carrying capacity (K), the value of r steadily decreases until at the carrying capacity it equals zero and the population stops growing. If N exceeds K, then r becomes negative and the population will decline.

By substituting Eqn 5.1 in Exp. 5.1, we obtain the logistic growth equation, first derived by the French mathematician Verhulst (1838), and independently derived by the American demographers Pearl and Reed (1920):

$$\frac{\delta N}{\delta t} = r_m N - r_m \frac{N^2}{K} \qquad \text{(Eqn 5.2)}$$

Equation 5.2 is frequently presented in two other equivalent forms:

$$\frac{\delta N}{\delta t} = r_m N \left(1 - \frac{N}{K} \right) \quad \text{or} \quad \frac{\delta N}{\delta t} = r_m N \left(\frac{K - N}{K} \right) \qquad \text{(Eqn 5.2a)}$$

One interpretation of Eqn 5.2 is that the rate of increase of the population ($\delta N/\delta t$) is equal to the biotic potential, i.e. the potential for exponential growth ($r_m N$), minus the resistance to growth that is created by the population itself, i.e. density-dependent effects ($r_m N^2/K$). This latter term can be considered to be a measure of intraspecific competition and is one component of what Darwin termed the 'struggle for existence'.

To express population density as a function of time, Eqn 5.2 is integrated following the rules of integral calculus to give the following complex equation:

$$N_t = \frac{K}{1 + \left(\dfrac{K}{N_0} - 1 \right) e^{-r_m t}} \qquad \text{(Eqn 5.3)}$$

This equation shows that the population density at time $t (N_t)$ is related to the starting population size (N_0), the carrying capacity (K) and the intrinsic rate of natural increase (r_m) in a complex way. However, if we wish to calculate r_m from a logistic growth curve, where we know the population densities at three points (N_0, N_t and K), it is easier to do this if Eqn 5.3 is rearranged to:

$$-r_m t = \ln\left\{\frac{K - N_t}{[(N_t K - N_t N_0)/N_0]}\right\}$$ (Eqn 5.4)

The following are examples of how these equations may be applied.

Example 5.1 *The growth of a laboratory culture of* Paramecium *was accurately predicted by the logistic growth equation. If the equilibrium density (K) is 400 individuals per ml, and the intrinsic rate of natural increase (r_m) is 0.7 per day, what is the predicted density of individuals after 10 days in a culture started with 5 individuals per ml?*

Use Eqn 5.3 to solve this. The value of $e^{-0.7 \times 10} = 0.000912$, and this is multiplied by ($400/5 - 1 = 79$) to obtain 0.072. Add one to this value (= 1.072), and then divide the sum into 400 to obtain the answer of 373 individuals per ml (rounded to the nearest integer).

Example 5.2 *A population of songbirds has an equilibrium density of 31 breeding pairs per hectare. A population was introduced into a new area at a density of one breeding pair per hectare and reached a density of 12 breeding pairs per hectare after 10 years. What is the intrinsic rate of natural increase (r_m) assuming that the population is growing logistically?*

Use Eqn 5.4 and set $t = 10$, $K = 31$, $N_t = 12$ and $N_0 = 1$. The answer is 0.294 per year.

Example 5.3 *What is the realized rate of increase per capita when there are 12 breeding pairs per hectare in the population in example 5.2?*

Use Eqn 5.1 to calculate this, where $r_m = 0.294$ per year, $N = 12$ and $K = 31$. The answer is approximately 0.180 per year. Note that r does not appear in Eqns 5.2 to 5.4. This is because these equations automatically calculate r from the r_m, N and K values.

5.2 Simulating logistic growth

The predictions of Eqns 5.1 to 5.3 may be investigated by completing a spreadsheet simulation (see Appendix 5.1). You may need to refresh your memory about how to do various operations by checking Appendices 4.1 and 4.2. The completed simulation provides graphs that are similar to Figs. 5.1 to 5.3.

The logistic model of population growth predicts that populations attain a stable carrying capacity (K). The form of growth is S-shaped for populations starting at a density below that of the carrying capacity (Fig. 5.1), and so it is sometimes called sigmoid growth. The precise shape of the curve depends on the starting density (N_0) and the final density or carrying capacity (K). The steepness of the curve is directly proportional to the value of the intrinsic rate of increase (r_m). Population densities never overshoot the carrying capacity and

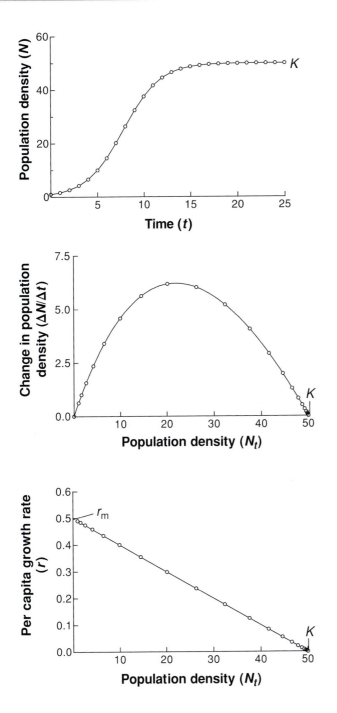

Fig. 5.1 Logistic growth of a population with a carrying capacity (K) of 50 and an r_m value of 0.5, starting from a population density (N) of one individual.

Fig. 5.2 The change in population size ($\Delta N/\Delta t$) as a function of density (N) for a population undergoing logistic growth.

Fig. 5.3 Per capita growth rates (r) as a function of density (N) for a population undergoing logistic growth. The value of r equals r_m when there are no effects of density (the y-intercept), and declines to zero at the carrying capacity (K).

so the growth curves have a smooth shape. This indicates a perfect adjustment of the per capita (i.e. per individual) growth rate, r, as the density changes.

Simulations show that populations starting at densities above the carrying capacity approach the carrying capacity more rapidly than populations starting at densities below the carrying capacity. This is because the inhibition to population growth (term r_mN^2/K in Eqn 5.2) is related to the square of the population density.

An examination of the S-shaped growth curve suggests that the population grows at its fastest rate at intermediate densities. This observation is confirmed when the population growth rate is plotted as a function of population density (Fig. 5.2). The maximum increase in numbers always occurs at half the carrying capacity (i.e. $K/2$).

The growth rate per capita, or the intrinsic rate of increase (r_m) as it is called, remains constant in exponential growth (Chapter 4). In contrast, the growth rate per capita (r) in the logistic growth model declines linearly as the density increases (Fig. 5.3). When the density is zero, r is equal to r_m because there are no effects of density, and r declines to zero when the density reaches the carrying capacity (K). At densities above the carrying capacity, r is negative. Assuming no immigration or emigration, the population adjusts the value of r in relation to density by altering the birth and death rates, and a stable equilibrium ($N = K$) is reached at a density where the birth rate is equal to the death rate.

The model has many unrealistic assumptions. It assumes that all individuals are identical, but in reality they vary in size, age, sex and genotype. These factors affect birth and death rates, and the use of resources, and so we cannot expect r_m and K to be constants. The model also assumes that individuals adjust their birth and death rates (i.e. r) instantaneously as the population changes in size, but in reality there will be time lags to any such response. Finally, it assumes that the environment is constant, but environments change over the course of time and this is another reason why we cannot expect r_m and K to be constants.

Let's now relax some of the restrictive assumptions of the model to see how the form of growth may change.

5.3 | Time lags

The logistic growth equation assumes that there is an instantaneous and continuous adjustment of the growth rate as the population changes in density, hence the smooth form to logistic growth curves (Fig. 5.1). It seems likely, however, that most populations have time lags in the way that they adjust their birth and death rates in relation to population density. For example, many species lay eggs which hatch independently of the parent, and so the birth rate cannot be adjusted if the population density changes between the times of laying and hatching of the eggs. In this case, the birth rate is related to the density at the time of egg deposition, not the time of hatching, and the time lag will correspond to the length of the incubation period. Similarly, when young are born, they are usually much smaller than adults. As they grow in size, they require more resources and the death rate may adjust as a consequence. In this case the time lag will be related to the developmental period of the young in some way.

There are various models to simulate time lags in logistic growth, but we will only consider one of them. The discrete version of the logistic model describes population growth by the following equation:

$$N_{t+1} = N_t + r_m N_t \left(1 - \frac{N_t}{K} \right) \qquad \text{(Eqn 5.5)}$$

If you subtract N_t from both sides of Eqn 5.5 it can be seen that this equation is analogous to the logistic equation of 5.2a, except that there is a built-in time lag of one time step because the population size at time $t + 1$ depends on the population size at time t. As the time lag is a constant, the response of the model depends solely on the intrinsic rate of increase (r_m).

5.3.1 Simulating time lags: a discrete version of the logistic growth model

A discrete version of the logistic growth model may be simulated by adding to the spreadsheet simulation we have developed for logistic growth (see Appendix 5.2).

The behaviour of the model is surprisingly complex. At low values of r_m, it behaves like the simple logistic model and smoothly approaches the carrying capacity in the familiar S-shaped pattern of growth (Fig. 5.4a). When r_m attains a value of about 1.1, the population first overshoots and then undershoots the carrying capacity in a series of damped oscillations. These oscillations are barely evident at first, but become more noticeable as r_m gets larger (Fig. 5.4b). When r_m is greater than 2.0, the population begins to oscillate about the carrying capacity in a stable two-point cycle (Fig. 5.4c). The cycle rapidly becomes more and more complex as r_m increases from 2.449 to 2.57, until at values above 2.57 the population fluctuates around the carrying capacity in a chaotic manner (Fig. 5.4d).

The growth of populations starting at similar, but not identical, densities are almost identical at low values of r_m (Fig. 5.4a,b,c), but once the fluctuations become chaotic, the two populations diverge from one another over time (Fig. 5.4d). Also note that when the population fluctuates around the carrying capacity (K) the average population size is less than K, because populations above the carrying capacity decline more rapidly in size than populations below the carrying capacity increase in size.

What does all this mean? For populations that grow in a series of steps, like many annual insects and plants, their form of growth may not appear to be logistic even when their birth and death rates are density dependent. Their form of growth depends on the value of r_m, which will be high for many of these species, and so we might expect their densities to be chaotic from one year to the next. However, there

Fig. 5.4 Behaviour of the discrete logistic growth model for a population with different values of r_m and a carrying capacity (K) of 50. Solid lines indicate a population starting at a population size of 1, and stippled lines indicate a population starting at a population size of 1.1. See text for details.

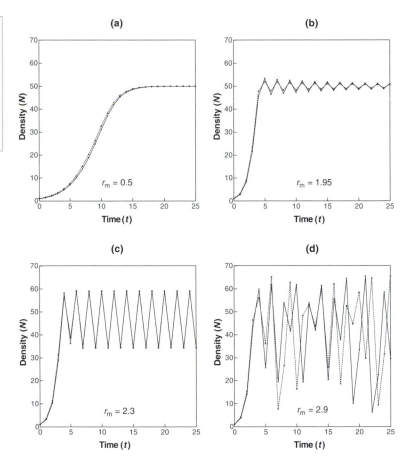

are limits to the size of these fluctuations, and we may still be able to detect density dependence. We will consider this aspect when we come to apply the models.

5.4 | Varying the carrying capacity

The carrying capacity is not constant because the environment varies both seasonally and from year to year. How do populations respond? From our analysis of time lags we can obtain an understanding of how populations will respond, because there will be an inevitable lag in the population's response to changes in the carrying capacity. How a population reacts will depend on its intrinsic rate of increase (r_m). Populations with high r_m values, such as many species of small mammals and insects, have a short time lag and so will tend to track the fluctuations in K. In contrast, populations with low r_m values, such as large mammals, have longer time lags and so react more slowly. They will vary less than the variation in carrying capacity, and will tend to persist at a density that is lower than the overall average of K.

Remember that fluctuations in density are asymmetrical about K, and that the mean density is below K (Fig. 5.4c,d). Excellent introductions to this topic are provided by May (1976) and Gotelli (1995).

5.5 | Analysing population growth

5.5.1 Yeast

One might anticipate that laboratory cultures of unicellular organisms are likely to exhibit a form of growth that is approximately logistic, because the conditions necessary for growth, and consequently the carrying capacity, can be held constant, and any time lags are likely to be short. Yeast is often presented as a classic case of logistic growth in textbooks (Fig. 5.5), and it may be seen that the logistic growth curve provides an excellent fit to these data (Table 5.1).

5.5.2 Fitting the logistic growth curve

How do we fit a logistic growth curve to these data? A reasonable fit can be made in the following way. First, we can rearrange Eqn 5.3 to the following expression:

$$\ln\left(\frac{K - N_t}{N_t}\right) = a - r_m t \qquad \text{(Exp. 5.3)}$$

In this expression, $a = \ln(K/N_0 - 1)$. If we plot the values for the left-hand side of the equation (i.e. y values) versus t (i.e. x values), the points should lie more or less on a straight line. We can then estimate a (the y-intercept) and r_m (the slope of the line) by fitting a linear regression. The trick is to estimate K correctly. Initially K is estimated by seeing where the slope levels off. We can then systematically alter K and see which value gives the best fit to the data. The procedure is described in Appendix 5.3 if you wish to try your hand at curve-fitting. I used this method to fit a logistic curve to the data in Table 5.1 (see Fig. 5.5). My estimates were $K = 664.3$, $a = 4.2017$ and $r_m = 0.5384$, which compare very favourably to the estimates by Pearl (1927) of $K = 665$, $a = 4.1896$ and $r_m = 0.5355$.

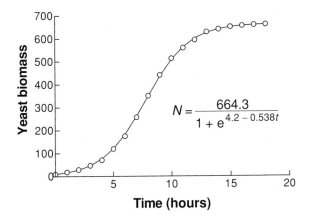

$$N = \frac{664.3}{1 + e^{4.2 - 0.538t}}$$

Fig. 5.5 Growth of a population of yeast cells (see Table 5.1 for data) showing the fit of a logistic growth curve. (Data from Carlson (1913), cited in Pearl 1927.)

| Table 5.1 | Growth of a yeast population in culture. The biomass (units not provided) of yeast was measured at hourly intervals |

Time (hours)	Yeast biomass
0	9.6
1	18.3
2	29.0
3	47.2
4	71.1
5	119.1
6	174.6
7	257.3
8	350.7
9	441.0
10	513.3
11	559.7
12	594.8
13	629.4
14	640.8
15	651.1
16	655.9
17	659.6
18	661.8

Source: Data from Carlson (1913), cited in Pearl (1927).

5.5.3 *Paramecium*

The growth of *Paramecium caudatum* does not describe such a near-perfect logistic growth form as yeast, although the pattern of growth is S-shaped (Fig. 5.6). It is also not as straightforward as before to fit the logistic growth model to these data because the population appears to fluctuate around the carrying capacity K. We cannot calculate the value of $\ln[(K-N_t)/N_t]$ when N_t is larger than K because we are trying to take the logarithm of a negative number. This happens by day 11 in the data presented (Table 5.2 and Fig. 5.6). What do we do? The solution is to trim the data so that we only use the data up to, but not including the day on which N_t exceeds K. We then use these trimmed data to fit the growth curve as we did for yeast. Using the data for days 0 to 10 in Table 5.2 provides a reasonable fit (Fig. 5.6) when $K = 202$, $a = 5.1$ and $r_m = 0.74$.

The growth form of *Paramecium* suggests that the population may be oscillating about the carrying capacity. There are two possible reasons for this. There may be a time lag operating, although the value of r_m does not suggest this would result in sustained oscillations (see section 5.3). Alternatively, the population may be responding to periodic fluctuations in the environment (i.e. a variable K), such as the addition of food at fixed intervals.

Table 5.2 Growth of *Paramecium caudatum* population in the medium of Osterhout. Density (number of individuals in 0.5 ml of medium) represents the mean of four different cultures started simultaneously

Day	Density
0	2
2	10
3	10
4	11
5	21
6	56
7	104
8	137
9	165
10	194
11	217
12	199
13	201
14	182
15	192
16	179
17	190
18	206
19	209
20	196
21	195
22	234
23	210
24	210
25	180

Source: Data from Table 3 in Appendix I of Gause (1934).

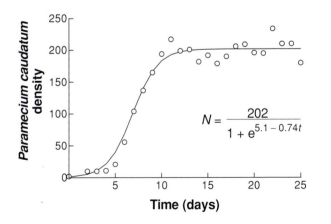

$$N = \frac{202}{1 + e^{5.1 - 0.74t}}$$

Fig. 5.6 Growth of *Paramecium caudatum* in laboratory culture (see Table 5.2 for data) showing the fit of a logistic growth curve. (Data from Gause 1934.)

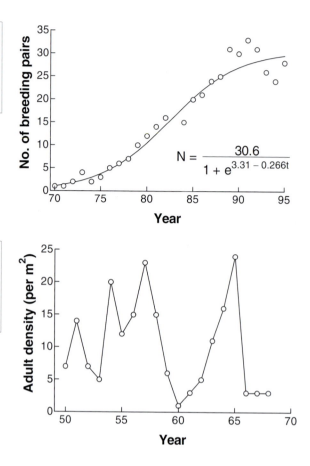

Fig. 5.7 Increase in the number of breeding pairs of merlins in Saskatoon, Canada from 1970 to 1995, with a fitted logistic growth curve. (Data from Oliphant and Haug 1985 and Lieske 1997.)

$$N = \frac{30.6}{1 + e^{3.31 - 0.266t}}$$

Fig. 5.8 Density of winter moth adults (*Operoptera brumata*) in Wytham Wood near Oxford, England from 1950 to 1968. (Data from Varley, Gradwell and Hassell 1973.)

5.5.4 Merlins

In Chapter 4, we saw that the merlin population in Saskatoon, Canada increased approximately exponentially from one to 16 breeding pairs during the period 1970 to 1982. If the population had continued to increase exponentially at the same rate, there would have been 365 breeding pairs in 1995. In fact, only 28 pairs were recorded, which is not surprising in view of the limitation on suitable nest sites and food availability.

The number of breeding pairs was recorded during the 26-year period and it can be seen that population growth was approximately logistic during this time (Fig. 5.7). It is unlikely that the carrying capacity (*K*) will remain constant, however, because the availability of nest sites, which are almost always located in mature spruce trees, will change as landowners cut down and replace old trees, and as trees mature in newer neighbourhoods.

5.5.5 Winter moth

Our next example considers the winter moth (*Operoptera brumata*) in Wytham Wood near Oxford, England where they were studied from 1950 to 1968 (Varley *et al.* 1973). The density of adult moths fluctuated erratically during this period (Fig. 5.8) and it would seem pointless

trying to fit a logistic growth curve to such data, unless one at-
tempted to fit the time-lag model where there are chaotic fluctuations
(section 5.3.1).

Varley and his co-workers conducted a detailed study of the population dynamics of this species to try to understand the key factors
that governed its density. They concluded that the observed variation
in winter moth density (Fig. 5.8) was a result of a complex interaction of destabilizing factors at the time of egg hatching, and stabilizing factors during the pupal stage. The weather at the time of
egg hatching, and the synchrony between egg hatch and the opening
of the leaf buds (on which the emerging larvae feed), were critical
to the survival of the emerging larvae. If the weather was good, and
if the hatching of the eggs coincided with the opening of the leaf
buds, larval survival was good; if not, there was a poor survival of
larvae. Larval densities were more variable than egg densities, and so
the population was being pushed away from an equilibrium density,
i.e. the factors were destabilizing. In contrast, after the mature larvae
pupated in the soil they were subjected to predation by small mammals and various ground beetles, and the proportion of pupae eaten
increased as pupal density increased, i.e. predation was directly density dependent. Adult densities were less variable than pupal densities
and so predation tended to stabilize the population density.

The question is, can we detect density dependence from these
census data of adult density or not? We will use a quick method of
doing this, which has some statistical problems, but relates well to
the theory of logistic growth. From our analysis of logistic growth, we
know that the growth rate per capita (r) is inversely related to population density (Fig. 5.3) if growth is density dependent. The r values are
calculated for each year, by taking the natural logarithm of the multiplication rate (λ) from one year to the next, and these are plotted
against population density (Fig. 5.9). An overall inverse relationship is
observed between the per capita growth rate and population density
(Fig. 5.9), which suggests that density-dependent factors are operating
on this population.

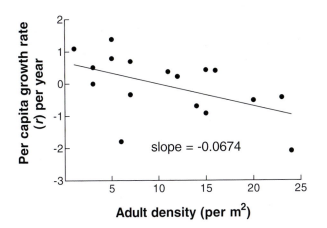

slope = -0.0674

Per capita growth rate (r) per year

Adult density (per m^2)

Fig. 5.9 Relationship between
the annual per capita growth rate
and adult density of winter moths.
The data are calculated from those
presented in Fig. 5.8. The slope of
the least-squares regression is
significantly different from zero
($P < 0.05$).

5.5.6 Maximum sustainable yield

The largest rate of increase in numbers occurs at half the carrying capacity ($K/2$) for those populations that are growing logistically (see Fig. 5.2). This feature has been utilized to optimize the harvest of certain fisheries to maximize the sustainable yield. The objective is to harvest the population until it reaches $K/2$ and then maintain the population at that density by harvesting the yield, i.e. the increase in numbers or biomass ($\delta N/\delta t$). However, in most cases we do not know what the carrying capacity is or whether the population is growing logistically. It can be shown that if population growth is S-shaped, there is a relationship between the catch, representing the yield ($\delta N/\delta t$), and the fishing intensity, which can be related to population density (N). This relationship describes a parabola which is similar to our theoretical relationship illustrated in Fig. 5.2.

The theory has been applied to certain fisheries with varying degrees of success (see Krebs 1994). There have been many cases where its application has led to the collapse of the fishery, primarily because of overfishing. Once one drives the fishing parabola over the crest of the yield parabola, continued heavy fishing rapidly drives the population to lower densities and consequently to low recruitment levels. The problem is particularly acute where there is a variable carrying capacity, because it is difficult to define the harvest parabola and one should therefore always underestimate the sustainable yield in such cases. This is often politically unacceptable even though the consequences of overfishing are disastrous in the long term. Once a fishery has collapsed, its recovery is by no means assured even when fishing levels are reduced.

5.6 | Summary and conclusions

The logistic growth curve describes the growth of a population of identical individuals, that are growing in a constant environment of defined limits or size, and which are able to adjust their growth rates instantaneously as they utilize the fixed resources of the environment. The model describes an S-shaped form of growth to a stable carrying capacity, K, which depends on the characteristics of the population and the amount of resources available in the environment, and the steepness of the curve depends on the per capita rate of increase, r.

The restrictive assumptions of the model may be relaxed to analyse how factors such as time lags and a variable environment affect the form of population growth. These analyses show that time lags have surprisingly little effect on the form of population growth for populations with low r values, but that population densities oscillate more and more, and may become unpredictable (or chaotic), as r increases to high values. The response of populations to environmental variation (affecting K) are also influenced by r. Populations with high r values track the changes in environment, whereas populations with low r values tend to average the environmental fluctuations over time.

The basic model has great heuristic value in spite of its restrictive assumptions because it can be used as a basis to investigate the pattern of population growth. Departures from the idealized S-shaped form of growth may be analysed to determine if they are related to internal factors, such as time lags, or external factors, such as a variable environment.

5.7 | Problems

The summary of equations (Box 5.1) should help you with the following problems. You will also need to remember the equations relating to exponential growth (Box 4.1).

1. Compare the relationship between (a) the rate of increase per capita (r) and density (N), and (b) the population rate of increase ($\delta N/\delta t$) and density (N), for the exponential and logistic growth models.
2. (a) You set up a colony of worms to sell to local fishermen. Starting with only five individuals, you are delighted to find that they have increased to 1044 individuals after one month (28 days). What is the value of r_m per day assuming exponential growth?
   (b) Using the information in part (a) calculate the expected size of the population after 15 weeks (from the original starting time) assuming a constant rate of increase per capita (r_m).
   (c) You have dreams of becoming a millionaire but your hopes are dashed when you discover that there are only 2500 worms after 15 weeks and their numbers stay approximately constant thereafter. Calculate the value of r_m assuming logistic growth.
   (d) Why are the values of r_m different in parts (a) and (c)?
   (e) What is the maximum sustainable daily harvest for this population if you assume logistic growth?
3. A population takes 10 days to double in size from 20 to 40 individuals. How long will it take to double in size again if (a) it grows exponentially, or (b) it grows logistically and $K = 100$?
4. (a) The growth of a microbial population was found to be accurately predicted by the logistic growth equation. If the equilibrium density of cells (K) is 5.0×10^6 cells per ml, what is the predicted density

Box 5.1 | Summary of equations for logistic growth

$$r = r_m \left(1 - \frac{N}{K} \right) \tag{Eqn 5.1}$$

$$\frac{\delta N}{\delta t} = r_m N \left(1 - \frac{N}{K} \right) = r_m N - r_m \left(\frac{N^2}{K} \right) = r_m N \left(\frac{K - N}{K} \right) \tag{Eqn 5.2}$$

$$N_t = \frac{K}{1 + \left(\dfrac{K}{N_0} - 1 \right) e^{-r_m t}} \tag{Eqn 5.3}$$

$$-r_m t = \ln \left[\frac{K - N_t}{((N_t K - N_t N_0)/N_0)} \right] \tag{Eqn 5.4}$$

after 3 hours in a culture started with a density of 2×10^3 cells per ml if the intrinsic rate of natural increase is 0.29 per hour?

(b) What is the maximum sustainable yield per hour for this population?

(c) How long will it take to start harvesting at the maximum sustained rate starting from the density given in part (a)?

Appendix 5.1 Simulating logistic growth

1. Open your spreadsheet and give your simulation a title of **Logistic (Sigmoid) Population Growth**

2. Enter the constants we need for the model by typing $r_m =$ in A3 and entering the value of **0.5** in B3, and typing **K =** in A4 and entering the value of **50** in B4.

3. Enter the following column headings in rows 8 and 9 of columns A–E. You will need to adjust the width of some of the columns.
   Row 8: In column A **Time**, in B **Density (1)**, in C **delta N**, in D **f(N)** and in E **Density (2)**.
   Row 9: In column A **(t)**, in B **Nt (1)**, in C $(N_{t+1} - N_t)$, in D $r = r_m \text{-} r_m$ N/K and in E **Nt (2)**

4. Enter the starting time of **0** (zero) in A10; then enter = A10+1 in A11 and copy A11 to cells A12 to 35 to create a sequence of times from 0 to 25.

5. Enter **1** in B10 (equals N_0); then type = $B$4/(1+($B$4/$B$10-1)^*$ EXP(-$B$3^*A11)) in B11 and copy B11 to cells B12 to B35. This formula represents Eqn 5.3.

6. Type = $ B$3^*B10^*(1-B10/$B$4) in C10 and copy C10 to cells C11 to C35. This formula represents Eqn 5.2a.

7. Type = $B$3-$B$3^*B10/$B$4 in D10 and copy D10 to cells D11 to D35. This formula represents Eqn 5.1.

8. To examine population growth where N_0 is greater than K, enter **99** in E10; then enter = $B$4/(1+($B$4/$E$10-1)^*EXP(-$B$3^*A11)) in E11 and copy E11 to cells E12 to E35. This formula represents Eqn 5.3.

9. Make three graphs of the following relationships. (You may need to refresh your memory of how to do this by checking steps 9 and 10 in Appendix 4.1.)

   (a) Population density (N) over time (t). Enter two y-series: B10 . . B35 and E10 . . E35; the x-series is A10 . . A35. The graph of the first y-series should be similar in form to Fig. 5.1.

   (b) Change in density $(\delta N/\delta t)$ versus density (N). The y-series is C10 . . C35 and the x-series is B10 . . B35. Your graph should be similar to Fig. 5.2.

   (c) Per capita growth rate (r) versus density (N). The y-series is D10 . . D35 and the x-series is B10 . . B35. Your graph should be similar to Fig. 5.3.

10. Before you leave your simulation you should change the constants r_m and K and see that the general shape of the relationships does not change. Note that if K exceeds the value of 99 the second

series of density in column E will not be starting from above K. In this case, adjust the value of E10.

11. Save the spreadsheet because we will return to it later.

Appendix 5.2 Simulating a discrete form of the logistic growth model

1. Open your saved spreadsheet for the logistic growth model.
2. Enter column labels: **Discrete** and **model** in rows 8 and 9 of column F, and **Discrete** and **model (2)** in rows 8 and 9 of column G.
3. Enter starting population sizes of **1** and **1.1** in cells F10 and G10, respectively.
4. Enter $=$ F10+$B$3*F10*(1-F10/$B$4) in F11 and copy to cells F12 to F35 and Cells G11 to G35. This formula is equivalent to Eqn 5.5.
5. Graph population size over time. There will be two y-series: F10 . . F35, and G10 . . G35, and the x-axis is A10 . . A35.
6. Progressively increase the value of r_m from the existing value of 0.5 to at least 2.8. The results will surprise you. You should obtain a sequence of graphs similar to those presented in Fig. 5.4.
7. When you have finished, save and close your spreadsheet.

Appendix 5.3 Fitting logistic growth curves to data

1. Open your spreadsheet and title your program appropriately.
2. Type **Trial K =** in A3 and the value **665** in B3.
3. Starting in row 5, label column A **Time**, column B **Observed N**, column C **ln((K-N)/N)**, column D **Estimated N** and column E **Error**.
4. Below your column labels do the following:
   (a) In column A enter your sequence of time values from 0 to 18 (see Appendix 4.1).
   (b) In column B enter the corresponding N values (biomass) from Table 5.1.
   (c) Type $=$ LN(($B$3 $-$ B7)/B7) in C7 (assuming that the starting time 0 is in row 7); then copy C7 to cells C8 to C25.
   (d) In Quattro Pro click Tools, Numeric Tools, Regression. The Independent variable is A7 . . A25, the Dependent variable is C7 . . C25, and the Output is B27. Click OK, and your program will calculate a regression of $\ln[(K - N)/N]$ against t. The Constant in E28 is the estimate of a, and the x Coefficient in D34 is $- r_m$. In Excel click Tools, Data Analysis, Regression; the y values are C7:C25, the x values are A7:A25, and enter B27 for Output range. In the output of the regression statistics the Intercept $= a$ and the x variable $= r_m$. If Data Analysis does not appear as an option when you click Tools, select Add-Ins and then check the Analysis Tools box. Then try again.

(e) In Quattro Pro Type $= $ B$3/(1+EXP($E$28+$D$34*A7))$ in D7 and copy D7 to cells D8 to D25. This calculates our expected values of N for K $= 665$, using a rearranged form of Eqn 5.2. In Excel, substitute C43 for E28, and C44 for D34 in the formula.

(f) Type $= (B7 \quad D7)^\wedge 2$ in E7 and copy E7 to cells E8 to E25. This squares the deviations between our observed and expected N values and is a measure of how different they are. Highlight cells E7 to E26 and click on Σ in the tool bar. The total of the squared deviations will appear in E26.

5. Make a note of the value of E26 (this is a measure of our goodness of fit to the data) and also of your trial K value. Now systematically alter your K value in B3. When you do this, only the values in column C will change. *Each time you alter K you will have to repeat step 4(d) to fit a new regression.* Note your new values of K and E26. If the value of E26 increases, reverse the direction of your modification of K. I made the following changes in K, starting from the value of 665: 664, 663, 664.5, 664.6, 664.4, 664.3, 664.2, and back again to 664.3 my best fit.

6. You may wish to graph both the observed and estimated N values over time to see how well your logistic growth curve fits the data (see Appendix 4.1 for procedure).

7. Save your program if you wish to use it again.

Part III

Population genetics and evolution

There are two conditions that are necessary for evolution to occur. First, the characteristics of an organism must vary in the population, and that variation must be related to differences in survival or reproductive success. Second, the variation must also have a genetic basis, at least in part. As a consequence, evolution changes the gene frequencies of populations. In Part I, we noted that Darwin made a strong argument that natural selection was the main force driving evolution. However, the gene frequencies in populations can also be changed by other forces, such as mutation, migration, and even chance, and so we need to assess the importance of these factors on the evolution of populations.

The main purpose of the following eight chapters is to make a quantitative assessment of the various factors that affect the gene frequencies of populations. How do we measure the allelic and genotypic frequencies in populations, and how are they affected by sexual reproduction (Chapter 6)? How does genetic variation arise in populations and how is it maintained (Chapter 7)? How are gene frequencies in populations affected by mutation (Chapter 7), chance (Chapter 8), migration (Chapter 9) and selection (Chapters 10 to 12)? What are the relative strengths of these factors and how do they interact with one another (Chapter 13)? Thus, we will try to make an objective assessment of Darwin's theory of evolution by natural selection to see if it is supported by the theory of population genetics. It is assumed that the reader will have an elementary knowledge of Mendelian genetics.

Chapter 6

Gene frequencies and the Hardy–Weinberg principle

Population genetics considers how the frequencies of alternative states of genes in populations are maintained or changed from generation to generation. First, however, it is important that we understand the terms that are used; otherwise, it is easy for beginners to become confused. It is also important to know how the terms will be used in this book, because many of the terms are not used consistently in the wider literature.

6.1 | Terminology

The following should clarify how the various terms introduced in this chapter are used throughout the book.

phenotype The morphological, physiological, behavioural or biochemical characteristic of an individual, or a group of individuals in a population. Typically, the term refers to a single characteristic, such as body colour or blood group type, but can also refer to more than one characteristic. Almost invariably, there is more than one phenotype for a given characteristic. For example, there may be both short and tall plants in a population.

genotype This is the genetic constitution of an individual, or a group of individuals in a population, which is related by simple Mendelian rules to the phenotype. The theory in this book mainly considers genes with just two different alleles in the population, e.g. A and B, so that there will be just three different genotypes, AA, AB and BB. These will result in three different phenotypes if there is no dominance, but only two if there is dominance. If genotypes AA and AB give rise to the same phenotype, A is considered to be dominant to B, and if AB and BB give the same phenotype, B is considered dominant to A. Theory relating to multiple genes and alleles is considered in Chapter 12.

locus This is a site on a chromosome and we will consider a gene to occupy a particular locus.

Table 6.1 The frequencies of M–N blood groups in a New York City black population

Phenotype (blood group)	M	MN	N	Total
Genotype	MM	MN	NN	
Number in sample	119	242	139	500
Genotypic frequency	0.238 = P	0.484 = H	0.278 = Q	1.0 = P + H + Q
Number of alleles M	238	242	0	480 ⎫
N	0	242	278	520 ⎬ = 1000
Allelic frequency M				0.48 = p
N				0.52 = q

Source: Data from Mourant *et al.* (1976).

gene The definition of this term is complicated because it is used in different contexts. A gene can be considered to occupy a particular locus on a chromosome and code for a particular characteristic of the organism, such as body colour. There may be alternative states, or alleles (see next definition), of the gene. For example, there may be two alleles for flower colour, one coding for red flowers and the other for white flowers. However, the term gene is often used as a synonym for allele, although I have tried to avoid this in this book. For example, we may talk of the gene for cystic fibrosis, or some other genetic disease, but only one form of the gene (i.e. one allele) gives rise to that particular phenotype.

allele One of the alternative states of a gene. An individual may have only one type of allele, in which case it is said to be homozygous for that particular gene or trait, or an individual may have two different alleles (assuming we are dealing with diploid organisms) and is said to be heterozygous for that gene.

6.2 Frequencies of alleles, genotypes and phenotypes

We can understand the relationship between the frequencies of alleles, genotypes and phenotypes in populations by considering a simple example (Table 6.1).

It may be seen that each of the three genotypes gives rise to a different blood group because there is no dominance (the two alleles, M and N, are said to be codominant). The blood groups were screened in a sample of 500 individuals from the population, and it is a simple matter to calculate the genotypic frequencies in the population from the results. The frequency (P) of MM is $119/500 = 0.238$; the frequency (H) of MN is $242/500 = 0.484$; and the frequency (Q) of NN is $139/500 = 0.278$. Note that $P + H + Q = 1$. Similarly, it is easy to calculate the allelic frequencies. The frequency (p) of M is $(238 + 242)/1000 = 0.48$ (or $(2P + H)/2$); and the frequency (q) of N is $(278 + 242)/1000 = 0.52$ (or $(2Q + H)/2$), because each individual has two alleles. Note that $p + q = 1$.

We can summarize these relationships for a system of two alleles and three genotype as follows:

Genotypic frequency $P = n_P/N$

$$H = n_H/N$$

$$Q = n_Q/N$$

and $P + Q + H = 1$ (Exp. 6.1)

where N is the number of individuals in the sample, and the number of individuals of each genotype are n_P, n_H and n_Q. Similarly:

Allelic frequencies $p = P + \dfrac{1}{2}H$ (Exp. 6.2)

$$q = Q + \dfrac{1}{2}H$$ (Exp. 6.3)

and $p + q = 1$ (Exp. 6.4)

In this example each genotype corresponds to a different phenotype and so the genotypic and phenotypic frequencies are the same. If one allele is dominant over the other, there will only be two phenotypes. If one cannot distinguish the heterozygous individuals from the homozygous dominant individuals, the estimation of the allelic frequencies becomes less accurate (see section 6.4.1). The estimation of allelic frequencies where there are three or more alleles can also be troublesome (see Hartl and Clark 1989).

6.3 | The Hardy–Weinberg principle

Shortly after the rediscovery of Mendel's work, people began to speculate about its implications for the genetic structure of populations. It was suggested that as dominant characteristics assumed a 3:1 ratio in classic Mendelian crosses, this meant that any dominant character or phenotype should eventually appear in 75% of the population. This apparent consequence of Mendelian genetics was clearly not true for certain dominant traits, like bradydactyly (stubby fingers) in humans, which remained extremely rare, and so some scientists questioned the very foundation of Mendelian genetics. These misconceptions were brought to the attention of a Cambridge University mathematician, G. H. Hardy, and a German clinical physician, W. Weinberg (pronounced Vineberg), who showed independently that dominance *per se* had no effect on allelic frequencies, and furthermore that allelic frequencies would not change as a result of sexual reproduction. Their elegant proofs for populations breeding at random, published in 1908, formed the basis of the new field of population genetics.

The Hardy–Weinberg principle can be stated as follows: *In a large population where there is no genetic drift,[1] and in the absence of selection, migration and mutation, the allelic frequencies remain constant from generation to generation. If mating is random, the genotypic frequencies are related*

---

[1] Genetic drift is the chance change in allelic frequencies as a result of sampling error (see Chapter 8).

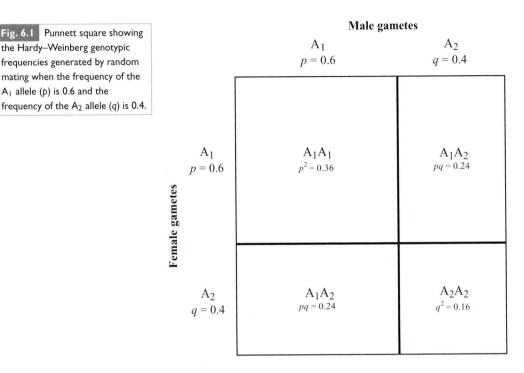

Fig. 6.1 Punnett square showing the Hardy–Weinberg genotypic frequencies generated by random mating when the frequency of the A_1 allele (p) is 0.6 and the frequency of the A_2 allele (q) is 0.4.

to the allelic frequencies by the square expansion of allelic frequencies. Thus, for autosomal genes in diploid organisms in which there are two alleles with frequencies p and q, the frequencies of the three genotypes are predicted by the formula $(p + q)^2 = p^2 + 2pq + q^2$. Furthermore, *for autosomal genes the equilibrium genotypic frequencies at any given locus are attained in a single generation providing there is no overlapping of generations.*

The principle can be demonstrated most simply by a Punnett square diagram (Fig. 6.1), which represents the union of gametes by random mating of an entire breeding population. A single gene locus is shown, with two alleles (A_1 and A_2) with frequencies of p and q. The random combination of these alleles in sexual reproduction results in the genotypic frequencies of p^2 for A_1A_1, $2pq$ for A_1A_2 and q^2 for A_2A_2. Thus, the genotypic frequencies for a two-allele system are as follows:

$$p^2 + 2pq + q^2 = 1 \qquad \text{(Eqn 6.1)}$$

The allelic frequencies do not change as a result of this reproduction. We can see from Fig. 6.1, or from Exp. 6.2, that the frequency (p_1) of A_1 after one generation of random breeding is given by:

$$p_1 = p^2 + \frac{1}{2}(2pq)$$
$$= p^2 + pq$$
$$= p(p + q)$$

But $p + q$ is equal to 1. Therefore, p_1 is equal to p, which is the original frequency of the A_1 allele. In a similar fashion we can show

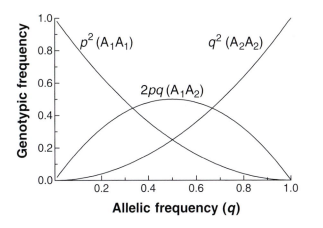

Fig. 6.2 The Hardy–Weinberg genotypic frequencies at a gene locus with two alleles as a function of the frequency (q) of the A_2 allele. Note that the heterozygotes are most common at intermediate allelic frequencies (between 0.33 and 0.67).

that the frequency of the A_2 allele in the offspring equals q. Thus, when there is random breeding, the allelic frequencies stay constant from generation to generation.

It is a simple matter to relate the genotypic frequencies to the allelic frequencies using Eqn 6.1 (Fig. 6.2). For example, if the frequency of the A_2 allele (q) is 0.3 then genotype A_2A_2 has a frequency of q^2 ($0.3^2 = 0.09$), genotype A_1A_2 has a frequency of $2pq$ ($2 \times 0.7 \times 0.3 = 0.42$), and genotype A_1A_1 has a frequency of p^2 ($0.7^2 = 0.49$). It may be seen from Fig. 6.2 that heterozygotes are most common at intermediate allelic frequencies.

6.3.1 Neutral equilibrium

The Hardy–Weinberg equilibrium is a neutral equilibrium. This means that the allelic and genotypic frequencies do not change because of random mating, but if some other force, such as selection or migration, changes the frequencies of the alleles to new values, the genotypic frequencies automatically shift according to the formula $p^2 + 2pq + q^2$. Thus, the genotypic frequencies do not return to their previous values but are defined by the new allelic frequencies. If no other force is applied, the population will remain at this new equilibrium. This neutral equilibrium differs from a stable equilibrium, like the carrying capacity K in logistic growth, because the latter returns to a fixed equilibrium value (K) if disturbed.

6.4 Applying the Hardy–Weinberg principle to autosomal genes with two alleles

The Hardy–Weinberg principle is elegant, but how useful is it? It all seems so idealistic: random breeding, no evolutionary forces such as selection or mutation operating, no overlapping of generations, and so on. Let us consider some of these apparently idealistic conditions when we apply the principle, and see how useful it can be.

Table 6.2 The frequencies of M–N blood groups using the data from Table 6.1, assuming that M is dominant to N for the purposes of illustration

Phenotype (blood group)	M	N	Total
Genotype	MM + MN	NN	
Number in sample	361	139	500
Frequency in sample	0.722	0.278	1.0
Theoretical frequency	$p^2 + 2pq$	q^2	$p^2 + 2pq + q^2 = 1$
Estimated allelic frequency of N	$= \sqrt{(q^2)} = \sqrt{(0.278)} = 0.5273$		
Estimated allelic frequency of M	$= 1 - q = 1 - 0.5273 = 0.4727$		

6.4.1 Estimating allelic frequencies when one allele is dominant to another

In section 6.2, we learned how to estimate allelic frequencies from the genotypic frequencies (see Exps. 6.2 and 6.3). However, if one allele is dominant to the other, and we cannot distinguish between the homozygous dominant and heterozygous individuals, we have to estimate the allelic frequencies in another, less accurate, way. To illustrate this, we will use the M–N blood group data from Table 6.1, but imagine that the M allele is dominant to the N allele.

If there were dominance, we would observe two phenotypes, M and N. The M phenotype would include both the MM and MN genotypes, and so there would be $119 + 242 = 361$ of this phenotype (see Table 6.1). The frequencies of the two phenotypes are $361/500 = 0.722$ and $139/500 = 0.278$. We cannot estimate the frequency of M alleles directly because some individuals of phenotype M have both M and N alleles. However, phenotype N consists of a single genotype, and if we assume random breeding this has a theoretical frequency of q^2 in the population, according to the Hardy–Weinberg equilibrium (Eqn 6.1). Consequently, we can estimate the allelic frequency (q) of N as $\sqrt{(q^2)}$ and this gives us an estimate of 0.5273. The allelic frequency (p) of M is 0.4727 from the relationship $p = 1 - q$ (a transformation of Exp. 6.4).

These estimates are very similar to those based on the entire sample (Table 6.2), and the two sets of estimates only differ by approximately 1.5%. However, the error increases as the frequency of the homozygous recessive individuals becomes lower in the population.

6.4.2 Random mating

It is important to understand that when we talk of random mating, we do not mean promiscuous mating, we only mean that mates are chosen without regard to the genotype at the gene locus being considered. It is possible for mating to be random with respect to some traits and, simultaneously, to be non-random with respect to other traits. In humans, for example, mating appears to be random with respect to blood groups and many enzyme systems, but is non-random with respect to skin colour, height and IQ.

Table 6.3 Comparison of observed and expected numbers of M–N phenotypes, assuming random breeding, in a sample of 500 individuals (data from Table 6.1)

Blood group	MM	MN	NN	Total
Observed number	119	242	139	500
Expected number	115.2	249.6	135.2	500
χ^2 value	$\frac{(119-115.2)^2}{115.2}$	$+ \frac{(242-249.6)^2}{249.6}$	$+ \frac{(139-135.2)^2}{135.2} = 0.4635$	
	$df = 3 - 2 = 1$	$P = 0.5$		

We can see how well the genotypic frequencies in a population correspond to the expected Hardy–Weinberg frequencies by looking at the data from our first example (Table 6.3). The expected number for each genotype was calculated by multiplying the expected frequencies of $p^2 + 2pq + q^2$ by the total number of the sample. Thus the expected number of the MM genotype is $0.48^2 \times 500 = 115.2$, and so on. It may be seen that the observed and expected numbers are in close agreement. This is not too surprising when we consider that most people live, choose a mate, reproduce, and so on without ever knowing their MN blood type. Thus, mates are chosen without regard to blood type and so breeding is random with respect to blood type.

How different would the observed and expected numbers have to be before we considered them to be significantly different? We can make a statistical comparison of the two sets of numbers using the chi-squared test (χ^2-test), a standard procedure that is explained in virtually any textbook on statistics. In our example, the χ^2 value is 0.4635, with one degree of freedom (we lose two degrees of freedom because the total numbers and the allelic frequencies are the same in the observed and expected series). The probability is about 0.5, which is not significant (see below). We can conclude, therefore, that mating is random with respect to the M–N blood groups in this population.

The χ^2 test gives an objective way of assessing the agreement between the observed and expected results. As the difference between the observed and expected results gets larger, the χ^2 value also gets larger. When it reaches 3.84 or higher (df = 1), and the probability (P) becomes 0.05 or lower, we can conclude that the observed and expected results are significantly different from one another. At this point we consider that the population is not in Hardy–Weinberg equilibrium, i.e. is not breeding at random with respect to the character in question.

6.4.3 Violation of strict assumptions

The Hardy–Weinberg principle is not very sensitive to certain violations of the assumptions. For this reason, we cannot say that there is no selection, mutation, etc. if we find that the genotypic frequencies conform to the expected values. Let us consider two examples to show this.

Sickle-cell anaemia is prevalent in tropical Africa where there is a high incidence of malaria. Humans from this area have two forms of

Table 6.4 Frequencies of haemoglobin types in samples of 287 infants and 654 adults in Tanzania

Genotype	AA	AS	SS	Total	Frequency of S allele
Observed number of infants	189	89	9	287	0.1864
Expected H–W numbers	190	87	10	287	
	χ^2 value $= 0.15$; df $= 1$; $P > 0.5$				
Observed number of adults	400	249	5	654	0.1980
Expected H–W numbers	420.7	207.7	25.6	654	
	χ^2 value $= 25.8$; df $= 1$; $P < 0.001$				

Source: Data from Allison (1956).

haemoglobin: a normal form, A, and a sickle form, S. The three genotypes have the following characteristics: AA has 'normal' haemoglobin and red blood cells; SS individuals have abnormal haemoglobin and their red blood cells have a characteristic sickle shape; and heterozygous AS individuals have red blood cells that assume a sickle shape only when the blood is deoxygenated. Homozygous SS individuals mainly die an early death from a wide variety of disorders (see Chapter 7), but heterozygous (AS) individuals have a resistance to malaria and survive better than 'normal' individuals in areas where malaria is prevalent. Thus, there are strong selection pressures operating on this gene system.

Samples of a Tanzanian population show that the infant genotypes are in Hardy–Weinberg equilibrium but the adults are not (Table 6.4). There are fewer homozygotes than expected in adults because AA individuals have a higher death rate from malaria than other genotypes and SS individuals have a high death rate from the effects of sickle-cell anaemia, and consequently there are more heterozygotes than expected because they are at a selective advantage. The surviving adults mate at random with respect to this gene and the fertility of the different genotypes is equal. Consequently, the genotypes of the next generation of children occur at Hardy–Weinberg frequencies because this equilibrium is attained in a single generation (see section 6.3). Selection is operating, but the genotypic frequencies of the young are in Hardy–Weinberg equilibrium.

The second example concerns the rare Tay–Sachs disease, a disorder involving lipid metabolism which results in the accumulation of a specialized type of lipid known as ganglioside in the nerve cells. Tay–Sachs is a recessive disorder that is lethal in early childhood. There is no known cure. The disease occurs at an incidence of about 1 in 550 000 births in the non-Jewish Canadian population (it has a higher incidence in Jews who originally came from Europe). The homozygous 'normal' individuals (AA) and heterozygous individuals (Aa) are generally indistinguishable, although heterozygous individuals can be detected by screening a certain enzyme in the blood.

According to the Hardy–Weinberg principle, the frequency of the homozygous recessive (aa) in the population is q^2. Assuming random breeding, we can estimate the frequency of the Tay–Sachs allele as follows: $q^2 = 1/550\,000 = 0.000\,001\,82$, therefore $q = \sqrt{(0.000\,001\,82)} = 0.001\,348$. Are we justified in making this assumption of random breeding? The answer is probably yes. It is unlikely that AA and Aa individuals are aware of their condition relative to this gene locus, and so mating within this segment of the population is probably random with respect to Tay–Sachs. It is true that the homozygous recessive individuals cannot breed, but this is such a trivial proportion of the population that it can safely be ignored.

We can estimate the frequency of heterozygous individuals, who are carriers of Tay–Sachs, using the formula $2pq$. This gives us a frequency of $0.002\,693$ or approximately 1 in 371 individuals in the population. It may surprise you that the number of carriers is so high considering that the incidence of the disease is so low (1 in 550 000). This reveals another interesting implication of the Hardy–Weinberg principle, which is that rare alleles exist mainly in heterozygous rather than homozygous individuals in the population. The ratio of recessive alleles in heterozygotes to those in homozygous recessives $= pq/q^2 = p/q$; but p is approximately 1 when q is very small, therefore $p/q \approx 1/q$. In our example of Tay–Sachs, this approximation gives us a ratio of approximately 742 which is very similar to the more precise calculation of 741 (calculated from pq/q^2).

6.5 | Complications

We will briefly consider how the Hardy–Weinberg principle applies to situations other than autosomal genes with two alleles.

6.5.1 Multiple alleles

The Hardy–Weinberg principle can easily be extended to include three or more alleles at a gene locus. The number of possible genotypes increases as the number of alleles increases. This is illustrated for an autosomal gene with three alleles, with frequencies of p, q and r (Fig. 6.3).

It may be seen that there are six possible genotypes with the following set of frequencies: $A_1A_1 = p^2$, $A_1A_2 = 2pq$, $A_1A_3 = 2pr$, $A_2A_2 = q^2$, $A_2A_3 = 2qr$, and $A_3A_3 = r^2$. If the alleles are all codominant, the calculation of the allelic and genotypic frequencies is straightforward, but if certain alleles are dominant to others it becomes more complicated to solve. For example, in the ABO blood group system, A and B are codominant, but are dominant to O. Thus, if we set $A = A_1$, $B = A_2$, and $O = A_3$, we can see from Fig. 6.3 that blood type A has a phenotypic frequency of $p^2 + 2pr$, blood type B a frequency of $q^2 + 2qr$, blood type AB a frequency of $2pq$, and blood type O a frequency of r^2. Although we can estimate the frequency of the O allele as $\sqrt{(r^2)}$, we cannot estimate the frequencies of the A and B alleles directly, and

Fig. 6.3 The relationship between the allelic frequencies (p, q and r) and the resulting genotypic frequencies (A_1A_1, A_1A_2, A_1A_3, etc.) when there is random mating between individuals carrying a gene with three alleles.

	A_1 p	A_2 q	A_3 r
A_1 p	$A_1A_1 = p^2$	$A_1A_2 = pq$	$A_1A_3 = pr$
A_2 q	$A_1A_2 = pq$	$A_2A_2 = q^2$	$A_2A_3 = qr$
A_3 r	$A_1A_3 = pr$	$A_2A_3 = qr$	$A_3A_3 = r^2$

have to use a maximum likelihood procedure (see Hartl and Clark 1989 for more details).

6.5.2 Sex-linked genes

In the case of sex-linked genes, individuals of the heterogametic sex have a single allele, whereas individuals of the homogametic sex have two alleles, the same as autosomal genes. Let us consider the situation where the heterogametic sex (XY) is male and the homogametic sex (XX) is female. If the allelic frequencies are the same in both males and females, the equilibrium genotypic frequencies are established in a single generation, like the autosomal genes. However, if the allelic frequencies are different between males and females, the allelic frequencies in the two sexes will undergo a series of damped oscillations about the overall allelic frequency (i.e. of the two sexes combined), and the genotypic frequencies will also oscillate. To assess the effects of this instability, let us consider an extreme example where a population starts with an allelic frequency of $q_f = 1$ in the females and $q_m = 0$ in the males. The allelic frequency in the males in any subsequent generation will be the allelic frequency of the females in the preceding generation, because all of their alleles are derived from those females. The allelic frequency in the females, however, will be the arithmetic average of q_f and q_m of the preceding generation, because half of their alleles are derived from the males and half from the females from the previous generation. The result is a series of oscillations which rapidly dampen until the equilibrium frequency $q = 0.67$ is attained by both sexes (see Fig. 6.4). In most cases, however, the difference between the allelic frequencies of the males and females would be much smaller than this and would probably attain equilibrium within two or three generations.

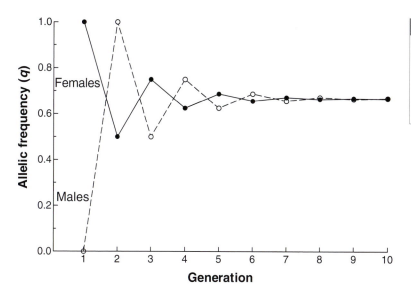

Fig. 6.4 Random mating for a sex-linked gene, showing the approach to equilibrium of the allelic frequencies for each sex, when the starting allelic frequency is 1 ($= q_f$) for females and 0 ($= q_m$) for males.

6.5.3 Multiple loci

The Hardy–Weinberg principle can also be extended to deal simultaneously with more than one locus of genes. Similar to the situation with sex-linked genes, however, an equilibrium will not be reached in a single generation if the genotypes are not in equilibrium. A simple example will make this clear. Imagine that we start a population with two genotypes: $A_1A_1B_1B_1$ and $A_2A_2B_2B_2$. In the next generation there will be only three possible genotypes: $A_1A_1B_1B_1$, $A_1A_2B_1B_2$ and $A_2A_2B_2B_2$ in a $1:2:1$ ratio. Thus, the genotypes $A_1A_1B_2B_2$, $A_2A_2B_1B_1$, etc. are not produced immediately, but they occur in subsequent generations of random mating and the genotype frequencies converge to a stable equilibrium after about seven generations. However, if the loci are linked, this reduces the amount of recombination between the two genes and slows the approach to equilibrium. The tighter the linkage between two gene loci, the longer it takes to reach equilibrium.

6.5.4 Non-random mating

If mating is non-random and the mating system is unrelated to the allelic frequencies being considered (i.e. one allele or another is not favoured in the mating process), the allelic frequencies and genotype ratios will remain stable from generation to generation. However, the equilibrium genotypic frequencies will differ from those predicted by the Hardy–Weinberg principle. In the case where like tend to breed with like, called assortative mating, homozygotes have a higher frequency, and heterozygotes a lower frequency, than what would be predicted by the Hardy–Weinberg equilibrium. This type of mating does not lead to a change in allelic frequencies. If there is a preference for different phenotypes to mate with each other, called disassortative mating, heterozygotes increase in the frequency at the expense of homozygotes. These facts are intuitively obvious. What is not obvious, however, is that disassortative mating leads to a change in allelic frequencies. Rarer alleles are favoured because the rarer phenotype has a better chance of mating than the commoner phenotype; it is easier for them to find a dissimilar mate. As a result, the frequency of the rarer allele increases so that the allelic frequencies become similar. This has been observed in some plants with self-sterility mechanisms based on multiple alleles, which coexist at approximately equal frequencies in the population (see Falconer and Mackay 1996).

6.6 | Summary and conclusions

The frequencies of the alleles, genotypes and phenotypes relating to a particular trait, such as blood type or flower colour, are determined by calculating their proportions in the total breeding population. Sexual reproduction does not usually lead to a change in these frequencies, provided the type of mating remains constant. When mating is random, the genotypic frequencies have a characteristic relationship to the allelic frequencies for autosomal genes, called the Hardy–Weinberg ratio, which remains constant from generation to generation provided there are no other forces operating on the system. Departures from the characteristic Hardy–Weinberg ratio may indicate that mating is not random, or that there is some other factor such as selection that is changing the allelic frequencies. The Hardy–Weinberg ratio or equilibrium is attained in a single generation for a single autosomal gene, but may take several generations to attain if a trait is determined by more than one gene, or by a sex-linked gene. There are two types of non-random mating. When like tend to breed with like (assortative mating), the proportion of homozygotes is higher, and the heterozygotes are lower, than that predicted by the Hardy–Weinberg equilibrium. When different phenotypes prefer to mate with each other (disassortative mating), the proportion of heterozygotes is higher than that predicted by the Hardy–Weinberg equilibrium, and this type of mating changes the allelic frequencies until they are all similar to one another.

6.7 | Problems

1. The rhesus (Rh) blood factor in humans is controlled by three tightly linked genes with two basic categories of alleles: R, which produces an antigen on the surface of red blood cells, and r, which does not. The R allele is dominant, and the RR and Rr genotypes are said to be rhesus positive (Rh$^+$). The frequency of the R allele is 0.9 in a Caucasian population. Assuming that mating is random with respect to this factor, (a) what is the frequency of heterozygous individuals in the population, and (b) what fraction of rhesus positive people are heterozygous?
2. The following frequencies of M–N blood groups were collected on a sample of 203 Guatemalan Indians (data from Mourant *et al.* 1976): MM 112, MN 74, and NN 17. Calculate the expected Hardy–Weinberg equilibrium frequencies of these genotypes. Do they conform to what is observed?

3. Spooner *et al.* (1973) studied the amylase locus in Friesian milk cows. The genotypic distribution of the milk herd was BB 86, BC 402 and CC 74. Is the distribution of genotypes in Hardy–Weinberg equilibrium? How can you account for these results given that the genotypic frequencies of young calves conform to the Hardy–Weinberg equilibrium?

4. The frequency of cystic fibrosis, an autosomal recessive condition causing severe respiratory problems, is approximately 1 in 2000 live births. What is the frequency of heterozygous carriers, assuming random mating?

5. In the peppered moth (*Biston betularia*) there is a *carbonaria* allele (C) which codes for a dark body colour and which is dominant to the *typica* allele (c) which codes for a light, speckled body colour. In one population that was surveyed, 96% of the moths were dark coloured. Assuming random mating, what is the frequency of the *carbonaria* allele in the population?

Chapter 7

Mutation and the genetic variation of populations

There must be genetic variation for evolution to occur. Mutation is the ultimate source of genetic variation, which is amplified by recombination during sexual reproduction. Mutations will only play a role in evolution if they are heritable. In most organisms this means that only the mutations occurring in the germ line leading to the production of gametes may have evolutionary consequences.

7.1 | Gene mutations

The word mutation may refer to any change in the genetic material, ranging from a change to a single base pair in DNA, to changes in the structure and number of chromosomes. The discussion of mutation and genetic variation in this book will only consider mutations within a gene, and this gene mutation can be simply thought of as a change in the sequence of DNA. In principle the DNA must be sequenced to detect a mutation, but in practice most mutations are identified and named by their phenotypic effects.

The simplest kind of gene mutation is the substitution of one base pair by another. These point mutations, as they are called, may result in the replacement of one amino acid by another, but in many cases there is no change in the amino acid because of the redundancy of the genetic code (Fig. 7.1). In the example of isoleucine, two of the three substitutions in the third position do not result in a change of amino acid. Where there is no change in amino acid (called a silent mutation) one might expect there to be no effect on the organism. This is usually the case, but there are situations where silent mutations influence gene expression and the fitness of an organism by changing the secondary structure (i.e. folding) of DNA (see Hartl and Clark 1989).

Where there is a change in amino acid, the effect is very variable. It depends partly on the degree of difference between the chemical properties of the substituting amino acid and the original amino acid. In isoleucine (Fig. 7.1), for example, three of the possible new amino acids, arginine, lysine and threonine, have chemical properties

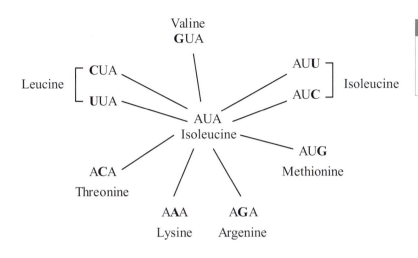

that differ sharply from isoleucine, and so potentially could affect the function of a gene. It also depends, however, on where the substitution takes place, and whether the substitution affects the active site of an enzyme or the secondary structure of the protein being coded for. Thus, in some cases there is no discernible effect on the function of the protein product, but in other cases there are profound effects on the protein product and on the physiology of the organism. Examples of changes of a single amino acid leading to severe genetic disorders in humans, include phenylketonuria, albinism and sickle-cell anaemia. In the mutation of sickle-cell anaemia, a point mutation substitutes adenine for thymine at a critical point in the DNA molecule. This changes the normal codon from CTT (or CTC) to CAT (or CAC), and the corresponding codon on the messenger RNA molecule is changed from GAA (or GAG) to GUA (or GUG). The result is that the sixth amino acid in the 146-chain of amino acids in the β chain of the haemoglobin molecule is changed from glutamic acid to valine (Fig. 7.2).

This seemingly inconsequential change results in an abnormal haemoglobin which, in the homozygous condition, causes the red blood cells to assume a characteristic sickle shape. The sickle shape of the red blood cells causes them to clump and interfere with blood circulation. This leads to local failures in blood supply, causing such things as heart failure, brain damage and subsequent paralysis, kidney damage and failure, lung damage promoting susceptibility to pneumonia, etc. The body destroys the sickle cells more rapidly than normal red blood cells, and this leads to anaemia, weakness and lassitude, poor physical development and impaired mental function. There is also an increase in bone marrow activity which may result in the characteristic 'tower' skull shape. The sickle cells also collect in the spleen, causing enlargement and fibrosis of the spleen. It is not surprising that individuals homozygous for this condition have poor juvenile survival rates. The mutation is maintained in the population in malarial areas because heterozygous individuals have a resistance to malaria (see Chapter 11).

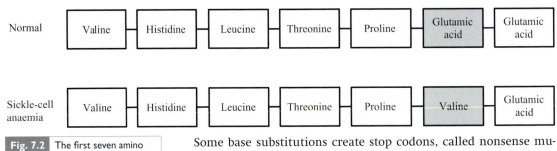

| Normal | Valine | Histidine | Leucine | Threonine | Proline | Glutamic acid | Glutamic acid |

| Sickle-cell anaemia | Valine | Histidine | Leucine | Threonine | Proline | Valine | Glutamic acid |

Fig. 7.2 The first seven amino acids in the β chain of human haemoglobin showing the substitution of valine for glutamic acid. This results in a severe condition in the homozygous state known as sickle-cell anaemia.

Some base substitutions create stop codons, called nonsense mutations, which usually destroy the function of the gene product, because protein synthesis ends before the complete polypeptide chain is formed. Similar effects are usually produced by the deletion or the insertion of a base pair in the DNA molecule, because all of the codons 'downstream' of that point will be incorrect and will code for the wrong amino acids. Such insertions or deletions are called frameshift mutations.

In addition to single point mutations, there are many other ways in which the sequence of base pairs in the DNA molecule of a gene can be changed. Those interested in learning more about the range of possible mutations are referred to Futuyma (1998). It should be clear that there is an extraordinary variety of possible gene mutations, which may have either inconsequential or dramatic phenotypic effects. We should also stress, however, that mutations alter pre-existing characteristics and do not create entirely new structures. For example, we see mutations modifying the pentadactyl limb of the vertebrates into legs for walking, wings for flying, and fins for swimming, etc., not the creation of entirely new developmental structures for these functions.

7.2 | The randomness of mutations

Mutations are considered to be accidental, undirected, random or chance events, but we should clarify what we mean by using these descriptors. Mutations are accidental or chance events in the sense that they are rare exceptions to the precise copying of DNA during replication. However, mutations are not totally random because some mutations occur more frequently than others, and genes may mutate in a particular way at a particular frequency. For example, we may know that a particular allele mutates to another allele at a frequency of 1 per 100 000 individuals per generation. However, even though the mutation rate may be predictable, we cannot predict which individual will mutate in a particular way.

The Darwinian view of evolution is that mutations are random or undirected, relative to the needs of the organism. In other words, mutations occur independently of whether they help or harm an organism in the environment in which it lives. Most mutations will be harmful because organisms have been selected over countless generations to suit, or fit, their environment. Very occasionally a mutation may increase the probability of survival of that genotype in subsequent generations. These favourable mutations are not considered to

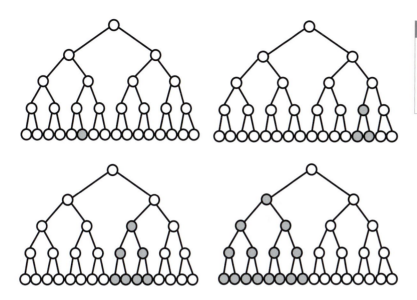

be adaptive responses of the organism to the environment, but rather are fortuitous accidents that proved to be adaptive after the event.

At one time, however, there were many scientists, particularly bacteriologists, who held the Lamarckian view that environments could induce favourable mutations. This was because it had been known for a long time that bacterial cultures, when confronted with a bactericide, regularly gave rise to new genetic strains that could cope with these adverse environments. However, experiments on bacteria in the 1940s and 1950s effectively killed this neo-Lamarckian viewpoint, and supported the Darwinian position.

Salvador Luria and Max Delbrück (1943) looked at the origin of mutations conferring phage (i.e. viral) resistance in bacteria. They established a large number of genetically identical bacterial cultures, starting with a single cell that was not phage resistant, and allowed them to grow to a constant population size. The cultures were then plated on individual agar plates covered with a bacteriophage. This treatment killed almost all the bacteria, but some colonies survived because individual cells had developed mutations for phage resistance during the growth of each culture. Consequently, the number of resistant cells, and therefore mutations, in each culture could be counted. To simplify the argument, let us imagine that after four generations of binary fission, the final size of each culture was 16 cells (Fig. 7.3) which were then exposed to the bacteriophage. Luria and Delbrück reasoned that if the mutations conferring phage resistance occurred at any point in the history of the cultures, many cultures would have 0 mutations (none survived), some cultures would have 1 mutation, some 2, others 4, and still others 8 (Fig. 7.3). Consequently, the number of mutations per culture would exhibit a clumped distribution, rather than an even or random distribution, around the mean number of mutations per culture. Statistical analysis showed that the mutations had a clumped distribution, which indicates that the majority of the mutations had occurred before exposure to the phage.

Thus, the mutation for phage resistance was a fortuitous preadaptation[1] rather than a response to the phage environment.

A second experiment by Joshua and Esther Lederberg (1952) showed even more directly that advantageous mutations occur without the organism being exposed to the environment in which they are favoured. They used a technique known as replica plating. They spread cultures of *Escherichia coli* that had never been exposed to penicillin onto 'master' agar plates without penicillin. Each cell on these plates gave rise to a distinct colony of cells. They then used a stamp covered with velvet cloth to transfer a sample of cells from each colony on the master plates to new 'replica' agar plates containing the antibiotic penicillin. A few colonies appeared on these replicate plates that were resistant to penicillin. Because the transferred cells on the replica plates had the same spatial arrangement as the parental cells on the master plates, they were able to identify which parental colony had given rise to the resistant colonies. When they tested the resistance of the colonies on the master plates, only those colonies that had given rise to resistant colonies were resistant to penicillin. This proved that the mutations for penicillin resistance had occurred before exposure to penicillin.

These classic experiments, and many other experimental results, have convinced biologists that mutations are random rather than directed by environmental need. In 1988, however, the controversy was revived by John Cairns and colleagues at Harvard University, who employed non-lethal selective agents (specific nutrients required for growth and reproduction) on *E. coli* rather than the lethal selective agents (viruses and antibiotics) used in the classic experiments (Cairns *et al.* 1988). For example, when a strain of *lac*− bacteria, that cannot utilize lactose as a source of carbon, was put in a medium where lactose was the only source of carbon they were not killed but entered a resting phase. However, some cells mutated to the *lac*+ strain in a pattern that they claimed could not be accounted for by random mutation, and they concluded that these mutations must have been directed or induced by the lactose environment. Similarly, Barry Hall of the University of Rochester, New York, worked on a strain of *E. coli* that had defects in two genes coding for enzymes needed to break down the amino acid tryptophan (Hall 1990). When he grew the bacteria in a tryptophan-based medium he discovered that some bacteria developed the required mutations in both genes and so could utilize the medium. The surprise was that the pair of mutations occurred 100 million times more often than expected from the mutation rates of the individual genes. These, and other similar claims of advantageous mutations being induced by the environment have been reviewed by Sniegowski and Lenski (1995), and they have convincingly demonstrated that these results can be explained by the orthodox Darwinian view that mutations are random with respect to need.

---

[1] A preadaptation is where an organism or part of an organism is well suited to live in a particular set of conditions it has yet to encounter.

7.3 | Mutation rates and evolution

Mutation rates are very low, typically ranging from 10^{-4} to 10^{-9} per cell per replication (Table 7.1). The mutation rates of bacteria and other microorganisms appear to be lower than those of large multicellular organisms, but the latter include somatic mutations during early development and so they are artificially elevated. One should also be aware, when comparing mutation rates, that the specificity of different mutations varies widely. In some cases the mutation involves a specific base pair substitution in the DNA molecule (for example, sickle-cell anaemia), whereas in other cases there may a variety of mutations that deactivate a gene but because they give rise to the same phenotypic expression they are grouped together as a single type of mutation.

Table 7.1 | Mutation rates of specific genes in various organisms (from a variety of sources)

Organism/character	Rate	Units
Bacteriophage – T2		
Lysis inhibition	1×10^{-8}	Per gene per replication
Host range	3×10^{-9}	
Bacteria – *Escherichia coli*		
Lactose fermentation	2×10^{-7}	Per cell per division
Resistance to T1 phage	3×10^{-8}	
Streptomycin resistance	4×10^{-10}	
Algae – *Chlamydomonas reinhardi*	1×10^{-6}	Per cell per division
Streptomycin resistance		
Fungi – *Neurospora crassa*		
Inositol requirement	8×10^{-8}	Mutant frequency among
Adenine independence	4×10^{-8}	asexual spores
Corn – *Zea mays*		
Shrunken seeds	1×10^{-5}	Per genome per sexual generation
Sugary seeds	2×10^{-6}	
Fruit fly – *Drosophila melanogaster*		
Eyeless	6×10^{-5}	Per genome per sexual generation
White eye	4×10^{-5}	
Brown eye	3×10^{-5}	
Mouse – *Mus musculus*		
Piebald coat colour	3×10^{-5}	Per genome per sexual generation
Dilute coat colour	3×10^{-5}	
Humans – *Homo sapiens*		
Normal to haemophilia A	3×10^{-5}	Per genome per sexual generation
Normal to albino	3×10^{-5}	
Normal to Huntington disease	1×10^{-6}	

The average mutation rate per locus per generation is estimated to be 10^{-6} to 10^{-5} as measured by phenotypic effects (Futuyma 1998). Let us consider the evolutionary implications of this level of mutation rates by examining how gene frequencies change in populations as a result of mutation pressure.

7.3.1 Non-recurrent mutation

If just a single new allele is created by mutation in the whole population, its chance of survival is very small even if it is advantageous. This is because there will be a single heterozygous individual in the population carrying this allele, and there is always a chance that it may not survive to reproduce, or if it does reproduce that the copies of this allele may not be passed on to the next generation. This low probability of survival will continue, generation after generation, as long as the allele remains at a very low frequency in the population. Indeed, in an infinitely large population, if the gene is selectively neutral, i.e. is neither advantageous nor disadvantageous compared to other alleles, its probability of survival is zero over the long term. In small populations, the chance of survival is increased because its initial frequency is much higher. For example, in a diploid population of 10 individuals the frequency of the allele is 1 in 20, or 0.05. Thus, novel mutations may occasionally lead to abrupt changes in the gene frequency of small populations, provided there is no selection against the allele.

7.3.2 Recurrent, non-reversible mutation

How quickly can gene frequencies change as a result of observed mutation rates? We will consider this question at first by ignoring the possibility of reverse mutations. Imagine that an allele A_1 mutates to another allele A_2 at a rate of μ per individual per generation. Let the allelic frequencies of $A_1 = p$ and $A_2 = q$, and their initial frequencies equal p_0 and q_0. The change in allelic frequency over one generation is:

$$\Delta q = q_1 - q_0 \qquad \text{(Exp. 7.1)}$$

But this is a result of allele A_1 (at frequency p_0) mutating at a rate of μ to allele A_2. Therefore:

$$\Delta q = \mu p_0 \qquad \text{(Exp. 7.2)}$$

Expressions 7.1 and 7.2 are equivalent, and so:

$$q_1 - q_0 = \mu p_0 \qquad \text{(Exp. 7.3)}$$

But $p_0 = 1 - q_0$, and substituting this for p_0 in Exp. 7.3 we obtain:

$$q_1 - q_0 = \mu(1 - q_0) \qquad \text{(Exp. 7.4)}$$

This may be rearranged to:

$$q_1 = \mu + (1 - \mu)q_0 \qquad \text{(Exp. 7.5)}$$

Similarly, we can show that in the second generation:

$$q_2 = \mu + (1 - \mu)q_1 \qquad \text{(Exp. 7.6)}$$

Substituting Exp. 7.5 for q_1 in Exp. 7.6 results in:

$$q_2 = \mu + (1 - \mu) \times [\mu + (1 - \mu)q_0] \qquad \text{(Exp. 7.7)}$$

which rearranges to:

$$q_2 = \mu + (1 - \mu)\mu + (1 - \mu)^2 q_0 \qquad \text{(Exp. 7.8)}$$

Note how Exps. 7.5 and 7.8 compare to one another. We can continue to develop this equation to predict q, generation after generation, to show that the general case after n generations is predicted by:

$$q_n = \mu + (1 - \mu)\mu + (1 - \mu)^2\mu + \cdots + (1 - \mu)^n q_0 \qquad \text{(Exp. 7.9)}$$

Mathematically, Exp. 7.9 is equivalent to:

$$q_n = 1 - (1 - \mu)^n + (1 - \mu)^n q_0 \qquad \text{(Exp. 7.10)}$$

We can factor and rearrange this expression to:

$$(1 - \mu)^n = \frac{1 - q_n}{1 - q_0} = \frac{p_n}{p_0} \qquad \text{(Exp. 7.11)}$$

This expression may be rearranged to obtain our first predictive equation:

$$p_n = p_0(1 - \mu)^n \qquad \text{(Eqn 7.1)}$$

This equation may be used to see how rapidly the frequency of A_1 is reduced as it mutates to A_2. If we start with a frequency of $A_1 = 1$, and use an average mutation rate (μ) per gene per generation of 1×10^{-5}, we find that after one generation the frequency of the A_1 allele will reduce to 0.999 99. After 100 generations the frequency will reduce to 0.999, and after 1000 generations the frequency will reduce to 0.99. Thus, it will take 1000 generations to reduce the frequency of the allele by approximately 1%! It takes 70 000 generations before the frequency of the A_1 allele is reduced to 0.497, or approximately half its initial value.

The conclusion from these calculations is obvious. Normal mutation rates can only produce very slow changes in allelic frequencies, and it takes many thousands of generations to change these frequencies by appreciable amounts. Thus, mutation pressure by itself can only cause large changes in the allelic frequencies of populations over vast periods of time. We have also ignored the possibility of reverse mutations, and these will obviously slow the rate of change still further. We will consider this complication next.

7.3.3 Recurrent, reversible mutation

Consider the following situation where a wild-type allele (the common form of the allele) A_1 is mutating to A_2 (the mutant form) at a rate u per generation, and A_2 is mutating back to A_1 at a rate v per generation. If the initial allelic frequency of A_1 is p and that of A_2 is q, the change in allelic frequency after one generation is:

$$\Delta q = up - vq \qquad \text{(Exp. 7.12)}$$

The situation will lead to an equilibrium, in which the change in A_1 to A_2 is exactly balanced by the change in A_2 to A_1. In this case $\Delta q = 0$ (there is no change in allelic frequencies) and $u\hat{p}$ equals $v\hat{q}$, where $\hat{p}$ and $\hat{q}$ represent equilibrium values. Thus:

$$\hat{p}u = \hat{q}v \qquad \text{(Exp. 7.13)}$$

This rearranges to:

$$\frac{\hat{p}}{\hat{q}} = \frac{v}{u} \qquad \text{(Eqn 7.2)}$$

Thus, if the forward mutation rate (u) is ten times the value of the reverse mutation rate (v) the frequency of the A_1 allele (p) will be one-tenth that of the A_2 allele (q). Setting $p = 1 - q$ in Exp. 7.11 and rearranging the modified expression we obtain:

$$\hat{q} = \frac{u}{u + v} \qquad \text{(Eqn 7.3)}$$

What can we conclude from these last two equations? First, although Eqn 7.2 sometimes predicts the frequencies of the two alleles in the population, more commonly it does not. We know from observation that forward mutation rates, u, are usually higher than the reverse mutation rates, v. Consequently, Eqn 7.2 predicts that the frequency, p, of the wild-type allele should be less than the frequency, q, of the mutant form, but this is not usually the case. We can conclude, therefore, that *the equilibrium frequencies of such genes are not usually the product of mutation rates alone; other factors, especially selection, are usually more important.*

Second, if there is a change in mutation rates by radiation, chemical mutagens, etc., Eqn 7.3 shows that the equilibrium allelic frequency, q, (and consequently p) will not change unless the forward mutation rate, u, is changed differently from the reverse mutation rate, v.

7.4 | Genetic variation of populations

As population geneticists began to consider the genetic structure of populations, two different models slowly developed. The classical model was the first to be developed, and was predominantly the viewpoint of the mathematical theoreticians and some of the laboratory geneticists. They believed that most gene loci were homozygous for the wild-type allele because natural selection had purged alleles of

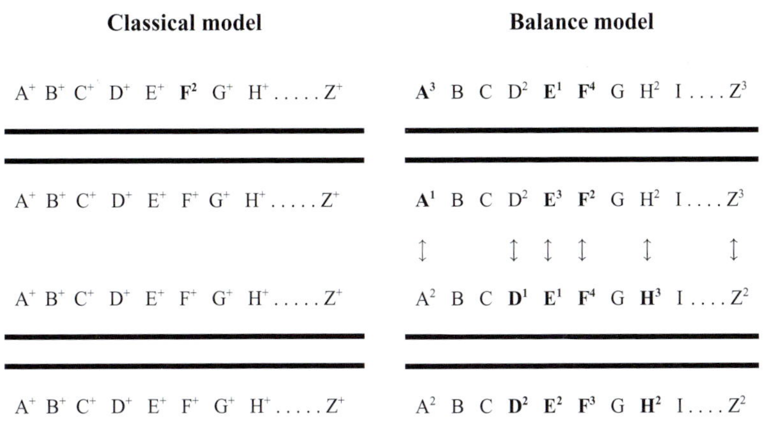

Classical model   **Balance model**

A^+ B^+ C^+ D^+ E^+ $\mathbf{F^2}$ G^+ H^+ ..... Z^+ A^3 B C D^2 $\mathbf{E^1}$ $\mathbf{F^4}$ G H^2 I .... Z^3

────────────   ────────────

A^+ B^+ C^+ D^+ E^+ F^+ G^+ H^+ ..... Z^+ A^1 B C D^2 E^3 $\mathbf{F^2}$ G H^2 I .... Z^3

$\updownarrow$ $\updownarrow$ $\updownarrow$ $\updownarrow$ $\updownarrow$ $\updownarrow$

A^+ B^+ C^+ D^+ E^+ F^+ G^+ H^+ ..... Z^+ A^2 B C $\mathbf{D^1}$ $\mathbf{E^1}$ $\mathbf{F^4}$ G $\mathbf{H^3}$ I .... Z^2

────────────   ────────────

A^+ B^+ C^+ D^+ E^+ F^+ G^+ H^+ ..... Z^+ A^2 B C $\mathbf{D^2}$ $\mathbf{E^2}$ $\mathbf{F^3}$ G H^2 I .... Z^2

Fig. 7.4 The genetic variation of populations as proposed by the classical and balance hypotheses. One pair of homologous chromosomes from two individuals is represented for each model. Capital letters denote gene loci, and numbers represent different alleles with the wild-type allele of the classical model being represented by a + sign. In the balance model, heterozygous gene loci within an individual are shown in bold type, and polymorphic gene loci within the population are indicated by $\updownarrow$ (see text).

lower fitness from the population, i.e. only the fittest alleles survived (Fig. 7.4). Occasionally, there would be a mutant allele. In most cases, these mutants would be purged from the population by natural selection, but in the rare case when the mutant allele was more fit than the wild-type allele, it would increase in frequency and eventually the mutant form would become the new wild-type allele.

An alternative hypothesis, the balance model, took longer to develop and represented the views of ecological geneticists (geneticists looking at wild populations) and some laboratory, experimental geneticists. They believed that a large proportion of the gene loci in a population were polymorphic, i.e. there was more than a single allele present in the population, and that individuals were heterozygous at many gene loci (Fig. 7.4). Initially it was proposed that the high level of heterozygosity was maintained by heterozygote superiority, i.e. heterozygotes were the most advantageous genotypes in the population. Later many different mechanisms were proposed to explain how the high level of genetic diversity in the population was maintained. For example, different alleles might be at a selective advantage in different environments, and so could be maintained in populations living in variable environments. There could also be frequency-dependent selection, where the selective advantage or disadvantage of a given phenotype might depend on its frequency in the population. The main point, however, of the hypothesis was that selection maintained high levels of genetic diversity in populations.

From the 1930s to the 1960s, biologists concerned with the genetic structure of populations belonged to one or other of these two camps. Either they believed in the classical hypothesis, which considered that natural selection purged the population of most genetic variation, or they believed in the balance hypothesis which considered that natural

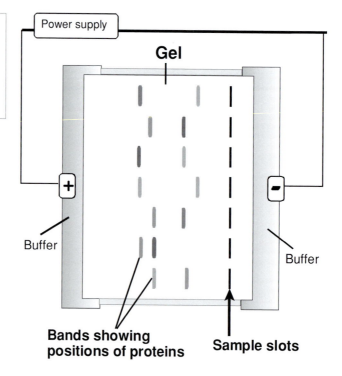

Fig. 7.5 A diagram of a gel electrophoresis apparatus. The buffers conduct electricity and provide a specific pH, and protein samples placed in the sample slots move according to their electrical charge and molecular weight.

selection maintained a large genetic diversity within the population. Note that the two views have different evolutionary consequences. If populations conform to the classical model, by and large individual populations do not respond to fluctuations in environmental conditions over time by changing their genetic structure. In addition, if there is an environmental change that requires a genetic response for the population to survive, for example the evolution of a resistant strain to pesticides or drugs, the population usually has to wait until the right mutation appears. In contrast, if populations conform to the balance model there is a large genetic diversity maintained within the population. Consequently, it is more probable that a resistant strain may already be present and so the population can respond more quickly to novel environmental changes. In addition, allelic frequencies will change in response to changes in the environmental conditions.

The controversy could not be resolved until the genetic diversity of populations could be measured. This was first made possible in the late 1960s using electrophoresis. This procedure utilizes the fact that most proteins have a different electrical charge in relation to their mass, and so will move at different rates through a suitable medium (usually a starch or polyacrylamide gel) if an electrical charge is applied across the medium (Fig. 7.5). Small samples of blood, or ground-up tissue, from different individuals are placed in slots near the edge of a gel and an electrical current is applied across the gel for several hours. The gel is then stained for specific enzymes by soaking it in a solution containing the substrate for the enzyme, along with

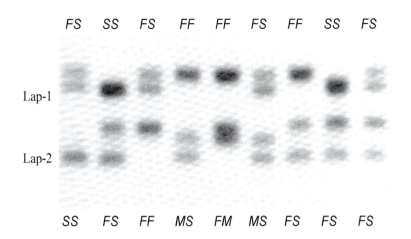

FS   SS   FS   FF   FF   FS   FF   SS   FS

Lap-1

Lap-2

SS   FS   FF   MS   FM   MS   FS   FS   FS

Fig. 7.6 Variation in two enzymes of the brown snail (*Helix aspersa*). The upper system is variable for two alleles (F and S) and the lower system is variable for three alleles (S, M and F). The genotypes are indicated above and below the gel for the Lap-1 and Lap-2 enzymes, respectively, for the nine individuals analysed. (From Selander 1976, with permission.)

a dye that precipitates where the enzyme-catalysed reaction occurs. A dark band will appear in the gel marking the position of the enzyme. If there is more than one form of the enzyme (called allozymes) because of amino acid substitutions, and if they carry different electrical charges, they will appear at different points on the gel (Fig. 7.6). Thus, it is possible to screen the genetic variation of specific gene loci in a population by looking at the protein product of the gene. This method does not detect all genetic diversity, because base substitutions which do not change in amino acids are not detected, but it is a way of screening a major proportion of the genetic diversity of populations. When a large number of individuals in a population are screened, the genetic diversity is measured in two ways: the average proportion of loci that are heterozygous in an individual, and the average proportion of loci that are polymorphic in the population (i.e. have two or more alleles detected).

The results of such electrophoretic surveys revealed a large amount of genetic variation in most populations (Table 7.2), and seemed to unequivocally support the balance model rather than the classical model. Most invertebrates appear to be highly polymorphic whereas the reptiles, birds and mammals are only about half as variable, and the fish and amphibia are intermediate in their variability on average (Table 7.2). No genetic variability has been detected in the northern elephant seal (*Mirounga angustirostris*) and the self-fertilizing snail (*Rumina decollata*). The elephant seal almost became extinct at the turn of the century, and the lack of genetic variability has been postulated as the result of the population's small size at that time, resulting in the fixation of alleles due to genetic drift (see Chapter 8). There have been many attempts to find patterns in the genetic variation of populations but the results are inconsistent. For example, there appears to be no relationship between genetic variability and environmental variability.

When the genetic diversity of populations was beginning to be assessed by electrophoretic methods in the late 1960s, a new theory was developed to account for protein polymorphism. This was the

Table 7.2 Genetic variation at allozyme loci in animals and plants

Taxon	Number of species examined	Average number of loci per species	Mean proportions of loci	
			Polymorphic per population	Heterozygous per individual
Insects				
Drosophila	28	24	0.529 ± 0.030	0.150 ± 0.010
Others	4	18	0.531	0.151
Haplodiploid wasps[a]	6	15	0.243 ± 0.039	0.062 ± 0.007
Marine invertebrates	9	26	0.587 ± 0.084	0.147 ± 0.019
Marine snails	5	17	0.175	0.083
Land snails	5	18	0.437	0.150
Fish	14	21	0.306 ± 0.047	0.078 ± 0.012
Amphibians	11	22	0.336 ± 0.034	0.082 ± 0.008
Reptiles	9	21	0.231 ± 0.032	0.047 ± 0.008
Birds	4	19	0.145	0.042
Rodents	26	26	0.202 ± 0.015	0.054 ± 0.005
Large mammals[b]	4	40	0.233	0.037
Plants[c]	8	8	0.464 ± 0.064	0.170 ± 0.031

[a]Females are diploid, males haploid.
[b]Human, chimpanzee, pigtailed macaque and southern elephant seal.
[c]Predominantly outcrossing species (i.e. not self-fertilizing).
Source: From Selander (1976) with permission.

neutral mutation–random drift theory of Kimura, who proposed that most of the different alleles of a gene are selectively neutral. Thus, most protein polymorphism is invisible to natural selection, in contrast to the selectionist argument of the balance hypothesis. With the demise of the classical model of genetic variation, the classical–balance controversy has been replaced by the neutralist–selectionist argument. Indeed, it has been suggested that the neutralist theory is simply a resurrection of the dead classical theory in a modified form.

Where does this leave us or, in the more blunt words of the average student, which theory is correct? Unfortunately, there is no neat and tidy ending to this story. The balance model considers that genetic variability is maintained in the population in a variety of ways by selection, whereas the neutral gene model considers that most of the observed genetic variability is neutral as far as natural selection is concerned. It may seem easy to prove one theory or the other but the fact is that it is impossible to test or discriminate between these two theories in any clear-cut way.

For those who are interested in learning more about the neutral-selectionist controversy, a very readable account is given in Merrell (1981). For our purpose, however, we only need to know that most populations have a high level of genetic diversity and it is not necessary to know how this diversity is maintained. We will now go on and consider some aspects of how genetic variation accumulates in populations and certain consequences of the observed genetic diversity.

7.5 | Mutations and variability

We can estimate how long it takes for mutations to accumulate to the observed levels of genetic diversity in populations by considering two examples, humans and *Drosophila* (Box 7.1).

It is estimated that the human genome consists of approximately 35 000 gene loci, whereas *Drosophila* have about 10 000 gene loci. Electrophoretic methods suggest that 0.067 (6.7%) of the gene loci are heterozygous in humans, and the corresponding estimate in *Drosophila* is 0.15 (15%). If this is the case, the number of heterozygous gene loci in humans and *Drosophila* is 2345 and 1500, respectively. The average mutation rate per gene locus per generation is estimated to be between 10^{-6} and 10^{-5} (section 7.3), and using the higher of these estimates the average number of mutations (M) per zygote is calculated to be 0.7 in humans and 0.2 in *Drosophila* (M = number of gene loci × number of alleles per locus (2 in diploid organisms) × average mutation rate per locus per generation). These estimates change to 0.07 in humans and 0.02 in *Drosophila* using the lower average mutation rate. On an individual basis, the ratio of the existing variation (i.e. heterozygous gene loci) to potentially new variation being introduced through mutation is measured in the thousands (3350 for humans and 7500 for *Drosophila*). We cannot use this ratio to estimate the minimum number of generations required to build up this level of variation because variation is incorporated on a population-wide basis, not an individual basis. As we shall see, large populations have an enormous capacity to produce mutations; however, most of the new mutations are either lost by chance (see section 7.3.1) or are purged from the population by natural selection. The observed level

Box 7.1 | Mutation and variability

Estimated parameter	Humans	Drosophila
Number of gene loci	35 000	10 000
Percentage heterozygous gene loci	6.7%	15%
Number of heterozygous gene loci	2345	1500
Average mutation rate per locus per generation	1×10^{-5}	1×10^{-5}
Average number of mutations per zygote	$35\,000 \times 2 \times 10^{-5} = 0.7$	$10\,000 \times 2 \times 10^{-5} = 0.2$
Ratio of existing variation to new variation introduced each generation (per individual)	$2345/0.7 = 3350$	$1500/0.2 = 7500$
Total population size	6×10^{9}	1×10^{8}
Number of new mutations per generation	$0.7 \times 6 \times 10^{9} = 4.2 \times 10^{9}$	$0.2 \times 1 \times 10^{8} = 2 \times 10^{7}$
Number of new mutations per locus per generation	$4.2 \times 10^{9}/35\,000 = 120\,000$	$2 \times 10^{7}/10\,000 = 2000$

of genetic variability in most populations has probably accumulated over the course of thousands of generations. Clearly, if the level of genetic variability is considerably reduced for some reason, it will require many thousands of generations of mutation to restore the genetic diversity of the population.

The frequency of mutation may also be calculated on either a population or a per locus basis (Box 7.1). The world human population is of the order of 6 billion, and *Drosophila* populations are estimated to be of the order of one hundred million individuals. Previously, we computed the average number of mutations per individual (i.e. zygote) per generation at approximately 0.7 for humans and 0.2 for *Drosophila*. The total number of mutations occurring in these populations is the product of these two estimates, giving values of 4.2 billion for humans and 20 million for *Drosophila*. If we divide these values by the number of gene loci we can compute that the average number of new mutations per gene locus is approximately 120 000 in humans and 2000 in *Drosophila*. Thus, the potential to create new variation by mutation is enormous, and we should not be surprised at the speed at which some populations develop a resistance to the novel poisons we have produced in our efforts to eradicate them. Obviously, population size is an important variable, and more abundant species have more potential to change than rare species.

Finally, how is the genetic diversity created by mutation amplified by sexual recombination? We have estimated that there are about 2345 heterozygous gene loci in the average person. Thus, theoretically each individual has the potential to produce 2^{2345}, or approximately 10^{706}, genetically different gametes. In practice we do not produce quite this variety of gametes because many gene loci are linked and move together during meiosis. Even so, the number of genetically different gametes is truly astronomical and it is almost impossible that any two gametes will be genetically identical. We can conclude that all individuals in the population are genetically unique, except in the rare case of identical twins where the zygote has split into two during development. We would reach the same conclusion for most sexually reproducing organisms, and so we can think of such populations being made up of an infinite variety of genetically unique individuals. In the next chapter, however, we will see how small population size can have a profound effect on the level of genetic variability.

7.6 | Summary and conclusions

Mutations change the sequence of bases in the DNA molecule, and this may lead to a change in phenotype. Mutations are random with respect to the needs of the organism, and so may be favourable, neutral or disadvantageous in terms of selection. Mutation rates are extremely low, of the order of 1 in 10 000 to 1 in 10 billion (10^9) per cell per replication, and consequently they can only cause extremely slow changes in the characteristics of populations unless aided by some other force, such as selection. Almost all populations contain a large amount of genetic variation. Typically, 5–15% of the genes in an individual are heterozygous, with the result that no two gametes will be genetically identical and so in most sexually reproducing populations all the individuals are genetically unique. At the population level, typically 20–60% of the genes are polymorphic, and this huge reservoir of genetic diversity means that populations can respond genetically to adapt to changes in the environment.

Chapter 8

Small populations, genetic drift and inbreeding

In randomly breeding populations, the allelic and genotypic frequencies remain constant from generation to generation and are predicted by the Hardy–Weinberg principle, provided there is no mutation, migration or selection, and the population is infinitely large (see Chapter 6). Population size is finite, however, and many species are structured into several more or less discrete populations (subpopulations or demes) which may be quite small in size. As a consequence there will be changes in allelic frequencies from generation to generation because of sampling error in the production of gametes.

What do we mean by sampling error? Consider a game of coin-tossing in which there is an equal chance of obtaining heads or tails. However, if we toss a coin repeatedly, there is not a sequence of heads, tails, heads, tails, and so on ad infinitum, but rather a random sequence in which there are groupings of heads and tails. Consequently, we would not be surprised if there were not exactly half heads and half tails in a small sample of coin tosses. We would expect the proportion of heads and tails to be distributed in some way around 50%.

Consider the results of a coin-tossing experiment (Fig. 8.1). When the coin was tossed 20 times, the percentage of heads ranged from 25% to 75% in individual trials, and the average across all trials was 49.55%. When the coin was tossed 200 times, the percentage of heads ranged from 42.5% to 57.5%, and the average across all trials was 50%. Obviously, the larger sample provided a much better representation of the expected 50% chance of obtaining heads in a coin toss.

We can relate our coin-tossing experiment to chance changes in the allelic frequencies in small populations, arising from sampling error of the gametes, in the following way. If a gene has two alleles, A and a, with equal frequencies in the population (i.e. $p = q = 0.5$), this is analogous to our coin-tossing game where heads and tails have equal chances of occurring. If there was a constant population size, N, of 10 individuals there would be $2N = 20$ gametes needed to produce the next generation, and this is equivalent to 20 coin tosses. One can see from Fig. 8.1 that the frequency of an allele might change, as a result of sampling error, from 0.5 to a value between 0.25 and

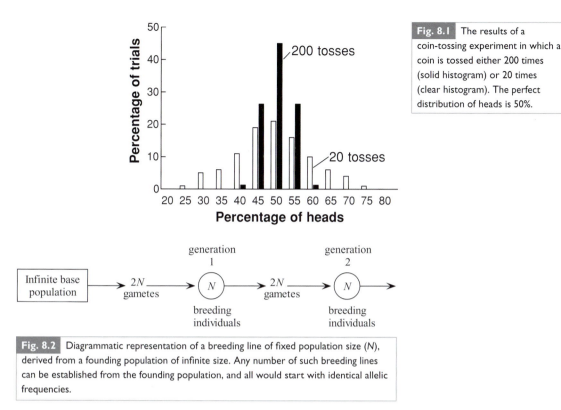

Fig. 8.1 The results of a coin-tossing experiment in which a coin is tossed either 200 times (solid histogram) or 20 times (clear histogram). The perfect distribution of heads is 50%.

Fig. 8.2 Diagrammatic representation of a breeding line of fixed population size (N), derived from a founding population of infinite size. Any number of such breeding lines can be established from the founding population, and all would start with identical allelic frequencies.

0.75 in one generation. If the population size were 100, and $2N = 200$, the potential change in allelic frequency would be smaller, but would still fluctuate around a value of 0.5. The distribution of sample values around the mean is predicted by the binomial theorem, and so we can use this mathematical approach to predict how allelic frequencies will change as a result of sampling error. This random fluctuation in allelic frequency is called genetic drift.

8.1 | Genetic drift in idealized populations

We will first consider the process of genetic drift in idealized randomly breeding populations of constant size, where there is no mutation, migration or selection, and there is no overlapping of generations. We will relax these assumptions later.

Consider what happens at a single gene locus, with two alleles with frequencies p_0 and q_0 in the founding base population, from which samples of $2N$ gametes (or alleles) are drawn at random to establish a series of populations, or lines, of N breeding individuals (Fig. 8.2). After one generation, the average allelic frequency q across all lines (i.e. in all populations combined) will be equal to that in the base population q_0, but the q_1 values in the individual populations will be distributed around this average value with a variance of $p_0 q_0 / 2N$. This is the binomial variance of sample means.

As all lines had the same initial allelic frequency, q_0, this is also the variance of $(q_1 - q_0)$ which is the change in allelic frequency (Δq). Consequently, we can predict the expected change in allelic frequency (Δq) after a single generation of drift in terms of its variance (σ^2):

$$\sigma^2_{\Delta q} = \frac{p_0 q_0}{2N}$$ (Eqn 8.1)

Thus, the process of genetic drift leads to a dispersion of allelic frequencies around an average value, and the variance of this dispersion is predicted by Eqn 8.1. The square root of the variance gives the standard deviation (s):

$$s = \sqrt{\frac{p_0 q_0}{2N}}$$ (Eqn 8.2)

When there is a large number of equal-sized populations, the distribution of allelic frequencies around the mean will correspond to a normal distribution, in which case 68.27% of the q_1 values are expected to lie within one standard deviation of the mean ($\bar{q} = q_0$), 95.45% within two standard deviations of the mean and 99.73% within three standard deviations of the mean. This allows us to predict if a particular change in allelic frequency (Δq) might be a result of genetic drift.

In the next (second) generation the sampling process is repeated, but as there is now a range of allelic frequencies in the different lines this leads to further variation or dispersion of allelic frequencies around the mean. Thus, the variance in allelic frequencies among lines is compounded each generation, and after t generations this variance equals:

$$\sigma^2_{\Delta q} = p_0 q_0 \left[1 - \left(1 - \frac{1}{2N} \right)^t \right]$$ (Eqn 8.3)

The derivation of this equation will not be dealt with here because it involves a consideration of the inbreeding aspects of genetic drift, which is not covered until the end of this chapter. What this equation predicts is that the variance in allelic frequency increases at a slower and slower rate as the number of generations increases, and attains a maximum value of $p_0 q_0$. For example, if $p_0 = 0.4$, the variance of the allelic frequency will approach a value of 0.24 when t is very large.

A simulation of the process of genetic drift shows the dispersion in allelic frequencies over the course of many generations and how this is affected by population size (Fig. 8.3). The allelic frequencies in the different lines fluctuate independently of one another, and individually they diverge from the initial base frequency ($q_0 = 0.5$) over time. The small populations showed a greater variation in allelic frequencies than the larger populations. This is exactly what we would expect from Eqn 8.1 which shows that the variation in allelic frequency is inversely related to population size (N).

To this point we have only considered a single gene locus, but we could make exactly the same sort of observation about different gene loci within a single line. Thus, the different lines in Fig. 8.3

Table 8.1 A comparison of the expected and observed range of frequencies after one generation of sampling error in the coin-tossing experiment illustrated in Fig. 8.1

Standard deviation (s) from Eqn 8.2	Expected range of allelic frequencies	Observed percentage of observations within expected range in coin-tossing experiment
$N = 10$, and $p = q = 0.5$		
$s = 0.1118$	68% between 0.3882 and 0.6118	77%
$2 \times s = 0.2236$	95% between 0.2764 and 0.7236	98%
$3 \times s = 0.3354$	99% between 0.1646 and 0.8354	100%
$N = 100$, and $p = q = 0.5$		
$s = 0.03535$	68% between 0.4647 and 0.5354	65%
$2 \times s = 0.0707$	95% between 0.4293 and 0.5707	95%
$3 \times s = 0.1061$	99% between 0.2939 and 0.6061	100%

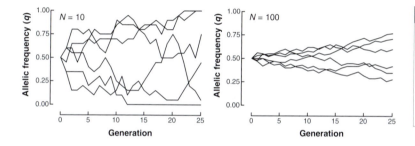

Fig. 8.3 Computer simulation of changes in allelic frequency as a result of genetic drift. Six populations with an initial allelic frequency (q_0) of 0.5 and population sizes (N) of 10 or 100 individuals were followed for 25 generations.

could represent the allelic frequencies of six different gene loci in one line, instead of one gene locus in six lines, provided they are not tightly linked to one another. This represents another way in which the different lines diverge from one another.

We can see how well Eqns 8.1 to 8.3 predict the changes in allelic frequencies as a result of genetic drift by applying them to the results of our coin-tossing experiment (Fig. 8.1) and our computer simulation (Fig. 8.3). The variance in allelic frequency (q) for a sample size (N) of 10 is predicted to be 0.0125 using Eqn 8.1. The observed values were 0.0106 for the coin-tossing experiment and 0.0154 for the computer simulation. Similarly, for a sample size (N) of 100 the predicted variance is 0.00125 and the observed values were 0.00142 for both the coin-tossing experiment and the computer simulation. Thus, the observations are reasonably well predicted by Eqn 8.1.

In the case of Eqn 8.2 the results of our computer simulations are not very useful because we only have six replications of each sample size, but we can use the results of the coin-tossing experiment because there were 100 independent trials. It may be observed from Table 8.1 that there is a reasonable correspondence between the expected and observed distribution of values.

Finally, Eqn 8.3 predicts that the variance in allelic frequency will increase over time, depending on the initial frequency and the

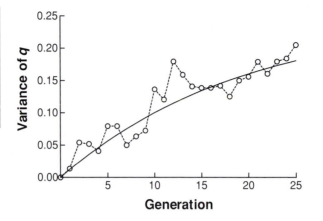

Fig. 8.4 Variance in allelic frequencies among lines in the computer simulation of genetic drift for $N = 10$ in Fig. 8.3. The points represent the observed values and the smooth line is the expected variance as calculated by Eqn 8.3.

population size (N). Figure 8.4 shows the predicted and observed variance of q over time for a population size of 10 individuals. It may be seen that the predicted values provide a good fit to the data, and that the variance increases at a slower and slower rate over time.

The variance of q among lines reaches a maximum value because q can only decrease to zero or increase to one. When one allele is lost ($q = 0$), the other allele becomes fixed ($p = 1$) in the population, and all individuals have the same genotype with respect to that gene, and so there is a limit to the dispersive process. One can see in Fig. 8.3 that three of the six lines became fixed during the 25 generations of drift when the population size (N) was 10. The fixation of alleles is proportional to their initial frequencies. If the frequency of the two alleles is initially the same, i.e. $p_0 = q_0 = 0.5$, the frequency of fixation of the two alleles will be the same, but if one allele has a frequency $p = 0.9$ and the other a frequency $q = 0.1$, p will become fixed nine times more frequently than the other allele (q).

We can summarize the consequences of genetic drift in the absence of other evolutionary forces as follows:

1. Allelic frequencies fluctuate at random, independently of one another in different populations or demes. The alleles of different loci within a population also fluctuate independently of one another, provided the loci are not linked to one another.
2. Thus, different populations or demes diverge in allelic frequencies and become genetically distinct from one another. The genetic diversity of all populations combined is increased compared to the situation where all individuals could interbreed freely within a single population.
3. Eventually, given enough time, a single allele will become fixed at each gene locus. The probability that a specific allele will eventually become fixed is equal to the frequency of the allele.
4. Thus, there is a reduction of genetic variation within a population or deme. There is an increase in the proportion of homozygotes at the expense of the heterozygotes. This may lead to an

increase in the incidence of deleterious recessive traits (which are only expressed in homozygous individuals), leading to a reduction in viability.

5. The rate at which these events occur is inversely related to population size. The smaller the population, the faster the process of genetic drift.

8.2 | Effective population size

So far we have considered genetic drift as if it is simply the total size of the population that is important. In reality, however, it is the size and structure of the breeding component of the population that is important, and so we need to know the *effective population size*, N_e. This is usually much less than the total population size for a variety of reasons. For example, in species that are subdivided into more or less discrete populations or demes, a proportion of each deme may consist of juveniles and non-breeding adults, or some animals have skewed sex ratios where only a small fraction of the dominant males breeds successfully. In large continuous populations, like those of the boreal forest, the overall population may number in the millions and be spread over thousands of kilometres, but individuals breed with those within a certain neighbourhood, the size of which will depend on the dispersal of gametes (i.e. pollen) in plants or of juveniles in animals. In this situation, the overall population consists of a series of overlapping breeding neighbourhoods containing the effective breeding populations.

We will consider two examples of factors that influence effective population size. We will not concern ourselves with the derivation of the appropriate equations. Those who are interested in this topic are referred to Falconer and Mackay (1996).

8.2.1 Unequal numbers of males and females
If the population consists of N_m breeding males and N_f breeding females, the effective population size is given by:

$$N_e = \frac{4N_m N_f}{N_m + N_f} \qquad \text{(Exp. 8.1)}$$

Now consider a population of 100 zebra living in a small nature reserve. Approximately half of the population may consist of juveniles and other non-breeding individuals, and the remaining 50 breeding animals have an average harem structure of one male to four females. Thus, N_m is 10 and N_f is 40. Using Exp. 8.1, the effective population size, N_e, equals 32, or approximately one-third of the total population size. Note that in this example we have simplified the problem of dealing with overlapping of generations (see Falconer and Mackay 1996).

8.2.2 Unequal numbers in successive generations

If the population size varies dramatically from generation to generation, the effective population size is the harmonic mean of the numbers in each generation. Over a period of t generations, therefore:

$$\frac{1}{N_e} = \frac{1}{t}\left(\frac{1}{N_1} + \frac{1}{N_2} + \frac{1}{N_3} + \cdots + \frac{1}{N_t}\right) \qquad \text{(Exp. 8.2)}$$

The generations with the smallest numbers carry the greatest weight, because the process of genetic drift is greatest in small populations. The effects of genetic drift are not reversed or eliminated when the population increases in size again. Consider an insect where the breeding population decreases in size by an order of magnitude each generation from 10 000 to 10 individuals, and then increases in size by an order of magnitude each generation until it reaches its original size, i.e. the values of N_1 to N_7 are 10 000, 1000, 100, 10, 100, 1000, and 10 000. When we apply Exp. 8.2, we find that the effective population size (N_e) over these seven generations is approximately 57.

This example shows that populations that undergo a severe reduction in size, where genetic drift becomes an important factor, do not lose the effects of genetic drift when the population grows to a much larger size where genetic drift is unimportant. The reason for this will be explained when we consider inbreeding in section 8.5. This phenomenon is called a genetic bottleneck. A particularly interesting type of bottleneck occurs when a new population is formed by a small number of migrants or founders, and the resulting genetic drift is called a founder effect.

Further details on the calculation of effective population size may be found in Falconer and Mackay (1996). In addition to unequal numbers of males and females and fluctuations in population size, one needs to consider variation in the number of progeny per parent, the effect of overlapping generations, and the exclusion of closely related matings (e.g. self-fertilization). The amount of information required is considerable, so it perhaps not surprising that there are relatively few estimates of effective population size (N_e) in natural populations. However, in many cases the effective population size is within the range where genetic drift could be important (see section 8.5). For example, N_e has been estimated to be 10 or less in the house mouse (*Mus musculus*), between 82 and 114 for deer mice (*Peromyscus maniculatus*) in southern Michigan, between 46 and 112 in the leopard frog (*Rana pipiens*) in Minnesota, and about 10 in ash trees (*Fraxinus*).

8.3 | Empirical examples of genetic drift

Peter Buri made a classic experimental study of genetic drift on brown eye colour in *Drosophila melanogaster* (Buri 1956). He started 107 populations, each with eight males and eight females, that were heterozygous for two alleles (*bw* and *bw*[75]) so that the two alleles had an initial frequency of 0.5. Every generation, each line was propagated

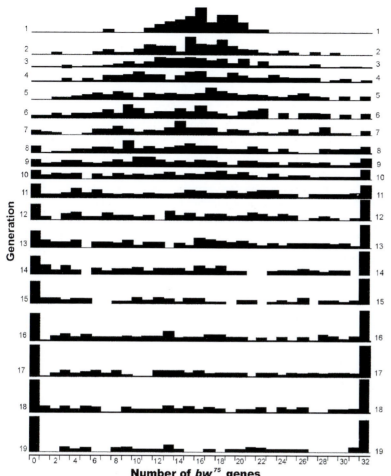

Number of *bw*⁷⁵ genes

by selecting eight flies of each sex at random and transferring them to a fresh vial. The three genotypes were distinguishable from one another and so he could directly count the number of bw^{75} alleles in each generation. This could range from 0 if the allele was lost (and bw became fixed) to 32 if bw^{75} became fixed (16 flies × 2 alleles).

The frequency of the bw^{75} allele varied rapidly among the populations or lines (Fig. 8.5). Fixation occurred from the fourth generation onwards for either the bw^{75} allele or the bw allele. By the nineteenth generation, fixation had occurred in more than half the lines, with 30 lines losing the bw^{75} allele and 28 lines fixing the bw^{75} allele.

The results matched what was expected from the theory of genetic drift. First, the allelic frequencies in each population tended to diverge more and more from the initial frequency of 0.5 (i.e. there was dispersion of allelic frequencies among lines as shown in Figs. 8.5 and 8.6a), but the overall allelic frequency for all subpopulations combined changed little from the initial allelic frequency of 0.5 (Fig. 8.6b).

Second, there was an increase in homozygotes and a corresponding decrease in heterozygotes as the various lines became fixed for one allele or the other (Fig. 8.7). However, the rate of drift was higher

Fig. 8.5 Distribution of allelic frequencies in 19 consecutive generations among 107 lines of *Drosophila melanogaster*, each with 16 individuals. (From Buri 1956, with permission.)

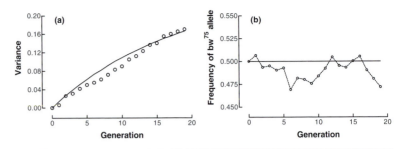

Fig. 8.6 (a) Observed (circles) and theoretical variation (line) of allelic frequencies among populations of *Drosophila* shown in Fig. 8.5, assuming an effective population size of 9 individuals. (From Buri 1956, with permission.) (b) The frequency of the bw^{75} allele in all populations combined compared to the starting frequency of 0.5.

Fig. 8.7 The observed reduction of heterozygotes (circles) in all lines of *Drosophila* shown in Fig. 8.5, compared to the theoretical frequency (line) calculated for an effective population size of 9 individuals. (From Buri 1956, with permission.)

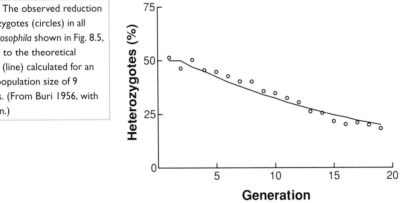

than expected for a population size of 16 individuals and Buri estimated that the effective population size was approximately nine. This simply means that on average there were nine breeding individuals each generation, and the other seven individuals did not produce offspring.

The increase in homozygotes, and consequently of the expression of deleterious recessive traits, is demonstrated in many isolated human populations, and for this reason medical geneticists regularly concentrate their work on such populations. For example, in certain isolated alpine villages in Italy the frequency of albino individuals in a village may be several percent, although the frequency in the general population is usually less than 0.000 1%. In other villages there may be remarkably high frequencies of deaf-mutes, of blind people, or of individuals with one or other type of mental deficiency, all of which are governed by recessive alleles (Bodmer and Cavalli-Sforza 1976). Other human groups isolate themselves because of religious beliefs, and in some of these groups there may be a high incidence of genetic disease. These are frequently linked to what is called founder effects.

8.3.1 Founder effects

When a population is founded by a small number of colonists they will not carry a perfect sample of alleles from the parental population, and will lose some genetic variation compared to the parental population. This change in allelic frequencies and genetic variation will be augmented by genetic drift until such time as the population increases to a large size.

In most cases it is the uncommon alleles in the parent population that are lost, but on occasion an uncommon allele may be included in the founding population and be at a much higher frequency than usual, even if it has deleterious effects. A spectacular example is Ellis–van Creveld syndrome, a rare form of dwarfism with polydactyly (a sixth finger), which is associated with Old Order Amish living in Lancaster County, Pennsylvania. During the 1960s, there were 43 cases of this syndrome in the approximately 8000 Amish living in that locality, approximately as many as were found in the rest of the world! The syndrome occurs in individuals homozygous for this trait and is a semi-lethal trait. Most individuals with this condition die soon after birth, but milder cases may reach adulthood and a few individuals may have children. A survey in 1964 revealed 43 people with the syndrome out of 8000 Amish, and so the genotypic frequency (q^2) is 43/8000. The allelic frequency of the recessive allele ($\sqrt{q^2}$) was estimated as $\sqrt{(43/8000)} = 0.0733$, or approximately 1 in 14 of the population.

All the Lancaster County families with the Ellis–van Creveld syndrome trace their ancestry back to a Mr and Mrs Samuel King who immigrated in 1744. The recessive allele was almost certainly present in one of these founders in heterozygous form. If the allele was only present in Mr or Mrs King, the frequency among the founding population would have been about 1 in 400, because about 200 Amish people moved to Pennsylvania between 1720 and 1770. In any case, its frequency was not likely to be as high as its estimated value in 1964 of 1 in 14. Most probably the frequency increased because of genetic drift. It is known that the Kings and their descendants had larger families than others in the community and, as a consequence, the frequency of the deleterious allele 'drifted' to higher values, particularly in the early generations when the population was much smaller.

Another example is provided by populations of plains zebra (*Equus quagga antiquorum*) introduced into small nature reserves in KwaZulu-Natal, South Africa (Bowland *et al.* 2001). Wildlife officials noticed that these small populations of zebra had almost identical striping patterns, were smaller in size, and had higher mortality rates and numbers of stillbirths, compared with the large population in the Umfolozi Game Reserve from which they were derived. There was concern about inbreeding, and so the genetic diversity of the introduced and parent populations were assessed by two standard methods, the electrophoresis of allozymes and the variation in DNA polymerase chain reaction – randomly amplified polymorphic

Table 8.2 Genetic diversity as assessed by PCR-RAPD technique and allozyme electrophoresis for four populations of zebra. Animals were introduced from the Umfolozi Game Reserve into the three other areas 22 to 25 years ago

	Umfolozi Game Reserve	Vernon Crookes Nature Reserve	Albert Falls Nature Reserve	Harold Johnson Nature Reserve
Years isolated	–	25	25	22
Number of founders	–	19	12	8
Population size	2000	110	50	9
DNA analysis (105 loci)				
Number of polymorphic loci	41	38	30	21
Percentage polymorphism	39	36	29	20
Percentage of polymorphism lost	–	3	10	19
Allozyme electrophoresis				
Percentage heterozygosity	12.3	12.9	12.1	12.8
Percentage of polymorphic loci	28.1	28.1	28.1	28.1
Mean number of alleles per locus	1.3	1.3	1.3	1.3

Data from Bowland *et al.* (2001).

DNA using the (PCR-RAPD) technique. The results are summarized in Table 8.2.

The DNA analysis revealed a reduced genetic diversity in the small introduced populations, and the reduction in genetic diversity was inversely related to the size of the founding population as well as the current population size. This suggests that both founder effects and continuing genetic drift are important factors. However, the allozyme electrophoresis study did not support the DNA analysis because it failed to detect any reduction in genetic diversity! The reason for this is not clear. The authors point out that it would be possible to maintain the level of polymorphism (as detected by DNA analysis) close to the parental population in Umfolozi by reintroducing small numbers of animals periodically to each population. This migration would override the effects of genetic drift, as explained in section 8.4. Similar observations of reduced genetic diversity have been made on other African ungulates in small reserves, including blue wildebeest (*Connochaetes taurinus*) by Grobler and Van der Bank (1993), and impala (*Aepyceros melampus*) by Grobler and Van der Bank (1994).

8.3.2 Genetic bottlenecks

An electrophoretic survey of allozymes in the northern elephant seal (*Mirounga angustirostris*) revealed no variation in any of the 24 loci studied (Bonnell and Selander 1974). This is unusual because most natural populations are highly polymorphic. The lack of genetic diversity is attributed to the population experiencing a genetic bottleneck.

Historical records show that the population, which numbered tens of thousands of individuals in the mid nineteenth century, was hunted almost to extinction so that the population was reduced to about 20 individuals in the 1890s. The population has since recovered to about 30 000 seals. Although a genetic bottleneck is the most obvious explanation for the lack of genetic diversity in the northern elephant seal, it is not the only possible explanation. One would require a pre-bottleneck assessment of genetic diversity to be certain that genetic diversity had been lost by the dramatic reduction in population size.

Bouzat *et al.* (1998) measured the pre-bottleneck diversity in their study on the greater prairie chicken (*Tympanuchus cupido*) in Illinois. There were thought to have been millions of these birds in Illinois in the 1860s, but loss of their natural habitat led to a precipitous decline in population size to approximately 25 000 birds in 1933, to 2000 in 1962, 500 in 1972, 76 in 1990, and to less than 50 in 1993. Today there is a single population in Jasper County, Illinois although there are still large western populations of this species in Kansas, Minnesota and Nebraska. The DNA from museum specimens collected in the 1930s and 1960s, when the population was much larger than at present, was compared to that of the present Illinois population as well as the populations in Kansas, Minnesota and Nebraska. The number of alleles at six loci was estimated for these populations. The mean number of alleles per locus was similar in the pre-bottleneck Illinois population and the large western populations, although some alleles were unique to the different populations, but the mean number of alleles in the present Illinois population was only about 71% of the pre-bottleneck estimate. The missing alleles were almost all at low frequencies (<0.09) in the other large populations. All these observations are consistent with the argument that genetic bottlenecks lead to a loss of genetic variation.

8.4 Genetic drift in relation to mutation, migration and selection

We have seen that genetic drift is a dispersive process in which the allelic frequencies fluctuate at random. However, our description of this dispersive process has assumed that the systematic processes[1] of mutation, migration and selection are absent. We will now consider the conditions whereby these systematic processes may override or negate the effects of genetic drift.

Changes in allelic frequency will be governed primarily by genetic drift if, and only if:

$$N_e x \ll 1 \qquad \text{(Eqn 8.4)}$$

---

[1] Systematic processes like mutation, migration and selection change the allelic frequencies in a particular, predictive direction. In contrast, the dispersive process of genetic drift causes the allelic frequencies to change at random. Although the magnitude of the change can be predicted, one cannot predict the direction of change.

where N_e is the effective population size, x represents the mutation rate (Φ), the migration rate (m) or the selection coefficient (s), and the symbol $\ll$ means 'much less than' (Ayala and Valentine 1979). If $N_e x$ is approximately equal to or greater than 1, the changes in allelic frequency will be determined for the most part by systematic processes. We can now assess the effects of genetic drift relative to the other evolutionary processes.

The average mutation rate per gene locus per generation is estimated to be 10^{-5} or lower (Chapter 7). If we use this upper estimate in Eqn 8.4, we can see that N_e would have to be at least 100 000 for mutation to dictate changes in allelic frequency (i.e. $100\,000 \times 10^{-5} = 1$). Thus, mutation can only arrest the dispersive process of genetic drift, and prevent fixation, in extremely large populations.

If the migration rate (m) is 1% (or 0.01) and the effective population size is 100 individuals, then $N_e m = 1$, and so the allelic frequency will change toward the frequency in the population from which the migrants come. Indeed, a single migrant every fourth generation is sufficient to prevent fixation, whatever the size of the population. Thus, a small amount of interchange between populations or demes prevents them from diverging too far from one another.

Similarly, very small selection pressures are sufficient to direct the dispersive process in favour of a particular allele in all but the smallest populations. For example, if N_e is 100 individuals, a selection pressure of 0.01 against the disadvantageous allele (which would be difficult for us to measure except in ideal circumstances) would be sufficient to prevent the disadvantageous allele from being fixed by genetic drift. Thus, genetic drift will not overcome the effect of even modest selection pressures, and the latter will direct the change in allelic frequency.

In general terms, we can see that genetic drift may be important in small populations and may cause small populations to diverge in their allelic frequencies to some degree. This divergence will be held in check by any migration between populations, and may also be directed by selection for or against particular alleles.

8.5 | Inbreeding

In bisexual organisms, every individual has two parents, four grandparents, eight great grandparents, and so on. Theoretically, if we go back t generations, an individual may have 2^t ancestors in that generation. Consequently, the potential number of ancestors increases geometrically as we go back in time, but because real populations are finite we can infer that all individuals are related to some extent, i.e. have ancestors in common.

The degree of relatedness between individuals will be affected by population size. Imagine a population that has a constant population size of 1 000 000 individuals. If we go back 20 generations, each individual could potentially have more ancestors than the size of the population ($2^{20} = 1\,040\,576$). In reality, the number of ancestors 20 generations back would almost certainly be less than this because of matings between relatives, but even so we would expect all individuals in the population to be interrelated after about 20 generations. If the population had a constant size of 1000 individuals, however, we would expect all individuals to be related after 10 generations ($2^{10} = 1024$) following the same line of reasoning. Thus, the smaller the population, the more recent are the common ancestors, and so individuals in small populations are more closely related to each other (all other things being equal) than are individuals in large populations.

Matings between relatives, or inbreeding, is a form of assortative mating, which results in an increase in homozygotes and a decrease in heterozygotes, i.e. a change in genotypic frequencies, but not of allelic frequencies (see section 6.5.4).

The increase in homozygosity resulting from inbreeding may have adverse consequences because of the increased expression of deleterious recessive traits. An example of this is provided by the study of Ralls *et al.* (1979) on zoo populations. The young of parents that were inbred to some extent, generally had much lower survival rates than non-inbred young, born to parents brought in from the wild (Table 8.3), assuming that the latter were not related. This study demonstrates that small captive populations of animals require genetic management, and the same might be said of small populations in small nature reserves (see section 8.3.1).

8.5.1 Quantifying inbreeding

If two alleles at any locus originate from the replication of the same strand of DNA in a previous generation, they are said to be *identical by descent*, or autozygous. If not, they are said to be independent in descent, or allozygous. This does not imply that the alleles in all homozygous individuals are autozygous because it is possible that they arose from separate mutations. Identity by descent provides us with a measure of inbreeding, called the *coefficient of inbreeding* (F), which is the probability that the two alleles at a single locus are related by descent. If one goes back far enough, all alleles are related by descent, so in practice F is calculated for the population or individual by comparing it to a base population one or more generations before. The base population is considered to have an F value of zero.

We will examine the use of this measure from three different perspectives, to learn more about inbreeding and also genetic drift, because the two processes are closely related.

First, we can use the genotypic frequencies to measure the coefficient of inbreeding (F) for a population. If there is no inbreeding, $F = 0$, and the genotypic frequencies would be in Hardy–Weinberg equilibrium, i.e. $p^2 + 2pq + q^2$ at a locus with two alleles (see Chapter 6). In a fully inbred population, $F = 1$, all the alleles are autozygous, and so there are no heterozygotes and the genotypic

Table 8.3 | Juvenile mortality of inbred and non-inbred young of 16 species of ungulates

Species	Non-inbred young		Inbred young	
	Lived	Died	Lived	Died
Indian elephant	11	2	2	4
Zebra	20	7	3	2
Pygmy hippopotamus	139	45	23	28
Muntjac	18	4	12	6
Eld's deer	13	4	0	7
Père David's deer	15	2	19	3
Reindeer	19	10	9	12
Giraffe	11	3	2	3
Kudu	10	4	8	3
Sitatunga	15	1	31	28
Sable	18	4	3	7
Scimitar-horned oryx	35	2	0	5
Wildebeest	6	1	29	12
Dik-dik	10	7	7	8
Dorcas gazelle	36	14	17	25
Japanese serow	52	21	27	35

Source: Reprinted with permission from Ralls *et al. Science* 206: 1101–3. Copyright © 1979 American Association for the Advancement of Science.

frequencies will be $p + 0 + q$. In intermediate cases of inbreeding, the fraction of the population that is autozygous is F (and these can only be homozygous individuals), and the remainder $(1 - F)$ of the population is allozygous. If we split the genotypic frequencies into their autozygous and allozygous components we obtain the following:

Genotype	Allozygous	Autozygous	Genotypic frequency
A_1A_1	$p^2(1 - F)$	$+$	$pF = D$
A_1A_2	$2pq(1 - F)$		$= H$
A_2A_2	$q^2(1 - F)$	$+$	$qF = D$

The reader can confirm that when $F = 1$, the frequencies reduce to those noted before. Where F is greater than zero, there is a decrease of heterozygotes and an increase in homozygotes compared to the expected Hardy–Weinberg proportions, and this expresses in a quantitative manner our fourth general conclusion of genetic drift (section 8.1).

We can use the reduction in heterozygosity to obtain a measure of inbreeding for a population, as shown in the following example.

Example 8.1 *The genotypic frequencies at one gene locus in a self-fertilizing species of grass were observed to be 0.55 AA, 0.07 Aa and 0.38 aa. What is the coefficient of inbreeding in this population, assuming that genotypic frequencies are determined by the pattern of breeding?*

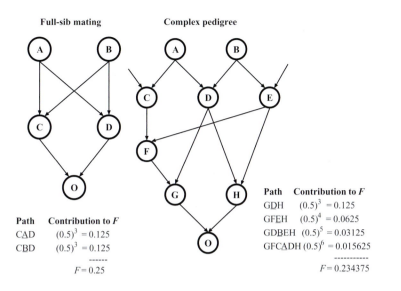

Full-sib mating

Complex pedigree

Path	Contribution to F
CAD	$(0.5)^3 = 0.125$
CBD	$(0.5)^3 = 0.125$

	$F = 0.25$

Path	Contribution to F
GDH	$(0.5)^3 = 0.125$
GFEH	$(0.5)^4 = 0.0625$
GDBEH	$(0.5)^5 = 0.03125$
GFCADH	$(0.5)^6 = 0.015625$

	$F = 0.234375$

We have shown that when there is inbreeding the frequency of heterozygotes is predicted by the equation $H = 2pq(1 - F)$, which may be rearranged to $F = (2pq - H)/2pq$. Note that as the level of inbreeding (F) increases, the observed frequency of heterozygotes (H) decreases from that predicted by the Hardy–Weinberg equilibrium (i.e. $2pq$). The allelic frequencies, p and q, may be calculated from the genotypic frequencies. Thus, $p = 0.55 + 1/2(0.07) = 0.585$, and similarly $q = 0.415$. The expected frequency of heterozygotes, based on the Hardy–Weinberg equilibrium, is calculated as $2 \times 0.585 \times 0.415 = 0.48555$, which is considerably higher than the observed value of 0.07. The coefficient of inbreeding is easily calculated as $F = (0.48555 - 0.07)/0.48555 = 0.8558$.

It is also possible to estimate the inbreeding coefficients of individuals, rather than of the population, from their pedigrees or genealogies. To explain the basis of the method, we will consider a full-sib mating between the offspring of A and B (Fig. 8.8), and calculate the coefficient of inbreeding for individual O, assuming that the grandparents A and B are not inbred. To do this, we need to calculate the probability of a gene being autozygous, i.e. identical by descent, from each of the grandparents. More concretely, what is the probability of individual O having a genotype of A_1A_1 or A_2A_2 where both copies have been derived from a single allele in one of the grandparents?

For the sake of simplicity, let each of the grandparents be genotype A_1A_2. First, we calculate the probability (Pr) of individual O having a genotype A_1A_1 from grandparent A as follows:

Pr (A_1 transmitted via C) $= (0.5)(0.5) = 0.25$
Pr (A_1 transmitted via D) $= (0.5)(0.5) = 0.25$
Therefore, Pr (genotype A_1A_1 in O) $= (0.25)(0.25) = 0.0625$.

In a similar fashion, we can calculate the probability of individual O having a genotype A_2A_2 from grandparent A to be also 0.0625.

Therefore, the probability of individual O being either genotype A_1A_1 or A_2A_2 derived from grandparent A is the sum of these two probabilities, i.e. $0.0625 + 0.0625 = 0.125$.

We can use the same reasoning to calculate that the probability of individual O being either genotype A_1A_1 or A_2A_2 derived from grandparent B is also 0.125. Thus, the inbreeding coefficient for individual O is 0.125 from grandparent A and 0.125 from grandparent B, for a total coefficient of inbreeding F_O of 0.25.

This all seems very involved and difficult. Fortunately, there is a simpler way of doing this calculation, although the logic is less easy to understand. First, we trace all the possible pathways between the parents of individual O and their common ancestors. In our full-sib mating example they are CAD and CBD, where the common ancestor is underlined. We then count the number of steps in each chain (n) and the inbreeding due to the common ancestor in each path is $(0.5)^n$. Thus, in our example it is $(0.5)^3 = 0.125$ for each grandparent, A and B, for a combined inbreeding coefficient of 0.25 for individual O.

Example 8.2 *Calculate the inbreeding coefficient of individual O using the complex pedigree in Fig. 8.8.*

The common ancestors of individual O are D, E, B and A. Using the procedure we have just outlined, the inbreeding coefficients due to the various common ancestors are calculated as follows:

Pathway	Number of steps	Inbreeding coefficient
GDH	(3)	$(0.5)^3 = 0.125$
GFEH	(4)	$(0.5)^4 = 0.0625$
GDEH	(5)	$(0.5)^5 = 0.03125$
GFCADH	(6)	$(0.5)^6 = 0.015625$

The overall coefficient of inbreeding for individual O is the sum of these inbreeding coefficients, or 0.234375.

This example shows that recent common ancestors contribute more to the overall inbreeding coefficient than common ancestors further back in time. This is not unexpected, but demonstrates in a different way that small populations will be more inbred than larger populations because on average their common ancestors will be more recent.

Finally, we will examine inbreeding from a third perspective to shed more light on the effects of founder populations and genetic bottlenecks. When we individually identify the four alleles in two parents and allow them to breed truly at random (i.e. they can self-fertilize as well as breed with each other), we see that four out of the 16 (or $1/2N$) possible combinations of alleles in the zygotes are identical by descent in the first generation of offspring.

Parents:	A_1A_2	×	A_3A_4	
Gametes:	A_1	A_2	A_3	A_4

	A_1	A_2	A_3	A_4
A_1	A_1A_1	A_1A_2	A_1A_3	A_1A_4
A_2	A_1A_2	A_2A_2	A_2A_3	A_2A_4
A_3	A_1A_3	A_2A_3	A_3A_3	A_3A_4
A_4	A_1A_4	A_2A_4	A_3A_4	A_4A_4

Thus:

$$F_1 = \frac{1}{2N} \qquad \text{(Exp. 8.3)}$$

In the second generation, individuals that are identical by descent can arise in two ways. The probability of new inbreeding by self-fertilization is again $1/2N$. The remaining proportion of the population $(1 - 1/2N)$ carries alleles that are independent in origin as a result of breeding in the present generation, but may be identical in origin because of inbreeding in the previous generation. Thus:

$$F_2 = \frac{1}{2N} + \left(1 - \frac{1}{2N}\right) F_1 \qquad \text{(Exp. 8.4)}$$

The same argument applies to subsequent generations and so the inbreeding coefficient in generation t is:

$$F_t = \frac{1}{2N} + \left(1 - \frac{1}{2N}\right) F_{t-1} \qquad \text{(Eqn 8.5)}$$

Note that the inbreeding coefficient is made up of two parts, new inbreeding as a result of self-fertilization $(1/2N)$ plus inbreeding from previous generations. If there is no self-fertilization, however, there are no alleles identical by descent from the preceding generation. This simply shifts the replication one generation further back, so that new inbreeding results from the replication of genes in the grandparents and previous inbreeding results from the replication of genes in the great-grandparents and previous generations.

Equation 8.5 illuminates why the founder effect and genetic bottlenecks have such long-lasting effects on populations. When a population is reduced to a small size, inbreeding and genetic drift affect the genetic structure of the population. If the population subsequently increases to a size where new inbreeding and genetic drift are trivial, the effects of this inbreeding do not disappear because the effects from previous generations, $(1 - 1/2N)F_{t-1}$, still remain. The loss of genetic variation through genetic drift, and the level of heterozygosity reduced by inbreeding, may be restored to some extent by mutation or more quickly by the immigration of different alleles from neighbouring populations. We will consider how migration between different populations influences their differentiation in the next chapter.

8.6 | Summary and conclusions

In small populations, allelic frequencies will either increase or decrease purely by chance, in a process called genetic drift. These changes in allelic frequencies occur independently of one another in different gene loci (provided they are not linked) and in different populations, so that different populations diverge and become genetically distinct from each other. Genetic drift is larger in small populations compared to large populations, and given enough time a single allele will become fixed at each gene locus provided that no other factors are operating. This reduction in genetic diversity within small discrete populations leads to an increase of homozygotes at the expense of heterozygotes. The effective population size that causes genetic drift may be much smaller than the total population size, and is related to the size of the breeding population during the course of its history, the sex ratio, and various other factors. Even though genetic drift may presently be insignificant, given the current size of a population, its effects may still be evident from past events, either from a founder effect, if the population was founded by a few migrants, or a genetic bottleneck, if the population was reduced to a small size at some point. The effects of genetic drift are countered by migration between populations, and may be directed by selection.

Inbreeding also occurs in small populations because individuals are more closely related than they are in large populations. Like genetic drift, inbreeding also increases homozygotes at the expense of heterozygotes, but it does not lead to a change in allelic frequencies. The degree of inbreeding may be calculated from the reduction of heterozygotes, or from the pedigrees of individuals. Finally, the theory of inbreeding helps explain why the founder effect and genetic bottlenecks have such long lasting effects on the genetic structure of populations.

Chapter 9

Migration, gene flow and the differentiation of populations

Ecologists and population geneticists view migration in very different ways. To the ecologist, migration is the movement of individuals or sometimes whole populations from one area to another. The movements often occur on an annual or seasonal basis, like the birds that overwinter in tropical and subtropical areas and then migrate north to breed in Holarctic regions during the spring or summer, or the caribou (*Rangifer tarandus*) herds that overwinter in the northern boreal forest and migrate north to calve on the tundra during the summer months. The movements may also be part of the life cycle, like in the Pacific sockeye salmon (*Oncorhynchus nerka*) that hatch in the headstreams of the rivers, move to the lower reaches of the rivers to feed, and then between the ages of three and seven years move to feed in the oceans before migrating back to their place of birth where they spawn and die. Ecologists seek to understand why animals migrate. Are they moving to take advantage of food resources that become available at different times and places, or is there some other explanation? Many of these migrations are spectacular and may cover huge distances, but to the population geneticist the issue is not how far they may have moved but whether there has been a movement of genes from one population to another. In other words, they are concerned about gene flow. There are many examples of animals that migrate thousands of kilometres but show an astonishing fidelity to the area where they were born and raised. In such cases the degree of gene flow may be extremely low, even though the individuals range over vast distances. What is important, then, is not how far individuals move or migrate, but how far they move or disperse from the site of their birth to where they produce their offspring and how this relates to the spatial structure of populations.

In the last chapter we noted that many organisms have a patchy distribution, where there are more or less discrete populations or demes. Examples include aquatic organisms in ponds and lakes, organisms restricted to patches of woodland, and the fauna and flora on oceanic islands. Gene flow between these populations can be modelled using *island* models and *stepping-stone* models. Other organisms have a continuous distribution over large areas, such as trees in a forest, grasshoppers in grasslands, and benthic organisms on the ocean floor. In these types of populations, each individual is the centre of a neighbourhood in which the probability of mating, and therefore of gene flow, declines with distance from the centre. The population as a whole consists of overlapping neighbourhoods, and gene flow can be modelled using *isolation by distance* or *neighbourhood* models (Wright 1969).

This chapter explores the consequences of gene flow, and how it interacts with genetic drift and selection, by analysing the various models of this process.

9.1 | Island models

If individuals move with equal probability among all discrete populations, the situation conforms to the basic island model. We need only consider a single population in the development of the model, and can then extend it to include as many populations as are necessary.

Let a large population receive a proportion, m, of new immigrants each generation (where m = the immigration rate). The other individuals $(1 - m)$ in the population are 'natives'. If the allelic frequency of natives is q_0, and that of the immigrants is q_m, the frequency of the allele after one generation of immigration will be:

$$q_1 = (1 - m)q_0 + mq_m \qquad \text{(Eqn 9.1)}$$

This equation rearranges to:

$$q_1 = m(q_m - q_0) + q_0 \qquad \text{(Exp. 9.1)}$$

The change in allelic frequency over one generation $(\Delta q = q_1 - q_0)$ is easily derived as:

$$\Delta q = m(q_m - q_0) \qquad \text{(Exp. 9.2)}$$

Thus, if there are no other evolutionary forces operating (i.e. mutation, genetic drift or selection), the change in gene frequency as a result of migration depends on the immigration rate (m) and the difference in allelic frequency between the immigrants and natives. This should be intuitively obvious. The immigration rate only includes those immigrants that successfully breed and mix their alleles into the native population's gene pool, which means that it can be difficult to measure immigration rates directly because we are not concerned with the immigrants that do not breed.

Marker genes (i.e. alleles which differ markedly in frequency between two populations) can sometimes be used to obtain the measure of the migration rate, m, between two populations. In order to use this approach we need know how the allelic frequencies change after a given number of generations, as well as the allelic frequency of the migrants. The predictive equations are developed as follows. First, we rearrange Eqn 9.1 to:

$$q_1 = q_0 - mq_0 + mq_m \qquad \text{(Exp. 9.3)}$$

The difference in allelic frequency between the local, resident, population and the immigrants after one generation is $q_1 - q_m$, and is calculated by subtracting q_m from both sides of Exp. 9.3:

$$q_1 - q_m = q_0 - mq_0 + mq_m - q_m \qquad \text{(Exp. 9.4)}$$

which factors to:

$$q_1 - q_m = (1 - m)(q_0 - q_m) \qquad \text{(Exp. 9.5)}$$

and rearranges to:

$$q_1 = (1 - m)(q_0 - q_m) + q_m \qquad \text{(Exp. 9.6)}$$

After two generations of migration, Eqn 9.1 modifies to:

$$q_2 = (1 - m)q_1 + mq_m \qquad \text{(Exp. 9.7)}$$

Substituting Exp. 9.6 for q_1 in Exp. 9.7 and rearranging yields:

$$q_2 = (1 - m)^2(q_0 - q_m) + q_m \qquad \text{(Exp. 9.8)}$$

Thus, the difference in allelic frequency between the local population and immigrants after two generations is:

$$q_2 - q_m = (1 - m)^2(q_0 - q_m) \qquad \text{(Exp. 9.9)}$$

This expression bears an obvious relationship to Exp. 9.5, and so we can infer that after t generations of migration:

$$q_t - q_m = (1 - m)^t(q_0 - q_m) \qquad \text{(Eqn 9.2)}$$

This equation may be rearranged to estimate the migration rate (m):

$$m = 1 - \left(\frac{q_t - q_m}{q_0 - q_m} \right)^{\frac{1}{t}} \qquad \text{(Eqn 9.3)}$$

We can use these equations in different ways. Three examples should make this clear.

Example 9.1   Estimation of migration rates (m)

Slaves were brought to the United States, mainly from West Africa, about 300 years ago. Since that time, Americans of African and Caucasian descent have been mixing their gene pools. This can be regarded as a one-way migration of alleles from Caucasian to African-American populations because individuals of mixed racial ancestry are regarded as African-Americans. Consequently, the allelic frequency in the local Caucasian population in the United States represents the value of q_m, because this is the group supplying the migrants. The original allelic frequency, q_0, in the African-American population can be estimated from populations in West Africa, and q_t is the allelic frequency in the present-day African-American population. The number of generations (t) of racial mixing is estimated to be 10.

The frequencies of the Fy^a allele of the Duffy blood groups were zero in West Africa ($q_0 = 0$); 0.045 in African-Americans in Georgia

Table 9.1 Estimates of the allelic frequencies of various blood groups in a slave-originating area in West Africa, and for African-American and Caucasian populations in one city in Georgia

Allele	West Africa	African-Americans (Claxton, Georgia)	Caucasians (Claxton, Georgia)	Migration rate $(m)^a$
R^0	0.630	0.533	0.022	0.017
R^1	0.066	0.109	0.429	0.013
R^2	0.061	0.109	0.137	0.095
r	0.248	0.230	0.374	−0.013
A	0.156	0.145	0.241	−0.012
B	0.136	0.113	0.038	0.026
M	0.474	0.484	0.507	0.035
S	0.172	0.157	0.279	−0.013
Hb^S	0.090	0.043	0.000	0.071

^{a}The migration rate from the Caucasian to the African-American population has been estimated using Eqn 9.3.
Source: Data from Adams and Ward (1973).

$(= q_t)$; and 0.422 in the Caucasian population in Georgia $(= q_m)$. If we substitute these values in Eqn 9.3, and set $t = 10$, we obtain an estimate of the migration rate (m) of 0.011 per generation. This implies an immigration rate of alleles from the Caucasian population to the African-American population of about 1% per generation.

The validity of this estimation method is questionable. If we use the allelic frequencies of other blood groups (Table 9.1), it may be seen that there is a wide variation in the positive values, and there are some negative values, which are not consistent with the model of migration that we are using. Some of the negative values may be a result of genetic drift. In the case of the sickle-cell (Hb^S) allele, the high value of apparent migration (7.1%) is known to represent a combination of both migration and selection. The allele is being selected against because as malaria has been eradicated in the United States, the allele is no longer advantageous in the heterozygous condition. The problem, however, is that it is impossible to know which are the 'good' genetic markers, i.e. alleles not subject to selection or genetic drift. Moreover, allelic frequencies vary throughout West Africa, and in the white and black populations in different areas of the United States. Consequently, it is not clear which allelic frequencies we should be using. All we can say is that the evidence suggests a low level of interbreeding between the two groups.

Example 9.2 Estimating the number of generations of migration

A farmer sows a small area of pasture to a pure line of white-flowered sweet clover $(q = 0)$. All the other farms in the neighbourhood have large areas of pasture planted with homozygous yellow-flowered sweet clover $(q = 1.0)$. How many generations will it take for the white-flowered area to have an allelic frequency of 0.5 for yellow flowers if the migration rate is 0.05 per generation?

The original allelic frequency of the 'native' population was zero, i.e. $q_0 = 0$, and eventually reaches a frequency (q_t) of 0.5, after an unknown number of generations (t) of immigration by migrant with an allelic frequency (q_m) of 1.0. Substituting these values in Eqn 9.2, we obtain $(0.5 - 1.0) = (1 - 0.05)^t \times (0 - 1.0)$. This reduces to $0.5 = 0.95^t$, and the logarithm of both sides yields $-0.6931 = -0.0513 \times t$. Consequently, the number of generations (t) is 13.51, or approximately 14.

Example 9.3 Estimating allelic frequencies after several generations of migration

Three equal-sized populations, A, B and C, with allelic frequencies of 0.2, 0.4 and 0.6, migrate according to the island model with a migration rate of 0.1 per generation. What are the expected allelic frequencies after 10 generations?

The allelic frequency of migrants (q_m) is the average of the allelic frequencies of the donor populations, and so for population A is $(0.4 + 0.6)/2 = 0.5$, and similarly for populations B and C are 0.4 and 0.3, respectively. Equation 9.2 is used to calculate q_t for each population separately, and for population A, $q_t = (1 - 0.1)^{10} \times (0.2 - 0.5) + 0.5 = 0.3954$. Similarly, populations B and C have values of 0.4 and 0.4046. The average allelic frequency after 10 generations remains at 0.4, and the three populations are steadily converging to this average allelic frequency. We should note two points when making these types of calculations. First, if the populations are of unequal size we need to weight the allelic frequencies of the donor populations accordingly when calculating q_m values; and second, the populations actually converge on their values of q_m, rather than the average allelic frequency across all populations, because we are not readjusting the q_m values over time. The solution to this problem is dealt with next.

9.2 | Simulation of island model and general conclusions

It is simple to simulate the island model to show how migration affects allelic frequencies by using Eqn 9.1 in an iterative fashion to calculate the allelic frequencies generation after generation (see Appendix 9.1). Populations converge to an allelic frequency equal to the average allelic frequency across all populations (Fig. 9.1). We can conclude that gene flow has the effect of making populations become genetically uniform, and that this process becomes more powerful as the migration rate increases. We have already shown that migration is a very powerful factor limiting the differentiation of populations as a result of genetic drift (section 8.4), but how effective is it countering the effects of selection?

To answer this question consider a situation where all of a mainland insect population possess wings but the insects are wingless on an offshore island because those with wings tend to be blown away on the strong prevailing winds (Fig. 9.2). In the absence of

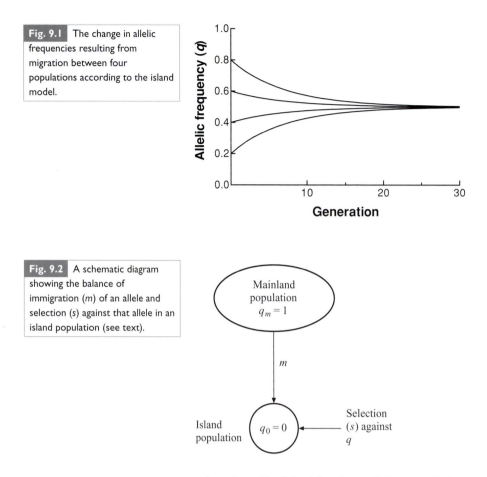

Fig. 9.1 The change in allelic frequencies resulting from migration between four populations according to the island model.

Fig. 9.2 A schematic diagram showing the balance of immigration (m) of an allele and selection (s) against that allele in an island population (see text).

migration, all of the island population would be wingless, i.e. $q_0 = 0$, because of selection, but how would this change if there is immigration of winged forms from the mainland? We can ignore migration from the island to the mainland because the island insects are wingless.

The joint effects of selection and migration can be assessed by determining the equilibrium frequency of wing alleles ($\hat{q}$) of the island population where the loss of alleles by selection is exactly balanced by the gain of these alleles by migration from the mainland. This may be predicted by the following equation:

$$\frac{s\,\hat{p}\hat{q}^2}{1 - s\hat{q}^2} = m(q_m - \hat{q}) \qquad \text{(Exp. 9.10)}$$

The gain of alleles by immigration over one generation is shown on the right-hand side of the equation, and is derived from Exp. 9.2. The loss of alleles by selection is shown on the left-hand side of Exp. 9.10, and is modified from Eqn 10.5, which assumes that the allele for wings is recessive to wingless.

We can simplify Exp. 9.10 by noting that the left-hand side of the equation is approximately $s\,\hat{p}\hat{q}^2$ because the value of $s\hat{q}^2$ in the denominator is so small, and that the right-hand side of the equation equals $m\hat{p}$ because $q_m = 1$ and so $1 - \hat{q} = \hat{p}$. After cancelling terms and rearranging the simplified equation we obtain:

$$\hat{q} \approx \sqrt{\left(\frac{m}{s}\right)} \qquad \text{(Exp. 9.11)}$$

To see what this predicts, assume that $m = 0.01$ and $s = 0.25$. Our predicted equilibrium frequency of wing alleles $(\hat{q}) = 0.2$, and so a 1% immigration rate of wing alleles results in 20% of the alleles for this trait in the population even though there is a fairly strong selection against them. Remember, however, that as wings are recessive in this example only 4% $(\hat{q}^2)$ of the population will have wings. If the immigration rate (m) increased to 0.1, the equilibrium value for wing alleles $(\hat{q})$ is predicted to be 0.6325, and 40% of the population would have wings. Although different cases of dominance (see Chapter 10) would change the precise values calculated in this example, we would still draw the same general conclusion that gene flow is also a powerful factor limiting the differentiation of populations as a result of selection.

9.3 | Stepping-stone model

The spatial distribution of many populations does not conform to the island model we have just considered. In most cases, individuals will tend to migrate to populations that are closest to them, so the spread of genes takes place in a stepping-stone fashion from a central source. Let's examine how this affects the genetic structure of a group of populations.

The simplest stepping-stone model is a linear model, which represents a sequence of populations $(1, 2, 3, 4, \ldots, n)$ along an environmental gradient. Examples include populations at increasing altitudes on a mountain, or populations along the shoreline of an estuary where the salinity varies in relation to location. There are various ways in which the model can be envisioned, but we will construct our model as shown diagrammatically in Fig. 9.3.

In this model we need to modify Eqn 9.1 for each population $(1, 2, 3, \ldots, n)$. For example, using the notation for migration in

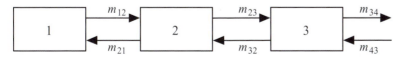

Fig. 9.3 Diagrammatic representation of a one-dimensional stepping-stone model along an environmental gradient. Each of the sequence of populations (2, 3, 4, etc.) exchanges migrants with the populations on either side. Between any two populations the exchange of migrants is balanced (i.e. $m_{12} = m_{21}$), but the migration rates can vary along the sequence of populations.

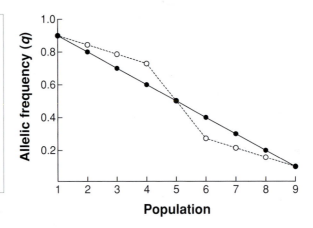

Fig. 9.4 The effects of migration on the allelic frequencies of a linear sequence of populations where the frequencies at either end of the chain (i.e. populations 1 and 9) are held constant at different frequencies as a result of selection. The migration rates are either held constant between all populations (solid symbols) or are reduced between populations 4 and 5 and 5 and 6 (open circles).

Fig. 9.3, the allelic frequency for population 2 after one generation of migration is:

$$q_1 = [1 - (m_{21} + m_{23})]q_0 + m_{12}q_{m_1} + m_{32}q_{m_3} \qquad \text{(Exp. 9.13)}$$

The allelic frequency of population 2 in the previous generation (i.e. prior to migration) is denoted by q_0, and the rate of loss of these alleles by migration to populations 1 and 3 is denoted by m_{21} and m_{23}, respectively. The increase of these alleles by immigration from populations 1 and 3 is denoted by $m_{12}q_{m_1}$ and $m_{32}q_{m_3}$, respectively, where q_{m_1} and q_{m_3} are the allelic frequencies of populations 1 and 3 prior to migration. Thus, migration is the only factor changing the allelic frequencies, and Exp. 9.13 is modified in an appropriate way for each population.

The simulation of this model is described in Appendix 9.2. In our simulation, the allelic frequencies of the populations at each end of the series are held constant by selection and the migration rates between any two populations are equal, i.e. $m_{12} = m_{21}$ and $m_{23} = m_{32}$, although this may not be the case in reality. However, the migration rates can vary between different pairs of populations, i.e. m_{12} and m_{21} may be greater or less than m_{23} and m_{32}. If selection maintains the allelic frequencies at different values at opposite ends of a sequence of populations, the allelic frequencies of the intermediate populations will fall on a gradient between these two values, depending on the migration rates. If the migration rates are similar among all populations, the gradient will be linear, but if there are regions where there are low levels of migration there will be abrupt changes in allelic frequencies at these points (Fig. 9.4).

We can conclude that gene flow limits the differentiation of adjacent populations and that abrupt changes in the characteristics of populations will be associated with geographical features that severely reduce the movement between populations.

Geographical trends in allelic frequencies, or morphological features, of populations are known as clines. In reality, the intermediate populations on such clines are unlikely to have their allelic frequencies determined solely by migration rates. Other factors, such as selection pressure and possibly genetic drift, will also have an effect. However, migration does have an effect because steep regions on a cline are often associated with barriers to movement.

McNeilly (1968) studied the copper tolerance in *Agrostis tenuis* around a copper mine in Britain and clearly demonstrated the interaction between gene flow and selection. As expected, the grass had developed a high tolerance to copper at the mine site, but copper-tolerant individuals are at a disadvantage to non-tolerant individuals in non-polluted areas and so copper tolerance tends to be low outside of the mine sites. The mine was located at the bottom of a steep-sided glacial valley that funneled the wind so that for most of the flowering season of the grass the wind blew in the same direction. McNeilly showed that there was a very sharp cline of copper tolerance on the upwind side of the mine, but copper tolerance spread a long way downwind of the mine, presumably because of the spread of wind-borne pollen. In addition, the copper tolerance of adults was higher than that of seedlings on the upwind side of the mine site, because of the inflow on non-tolerant genes, but downwind of the mine the seedlings had a higher tolerance to copper than the adult population because there was selection against tolerant individuals.

In the linear stepping-stone model, each population exchanges migrants with two populations on either side of it (Fig. 9.3). It is possible to extend this model to a two-dimensional model in which each population exchanges migrants with four populations surrounding it, i.e. each population is in contact with a neighbouring population in each of the four quadrants. This type of model is rather more complicated to simulate, but gives results that are similar to the isolation-by-distance or neighbourhood models that we briefly mentioned at the start of this chapter. We will not simulate either of these two models, and will conclude that the overall effect of gene flow between and within populations is to make them more genetically uniform and limit the spatial differentiation of populations resulting from genetic drift and selection.

9.4 | Problems

1. The frequency of G6PD deficiency in West Africa is 0.176, in African-Americans in Georgia is 0.118, and in the Caucasian population in Georgia is 0. Estimate the average migration rate (m) from Caucasians to Afro-Americans assuming there have been 10 generations of interbreeding between the two populations.
2. Four neighbouring populations of equal size have allelic frequencies of 0.2, 0.5, 0.8 and 0.9 and migrate according to the island model with $m = 0.05$. What are the expected allelic frequencies after five generations?
3. An island population of butterflies has an allelic frequency of 0.75 and the allelic frequency of the surrounding mainland population is 0.25 for the same allele. How many generations will it take for the island population to reach a frequency of 0.55 if the migration rate is 0.05?

Appendix 9.1 Simulating the island model

1. Open your spreadsheet and enter the title, **Island Model**, in A1.
2. Enter **m =** in cell A3, and a value of 0.1 in cell B3.
3. Enter titles in row 5 of columns A to E as follows: In A **Time**, B **Popn. 1**, in C **Popn. 2**, in D **Popn. 3**, and in E **Popn. 4**.
4. Enter starting values of 0, 0.2, 0.4, 0.6, and 0.8 in row 6 of columns A to E.
5. In column A generate times from 1 to 30 in cells A7 to A36 (see Appendix 4.1 step 5).
6. In cell B7 enter formula: $= (1\text{-}\$B\$3)^*B6 + \$B\$3^*(C6+D6+E6)/3$. This is equivalent to Eqn 9.1, with q_m calculated as an average of the donor populations. Enter modified versions of this formula in C7, D7 and E7. (E.g. the formula for C7 is: $= (1\text{-}\$B\$3)^*C6 + \$B\$3^*(B6+D6+E6)/3)$. Then copy cells B7 to E7 to cells B8 to E36.
7. Graph the changes in allelic frequency over time (see Appendix 4.1 step 9). The x axis is A6 . . A36, the 1st series is B6 . . B36, the 2nd series is C6 . . C36, the 3rd series is D6 . . D36, and the 4th series is E6 . . E36. Label the axes appropriately to obtain a graph similar to Fig. 9.1.
8. Change the migration rate in cell B3 and see how the slope of the graphs changes.
9. Save your work and exit.

Appendix 9.2 Simulating the stepping-stone model

1. Open your spreadsheet and type the title, **Stepping-stone model**, in A1.
2. In row 4, type **m values =** in column A, and then the value **0.2** in cells B4 to J4.
3. In row 5 type **Popn** in B5 and copy to cells C5 to J5.
4. In row 6 type **Time** in A6, and the integers **1** to **9** in cells B6 to J6.
5. In column A generate times from 0 to 200 in cells A7 to A207 (see Appendix 4.1 step 5).
6. In column B enter the allelic frequency of **0.9** in B7 and then copy this to cells B8 to B207. Similarly, in column J enter the allelic frequency of **0.1** in J7 and copy this value to cells J8 to J207. The allelic frequencies are now fixed at different values at opposite ends of the sequence of populations. Finally, copy B7 to cells C7 to I7 to provide a starting allelic frequency for each of the nine populations.
7. In cell C8 enter the formula: $=(1\text{-}(B\$4+C\$4))^*C7+B\$4^*B7+ C\$4^*D7$. This is equivalent to Exp. 9.10. Copy C8 to cells D8 to I8 to calculate the allelic frequencies after one generation of migration. Finally, copy cells C8 to I8 to all cells through to C207 to I207.

8. Graph the changes in allelic frequency after 200 generations of migration in relation to the sequence of populations (see Appendix 4.1 steps 9 and 10). The x axis is B6 . . J6, and the 1st series is B207 . . J207. Label the axes appropriately to obtain a graph like Fig. 9.4.

9. The allelic frequencies of populations 1 to 9 should lie on a linear series from 0.9 for population 1 to 0.1 for population 9. Now vary the migration rate (m) between certain pairs of populations. For example, if you reduce the migration rate for populations 4 and 5 (reduce m to 0.05 or 0.01) you will obtain a graph similar to the dashed line in Fig. 9.4. You will discover that wherever you reduce the migration rate between two populations (simulating a barrier to dispersal) there is a sudden shift in allelic frequency between adjacent populations.

10. Save your worksheet and exit.

Chapter 10

Quantifying natural selection: haploid and zygotic selection models

Natural selection occurs where there is heritable variation in a population and where there are differences in survival and fecundity associated with this variation. Thus, in order for natural selection to operate there must not only be phenotypic variation, there must also be an underlying genotypic variation. The relationship between phenotype and genotype can be very complex (see Schlichting and Pigliucci 1998) but we will confine ourselves to simple situations where there is a one-to-one mapping of genotype to phenotype, or to cases of complete dominance. Genotypes, and thereby alleles, leaving the most descendants will tend to increase in frequency in the population through the process of natural selection. You will note that this last statement is not absolute, because if the heterozygous genotype leaves the most descendants, the proportions of the various genotypes may remain constant from one generation to the next (see section 11.2.2).

The various equations that quantify natural selection are largely developed intuitively by the use of empirical examples. For those who are interested, the mathematical details of the derivations are confined to a few text boxes and an appendix, but it is not necessary to be able to derive the equations yourself in order to understand them. Simulations are used to analyse and show the predictions of the equations, but their application to the natural world is left until Chapter 11.

First, however, we need to define a few terms before we learn how to quantify them.

10.1 Defining fitness and selection

Absolute fitness is a measure of the growth rate of a genetically defined group within a population over the course of one or more generations. Thus, the fitness of an allele or a genotype depends on the number of copies in descendants in succeeding generations, and is measured by the multiplication rate, λ, of the allele or genotype, as defined for population growth in Chapter 4. Normally, however, we

Table 10.1 Calculation of the fitness of genotypes. Genotypes A, B and C may be haploid or diploid, although the calculations for diploid genotypes are not strictly correct (see example 11.3, section 11.1.2)

	Genotypes			
	A	B	C	Total
Number of individuals generation 0	50	60	40	140
Number of individuals generation 1	100	90	40	230
Multiplication rate per generation (λ)	$100/50 = 2$	$90/60 = 1.5$	$40/40 = 1$	
Relative fitness (W)	$2/2 = 1$	$1.5/2 = 0.75$	$1/2 = 0.5$	
Selection coefficient ($1-W = s$)	$1 - 1 = 0$	$1 - 0.75 = 0.25$	$1 - 0.5 = 0.5$	

are more interested in fitness relative to other genotypes or alleles, called relative fitness (W), because natural selection is the differential reproduction or survival of types.

The procedure for calculating fitness is shown in Table 10.1. First, the average multiplication rate per generation (λ) is calculated for each genotype (i.e. λ_A, λ_B, etc.). Then, the relative fitness (W_A, W_B, etc.) of each genotype is calculated relative to a reference genotype, which by convention is the genotype with the highest growth rate. Finally, the selection coefficient (s_A, s_B, etc.) operating on each genotype is defined as the difference between the relative fitness of a genotype and that of the reference genotype, which has a value of 1.0. Consequently, $s = 1 - W$ and $W = 1 - s$. Note that the selection coefficient can range in value from 0, which will be the case for the reference genotype, to 1.0, which indicates a completely lethal genotype (i.e. with $\lambda = 0$).

10.2 | Selection in action

Selection occurs throughout the life of an organism, as well as during the production of offspring. In organisms with a haploid life cycle (e.g. bacteria and some microorganisms), or in asexually reproducing organisms (e.g. many plants, aphids, and even a few vertebrates), fitness may be simply partitioned into two components: the probability of a genotype's survival from birth to reproduction, and the average production of offspring per individual of a genotype, or its fecundity.

Sexually reproducing species do not produce exact copies of themselves. They produce haploid gametes, and genetic information from two different individuals combine during reproduction to produce diploid zygotes for the start of the next generation. Such organisms have a life cycle that alternates between a haploid and a diploid phase. Either the haploid phase is dominant (e.g. many fungi and algae, and mosses) or the diploid phase is dominant (e.g. flowering plants and most animals). The overall fitness is determined by a combination of different components of selection that occur during the haploid stage (*gametic selection*) and the diploid phase (*zygotic selection*). For example,

Table 10.2 | The frequency of two genotypes, A and B, and the change in frequency (Δq) of the inferior genotype (B), in a population where genotype A quadruples each generation and genotype B doubles each generation

| Time (t) | Population size | | Frequency of genotype | | |
	Genotype A	Genotype B	A ($=p_t$)	B ($=q_t$)	Δq
0	1	99	0.0100	0.9900	−0.0098
1	4	198	0.0198	0.9802	−0.0190
2	16	396	0.0388	0.9612	−0.0359
3	64	792	0.0748	0.9252	−0.0644
4	256	1584	0.1391	0.8609	−0.1051
5	1024	3168	0.2433	0.7557	−0.1484
6	4096	6336	0.3926	0.6704	−0.1712
7	16 384	12 672	0.5639	0.4361	−0.1573
8	65 536	25 344	0.7211	0.2789	−0.1168
9	262 144	50 688	0.8380	0.1620	−0.0739

one genotype may have a lower viability of the offspring than another genotype, but this reduction in fitness may be compensated in whole or in part by the genotype having a higher fecundity. The different components of selection, such as gamete viability, fertilization success, mating success of adults, etc., will not be described here. They are difficult to measure individually and we will not be using them in our selection models. Readers who wish to learn more about specific components of selection are referred to Futuyma (1998).

There are many different models of selection which are appropriate for different situations. We will start with the simplest models and gradually build in the complications.

10.3 | Modelling haploid selection

This is the simplest model of selection. Each genotype is independent of the others, and so the growth of each genotype can be measured directly. This model may be applied to organisms with haploid life cycles, such as bacteria and certain microorganisms, and can also be applied to organisms that reproduce asexually, whether they are haploid or diploid, although in the latter case we might refer to phenotypes rather than genotypes.

Consider the example illustrated in Table 10.2, in which genotype A has a multiplication rate twice that of genotype B. Obviously, the relative fitness of B is half that of A ($W_B = \lambda_B/\lambda_A = 2/4 = 0.5$), and the selection coefficient against genotype B ($s_B = 1 - W_B$) is also 0.5. It is a simple matter to calculate the growth and frequency of each genotype, and also the change in genotypic frequency (Δq), generation by generation. If we set the relative fitness of the superior genotype to 1 and that of the less fit genotype to $1 - s$ ($= W$), we can develop a

Box 10.1 Quantifying haploid selection with two genotypes

Consider a population with two genotypes, A and B, with initial frequencies of p and q and relative fitness of 1 and $1 - s$, respectively. Their frequencies after one generation of selection are calculated by multiplying the initial frequency of each genotype by its relative fitness. Thus:

	Genotype		Total population
	A	B	
Initial frequency	p	q	$p + q = 1$
Relative fitness (W)	1	$1 - s$	
Frequency after one generation	p	$q(1 - s)$	$p + q(1 - s) = 1 - sq$

The frequency of genotype B after one generation of selection is:

$$q_1 = \frac{q(1 - s)}{1 - sq} \qquad \text{(Exp. 10.1)}$$

The change in frequency (Δq) over one generation is $q_1 - q$. Substituting Exp. 10.1 for q_1 we obtain:

$$\Delta q = \frac{q(1 - s)}{1 - sq} - \frac{q(1 - sq)}{1 - sq} \qquad \text{(Exp. 10.2)}$$

This simplifies to:

$$\Delta q = \frac{-sq(1 - q)}{1 - sq} \qquad \text{(Eqn 10.1)}$$

This equation predicts the change in frequency of the genotype (B) over a single generation. To predict the genotypic frequency (q) after several generations of constant selection we need to sum these changes over the required number of generations. If the selection coefficient (s) is very small, then Δq will also be small and approximates $\delta q / \delta t$, and the denominator ($1 - sq$) is almost equal to 1.0. Consequently, we can estimate q after t generations by integrating the numerator, following the rules of integral calculus, which is equivalent to adding up all of the small changes over t generations. The solution is:

$$q_t = \frac{q_0}{q_0 + (1 - q_0)e^{st}} \text{ approx.} \qquad \text{(Exp. 10.3)}$$

To simplify the calculation of the selection coefficient (s) or the number of generations (t) required to change the frequency from q_0 to q_t, this expression may be rearranged to:

$$st = \ln\left[\frac{q_0(1 - q_t)}{q_t(1 - q_0)}\right] \text{ approx.} \qquad \text{(Exp. 10.4)}$$

Note that Exps. 10.3 and 10.4 are only accurate when s is small (0.01 or less).

general formulation of how genotypic frequencies change from one generation to the next. This is developed algebraically in Box 10.1 for the inferior genotype to produce the following equation:

$$\Delta q = \frac{-sq(1-q)}{1-sq} \qquad \text{(Eqn 10.1)}$$

This equation provides an exact prediction of the change in allelic or genotypic frequency for any selection coefficient (s), and this can be confirmed by substituting the values for s and q in the equation for any of the generations in Table 10.2. Note that the values are negative, because the inferior genotype declines in frequency.

To make predictions over several generations we need to add up or integrate these changes generation by generation. We can do this by using Eqn 10.1 in an iterative fashion (see Appendix 10.2), which gives exact solutions, or we can integrate a simplified form of the equation to obtain Exps. 10.3 and 10.4 (see Box 10.1). These are standard equations (see Hartl and Clark 1989) that provide approximate predictions for q_t, s or t, after many generations of constant selection. They are only accurate if the selection coefficient (s) is small (0.01 or less), and the error increases rapidly as s increases in value. They give very inaccurate estimates of the various parameters for our example in Table 10.2. Expression 10.3 estimates $q_t = 0.5238$ after nine generations of selection, when $s = 0.5$ and $q_0 = 0.99$, rather than the true value of 0.1620, and Exp. 10.4 estimates the selection coefficient (s) = 0.6931 when $t = 9$, $q_0 = 0.99$, and $q_t = 0.1620$, rather than the true value of 0.5.

It is tempting to assume that it is always better to use the exact iterative simulation method (Appendix 10.2), but if s is very small you might have to do thousands of iterations to show much change in genotypic frequency. In this situation it would be better to use the analytical method, because it provides reasonably accurate solutions. So when should one switch from one method to the other? Fortunately, there is an alternative analytical method that gives exact solutions for all parameters.[1] The formal derivation of Eqns 10.2 and 10.3 is complex (see Appendix 10.1), but they are relatively easy to use.

$$q_t = \frac{q_0}{q_0 + (1-q_0)(1-s)^{-t}} \qquad \text{(Eqn 10.2)}$$

$$[\ln(1-s)]\,t = \ln\left[\frac{q_t(1-q_0)}{q_0(1-q_t)}\right] \qquad \text{(Eqn 10.3)}$$

If we apply these equations to the example in Table 10.2 we find that both equations calculate exact values for q_t, s and t when the correct values for the other terms in the equation are substituted.

---

[1] When simulating haploid selection (Appendix 10.1) I noticed that Exp. 10.4 calculated a value for the selection coefficient, s, equal to the true value of $-\ln(1-s)$, or $-\ln(W)$. It was a simple matter to modify Exps. 10.3 and 10.4 to obtain Eqns 10.2 and 10.3, which provide exact solutions for all parameters. Professor Jacek Banasiuk of the University of Natal, Durban, formally derived these equations from Eqn 10.1 (see Appendix 10.1).

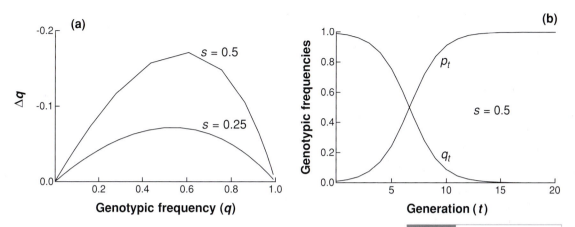

The simulation of haploid selection, described in Appendix 10.2, shows that Eqns 10.1, 10.2 and 10.3 provide exact solutions or predictions, whatever the selection coefficient. However, Exps. 10.3 and 10.4 only provide reasonably accurate estimates when the value of s is very low. Thus, the simulation confirms our assessment of the models so far. The simulation also helps us make some general conclusions about haploid selection, which are listed in the following section.

Fig. 10.1 (a) Change in frequency (Δq) of the inferior genotype in relation to the frequency (q) of the genotype in the population, as a result of selection (s). (b) Change in genotypic frequencies over time as a result of selection.

10.3.1 Conclusions

1. Equation 10.1 shows that the change in frequency of genotypes depends not only on the selection coefficient (s), but also on the frequencies of the two genotypes (note that $p = 1 - q$) in a complex way. An examination of Table 10.2 shows that genotypic frequencies change most rapidly at intermediate values of p and q, and change slowly when one genotype or the other is at a low frequency. The simulation of haploid selection (Appendix 10.2) confirms this observation (Fig. 10.1a). It may also be seen that the frequency of the advantageous genotype increases sigmoidally, whereas the disadvantageous genotype decreases sigmoidally (Fig. 10.1b). There is an obvious relationship between these observations and logistic growth (see Chapter 5).

2. Thus, the frequency of a new advantageous mutation in the population will only increase slowly at first. Its survival is precarious while it remains at a low frequency, because it may be lost by chance from the population (see Chapter 7).

3. It is the relative growth rates of genotypes that are important in determining the genotypic frequencies, not the actual growth rates. Thus, if the multiplication rates (absolute fitness) of genotypes A and B are respectively, 4 and 2, or 1 and 0.5, or 0.9 and 0.45, the change in genotypic frequencies over time will be identical because the relative fitness of genotype B (W_B) is 0.5 in each case.

4. The overall absolute fitness of the population (λ) steadily increases as the frequency of the superior allele or genotype increases in the population (Fig. 10.2). Thus, selection serves to increase the overall fitness of the population.

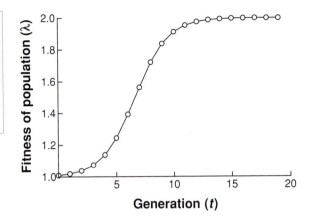

Fig. 10.2 Increase in overall fitness (λ) over time for a population represented by two genotypes, A and B, with multiplication rates of 2 and 1, respectively, and starting with one individual of genotype A and 99 individuals of genotype B.

10.4 | Zygotic selection models

Zygotic selection models are developed in exactly the same way as the basic haploid selection model. They are more complex because the growth rates of different genotypes are not independent of each other and so it is more difficult to calculate their growth rates and relative fitness. We will leave this problem until Chapter 11 when we apply the models to actual data. We also have to take into account the effects of dominance, and we will illustrate how we do this by considering four examples that correspond to different cases of dominance (Table 10.3).

Many insects use camouflage to reduce the risk of predation populations by birds, which act as a powerful selective agent on body colour by preferentially eating those insects that least resemble the background colour of their environment. This is illustrated in Table10.3, where the phenotype with the highest relative fitness or growth rate is the one that matches the colour of the vegetation. In Cases B and E (Table 10.3) there are two codominant alleles, A_1 and A_2, and the three genotypes give rise to green, olive and brown phenotypes. Early in the growing season the insects are living in a lush green environment, and selection occurs against both the olive and brown phenotypes, with the selection against olive being exactly half that against brown. This conforms to the relative fitness of our Case B model. Later in the season the vegetation becomes darker and now the olive individuals have the best camouflage (Case E). The olive individuals increase in frequency because of the selection against the two homozygous phenotypes (green and brown), and this conforms to our Case E model of heterozygote superiority.

In Cases C and D (Table 10.3) the allele for green is completely dominant to brown and so there are only two phenotypes. Early in the growing season the insects are living in a lush green environment, and there is selection against the homozygous recessive brown types (Case C). Late in the season, however, the vegetation dries and becomes brown, and now it is the brown insects that are better camouflaged

Table 10.3 Zygotic selection on the body colour of an insect as a result of differential predation by birds (see text). The fitness of genotypes is calculated as shown in Table 10.1, and selection is always against the A_2 allele, which has a frequency of q

Case B   No dominance, selection against A_2 allele

Colour of vegetation	Green		
Phenotype	Green	Olive	Brown
Genotype	A_1A_1	A_1A_2	A_2A_2
H–W equilibrium frequency	p^2	$2pq$	q^2
Numbers in generation 0	25	50	25
Numbers in generation 1	28	50	22
Absolute fitness, λ	1.12	1.0	0.88
Relative fitness, W	1.0	0.893	0.786
Model relative fitness	1	$1 - \frac{1}{2}s$	$1 - s$

Case C   Complete dominance, selection against recessive

Colour of vegetation	Green	
Phenotype	Green	Brown
Genotype	$A_1A_1 + A_1A_2$	A_2A_2
H–W equilibrium frequency	$p^2 + 2pq$	q^2
Numbers in generation 0	75	25
Numbers in generation 1	84	16
Absolute fitness, λ	1.12	0.64
Relative fitness, W	1.0	0.57
Model relative fitness	1 1	$1 - s$

Case D   Complete dominance, selection against dominant

Colour of vegetation	Brown	
Phenotype	Brown	Green
Genotype	A_1A_1	$A_1A_2 + A_2A_2$
H–W equilibrium frequency	p^2	$2pq + q^2$
Numbers in generation 0	16	84
Numbers in generation 1	25	75
Absolute fitness, λ	1.5625	0.8929
Relative fitness, W	1.0	0.57
Model relative fitness	1	$1 - s$ $1 - s$

Case E   Heterozygote superiority

Colour of vegetation	Olive		
Phenotype	Green	Olive	Brown
Genotype	A_1A_1	A_1A_2	A_2A_2
H–W equilibrium frequency	p^2	$2pq$	q^2
Numbers in generation 0	28	50	22
Numbers in generation 1	20	60	20
Absolute fitness, λ	0.71	1.2	0.91
Relative fitness, W	0.595	1	0.758
Model relative fitness	$1 - s_1$	1	$1 - s_2$

Table 10.4 Summary of zygotic selection equations. Selection is always against the A_2 allele, which has a frequency of q, and in Case E selection also occurs against the A_1 allele

Fitness of genotypes			Change in A_2 allele over one generation	Change in A_2 allele over many generations
$A_1 A_1$	$A_1 A_2$	$A_2 A_2$		

Case B No dominance, selection against A_2

When $s \ll 1$, approximate solution:

1	$1 - \frac{1}{2}s$	$1 - s$	$\Delta q = \frac{-\frac{1}{2}spq}{1-sq}$ (Eqn 10.4)	$st = 2\ln\left[\frac{q_0(1-q_t)}{q_1(1-q_0)}\right]$ (Eqn 10.8)

When $s = 1$ (i.e. lethal)

$$q_t = q_0 0.5^t \quad \text{(Eqn 10.9)}$$

$$t = \frac{\ln(q_t/q_0)}{\ln 0.5} \quad \text{(Eqn 10.10)}$$

Case C Complete dominance, selection against recessive

When $s \ll 1$, approximate solution:

1	1	$1 - s$	$\Delta q = \frac{-spq^2}{1-sq^2}$ (Eqn 10.5)	$st = \frac{q_0 - q_t}{q_0 q_t} + \ln\left[\frac{q_0(1-q_t)}{q_t(1-q_0)}\right]$ (Eqn 10.11)

When $s = 1$ (lethal)

$$q_t = \frac{q_0}{1+tq_0} \quad \text{(Eqn 10.12)}$$

$$t = \frac{1}{q_t} - \frac{1}{q_0} \quad \text{(Eqn 10.13)}$$

Case D Complete dominance, selection against dominant

1	$1 - s$	$1 - s$	$\Delta q = \frac{-sp^2q}{1-2sq+sq^2}$ (Eqn 10.6)	When $s \ll 1$, approximate solution:

$$st = \frac{q_0 - q_t}{(1-q_t)(1-q_0)} + \ln\left[\frac{q_0(1-q_t)}{q_t(1-q_0)}\right]$$

$$\text{(Eqn 10.14)}$$

Case E Heterozygote superiority

$1 - s_1$	1	$1 - s_2$	$\Delta q = \frac{+pq(s_1 p - s_2 q)}{1 - s_1 p^2 - s_2 q^2}$ (Eqn 10.7)	$\hat{q} = \frac{s_1}{s_1 + s_2}$ (Eqn 10.15)

and increase in frequency, and so there is selection against the dominant (green) type (Case D). Note that Cases C and D are mirror images of each other, and that to conform to the model we switch the labelling of the alleles so that the inferior allele always has a frequency of q.

How do these different cases of dominance influence how the allelic frequencies change as a result of selection? A complete list of equations is presented in Table 10.4, and although it looks quite formidable a quick review will reveal that it is simple to use.

The left-hand column lists the relative fitness of genotypes in the four cases that we developed in Table 10.3. In the next chapter we will show how to match the various studies to these four cases.

The middle column of equations (i.e. Eqns 10.4 to 10.7) shows how the A_2 allele changes in one generation of selection for each case. These equations are developed in a similar way, and this is shown for Eqn 10.4 in Box 10.2. Note that in Cases B, C and D the equations are negative, and this is because the A_2 allele is at a disadvantage to the other allele and so it will decline until it is eliminated, unless other forces intervene. Equation 10.7 is positive because neither allele is eliminated. Case E leads to a stable equilibrium of allelic frequencies, and this occurs when the term $(s_1 p - s_2 q)$ in the numerator equals

---

Box 10.2 | Zygotic selection – Case B: No dominance selection against A_2

	Genotypes			
	A_1A_1	A_1A_2	A_2A_2	Total population
Initial frequencies	p^2	$2pq$	q^2	$p^2 + 2pq + q^2 = 1$
Fitness	1	$1 - \frac{1}{2}s$	$1 - s$	
Frequency after selection^a	p^2	$2pq(1 - \frac{1}{2}s)$	$q^2(1 - s)$	$1 - sq$

^{a}Determination of total after selection: Total$=p^2+2pq(1-\frac{1}{2}s)+q^2(1 - s)$, which expands to $p^2 + 2pq - spq + q^2 - sq^2$. But $p^2 + 2pq + q^2 = 1$, and so the total $= 1 - spq - sq^2$. But $p = 1 - q$ and so the last expression expands to $1 - sq(1 - q) - sq^2$ or $1 - sq + sq^2 - sq^2$, which simplifies to $1 - sq$.

The frequency of the A_2 allele after one generation of selection is:

$$q_1 = \frac{q^2(1 - s) + \frac{1}{2}[2pq(1 - \frac{1}{2}s)]}{1 - sq} \qquad \text{(Exp. 10.16)}$$

The change in allelic frequency over one generation of selection $\Delta q = q_1 - q$. Therefore:

$$\Delta q = \frac{q^2(1 - s) + \frac{1}{2}[2pq(1 - \frac{1}{2}s)]}{1 - sq} - \frac{q(1 - sq)}{1 - sq} \qquad \text{(Exp. 10.17)}$$

Expanding this expression and setting $pq = q - q^2$ we obtain:

$$\Delta q = \frac{q^2 - sq^2 + q - q^2 - \frac{1}{2}spq - q + sq^2}{1 - sq} \qquad \text{(Exp. 10.18)}$$

This simplifies to:

$$\Delta q = \frac{-\frac{1}{2}spq}{1 - sq} \qquad \text{(Eqn 10.4)}$$

---

zero. If the equilibrium frequencies are denoted $\hat{p}$ and $\hat{q}$, at equilibrium $s_2\hat{q} = s_1\hat{p}$, but $\hat{p} = 1 - \hat{q}$, and so $s_2\hat{q} = s_1 + s_1\hat{q}$. This equation may be rearranged to Eqn 10.15 in the third column of Table 10.4, and shows that the equilibrium value of the allelic frequencies depends on the relative selection pressures against the two homozygote genotypes.

The remainder of the third column of Table 10.4 (Eqns 10.8 to 10.14) shows how the A_2 allele declines in frequency over many generations of selection in the various cases. Presently, we only have exact solutions when the A_2 allele is lethal (i.e. $s = 1$), and these are developed in Box 10.3 for Cases B and C. In Case D, the carriers of a lethal allele would all die, and the allele would be eliminated in a single generation. For lower selection pressures we integrate the numerators of Eqns 10.4 to 10.6, as outlined in Box 10.1 for Exp. 10.4, and

Box 10.3	Speed of evolutionary change with lethal alleles $(s = 1)$ in Cases B and C

Case B No dominance

	Genotypes			
	A_1A_1	A_1A_2	A_2A_2	Total population
Initial frequencies	p_0^2	$2p_0q_0$	q_0^2	1
Fitness	1	0.5	0	
Frequency after selection[a]	p_0^2	p_0q_0	0	$1 - q_0$

[a] Determination of total after selection: Total $= 1 - p_0q_0 - q_0^2$, or $1 - (1 - q_0)q_0 - q_0^2$ (as $p_0 = 1 - q_0$), which expands to $1 - q_0 + q_0^2 - q_0^2$ or $1 - q_0$.

The frequency of A_2 after one generation:

$$q_1 = \frac{\frac{1}{2}p_0q_0}{1 - q_0} \qquad \text{(Exp. 10.19)}$$

But $p_0 = (1 - q_0)$, therefore:

$$q_1 = \frac{\frac{1}{2}(1 - q_0)q_0}{1 - q_0} = \frac{1}{2}q_0 \qquad \text{(Exp. 10.20)}$$

Similarly,

$$q_2 = \frac{1}{2}q_1 = (\frac{1}{2})(\frac{1}{2})q_0 = 0.5^2 q_0 \qquad \text{(Exp. 10.21)}$$

Thus, the frequency of A_2 after t generations of selection is:

$$q_t = 0.5^t q_0 \qquad \text{(Eqn 10.9)}$$

which may be rearranged to estimate the number of generations to effect a given change in allelic frequency:

$$t = \frac{\ln(q_t/q_0)}{\ln 0.5} \qquad \text{(Eqn 10.10)}$$

Case C Complete dominance, selection against recessive

	Genotypes			
	A_1A_1	A_1A_2	A_2A_2	Total population
Initial frequencies	p_0^2	$2p_0q_0$	q_0^2	1
Fitness	1	1	0	
Frequency after selection	p_0^2	$2p_0q_0$	0	$1 - q_0^2$

The frequency of A_2 after one generation of selection is:

$$q_1 = \frac{\frac{1}{2}(2p_0q_0)}{1 - q_0^2} = \frac{p_0q_0}{(1 - q_0)(1 + q_0)} \qquad \text{(Exp. 10.22)}$$

But $p_0 = (1 - q_0)$, therefore:

$$q_1 = \frac{(1 - q_0)q_0}{(1 - q_0)(1 + q_0)} = \frac{q_0}{1 + q_0} \qquad \text{(Exp. 10.23)}$$

Similarly after two generations:

$$q_2 = \frac{q_1}{1 + q_1} = \frac{\frac{q_0}{1 + q_0}}{1 + \frac{q_0}{1 + q_0}} = \frac{q_0}{1 + 2q_0} \qquad \text{(Exp. 10.24)}$$

and after three generations of selection:

$$q_3 = \frac{q_0}{1 + 3q_0} \qquad \text{(Exp. 10.25)}$$

and so after t generations of selection:

$$q_t = \frac{q_0}{1 + tq_0} \qquad \text{(Eqn 10.12)}$$

Rearranging Eqn 10.12 to determine the number of generations to effect a given change in allelic frequency results in:

$$t = \frac{1}{q_t} - \frac{1}{q_0} \qquad \text{(Eqn 10.13)}$$

the resulting equations (10.8, 10.11 and 10.14) provide approximate solutions for the speed of selection.

We will show how to use these equations in the next chapter. Zygotic selection is simulated in Appendix 10.3, and the exercises there should aid your understanding of this type of selection, and help us make the following summary and conclusions.

10.4.1 Conclusions

1. Equations 10.4 to 10.7 show that the change in allelic frequency (Δq) is related to the selection coefficient, allelic frequency (q) and dominance in a complicated way. These relationships are illustrated in Fig. 10.3.

2. Where heterozygotes have the highest fitness (Case E), Δq is negative at high values of q and positive at low values of q Fig. 10.3b. This means that the allelic frequency will either increase or decrease to a stable equilibrium depending on the initial allelic frequency. Equation 10.15 predicts an equilibrium frequency ($\hat{q}$) of 0.4 when $s_1 = 0.2$ and $s_2 = 0.3$, and this is confirmed in Fig. 10.3b.

3. In Cases B, C and D, where one allele is favoured over another, the change in allelic frequency (Δq) is either exactly half (Case B) or approximately half (Cases C and D) that of haploid selection (compare Eqns 10.1 and 10.4). The shape of the curves (Fig. 10.3a) may be explained as follows. In Case C, where selection occurs against homozygous recessives, the recessive alleles in heterozygous individuals are protected against selection. Consequently, the greatest

Table 10.5 The number of generations (t) required to change the frequency of the favoured allele (p) by a given amount when the selection intensity, s, is 0.01. Values calculated by iteration from Eqns 10.4 to 10.6

Change in allelic frequency (p)		No dominance	Dominant favoured	Recessive favoured
From	To	(Case B)	(Case C)	(Case D)
0.001	0.01	459	231	90150
0.01	0.10	477	249	9 238
0.10	0.25	219	132	704
0.25	0.50	219	176	308
0.50	0.75	219	309	176
0.75	0.90	219	709	132
0.90	0.99	480	9 238	249
0.99	0.999	462	90 150	231

Source: After Crow (1986).

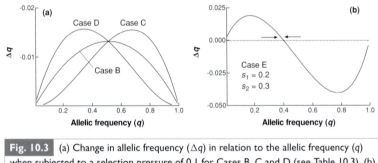

Fig. 10.3 (a) Change in allelic frequency (Δq) in relation to the allelic frequency (q) when subjected to a selection pressure of 0.1 for Cases B, C and D (see Table 10.3). (b) The change in allelic frequency (Δq) in relation to the allelic frequency (q) in the case of heterozygote superiority (Case E).

change in allelic frequencies occurs at high values of q where there is a greater proportion of recessive homozygotes in the population. In fact, Δq is at a maximum when $q = 0.67$ (Fig. 10.3a). In Case D, where selection is against the dominant, there is no protection against selection of the disadvantageous allele and so the maximum change in allelic frequencies occurs at low values of q when $q = 0.33$ (Fig. 10.3a). When there is no dominance (Case B), the maximum value of Δq occurs at an allelic frequency (q) of 0.5, as in gametic selection.

4. The approximate solutions to estimate the speed of evolutionary change (Eqns 10.8, 10.11 and 10.14 in Table 10.4) show that $s \times t$ is a function of the initial and final allelic frequencies. Consequently, the time (t) required to change the allelic frequency by a given amount is inversely related to the selection coefficient (s). Thus, if the selection pressure is doubled, it will halve the time required to change the allelic frequency by a given amount.

5. The speed of the directional changes in allelic frequencies in Cases B, C and D are shown in Fig. 10.4, and also in Table 10.5 where it is more obvious that Cases C and D are mirror images of each other.

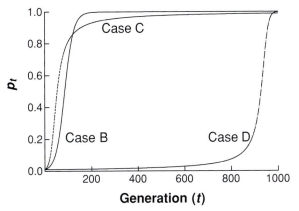

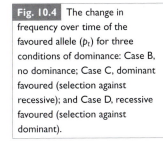

Fig. 10.4 The change in frequency over time of the favoured allele (p_t) for three conditions of dominance: Case B, no dominance; Case C, dominant favoured (selection against recessive); and Case D, recessive favoured (selection against dominant).

The allelic frequency of 0.001 in Table 10.5 seems quite low, but it only represents the occurrence of a single allele or mutation in a population of 500 individuals (remember that the number of alleles in a population is 2N). In a population of 100 000 individuals, a single favourable mutation would have a frequency of 0.000 005 and would increase even more slowly, particularly in Case D where the recessive is favoured.

6. The change in allelic frequencies is sigmoidal (Fig. 10.4), similar to haploid selection (Fig. 10.1b), and so the changes occur fastest at intermediate allelic frequencies. This illustrates Fisher's fundamental theorem of natural selection, which states that the rate of evolution (i.e. increase in fitness) is proportional to the genetic variance of the population (Fisher 1930). This makes intuitive sense, because if a population consists of mainly one type of allele there is little genetic variation for natural selection to work on and so it is difficult to change. However, if the alleles occur in equal numbers there is much more genetic variation, and if they differ in fitness selection can alter their frequency more easily. This is when $p = q = 0.5$ in haploid selection (Fig. 10.1a) and the increase in fitness of the population as a whole is illustrated in Fig. 10.2. The same is true for zygotic selection when there is no dominance (Case B, Fig. 10.3a), but where there is dominance the recessive allele has the same fitness as the dominant in the heterozygous state, and this distorts the curve so that the peak change is shifted to $q = 0.33$ or 0.67 (see point 3). Nevertheless, the change in allelic frequencies still follows Fisher's fundamental theorem.

7. The sigmoidal change in allelic frequencies when one allele is advantageous to another has two important results. First, the survival of an advantageous mutation is extremely precarious when it is at a low frequency in the population (see section 7.3), and this situation occurs for many generations, particularly when the favoured allele is recessive (Case D). Second, an advantageous allele is slow to become fixed in the population, particularly if it is dominant (Case C), and so a disadvantageous allele may be maintained in a population by relatively small opposing pressures of mutation or migration (gene flow).

10.5 | Using selection models

These models assume that allelic frequencies change as a result of selection on the gene in question, and not because of other forces, such as mutation, migration, genetic drift, or even selection on another gene that is linked to the gene we are observing. For this reason, the models are best used when the gene in question has a major effect on fitness, and other causes for changes in the allelic frequencies are trivial in comparison. We will see that this is frequently the case when we look at the application of the models in the next chapter.

Appendix 10.1 Derivation of haploid selection equations

The effects of haploid selection over many generations can be accurately predicted as follows. The formal derivation of Eqns 10.2 and 10.3 was developed by Jacek Banasiak, University of Natal, Durban.

In Box 10.1 we derived Eqn 10.1:

$$\Delta q = q_1 - q = \frac{-sq(1-q)}{1-sq} \tag{Eqn 10.1}$$

We can rewrite this equation in the form of a recurrence equation:

$$q_t - q_{t-1} = \frac{-sq_{t-1}(1-q_{t-1})}{1-sq_{t-1}} \tag{Exp. 10.5}$$

This simplifies to:

$$q_t = \frac{q_{t-1}(1-s)}{q_{t-1}(1-s) + 1 - q_{t-1}} \tag{Exp. 10.6}$$

As $W_B = (1-s)$, this is equivalent to:

$$q_t = \frac{q_{t-1}W_B}{q_{t-1}W_B + 1 - q_{t-1}} \tag{Exp. 10.7}$$

Introducing an unknown function (f_n) where:

$$q_t = \frac{f_t}{1+f_t} \tag{Exp. 10.8}$$

Substituting this in Exp. 10.7 gives:

$$\frac{f_t}{1+f_t} = \frac{\left(\dfrac{f_{t-1}}{1+f_{t-1}}\right)W_B}{\left(\dfrac{f_{t-1}}{1-f_{t-1}}\right)W_B + 1 - \left(\dfrac{f_{t-1}}{1+f_{t-1}}\right)} \tag{Exp. 10.9}$$

This simplifies to:

$$f_t = W_B f_{t-1} \tag{Exp. 10.10}$$

We can see from the development of Eqn 4.2 in Chapter 4 that this forms a geometric sequence with the solution:

$$f_t = W_B{}^t f_0 \tag{Exp. 10.11}$$

in which f_0 is the initial frequency of genotype B. If we rearrange Exp. 10.8 we can show that $f_t = q_t/(1 - q_t)$. Substituting this expression in Exp. 10.11 we obtain:

$$\frac{q_t}{1 - q_t} = W_B \left(\frac{q_0}{1 - q_0} \right) \qquad \text{(Exp. 10.12)}$$

Expression 10.12 simplifies to:

$$q_t = \frac{q_0 W_B{}^t}{1 - q_0 + q_0 W_B{}^t} \qquad \text{(Exp. 10.13)}$$

But $W_B = 1 - s$, and substituting this expression gives:

$$q_t = \frac{q_0(1 - s)^t}{1 - q_0 + q_0(1 - s)^t} \qquad \text{(Exp. 10.14)}$$

which simplifies to:

$$q_t = \frac{q_0}{q_0 + (1 - q_0)(1 - s)^t} \qquad \text{(Eqn 10.2)}$$

We can rearrange Eqn 10.2 to:

$$-[\ln (1 - s)]t = \ln \left[\frac{q_0(1 - q_t)}{q_t(1 - q_0)} \right] \qquad \text{(Exp. 10.15)}$$

which bears an obvious relationship to Exp. 10.4, in which the selection coefficient (s) is equal to $-[\ln(1 - s)]$ in Exp. 10.15. We may further simplify Exp. 10.15 to:

$$\ln [1 - s]t = \ln \left[\frac{q_t(1 - q_0)}{q_0(1 - q_t)} \right] \qquad \text{(Eqn 10.3)}$$

We should emphasize that Eqns 10.2 and 10.3 provide accurate estimates of q_t, s and t, whereas the more conventional Exps. 10.3 and 10.4 provide inaccurate estimates of these parameters.

Appendix 10.2 Simulating haploid selection

This simulation examines the predictions of the various equations to gain a better understanding of the process. Consider a simple situation where there are two genotypes, A and B, where genotype A quadruples each generation (i.e. $\lambda_A = 4$) and genotype B doubles each generation (i.e. $\lambda_B = 2$). As growth is geometric, we can simulate population sizes in future generations using Eqn 4.2. The two genotypes have a relative fitness of $W_A = 1.0$ (by definition), and $W_B = \lambda_B/\lambda_A = 2/4 = 0.5$. The selection coefficient against genotype B remains constant over time, and $s_B = 1 - W_B = 1 - 0.5 = 0.5$.

1. Open your spreadsheet and enter the title **Haploid Selection Model** in A1.
2. In row 3 of columns D and E type **Genotype A** and **Genotype B**. In row 4 type **Absolute Fitness (lambda)** = in column A, and enter the values **4** (for genotype A) and **2** (for genotype B) in columns D and E. In row 5 type **Selection coefficient (s_B)** = in column A, and enter the equation = **1 − E4/D4** in column E. This equation

represents $s_B = 1 - W_B$, where $W_B = \lambda_B/\lambda_A$. The value for the selection coefficient against genotype B should equal 0.5.

3. In rows 8 and 9 type the following headings in each column (you may have to alter column width): Column A: **Time** and **(t)**; column B: **# Genotype** and **A**; column C: **# Genotype** and **B**; column D: **Freq. of A** and **(p$_t$)**; column E: **Freq. of B** and **(q$_t$)**; column F: **delta q**; leave a blank column; column H: **ABS(delta q)** and **ABS (Eq.10.1)** (note we will be calculating the absolute value of Δq for the purposes of graphing); column I: **(q$_t$)** and **Eq. 10.2**; column J: **s$_B$** and **Eq. 10.3**; column K: **(q$_t$)** and **Exp. 10.3**; and in column L: **s$_B$** and **Exp. 10.4**. These last five columns are for the purpose of checking the predictions of the haploid selection models. Leave a blank column and in column N type **popn fitness** and **(lambda)**.

4. Next we simulate the growth of the two genotypes according to the laws of geometric growth and calculate the genotypic (or allelic) frequencies and the change in frequency from these data. Do the following:

   (a) In column A enter times from **0** to **20** in rows 10 to 30 (see step 5 in Box 4.1).

   (b) In column B enter a population size of **1** in B10; then type = **$B$10*$D$4^A11** in B11 and copy to cells B12 to B30. This equation is equivalent to Eqn 4.2.

   (c) Similarly, in column C enter a starting population size of **99** in C10; then type = **$C$10*$E$4^A11** in C11 and copy to cells C12 to C30.

   (d) In cell D10 type = **B10/(B10+C10)** and copy this cell to cells D11 to D30; and in cell E10 type = **C10/(B10+C10)** and copy this cell to cells E11 to E30. These formulae calculate the frequencies of genotype A (p) and genotype B (q).

   (e) In cell F10 type = **E11-E10** and copy this cell to cells F11 to F29. This calculates Δq.

5. We can now check to see if the various equations of haploid selection predict these observations. In columns H to L enter the following equations:

   (a) In H10 type = **$E$5*E10*(1-E10)/(1-$E$5*E10)** and copy to H11 to H30. This is equivalent to Eqn 10.1.

   (b) In I10 type = **$E$10/($E$10+(1-$E$10)*(1-$E$5)-A10)** and copy to cells I11 to I30. This is equivalent to Eqn 10.2.

   (c) In J11 type = **1-((E11*(1-$E$10)/($E$10*(1-E11)))^(1/A11)** and copy to cells J12 to J30. This is equivalent to Eqn 10.3 that has been rearranged to solve for s.

   (d) In K10 type = **$E$10/($E$10+(1-$E$10)*@EXP($E$5*A10))** and copy to cells K11 to K30. This is equivalent to Exp. 10.3.

   (e) In L11 type = **(@LN(($E$10*(1-E11))/(E11*(1-$E$10))))/A11** and copy to cells L12 to L30. This is equivalent to Exp. 10.4 that has been rearranged to solve for s.

6. If you have done step 5 correctly, the values of Δq in column H match the observed values in column F, except they are positive rather than negative; the values of q_t in column I equal the

observed values in column E; and the value of s_B in column J equals the value in E5. Systematically alter the value of λ_B in cell E4 and note that these relationships hold true in all cases. Thus, this haploid selection model provides exact solutions. Note, however, that the values in column K deviate more and more from the true values as the number of generations increases, and that the value in column L is equal to $-\ln(1 - s)$. Obviously, the approximation method, detailed in Box 10.1, gives poor predictions when s is large. Systematically alter the value of λ_B in cell E4, so that it approaches the value of cell D4, and note that the approximate values approach the true values as s decreases.

7. Finally in N10 type $=$ (B11+C11)/(B10+C10) and copy to cells N11 to N29. This calculates the multiplication rate, λ, for the population from one generation to the next, which is a measure of the overall fitness of the population.

8. We will now graph some of the relationships in order to understand the model a little better (see steps 9 and 10 in Appendix 4.1). The various graphs are discussed in the text.

   (a) First construct a graph of Δq (cells H10 . . H30) against q (the x-series is either E10 . . E30 or I10 . . I30). You should obtain a graph similar to Fig. 10.1a (set E4 to 2) which you can label in a similar way. Note that Δq is highest at intermediate values of q, although the curve is skewed slightly to the right with a peak at $q = 0.6$. If you progressively increase E4 from 2 to 3 you will see that the shape of the curve becomes more symmetrical with the peak Δq at $q = 0.5$.

   (b) Next graph the genotypic frequencies p_t (D10 . . D30) and q_t (E10 . . E30) against time (x-series is A10 . . A30). You should obtain a graph similar to Fig. 10.2. Note that the genotypic frequencies either increase or decrease sigmoidally. The genotypic frequency q_t is predicted by Eqn 10.2.

   (c) Finally, graph the overall multiplication rate or fitness, λ, of the population (N10 . . N29) against generation time (the x-series is A10 . . A29). You should obtain a graph similar to Fig. 10.2, which shows that fitness increases over time.

9. Close and save your simulation.

Appendix 10.3 Simulating zygotic selection

The purpose of this simulation exercise is to examine the predictions and relationships between the various equations listed in Table 10.4 in order to make some general conclusions about zygotic selection. The various conclusions are listed in section 10.4.1, and so you may wish to refer to this section once you have completed different stages of the simulation.

1. Open your spreadsheet and title your simulation.
2. First we will examine the relationship of Δq versus q. Enter the following:

In A4: **Selection coefficient against A_1A_1 genotype (s_1)** = and enter **0.2** in G4.

In A5: **Selection coefficient against A_2A_2 genotype (s_2)** = and enter **0.3** in G5.

In A6: **Selection coefficient against A_2 allele (s)** = and enter **0.1** in G6.

In A9: **Freq. A_2** and in B9: **Change in frequency of A_2 allele (delta q)**

In A10: **(q)** and in C10 to F10: **Case B, Case C, . . . , Case E**

3. Now make the following calculations:

   (a) In cells A11 to A31 enter allelic frequencies (q) of 0 to 1 in 0.05 increments.

   (b) In C11 type: = **(0.5*$G$6*(1-A11)*A11)/(1-$G$6*A11)** and copy C11 to cells C12 to C31. This represents Eqn 10.4.

   (c) In D11 type: = **($G$6*(1-A11)*A11^2)/(1-$G$6*A11^2)** and copy to cells D12 to D31. This represents Eqn 10.5

   (d) In E11 type: = **($G$6*(1-A11)^2*A11)/(1-2*$G$6 *A11 +$G$6* A11^2)** and copy to cells E12 to E31. This represents Eqn 10.6.

   (e) In F11 type = **((1-A11)*A11*($G$4*(1-A11)- $G$5*A11))/(1-$G$4 *(1-A11)^2 -$G$5*A11^2)** and copy to cells F12 to F31. This represents Eqn 10.7.

4. The equations in step 3 are equivalent to the equations in Table 10.4, but we have calculated the absolute values of Δq in Cases B to D by omitting the negative sign at the start of the relevant equations.

5. Graph the absolute values of Δq versus q for Cases B to D in the usual manner. The x-series is A11 . . A31 and your y-series are C11 . . C31; D11 . . D31 and E11 . . E31. Your graph should be similar to Fig. 10.3a. Make a similar graph for Case E, which should be similar to Fig. 10.3b. These relationships are discussed in section 10.3.2.

6. We will now examine the speed of evolutionary change. Enter the following:

   (a) In A35: **Starting allelic frequency (q_0)** = and enter the value **0.99** in cell D35.

   (b) In A36: **Selection coefficient (s)** = and enter the value **0.1** in cell D36.

   (c) In A38: **Generation**; in B38: **Allelic frequency (q_t)**; and in E38: **Allelic frequency (p_t)**

   (d) In A39: **(t)**; in B39 to D39: **Case B . . Case D**; and in E39 to G39: **Case B . . Case D.**

7. Now make the following calculations:

   (a) In column A enter times from 0 to 1000 in cells A40 to A1040. (Use an equation!)

   (b) Enter = **$D$35** in cells B40, C40 and D40 and = **1-B40 . . 1-D40** in cells E40 to G40. The entries in cells B40 to D40 are the q_0 values for Cases B to D, and the entries in cells E40 to G40 are the p_0 values because $p = (1 - q)$.

(c) Type: = **B40-(0.5*$D$36*E40*B40)/(1-$D$36*B40)** in B41; type = **C40-($D$36* F40*C40^2)/(1-$D$36*C40^2)** in C41; and type = **D40-($D$36*G40^2*D40)/(1-2*$D$36*D40+ $D$36*D40^2)** in D41. These formulae calculate the frequencies of the disadvantageous allele (q) for the first generation of Cases B, C and D, by combining the frequency of the allele in the starting generation with the value of Δq calculated by Eqns 10.4 to 10.6.

(d) Copy cells B41 . . D41 to B42 . . D1040 to calculate q_t values for 1000 generations of selection. Then copy cells E40 . . G40 to cells E41 . . G1040 to calculate the corresponding p_t values.

8. Make a graph of the p_t values versus generation time (t) where the x-axis is A40 . . A1040, and the y-axes are E40 . . E1040, F40 . . F1040 and G40 . . G1040. The resulting graph should resemble Fig. 10.4. You will see that the speed of incorporation of a favoured allele (p_t) is varies greatly for the different cases of dominance. This is discussed further in section 10.4.1. Change the initial frequency of q_0 from 0.99 to 0.995 and note that there is almost no change in the allelic frequencies in Case D. Now progressively reduce q_0 and see that the favoured allele is fixed more and more rapidly, until at $q_0 = 0.8$ it is most rapidly fixed in Case D. You can also affect the speed of change by altering the value of s. Return to your original values of 0.99 for q_0 and 0.1 for s.

9. To determine the utility of the approximation equations in Table 10.5 do the following:

(a) Type: **Case B** in I60, **Case C** in J60, **Case D** in K60, and **true value** in L60.

(b) Type: **st =** in H61, **s =** in H62, **t =** in H63; then = **$D$36** in L62 and **100** in L63.

(c) Type = **2*@LN(B40*E140/(B140*E40))** in I61; = **(C40-C140)/(C40*C140)+ @LN (C40*F140/(C140*F40))** in J61; and = **(D40-D140)/(G140*G40)+ @LN(D40 *G140/(D140*G40))** in K61. These formulas represent Eqns 10.8, 10.11 and 10.14 in Table 10.4.

(d) Finally, type: = **I61/$L$63** in I62 and copy to cells J62 and K62, and type = **I61/$L$62** in I63 and copy to cells J63 and K63.

(e) You will see that the estimates are approximately 4–11% in error when $s = 0.1$, but if we reduce s to 0.01 the error is <1%.

10. Now save and close your spreadsheet.

Chapter 11

Applying zygotic selection models to natural systems

Before we can apply the range of equations describing zygotic selection to natural populations, we must be able to estimate the fitness of the different genotypes. This can be difficult to do in practice.

11.1 Estimating fitness and selection

We will consider three basic methods of calculating fitness for natural populations. A more complete discussion of these and some additional methods may be found in Johnson (1976).

11.1.1 Direct calculation of partial-generation selection coefficients

Frequently, survival or viability is measured over part of the life cycle. If we use this information to estimate fitness for our selection model, we assume that the other components of fitness, such as number of viable offspring, are the same for the different genotypes. In other words, we are assuming that the coefficients we calculate for part of the life cycle, i.e. the partial-generation coefficients, are the same as those for the full life cycle (full-generation coefficients). It should be recognized that these estimates are only approximations.

Example 11.1 *A sample of newly weaned mice was marked just prior to the winter, and the following spring, when they had reached reproductive age, they were live-trapped to estimate their pre-reproductive survival. Other evidence suggested that the different genotypes did not differ in their fertility or fecundity during their brief reproductive lives. Calculate the relative fitness and selection coefficients of the different genotypes from the following data.*

Phenotype	Long tail	Medium tail	Short tail	
Genotype	A_1A_1	A_1A_2	A_2A_2	Total
No. weaned	25	50	25	100
No. reproducing	20	30	10	60

We can directly calculate the survival rates from birth to reproductive age for each genotype as follows: $A_1A_1 = 20/25 = 0.8$, $A_1A_2 = 30/50 = 0.6$, and $A_2A_2 = 10/25 = 0.4$. The genotype with the highest survival rate has the highest absolute fitness and so the relative fitness and selection coefficients for the different genotypes can be calculated directly. Relative fitness: $W_{A_1A_1} = 0.8/0.8 = 1$, $W_{A_1A_2} = 0.6/0.8 = 0.75$, $W_{A_2A_2} = 0.4/0.8 = 0.5$. Selection coefficients: $s_{A_1A_1} = 1- W_{A_1A_1} = 0$, $s_{A_1A_2} = 1- W_{A_1A_2} = 0.25$, $s_{A_2A_2} = 1- W_{A_2A_2} = 0.5$.

Thus, short-tailed mice only have half the chance of reaching reproductive age compared to long-tailed mice, and mice with medium-length tails. This corresponds to Case B where there is no dominance with respect to fitness.

Example 11.2 *Bishop (1972) estimated daily death rates and survival rates for two phenotypes of the peppered moth (Biston betularia) by placing frozen moths on their natural resting sites on tree trunks and observing the number eaten by birds after one day of exposure. At one locality, Sefton Park, 42 of the 56 carbonaria phenotype survived for one day, whereas only 39 of the 56 typica phenotype survived over the same time period. What is the relative fitness of typica to carbonaria?*

The daily survivorship of adults is estimated to be 39/56, or 0.6964, for *typica* and 42/56, or 0.75, for *carbonaria*. Thus, the relative fitness of *typica* to *carbonaria* would appear to be 0.6964/0.75, or 0.9286. However, the true relative fitness of the two phenotypes is not calculated as simply as this. If we follow the number of survivors of the two phenotypes, assuming constant daily survival rates of 0.6964 for *typica* and 0.75 for *carbonaria*, we find that the ratio of the two morphs varies over time as follows:

Time (days)	0	1	2	3
Surviving *typica*	56	39	27.16	18.92
Surviving *carbonaria*	56	42	31.50	23.63
Ratio of survivors	1.0	0.9286	0.8622	0.8007

If we had measured their survival over two days instead of one day the ratio would have been 0.8622, rather than 0.9286, and so the relative fitness appears to be declining with time. What do we do? If the daily survival rates are constant, the adult populations decline exponentially (Fig. 11.1a). In Chapter 4 we noted that exponential series are linear when the logarithm of the numbers is plotted versus time, and this is true for our survivorship series (Fig. 11.1b). The ratio of the two slopes provides us with the true measure of relative survival rates (they are actually instantaneous survival rates analogous to our r_m values in exponential growth). Thus, the relative fitness of *typica* to *carbonaria* is actually $-0.2877/-0.3618$, or 0.795 (Fig. 11.1b). Fortunately, there is a simpler way of calculating this. The relative fitness is provided by the ratio of the natural logarithms of the two survival rates (i.e. $\ln(0.75)/\ln(0.6964) = -0.2877/-0.3618 = 0.795$). We would

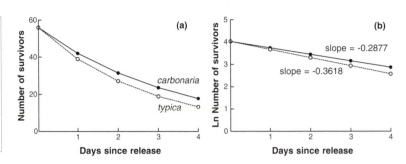

Fig. 11.1 The number of survivors each day after release of 56 *typica* and 56 *carbonaria* forms of the peppered moth (*Biston betularia*) where the daily survival rate is 0.6964 for *typica* and 0.75 for *carbonaria*. (a) On an arithmetic scale, and (b) on a logarithmic scale.

have obtained the same value if we had estimated the survival rates over two or more days, and you may check this by using the values for different days in the table above (there will be some minor fluctuations because of rounding errors in the calculation of numbers of survivors).

Thus, the true adult survival rate of adult *typica* is only 79.5% that of adult *carbonaria*, and the selection coefficient against *typica* is $1 - W$, which is $1 - 0.795 = 0.205$. If we assume that the different genotypes have equal fecundity, and equal egg and larval survival rates, the adult survival rates provide an approximation of the fitness of the different genotypes and phenotypes.

11.1.2 Indirect calculation of fitness using Hardy–Weinberg ratios

This approach is best used when we can measure the proportions or numbers of the different genotypes from one generation to the next. We use the Hardy–Weinberg law to allow for the effects of recombination, assuming random mating. A simple example will make this clear.

Example 11.3 *The following data were collected for a population of annual flowers in two successive years. Calculate the relative fitness of the three genotypes.*

Phenotype (flower colour) Genotype	Red $R_1 R_1$	Pink $R_1 R_2$	White $R_2 R_2$	Total
Number in year 1	270	410	180	860
Number in year 2	350	444	180	974

1. First calculate the allelic frequencies in the first year. The frequency of the red allele (p) is $(270 + \frac{1}{2}(410))/860$, or 0.5523, and the frequency of the white allele (q) is $1 - p$, or 0.4477.
2. Then calculate the expected numbers of different flower colours in the second year, assuming they are in Hardy–Weinberg equilibrium (i.e. random mating).
   Red $= p^2 \times$ total year 2 $= (0.5523)^2 \times 974 = 297.13$
   Pink $= 2pq \times$ total year 2 $= 2 \times 0.5523 \times 0.4477 \times 974 = 481.67$
   White $= q^2 \times$ total year 2 $= (0.4477)^2 \times 974 = 195.20$

3. We can now calculate the true multiplication rates, λ, for the different genotypes by comparing the observed numbers to the expected numbers calculated in step 2.

Red $\lambda_{R_1 R_1}$ = Observed/Expected = 350/297.13 = 1.1779
Pink $\lambda_{R_1 R_2}$ = 444/481.67 = 0.9218
White $\lambda_{R_2 R_2}$ = 180/195.20 = 0.9221

4. It is now a simple matter to calculate the relative fitness of each genotype:

Red $W_{R_1 R_1}$ = 1.0 (by definition, because it has the highest λ)
Pink $W_{R_1 R_2}$ = 0.9218/1.1779 = 0.7826
White $W_{R_2 R_2}$ = 0.9221/1.1779 = 0.7828

We can make three observations about this example. First, it approximates to a Case D selection model, where there is selection against the dominant allele (see Table 10.2). The white allele is dominant with respect to fitness because white and pink individuals have approximately the same fitness. Selection is against the dominant because the fitness of these two genotypes is lower than that of red individuals. Second, we see in this example that dominance with respect to fitness is different than that with respect to flower colour (where there is no dominance). This is an example of pleiotropy. In our selection models we are only concerned about dominance with respect to fitness. Third, if we had simply calculated the growth rates of the different genotypes without allowing for the effects of random breeding between genotypes, we would have obtained erroneous results (λ for red flowers = 350/270 = 1.2963, λ for pink flowers = 444/410 = 1.0829, and λ for white flowers = 180/180 = 1.0).

A cautionary note

Great care must be taken if this method is used to calculate partial-generation coefficients. In Example 11.1, we had the following data:

Genotype	$A_1 A_1$	$A_1 A_2$	$A_2 A_2$	Total
Number weaned	25	50	25	100
Number after selection	20	30	10	60

We can calculate the relative fitness of the different genotypes using genotypic frequencies as follows:

Genotype	$A_1 A_1$	$A_1 A_2$	$A_2 A_2$
Frequency at birth	0.25	0.5	0.25
Frequency after selection	0.333	0.5	0.167
Absolute fitness, λ	1.333	1.0	0.667
Relative fitness, W	1.0	0.75	0.5

These are all simple direct calculations because we do not have to allow for any recombination between genotypes when we are only considering survival. You will note that we obtain the same estimates as in Example 11.1.

Now imagine instead that we only had frequency data after selection, and had assumed that before selection the genotypic frequencies were in Hardy–Weinberg equilibrium. We would calculate the allelic frequencies (A_1 (p) = 0.5833 and A_2 (q) = 0.4167), and then calculate the expected Hardy–Weinberg genotypic frequencies based on this information (i.e. $A_1A_1 = p^2$, $A_1A_2 = 2pq$ and $A_2A_2 = q^2$. Our results would be as follows:

Genotype	A_1A_1	A_1A_2	A_2A_2
Observed frequency	0.333	0.5	0.167
Expected (H–W) frequency	0.3403	0.4861	0.1736
λ = observed/expected	0.9796	1.0286	0.96
Relative fitness, W	0.9524	1.0	0.9333

This suggests heterozygote superiority (Case E), even though selection only occurred against the A_2 allele. What have we done incorrectly? The expected Hardy–Weinberg frequencies were calculated assuming that the allelic frequencies were the same as those occurring before selection, but p prior to selection was 0.5 whereas after selection it was 0.5833. This difference in frequency leads us to erroneous conclusions. We can only apply this method to partial-generation data if the allelic frequencies remain the same before and after selection, i.e. are in equilibrium, and this only occurs when there truly is heterozygote superiority.

11.1.3 Calculating selection over many generations using selection models.

In this method we observe a systematic change in phenotypic or genotypic frequencies over a known number of generations. We then apply the appropriate model from Chapter 10 and use it to calculate the average selection coefficient, and hence fitness, of the various genotypes.

Example 11.4 *A snail with an annual life cycle has either brown or green shells in which brown is completely dominant to green. Over a prolonged period of drought the frequency of green-shelled snails is observed to decrease from about 81% of the population to 49% over a period of five years. What is the relative fitness of green- to brown-shelled snails?*

We can represent this information as follows:

Phenotype	Brown		Green
Genotype	BB	Bb	bb
Initial frequency		0.19	0.81
Frequency after five generations		0.51	0.49

Selection is occurring against green snails because they are declining in frequency. Thus, the green allele has a frequency of q. As green is the homozygous recessive genotype, its frequency is q^2 according to the Hardy–Weinberg equilibrium. Consequently, we can estimate the initial allelic frequency, q_0, as $\sqrt{0.81} = 0.9$, and q_t after five generations as $\sqrt{0.49} = 0.7$.

Selection is occurring against the recessive, and so it is most likely that we have Case C – complete dominance, selection against the recessive. We can use Eqn 10.11 (see Table 10.3) to obtain an approximate solution for s. If we substitute the values for q_0 and q_t that we have derived, we obtain: $s \times 5 = 0.3175 + 1.3499$, and so the selection coefficient (s) is approximately 0.3335. The relative fitness of green to brown snails is, therefore, $1 - s$, or 0.6665.

Note, that when you apply any of the models applying to Cases B, C or D then q_0 must be larger than q_t. If it is not, then you have made a mistake somewhere.

11.2 | The application of zygotic selection models to natural selection

Examples of natural selection abound in nature. We will look at four examples to show how the single-locus zygotic selection models can shed light on the process of natural selection. The various equations are found in Table 10.4.

11.2.1 Industrial melanism

One of the most thoroughly studied cases of evolutionary change involves an evolutionary response by a whole variety of insects and spiders to man-made pollution from the burning of coal. The smoke changed the colour of tree trunks from a general light colour to a dark brown because of the deposition of soot and the killing of the light-coloured crustose and foliose lichens by sulphur dioxide. In response, many insects and spider populations changed over time from a light body colour to a dark melanic form, a process called industrial melanism. It is significant that many species exhibiting this type of response rely on their cryptic coloration to avoid predation. The various species tend to rest in exposed places during the day and so are vulnerable to predation.

The best-studied case of industrial melanism involves the peppered moth (*Biston betularia*) which is common in England (Fig. 11.2). Prior to the Industrial Revolution, during the eighteenth and nineteenth centuries the common form of this moth had a light speckled coloration, called *typica*. The first known melanic form, called *carbonaria*, was caught at an unknown locality prior to 1811 and exists in a collection at Oxford University. Another *carbonaria* was collected in 1848 in Manchester by a local lepidopterist and is the only *carbonaria* in his collection, so we can assume that this form of the moth was rare at that time because insect collectors prize unusual varieties. The melanic form increased rapidly in frequency in the Manchester area, until by 1890, it made up more than 90% of the population. This dark form of the moth appeared to spread by migration from

Fig. 11.2 Two peppered moths (*Biston betularia*) rest on the dark bark of a tree in a highly polluted area near Liverpool (top) and on the light-coloured, lichen coated bark of a tree in an unpolluted area of rural Wales (below). The melanic, or *carbonaria*, form is better camouflaged in polluted areas and the light, or *typica*, form is better camouflaged in unpolluted areas. (From Bishop and Cook 1975, with permission.)

the Manchester area and rapidly became the dominant type in the industrial areas of Britain.

Work by Mendelian geneticists established that body and wing colour were controlled by a single gene with multiple alleles. The *typica* form is a pale speckled colour, which blends well with many lichens. It is recessive to a series of darker speckled forms, called *insularia*, which are relatively rare and tend to occur in slightly polluted areas. Finally, the coal-black *carbonaria* is dominant to all other forms. In the following account we will ignore the *insularia* forms and discuss the evolution of industrial melanism in *B. betularia* as though it only involved two alleles: *carbonaria* which is dominant to *typica*.

In 1924, J. B. S. Haldane (one of the major theoreticians in population genetics along with Ronald Fisher in England and Sewall Wright in the United States) showed that there must have been a strong selection pressure to cause such a rapid change in the frequencies of the *carbonaria* and *typica* morphs. He estimated that the frequency of *carbonaria* in the Manchester area had changed from about 1% in 1848 to 99% in 1898, i.e. had changed from being rare to almost the entire population in about a 50-year period. This change had occurred in 50 generations because there is only a single generation of the moth each year. We can follow Haldane's approach by laying out the available information as follows:

Phenotype	*carbonaria*	*typica*	
Genotype	CC Cc	cc	
Frequency in 1848	1% = 0.01	0.99 = q_0^2	$q_0 = (\sqrt{0.99}$ or 0.995)
Frequency in 1898	99% = 0.99	0.01 = q_t^2	$q_t = (\sqrt{0.01}$ or 0.10)

Selection is occurring against the recessive allele because the frequency of *typica* is declining over time. Haldane reasoned that the change in allelic frequencies corresponded to a case of complete dominance with selection against the recessive (Case C in our system), and so could use an equation equivalent to Eqn 10.11 to obtain an approximate estimate of the selection coefficient, *s*, against the *typica* allele. When the appropriate values of q_0, q_t and *t* are inserted in Eqn 10.11, we have:

$$s \times 50 = \frac{0.995 - 0.1}{0.995 \times 0.1} + \ln\left[\frac{0.995(1 - 0.1)}{0.1(1 - 0.995)}\right]$$

The solution is $s = 0.3297$, and the relative fitness of *typica* to *carbonaria* (*W*) is $(1 - s)$, or approximately 0.67.

For those who are interested in historical accuracy, Haldane used a variant of this model in which the relative fitness of *typica* = 1.0, and the relative fitness of the *carbonaria* was $1 + s$. Thus he considered the change in allelic frequencies to be a result of the relative advantage of *carbonaria* rather than the disadvantage of *typica*. This is easily calculated as the reciprocal of our estimate of the relative fitness of *typica*, i.e. $1/0.67 = 1.4925$, or approximately a 50% advantage of the *carbonaria* form.

Haldane's estimate of selection appeared to have little impact on the thinking of evolutionary biologists and population geneticists over the next three decades. The general assumption was that selection coefficients were small, of the order of 0.001, and that evolutionary changes occurred slowly. The other problem was that Haldane did not know the reason for the change in body colour in the peppered moth.

Approximately 30 years later, Kettlewell (1955, 1956) reported the results of field experiments on the survival of adult *B. betularia* in a polluted wood near Birmingham and a non-polluted wood in Dorset, England. He released marked individuals of both morphs, and then with the aid of light traps recaptured as many as possible a few days later (Table 11.1). His results showed that there was a strong

Table 11.1 Results of field experiments on the survival of adult *Biston betularia*

		carbonaria	*typica*
Polluted wood near Birmingham	Released	154	64
	Recaptured	82	16
	Survival rate	0.5325	0.25
	W (no correction)	1	0.4695
	s (no correction)	0	0.5305
	W (corrected)[a]	1	0.4546
	s (corrected)	0	0.5454
Non-polluted wood in Dorset	Released	473	496
	Recaptured	30	62
	Survival rate	0.0634	0.1250
	W (no correction)	0.5074	1
	s (no correction)	0.4926	0
	W (corrected)[a]	0.7540	1
	s (corrected)	0.2460	0

[a]Corrected values calculated from the ratio of the logarithm of survival rates (see Example 11.2).
Source: Kettlewell (1956).

selection for *carbonaria* and against *typica* in polluted areas and a strong selection for *typica* and against *carbonaria* in non-polluted areas. Moreover, he observed that differential survival of the two morphs was linked to differential predation of the resting moths by various species of birds. These birds mainly ate the less cryptic moths, i.e. the pale *typica* in polluted areas and the black *carbonaria* in unpolluted areas.

Initially his results were greeted with scepticism. Evolutionists 'knew' that selection coefficients were much lower than he had estimated, ornithologists did not believe that birds were capable of eating the numbers of moths that Kettlewell claimed, and lepidopterists had never observed birds eating cryptic moths in the wild. Undeterred, Kettlewell repeated his experiments and, with the help of Niko Tinbergen, filmed birds eating the resting moths. He quickly converted the sceptics into believers.

Kettlewell and other researchers have mapped the distribution of the different morphs in different areas of Britain (Fig. 11.3), and showed that *carbonaria* was largely confined to the polluted industrial areas and that *typica* was most common in the rural, unpolluted areas. The discrepancy of *carbonaria* being the most common form in the rural areas of Norfolk and Lincolnshire was explained by the fact that these areas were downwind of the industrial Midlands.

The distribution of melanic moths is not entirely predicted by differential predation by birds. For example, *carbonaria* used to make up at least 95% of the population in the industrial Liverpool–Manchester area of north-western England, and the percentage of this form declined as one proceeded to the south-west into unpolluted areas

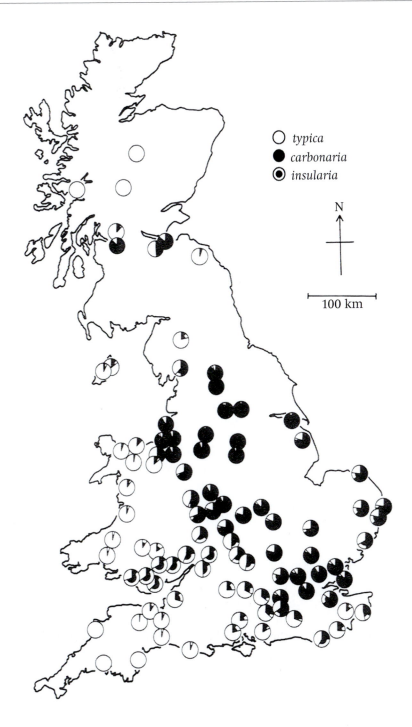

○ *typica*
● *carbonaria*
◉ *insularia*

N

100 km

Fig. 11.3 Frequencies of the different morphs of the peppered moth (*Biston betularia*) at various localities in Britain. (Reprinted from *Genetic Consequences of Man-Made Change* (eds. J. A. Bishop and L. M. Cook), Lees, D. R. Industrial melanism: genetic adaptation of animals to air pollution, pp. 129–76, Copyright 1981, with permission from Elsevier Science.)

of Wales (Fig. 11.3). The fitness of *typica* relative to *carbonaria*, at various points along this cline, was calculated from the differential survival of adult moths as a result of bird predation (Bishop 1972; see Example 11.2). The expected distribution of the two morphs did not fit the observed distribution along this cline (Fig. 11.4). There are two discrepancies: first, *typica* should have been eliminated from the

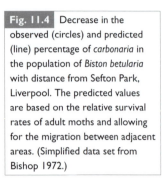

Fig. 11.4 Decrease in the observed (circles) and predicted (line) percentage of *carbonaria* in the population of *Biston betularia* with distance from Sefton Park, Liverpool. The predicted values are based on the relative survival rates of adult moths and allowing for the migration between adjacent areas. (Simplified data set from Bishop 1972.)

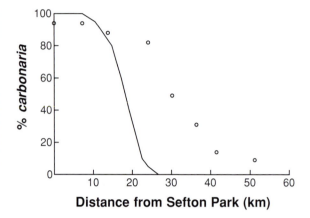

industrial areas of Liverpool and Manchester because selection is so strong, and secondly, *carbonaria* was much more frequent than expected in the non-polluted areas.

It is possible that migration might explain why *typica* was not eliminated from the industrial areas, because a few adult males migrate several kilometres and the industrial areas are downwind from the non-polluted areas making immigration of *typica* more likely. We can use our models of selection and migration to help us assess the likelihood of this factor being responsible for the maintenance of *typica* in industrial areas. If *typica* stabilizes at a frequency of 0.04 (i.e. 4%) in Sefton Park, we can calculate its expected reduction in frequency over one generation of selection by using Eqn 11.2 (i.e. Case C – complete dominance, selection against the recessive). This decrease should be balanced by an increase in the frequency of the *typica* allele resulting from immigration, given by Exp. 9.2, if this factor is solely responsible for maintaining the frequency of *typica* at 0.04 in the population. Thus:

$$\frac{spq^2}{1 - sq^2} = m(q_m - q_0) \tag{Exp. 11.1}$$

The selection coefficient (s) against *typica* in this locality was calculated as 0.205 (see Example 11.2). The frequency of the *typica* allele (q) is $\sqrt{0.04}$, or 0.2, which is also the frequency (q_0) because it has stabilized in the population, and $p = 1-q$, or 0.8. The allelic frequency of migrants (q_m) is estimated by assuming that 10% of the migrants are *typica*, because most areas within 10 km of Sefton Park have at least 90% *carbonaria*. So q_m is $\sqrt{0.1}$, or 0.3162. If we substitute these values in Exp. 11.1, we can calculate the migration rate, m, that would be required to maintain this balance. Thus:

$$\frac{0.205 \times (1 - 0.2) \times 0.2^2}{1 - 0.205 \times 0.2^2} = m(0.3162 - 0.2)$$

This gives us an estimate of $m = 0.057$, which suggests that a migration rate of close to 6% would be required to maintain *typica* at an equilibrium frequency of 4% in the population. However, estimates of migration rates using mark-and-recapture methods are of the order of 1% or 2%, and so although migration may play a role, it is unlikely to be the only factor involved.

It is also possible that heterozygote superiority might account for the maintenance of *typica* in polluted areas, because there is some experimental evidence that heterozygotes survive better than homozygotes during the larval stage of development. We can assess the effect of this factor by considering a general model of selection in polluted areas as follows:

Phenotype	*carbonaria*		*typica*
Genotype	CC	Cc	cc
Relative fitness (bird predation)	1	1	$1 - s$
Relative fitness (larval survival), $1 - s_1$	$1 - s_1$	1	$1 - s_1$
Overall fitness	$1 - s_1$	1	$1 - s_2$
			(where $s_2 = s + s_1$)

Selection coefficients acting on different stages of the life cycle are additive, and so can be combined to obtain an estimate of overall fitness of the different genotypes. The situation conforms to Case E, described by Eqn 10.15, in which the equilibrium frequency ($\hat{q}$) is 0.2, selection as a result of bird predation (s) is 0.205, as noted previously. If we substitute these values in Eqn 10.15, we can obtain an estimate of s_1:

$$0.2 = \frac{s_1}{s_1 + (0.205 + s_1)}$$

Thus, s_1 is 0.068, which corresponds well to the estimates of heterozygote advantage, of between 5% and 15%, determined by Clarke and Sheppard (1966). Consequently, it is quite possible that heterozygote superiority maintained *typica* at a low frequency in industrial areas.

Toward the other end of the cline, *carbonaria* occurred much more frequently then expected (Fig. 11.4). Migration is unlikely to be important in maintaining this discrepancy because *carbonaria* would be migrating against the prevailing winds. Similarly, if we consider our general model of heterozygote superiority:

Phenotype	*carbonaria*		*typica*
Genotype	CC	Cc	cc
Relative fitness (bird predation)	$1 - s$	$1 - s$	1
Relative fitness (larval survival)	$1 - s_1$	1	$1 - s_1$
Overall fitness	$1 - s_2$	$1 - s$	$1 - s_1$

We can see that s_1 must be larger than s in order for heterozygotes to be at an advantage, otherwise *typica* would have an overall fitness equal to, or greater than, the heterozygotes. However, the selection coefficient against *carbonaria* (s) resulting from differential bird predation was as high as 0.55 at some localities on the cline, and so it is extremely unlikely that differential larval survival (s_1) is of this magnitude. Consequently, *carbonaria* is not maintained in non-polluted areas by heterozygote superiority.

So how is *carbonaria* maintained in some non-polluted areas in the face of an apparent strong selection by birds? The most likely explanation is that the method of calculating selection pressures, by observing the relative adult survival of the two phenotypes on exposed tree trunks, is too simplistic. This treats the environment as if it is uniform, and assumes that all moths select the same resting sites. Thus, in unpolluted areas it is as if all of the resting places for moths are light in colour. This is not the case. It has been shown that moths placed in the shaded area below a branch have a better chance of survival than those placed in exposed areas of the tree trunk (Majerus 1998), and this difference in survival is especially marked for *carbonaria*. Thus, there are resting sites in unpolluted areas where the melanic forms are cryptic. If the moths tended to select the appropriate patches in which to rest, we could have frequency-dependent selection. For example, if the ratio of dark to light resting places was 5:95, we might expect *carbonaria* to comprise 5% and *typica* 95%, of the population. Selection against *carbonaria* would vary according to its frequency in the population, in relation to the availability of suitable cryptic resting sites. Majerus (1998) suggested that the selection of resting sites by moths needs to be studied to understand, and better estimate, the predation selection pressure against the different-coloured adults.

Finally, the overall pattern of the distribution of the two moths has changed dramatically over the last few decades. During the 1950s, the government enacted legislation to introduce smokeless fuels to decrease air pollution. The once grimy, dark industrial regions have slowly changed. No longer is soot covering the trees, and the regrowth of lichens is favouring the pale-coloured forms even in industrial areas. For example, in one garden area in West Kirby, just outside Liverpool, 93% of the population of peppered moths was black in 1959, but the proportion had reduced to 84% by 1976 and to 33% by 1990. We can determine the approximate selection pressures involved as follows:

Phenotype	*carbonaria*	*typica*
Genotype	CC Cc	cc
Frequency 1959	0.93	$0.07 = p^2$ Thus, $p = 0.2646$ and $q = 0.7354$
Frequency 1976	0.84	$0.16 = p^2$ Thus, $p = 0.4$ and $q = 0.6$
Frequency 1990	0.33	$0.67 = p^2$ Thus, $p = 0.8185$ and $q = 0.1815$

We can see that selection is occurring against the *carbonaria* allele (C) which has a frequency of q (in our models the inferior allele always has a frequency of q). The expected Hardy–Weinberg frequency of the *carbonaria* genotype is $q^2 + 2pq$ and so q cannot be solved for directly. The *typica* genotype has a frequency of p^2, which allows us to estimate the frequency of p, and hence q (because $q = 1 - p$). The situation conforms to Case D (complete dominance, selection against the dominant) and so we can use Eqn 10.14 to obtain approximate estimates of s. Our estimates of selection against *carbonaria* are 0.1115 from 1959 to 1976, 0.2279 from 1976 to 1990, and an overall value of 0.164 from 1959 to 1990. We would anticipate that selection would be slow at first, and then accelerate as the effects of the clean-up of the environment became more and more evident, and these estimates are consistent with this observation.

In summary, air pollution during the Industrial Revolution changed the colour of tree trunks from a light colour to black. Moths, like *B. betularia*, responded genetically to these changes during the nineteenth century. A black mutant phenotype, called *carbonaria*, rapidly became the most common form in industrial areas, while the light *typica* phenotype maintained its predominance in non-polluted areas. It was believed initially that these changes were the result of differential selection by birds, which preferentially ate light-coloured moths in industrial areas and dark-coloured moths in unpolluted areas, and simple selection models were used to analyse these changes. Further studies have revealed that the genetic changes are more complex than this, and that migration and larval survival might also be important. Clean-air legislation has reduced the level of air pollution to the extent that the *typica* phenotype is now favoured even in industrial areas. If present trends continue, the moth population will conform to the situation that was once found in pre-industrial times.

11.2.2 Sickle-cell anaemia

We saw in Chapter 7 (section 7.1) that the S form of haemoglobin, resulting from a single point mutation from the 'normal' A form of haemoglobin, produces drastic consequences. The majority of the homozygous SS individuals die an early death from a complex of disorders, known as sickle-cell anaemia, whereas heterozygous AS individuals are resistant to malaria. Haemoglobin S exists in a balanced polymorphism with 'normal' haemoglobin A, in areas of endemic malaria such as tropical Africa.

The selective forces involved in maintaining this polymorphism may be calculated from data provided by Allison (1956), who screened 287 infants and 654 adults in an area of Tanzania (Table 11.2). Ideally, infants would be screened at birth, and the survival of those same individuals would be followed to adulthood. However, dividing the adult by the infant genotypic frequencies gives a measure of differential survival, and hence fitness, of the different genotypes. It is a simple matter to calculate the relative fitness of each genotype, assuming that the different genotypes are equally fertile. This is unlikely, but

Table 11.3 | Frequency of haemoglobin genotypes in Tanzania and calculations of their fitness

	Genotype			Total	Frequency of S allele
	AA	AS	SS		
Number of infants	189	89	9	287	
Number of adults	400	249	5	654	
Frequency in infants	0.6585	0.3101	0.0314		0.1864
Frequency in adults	0.6116	0.3807	0.0076		0.1980
Absolute fitness	0.9288	1.2277	0.2420		
Relative fitness	0.7565	1	0.1971		
Selection coefficient	$s_1 = 0.2435$		$s_2 = 0.8029$		

Source: Allison (1956).

we will ignore the problem here. The situation conforms to Case E – heterozygote superiority, in which there is a strong selection against homozygous SS due to complications arising from sickle-cell anaemia (see Chapter 7), and a smaller selection against homozygous AA resulting from the effects of malaria. This results in a stable polymorphism in which the frequencies of the two alleles and the three genotypes remain constant from generation to generation.

A stable polymorphism will only be maintained in the presence of malaria. There is no malaria in North America, where Africans were transported as slaves, and the incidence of sickle-cell anaemia has been reduced. After ten generations there has been about a 7% decrease in the S or Hb^S allele each generation (see Table 9.1). Probably a decrease of about 1–2% per generation is a result of migration of Caucasian alleles into the African-American population (see Chapter 9), but the majority of the reduction is undoubtedly the result of strong selection against the S allele.

11.2.3 Eugenics

It is tempting to believe that one can improve the fitness of human populations by preventing those with deleterious genetic traits from having offspring. This type of policy is misguided, not only because it involves a clash between individual and societal rights, but because the results are simply not worth the effort involved, as the following fictitious example should make clear.

Example 11.5 *A dictator of a small country is angered to learn that there is one four-toed individual for every 10 000 people in what he considers to be his genetically superior nation. He orders that all four-toed individuals must be sterilized at birth and asks his Minister of Health to inform him when the incidence drops to below one in 1 000 000 people, at which point it would effectively be eliminated from his nation. How long would this take, knowing that the trait for four-toes in humans is controlled by a single recessive gene, and that there are approximately four generations per century?*

The incidence of the four-toed trait is one per 10 000 ($= 10^{-4}$), which is q_0^2, and the target frequency is one per 1 000 000 (10^{-6}) which is q_t^2. The dictator has made the four-toed genotype lethal, i.e. $s = 1$, and so we need to solve Eqn 10.2 in order to solve for the number of generations (t). Thus:

$$t = \frac{1}{q_t} - \frac{1}{q_0} \quad \text{where } q_t = \sqrt{10^{-6}} \text{ or } 10^{-3}, \quad \text{and } q_0 = \sqrt{10^{-4}} \text{ or } 10^{-2}$$

The solution is $t = 1000 - 100$, or 900 generations. At four generations per century, it will take $900/4 = 225$ centuries, or 22 500 years to reach the incidence the dictator desires. This assumes, of course that there are no mutations to the four-toed allele during this time.

The reduction in frequency of a recessive allele occurs slowly, even when it is lethal. Many of the deleterious traits that people would like to eliminate from the population, because of the pain and suffering they cause, are likely to have a high selection against them, and so increasing the selection pressure to 1.0 (i.e. making it lethal) will not change things very much. These traits are probably held at a low incidence in the population by a balance of mutation and selection, which we will now consider.

11.2.4   The balance between selection and mutation

Consider the situation where highly deleterious traits may be maintained in a population by recurrent mutation. As fast as deleterious alleles are being removed by selection, they are being replaced by mutation. The development of the appropriate equations (Eqns 11.1 to 11.3) is given in Box 11.1. These equations show that the deleterious allele will be maintained at an equilibrium frequency ($\hat{q}$), which is related to a certain ratio of the mutation rate (u) and selection coefficient (s). In Case D, the equilibrium is expressed in terms of the heterozygotes (H) because homozygotes of the deleterious allele seldom, if ever, occur in the population. To see how to use these equations, consider the following example.

Example 11.6   *In a classic study of achondroplasia (short-limbed dwarfism) Mørch (1941) noted 10 infants with this condition out of 94 075 births over a 30-year period in Denmark. Eight of these 10 achondroplastic individuals had normal parents. Looking at records covering a period of many years, he noted that 108 individuals with achondroplasia had produced a total of 27 offspring, whereas 457 of their normal siblings produced a total of 582 offspring.*

The relative fitness of achondroplasia may be calculated from these data as follows:

Phenotype	Achondroplasia	Normal
Average number of offspring	$27/108 = 0.25$	$582/457 = 1.2735$
Relative fitness (W)	$0.25/1.2735 = 0.1963$	1
Selection coefficient	$1 - 0.1963 = 0.8037$	

Achondroplasia is a dominant mutation, and so we must use Eqn 11.3 to estimate the mutation rate (u). We may note that all of the

Box 11.1 | Balance of selection and mutation

The decrease in allelic frequency (q) as a result of selection (Eqns 10.4, 10.5 and 10.6) is balanced by the increase in allelic frequency as a result of recurrent, reversible mutation (Exp. 7.12), where u is the forward mutation rate (p to q) and v is the reverse mutation rate. Note that $s = 1$, or nearly so, and the frequency of the deleterious allele (q) will be very small.

Case B – no dominance

$$\frac{1/2spq}{1 - sq} = up - vq \qquad \text{(Exp. 11.2)}$$

If we make two trivial sacrifices of error, we can simplify the equation considerably. First, $1 - sq$ is approximately 1 because q is very small, and vq can be eliminated for the same reason. Thus:

$$1/2spq = up \qquad \text{(Exp. 11.3)}$$

This simplifies to:

$$\hat{q} = \frac{2u}{s} \qquad \text{(Eqn 11.1)}$$

We can derive the equations for Cases C and D following the same kind of reasoning.

Case C – complete dominance, selection against recessive

$$\hat{q} = \sqrt{\frac{u}{s}} \qquad \text{(Eqn 11.2)}$$

Case D – complete dominance, selection against dominant

$$\hat{H} = \frac{2u}{s} \qquad \text{(Eqn 11.3)}$$

In these three equations, $\hat{q}$ = the equilibrium frequency of the deleterious allele, H = the equilibrium frequency of heterozygotes, u = the mutation rate of the deleterious allele from the 'normal' allele, and s = the selection coefficient against the inferior genotype.

achondroplastic individuals are heterozygous because homozygotes for this condition are lethal. Thus, the frequency of heterozygotes (H) is 10/94 075, or 0.000 106. Substituting this, and the selection coefficient determined above, in Eqn 11.3 we obtain:

$$0.000\,106 = \frac{2u}{0.803\,7}$$

This provides an indirect estimate of the mutation rate (u) of 4.3×10^{-5}. We can also calculate the mutation rate directly, because eight of the achondroplastic individuals in the 94 075 births were the result of new mutations, i.e. had normal parents. This gives a direct estimate rate (u) of 8/(94 075 × 2), or 4.3×10^{-5} (note that the number of alleles available for mutation is twice the number of newborns because we are diploid). The exact match of the two estimates is fortuitous because they are both subject to large errors. For example, if all 10 of the individuals with achondroplasia had been born to normal parents, the direct estimate of the mutation rate of achondroplasia would have been 5.3×10^{-5}. Similarly, if the 108 achondroplastic individuals had produced slightly more or fewer offspring, the selection coefficient, and hence the indirect estimate of the mutation rate from Eqn 11.3, would have been different.

If we applied the principle of eugenics to this situation, and were able to make $s = 1$, the equilibrium level of heterozygotes in the population would be reduced to 0.000 085 from 0.000 106 (assuming the mutation rate is 4.3×10^{-5}). This is two fewer cases of achondroplasia per 100 000 of the population, and so eugenics has little impact when there is already a strong selection pressure against the condition.

Finally, it is unwise to use Eqn 11.2 to obtain an indirect estimate of the mutation rate when there is selection against recessives. This is because the equilibrium state is only approached very slowly, and so the observed frequency of the allele may not be the equilibrium frequency. It takes hundreds of generations to reach equilibrium in large populations, and unless $s = 1$ it is unlikely that selection pressures will remain constant over this period. Equilibrium is reached much faster in small populations, but in this situation the frequency of the mutant allele is subject to genetic drift while in the heterozygous state. In addition, inbreeding can greatly change the equilibrium value, because the proportion of homozygotes is increased (see Crow 1986).

11.3 | Summary and conclusions

Several examples are provided of ways to calculate the relative fitness of different phenotypes over part of a generation, a single generation, or over many generations for natural populations. The methods should be used carefully, because they all are based on assumptions that may or may not be realistic.

During the Industrial Revolution, many insects and spiders responded genetically to the effects of air pollution by incorporating a rare dark mutant form into the population so that it became the dominant phenotype in industrial areas. The simple zygotic selection model has helped us understand some of the complexities of these genetic changes.

Sickle-cell anaemia demonstrates how heterozygote superiority can account for the maintenance of an allele that is extremely disadvantageous in the homozygous state.

Zygotic selection models also show how the policy of eugenics, which tried to improve the fitness of human populations by preventing those with deleterious genetic traits from having offspring, is truly misguided. In many cases, such deleterious traits are held at stable levels in the population by a balance of mutation and selection.

11.4 | Problems

The equations listed in Table 10.4 and Box 11.1 are used to solve the following problems.

1. A grasshopper has its body colour controlled by a single gene with two codominant alleles, G and B. The following information was collected by sampling at random at a single locality.

Phenotype	Green	Olive	Brown	
Genotype	GG	GB	BB	Total
Number in generation 1	6	284	1172	1462
Number in generation 2	4	244	952	1200

   (a) Calculate the relative fitness (W) and selection coefficient (s) for each genotype.
   (b) What is the equilibrium frequency of the brown allele (B)?

2. In *Biston betularia*, the *carbonaria* form is dominant to *typica*. The fitness of the *typica* was estimated to be 0.67, relative to *carbonaria* in industrial areas of Britain.
   (a) How long would it take for *carbonaria* to change from 10% to 90% of the population, assuming no change in selection pressure and only one generation of moths each year?
   (b) The population consisted of 36% *carbonaria* in 1924. If the breeding population had remained stable at 5000 individuals, when was the *carbonaria* allele first introduced into the population? You may assume that the allele was first introduced by a single mutation.

3. The oak eggar moth (*Lasiocampa quercus*) exhibits industrial melanism but is unusual in that the melanic form, *carbonaria*, is recessive to *typica*. In one industrial area, the frequency of the melanic form increased from 50% to 90% of the population over a ten-year period.
   (a) What is the selection coefficient against *typica*, assuming that there is one generation of moths each year?
   (b) Using the selection coefficient calculated in part (a), how long would it have taken for the *carbonaria* allele to have increased from a frequency of 0.01 to 0.1, and how long would it have taken if *carbonaria* had been dominant to *typica*?
   (c) Adult survival was estimated by placing 50 frozen specimens of each phenotype on tree trunks and seeing how many were eaten by birds during the course of one day. A total of 29 *carbonaria* and 24 *typica* were not eaten, i.e. 'survived' the day. What is the selection against *typica*, and how does it compare with your answer from part (a)?

4. An annual flower has either red (genotype RR or Rr) or pink (genotype rr) flowers. A total of 270 flowers was counted in one area, of which 180 individuals had red flowers and 90 individuals had pink flowers. Five years later, a search of the same area revealed 227 red-flowered and 85 pink-flowered plants.
   (a) Calculate the selection coefficients (s) against pink flowers, assuming that the change in allelic frequency was the result of selection.
   (b) What will be the equilibrium frequency of the pink allele (r), assuming no change in selection pressure?

(c) Electrophoresis revealed that 118 of the red flowers were heterozygous in the first sample, and 156 of the red flowers were heterozygous in the second sample. Further studies revealed that the relative fitness of the heterozygotes was intermediate between the two homozygotes. Using this additional information, calculate a more accurate estimation of the selection coefficient (s) for pink flowered plants than was possible in part (a).

5. In *Dactylis glomerata*, as in many other grasses, there is a recessive mutation for chlorophyll deficiency which is lethal when homozygous (the plants have no chlorophyll).
   (a) A population is started with only heterozygous plants. How many generations will it take until only one in 100 plants is heterozygous?
   (b) The mutation rate to the chlorophyll deficiency allele is 4.3×10^{-4}. What is the expected equilibrium frequency of this recessive allele, assuming a balance of mutation and selection?
   (c) In fact the population stabilized at a frequency of about 0.14 for the recessive allele. Of 184 plants tested, 132 were found to be homozygous dominant and 52 were heterozygous for this trait. What is the relative fitness of the three genotypes?

6. Tay–Sachs disease is a degenerative neurological disorder. Individuals who exhibit this trait are homozygous, and die by the time they are two or three years old. There is no known cure. Heterozygous individuals (carriers) do not suffer from the disorder. The disease occurs at an incidence of about one in 550 000 births in the non-Jewish Canadian population, but at an incidence of approximately one in 3600 births in the Canadian Jewish population.
   (a) Compare the frequency of carriers of this disease in the Jewish and non-Jewish Canadian populations.
   (b) Estimate the mutation rate of Tay–Sachs from normal individuals for the two populations, assuming a balance between mutation and selection. Comment on the difference in your two answers.
   (c) If the mutation of normal to Tay–Sachs alleles is ignored, how long will it take for the frequency of Tay–Sachs in Jewish Canadians to drop to the frequency observed in non-Jewish Canadians, given that there are approximately four generations per century?

Chapter 12

Polygenic inheritance, quantitative genetics and heritability

So far we have considered characters determined by a single gene with two alleles, occurring in sharply contrasting states, which can have a major affect on the fitness of the organism. In some cases we are justified in modelling selection in this manner, but in many cases, probably the majority, we are not. It is possible to expand the basic theory to consider characters determined by two gene loci, but this approach is no longer useful when we consider characters that are determined by many genes. In these cases we may observe a general relationship between parent and offspring, which suggests that there is an underlying genetic basis to the trait, but we usually do not know how many genes are involved or how they interact. In addition, we may also be aware that the environment influences the trait to some extent. Consequently, in order to study these traits we examine their variability, and attempt to dissect this variation into its genetic and environmental components. This type of analysis is called quantitative genetics.

We can consider three types of quantitative traits (Hartl and Clark 1989):

1. *Meristic traits*, in which the phenotype is expressed in discrete, integral classes. Examples include litter size or number of seeds produced per individual, number of flower parts, and kernel colour in wheat.
2. *Continuous traits*, in which there is a continuum of possible phenotypes. Examples include height, weight, oil content, milk yield, human skin colour, and growth rate. In practice, similar phenotypes are often grouped together into classes for the purposes of analysis.
3. *Discrete traits*, in which an individual either does or does not express the characteristic. Multiple genetic and environmental factors combine to determine the risk or liability of expressing the trait. It is assumed that the liability has to be greater than some threshold before the trait is expressed. Examples include diabetes and schizophrenia in humans.

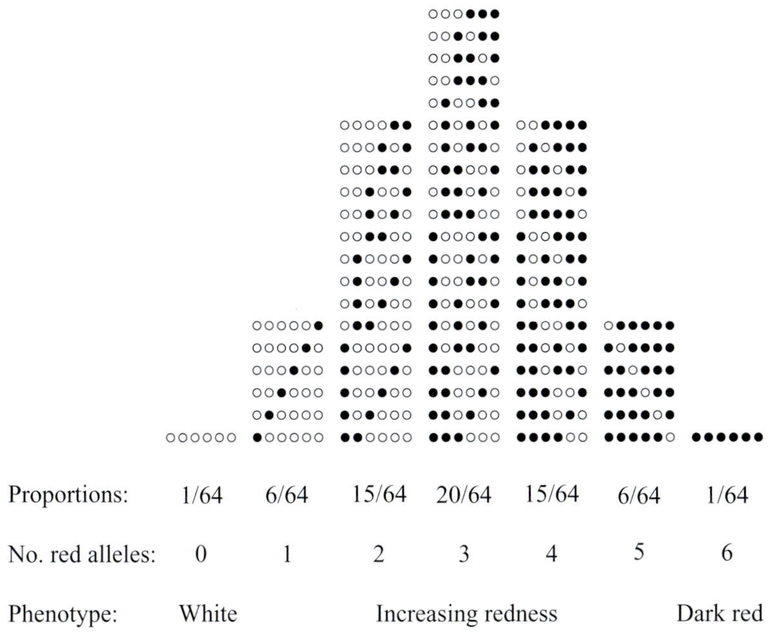

Fig. 12.1 Kernel colour in the F_2 generation of a cross between a white and a dark red variety of wheat. The colour difference is assumed to be due to three gene loci, and each red allele is denoted ● and each white allele is denoted ○. The 64 possible combination of alleles are grouped into the seven possible phenotypes, which occur in the proportions shown.

Proportions:	1/64	6/64	15/64	20/64	15/64	6/64	1/64
No. red alleles:	0	1	2	3	4	5	6
Phenotype:	White			Increasing redness			Dark red

12.1 Polygenic inheritance

Quantitative traits are influenced by many genes, called polygenes, each one of which contributes a small amount to the variation of a character. The first genetic analysis of a quantitative trait was made by the Scandinavian geneticist Nilsson-Ehle, in 1909. He studied red versus white kernel colour in wheat, and showed that there are three gene loci governing this trait. There are red alleles (R_1, R_2 and R_3) and white alleles (W_1, W_2 and W_3) at each locus, and there is no dominance in their effects. The alleles act in an additive manner, so that as the number of red alleles increases the intensity of the red colour increases, or conversely as the number of white alleles increases the intensity of the red colour decreases. Nilsson-Ehle crossed a homozygous white (denoted ○○○○○○) with a homozygous dark red strain (denoted ●●●●●●) and the kernels of the F_1 were an intermediate red colour (genotype ○●○●○●). The F_1 individuals can produce $2^3 = 8$ different types of gametes, and the $F_1 \times F_1$ cross will produce $8 \times 8 = 64$ unique combinations of these alleles in the F_2 generation. As there is no dominance there are 7 possible phenotypes corresponding to 0 to 6 red alleles, which occur in a $1:6:15:20:15:6:1$ ratio (Fig. 12.1).

We have considered a meristic quantitative trait in this example. It remains meristic because there is little environmental effect on kernel colour, and the alleles of the different genes act in a purely additive manner. Consequently, there are only seven discrete phenotypes. However, had the environment affected kernel colour, and if the alleles of the three different genes affected redness by slightly

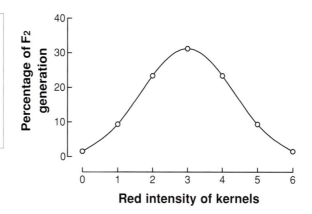

Fig. 12.2 Hypothetical continuous distribution of kernel colour in wheat. The proportions of the different genotypes remain the same as in Fig. 12.1, but environmental and other genetic effects blur the distinction between different genotypes (see text).

different amounts, the boundaries between the phenotypes would become blurred so that there would be more or less a continuum in kernel colour from white to dark red. In this case, the distribution of kernel colour would follow a smooth curve (Fig. 12.2) following the general shape of the histogram in Fig. 12.1. To analyse such a continuous distribution of kernel colour we might arbitrarily group the colours into seven classes which would be related in some way to the number of red alleles per individual. Thus, we can see that there is really no distinction between the first two types of quantitative traits (i.e. meristic and continuous).

12.2 Partitioning phenotypic variation into different components

The first attempt to partition phenotypic variation into its genetic and environmental components was made by East (1916) who began his experiments on the flower length of *Nicotiana longiflora* in 1912. We will use his data in the following two subsections to show how phenotypic variation can be partitioned into its various components. Our method of analysis is kept simple for obvious reasons, and you should be aware that it is not applicable in all situations. Some of the difficulties will be briefly mentioned as we develop our analysis, but for now let us consider our use of the similarity between parent and offspring to measure the genetic basis of a trait. Behavioural traits may be genetically transmitted from parent to offspring but may also be modified or taught by the parents, and our method of analysis does not distinguish between these two modes of transmission. A more complex example is provided by the body weight of eutherian mammals. An individual's body weight at the time of weaning depends on the body weight of the parents (genetic transmission), its weight at birth and the amount of milk it receives, which are influenced by the nutritional status of the mother and the litter size or number of siblings (transmission of maternal and sibling environmental effects).

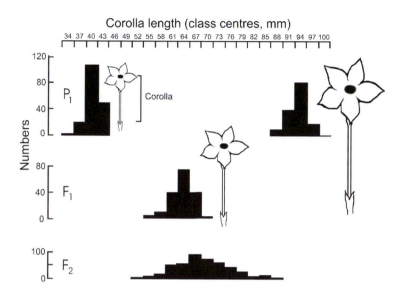

Fig. 12.3 Breeding experiments on flower length in *Nicotiana longiflora*. (Data from East 1916.)

Geneticists use a variety of methods to overcome these difficulties and more accurately partition the phenotypic variance into its different components (see Falconer and Mackay 1996), but they are more complex and are beyond the scope of this text.

12.2.1 Genetic and environmental components

The phenotypic variance can be calculated in a straightforward manner, described in any statistics text, as the average of the squared deviations about the mean phenotypic value. Phenotypic variation is divided into its genetic and environmental components by assuming that these sources of variation are additive. If this is the case, the total phenotypic variance (V_P) equals the fraction of the phenotypic variance that is a result of genetic differences between individuals (V_G) plus the fraction of the phenotypic variance resulting from differences in the environmental conditions to which individuals were exposed (V_E). Symbolically this is written:

$$V_P = V_G + V_E \qquad \text{(Eqn 12.1)}$$

East partitioned the variation in flower length in the following way. He crossed homozygous long-flowered plants with homozygous short-flowered plants, and the resulting F_1 plants, which were genetically identical to one another, had flowers of intermediate length (Fig. 12.3). There was no genetic variation (i.e. $V_G = 0$) in either of the parental varieties or the F_1 offspring, and so the observed variance within these groups (V_P) equals the environmental variance, V_E. The average variance of these three groups, V_E, equalled 5.2 for East's data.

East then made a cross of F_1 individuals to produce the F_2 generation. The alleles inherited from the two parental strains segregated, and so the total phenotypic variance of the F_2 was made up of both genetic and environmental variation. The total phenotypic variance (V_P) of the F_2 offspring was 40.5. The genetic variance (V_G) can then be calculated by rearranging Eqn 12.1 as $V_G = V_P - V_E$, which gives a value of 35.3.

In summary, by analysing East's data on the phenotypic variation of flower length in *Nicotiana*, it is possible to partition the total phenotypic variation $(V_P = 40.5)$ into its environmental $(V_E = 5.2)$ and genetic $(V_G = 35.3)$ components by assuming that these sources of variation are additive. Thus, in the F_2 generation approximately 87% of the variation was genetically based and 13% environmental based.

We can make two general points about this partitioning of phenotypic variation. First, the amount of variation (V_P) and the relative strengths of the genetic and environmental effects are not fixed entities. We may note that the value of V_G varied from zero, when the crosses were between genetically identical plants, to 35.3 for the $F_1 \times F_1$ cross, and it would be different again for crosses between other genotypes. In addition, if the plants had been grown in a more heterogeneous environment we would expect to see V_E increase for obvious reasons. Moreover, for some traits there can be genotype–environment interaction where some genotypes do better in some environments, and other genotypes do better in others. Consequently, the overall phenotypic variation and the relative importance of the genetic and environmental components vary according to the environment and the precise genetic make-up of the population.

Second, our partitioning of phenotypic variation does not give an unequivocal answer to the old genetics-versus-environment or 'nature-versus-nurture' debate. In our example of flower length it looks as though it is more important to have the 'right' genes rather than environment if we want a flower of a specific length. However, if we only had an inbred line with low genetic diversity, the reverse might be true. The debate has been highly emotional at times, and the opposing sides have often taken extreme positions, claiming either that only genetic variation is important (genetic determinism) or that the environment (nurture) is all-important. In reality it is a mixture of these two components that determines phenotypic expression, although their relative importance can vary. However, as we have seen, their relative importance is not fixed and so the debate continues without final resolution for some people. We will look at two examples of this debate in more detail, in section 12.6 of this chapter and in Chapter 19 (section 19.1).

12.2.2 Partitioning the components of genetic variation

The genetic variance (V_G) is also made up of a number of components. These components include the additive effects of all of the alleles that affect the trait, the dominance effects between alleles within gene loci, and epistatic interactions between different gene loci that modify the additive effects. To help us understand how the additive, dominance and epistatic effects can influence the genetic variance, consider the following hypothetical series:

Genotype	aabb	Aabb	AAbb	AABb	AABB
1. Additive effect					
Phenotypic score	0	1	2	3	4
2. Dominance effect					
Phenotypic score	0	2	2	4	4
3. Dominance plus epistatic effect					
Phenotypic score	0	0	0	4	4

Imagine that this corresponds to a situation similar to that of kernel colour in wheat (section 12.1), but there are only two gene loci involved and the red alleles are represented by capital letters. When there are purely additive effects, the red colour intensifies in a stepwise fashion (0–4) as each red allele is added. Now imagine that the red allele is completely dominant to white, as shown in the second example. The intensity of the red colour would be the same whether one or both alleles of a gene coded for red, and the phenotypic scores would be modified as shown. Finally, in the third example we can imagine that the A allele only exerts its effect in the presence of allele B, and so there would be a further modification of phenotypic scores as shown.

Thus, it is necessary to partition the genetic variance, V_G, into the various components as follows:

$$V_G = V_A + (V_D + V_I) \qquad \text{(Eqn 12.2)}$$

in which V_A is the variance due to the additive effects of alleles, V_D is the variance due to dominance effects between alleles and V_I is the variance due to epistatic interactions between the genes that affect the trait. In practice, it is difficult to separate V_D and V_I and consequently they are often grouped together as non-additive genetic variation.

The additive genetic variance (V_A) is the main cause of the resemblance between parents and their offspring, and between relatives. We can obtain a measure of this relationship by drawing a graph of the mean phenotypic score of offspring against the mean phenotypic score of their parents. Ideally, the parents should be mated at random when constructing these graphs, which can then be used to calculate V_A (see below). If we consider our example of flower length in *Nicotiana*, and use the data from crosses from the F_2 generation provided in East (1916), we obtain the following relationship between parent and offspring (Fig. 12.4).

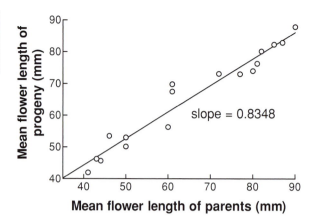

Fig. 12.4 The relationship of flower length between parents and offspring in *Nicotiana longiflora*. (Data from East 1916.)

The slope of the regression tells us how much the offspring resemble their parents, or what is called the *heritability in the narrow sense* (h^2_N) of the trait.[1] Thus, if the offspring have the same average phenotypic score as their parents, the slope of the regression (h^2_N) will be 1.0, and if there is no relationship in the phenotypic scores of parents and their offspring, then $h^2_N = 0$. Obviously, the higher the heritability (or slope of the regression) the larger the additive genetic component. The relationship between heritability (h^2_N), additive genetic variance (V_A) and phenotypic variance (V_P) is given by:

$$h^2_N = \frac{V_A}{V_P}$$ (Eqn 12.3)

From East's data (Fig. 12.4) we see that $h^2_N = 0.8348$ for flower length in *Nicotiana*. In section 12.2.1, we noted that $V_P = 40.5$, and so we can estimate V_A as $0.8348 \times 40.5 = 33.8$ by rearranging Eqn 12.3. We have previously estimated the genetic variance (V_G) as 35.3, and so from Eqn 12.2 we can estimate the non-additive genetic variance ($V_D + V_I$) as $35.3 - 33.8 = 1.5$.

This completes our partitioning of the phenotypic variation into its various genetic and environmental components, and the results are summarized in Table 12.1. The genetic variance (V_G) is the sum of the additive and non-additive genetic variances, and equals 35.3, or 87% of the total phenotypic variance.

12.3 Heritability

We have just seen that heritability in the narrow sense (h^2_N) is the proportion of the total phenotypic variation that is a result of additive genetic variation (Eqn 12.3). You should also be aware that there is another measure of heritability, called *heritability in the broad sense*

---

[1] The degree of genetic determination, or heritability, of a trait is symbolized as h^2 because it was first calculated as the square of the partial correlation coefficient (i.e. path coefficient) between the parental genotypes and the offspring's phenotype (see Feldman 1992).

Table 12.1 Partitioning of the variation of flower length in *Nicotiana longi-flora*. The components are expressed in terms of their variance and as percentages of the total phenotypic variance

		Variance	Percentage
Phenotypic variance	V_P	40.5	100
Additive genetic variance	V_A	33.8	83
Non-additive genetic variance	$V_D + V_I$	1.5	4
Environmental variance	V_E	5.2	13

Source: Data from East (1916).

(h^2_B) which is equal to V_G/V_P. We will not consider this measure any further, and wherever heritability is referred to in this chapter it means heritability in the narrow sense.

The term heritability has unfortunate connotations, and is frequently misunderstood, particularly by non-biologists. Many people believe it is a fixed property for a particular trait, and think that a character is genetically determined to a certain extent and is modified by the environment by some other, usually small, amount. This is not the case. Heritability is simply a ratio of two variances, and is only applicable to the population and environment in which it was measured. We can understand this if we expand Eqn 12.3 to:

$$h^2_N = \frac{V_A}{V_G + V_E} \qquad \text{(Exp. 12.1)}$$

The value of h^2_N is changed if we change the genetic constitution of the population because the variance of at least one of the genetic components will be altered. For example, if we had estimated the heritability of flower length for either of the two parental populations of *Nicotiana* we would have obtained values of 0 (zero), instead of the value of 0.8348 estimated in section 12.2.2. This is because there is no genetic variation (V_G and $V_A = 0$) in these two homozygous populations, and all of the variation is a result of environmental variation (V_E). Similarly, changes to the environment can also change the value of h^2_N. For example, height might have a high heritability for a population of plants grown under very uniform conditions, but if we grew the same genetic stock in an area where the soil and water conditions were extremely variable, the heritability would be lowered because the environmental variance (V_E) would increase.

Bearing this in mind when we compare the heritabilities of different characteristics, we find that the heritability of trivial, apparently unimportant characteristics is frequently high, whereas the heritability is usually low for characteristics that are closely related to fitness (Table 12.2). This is because selection on trivial characters will probably be low or non-existent, and so natural selection tolerates large genetic variability in these characteristics. However, there will be strong selection pressures on traits that play a vital role in the fitness of an organism, and so generally there will be much less genetic

Table 12.2 Approximate values of the heritability of various characters in certain domestic animal and plant species. Traits closely related to fitness (e.g. calving interval, eggs per hen, litter size of swine, yield and ear number of corn) tend to have low heritabilities

Species and trait	$h^2{}_N$
Cattle	
Wither height	0.60
Milk protein percentage	0.55
Feed efficiency	0.35
Milk yield	0.30
Calving interval	0.25
Poultry	
Egg weight	0.55
Body weight	0.50
Albumen content	0.40
Age of sexual maturity	0.35
Eggs per hen	0.10
Swine	
Back-fat thickness	0.60
Body length	0.53
Feed efficiency	0.35
Daily gain in weight	0.30
Litter size	0.15
Corn (Zea mays)	
Husk extension	0.67
Plant height	0.53
Ear height	0.45
Ear number	0.20
Yield	0.13

Source: Data from Hartl and Clark (1989).

variation because the inferior genotypes will be eliminated from the population.

Plant and animal breeders are interested in the heritabilities of different characteristics because the higher the heritability, the greater the response to selection. This leads us to our next topic where we consider the effect of selection on quantitative characters.

12.4 Response to selection

How do quantitative characters respond to selection? In many cases they will change, and we can illustrate this over two generations of selection using an abstract example (Fig. 12.5). The phenotypic score is arbitrary, and could correspond to such traits as the amount of oil in a seed, plant height, the degree of resistance to a particular insecticide, or body weight. We apply systematic selection to increase the size of the character in question. In the original population

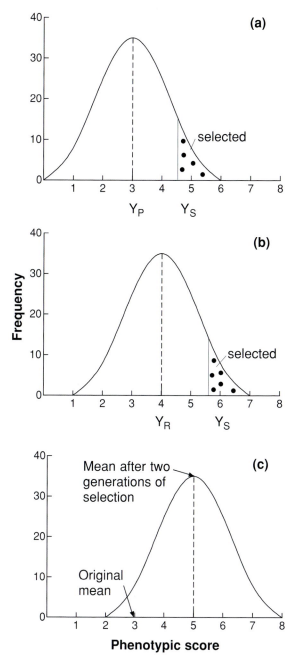

Fig. 12.5 Two generations of selection for increased size of a trait with a heritability of 0.5. The individuals selected to be the parents of the next generation are stippled (see text).

(Fig. 12.5a) we can see that the overall phenotypic mean of the parental population ($\bar{Y}_P$) is 3 units, and the group of individuals selected as parents of the next generation have an overall mean ($\bar{Y}_S$) of 5 units.

The intensity of selection, or selection pressure, being applied is called the *selection differential* (S), and is measured as the difference between the mean of the selected parents ($\bar{Y}_S$) and the mean of all the individuals in the parental population ($\bar{Y}_P$). Thus:

$$S = \bar{Y}_S - \bar{Y}_P \qquad \text{(Eqn 12.4)}$$

In our example we can see that $S = 5 - 3$, or 2 phenotypic units.

The response (R) to this selection differential is shown in Fig. 12.5b, and may be measured as the difference between the mean of the progeny ($\bar{Y}_R$) and the mean of the parental population ($\bar{Y}_P$). Thus:

$$R = \bar{Y}_R - \bar{Y}_P \qquad \text{(Eqn 12.5)}$$

In our example, $R = 4 - 3$, or 1 phenotypic unit.

We can also predict the response (R) of the population from the equation:

$$R = h^2_N S \qquad \text{(Eqn 12.6)}$$

On reflection, this last equation should be intuitively obvious. The heritability (h^2_N) is a measure of the similarity of the progeny to their parents, and if we multiply this by the selection differential (S) we can predict the overall change in the phenotype (or response, R). In our example, $R = 0.5 \times 2$, or 1 phenotypic unit, which is the same as that predicted by Eqn 12.5. Thus, the overall phenotypic score will change, or in this case increase because R is positive, by 1 phenotypic unit. The average phenotypic score of the progeny should be one unit larger than the mean score of the parents, i.e. $3 + 1 = 4$, which is what we observe.

When we repeat the operation, we see that after a second generation of selection at the same intensity ($S = 2$), the average phenotypic score of the population has increased by one more unit and now is 2 units larger than the original population (Fig. 12.5c). Thus, the population responds to selection generation after generation, and the response is directly related to the heritability (h^2_N) and the selection differential (S) being applied. If the heritability had been lower, the response to selection would have been lower. For example if h^2_N was 0.25 and $S = 2$ units, the mean phenotypic score would have increased by 0.25×2 or 0.5 units each generation, rather than the 1 unit observed in Fig. 12.5. Note, that unless the heritability $= 1.0$, the mean phenotypic score of the progeny will lie somewhere between the phenotypic score of those selected as parents ($\bar{Y}_S$) and the overall phenotypic score of the parental population ($\bar{Y}_P$). This slipping back toward the overall mean is known as regression (toward the mean).

12.5 | Empirical examples of selection of quantitative characters

Perhaps the best example of controlled, long-term selection is an experiment on the oil content of corn seed. The experiment was started in 1896 (even before the rediscovery of Mendel's laws) at the Illinois Experimental Station using a base population of 163 corn ears with oil contents ranging from 4% to 6%. Two experimental lines were started, one selecting for high oil content and the other for low oil

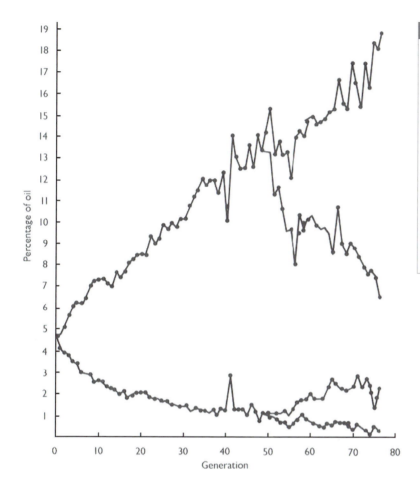

Fig. 12.6 Selection for high and low oil content in the seed of corn (*Zea mays*). The high line was formed from the 24 ears highest in oil content and the low line from the 12 ears with the lowest oil content in an initial population of 163 corn ears. Two additional lines of reverse selection were started in generation 46. (Reprinted from Dudley, J. W., in *Proceedings of the International Conference on Quantitative Genetics*) (eds. E. Pollock, O. Kempthorne and T. B. Bailey), pp. 459–73, Copyright 1977, with permission of Iowa State University Press.)

content and the results of the first 78 generations of selection are shown (Fig. 12.6).

It did not take long for the oil content of the two lines to be well outside of the original range of oil content. The low line has changed less than the high line because you cannot have an oil content of below zero. A careful examination of the trends shows that the rate of change was fastest during the first 10 to 20 generations of selection, but the lines are still diverging and so the additive genetic variance has still not been exhausted. Presumably, at some stage all the individuals within a line will come to have the same genotype for oil content, and the heritability (h^2_N) will be zero because there is no additive genetic variance (V_A). At this point there will be no further response to artificial selection unless there are new mutations affecting oil content. Heritability has declined to about one-third of its initial value in both lines (Table 12.3), but will take some time to decline to zero because there are at least 20 genes that affect oil content.

Selection is not always directional, it is often against the phenotypic extremes and intermediate phenotypes have higher fitness. Such selection is called stabilizing selection, because no change may

Table 12.3 | The heritability of oil content in corn seed after different numbers of generations of selection in the Illinois corn experiment illustrated in Fig. 12.6

	Heritability of oil content	
Generations	High line	Low line
1 – 9	0.32	0.50
10 – 25	0.34	0.23
26 – 52	0.11	0.10
53 – 76	0.12	0.15

Source: Reprinted from Dudley, J. W. in *Proceedings of the International Conference on Quantitative Genetics* (eds. E. Pollock, O. Kempthorne and T. B. Bailey), pp. 459–73, Copyright 1977, with permission of Iowa State University Press.

be seen in the phenotypic score generation after generation, even though there may be strong selection pressures on the character in question. A good example of this type of selection is seen in human birth weights (Fig. 12.7), where there is strong selection against large and small babies and the average birth weight is similar to the optimum predicted from infant mortality. A similar pattern of stabilizing selection is seen in clutch size in birds (see Chapter 16) where intermediate clutch sizes give rise to largest number of survivors.

12.6 | Intelligence, race and societal class

In recent decades there has been a controversy about the reasons for differences in IQ (intelligence quotient) scores between different segments of society, particularly in North America. For example, Jensen (1969) and Herrnstein and Murray (1994) have presented overwhelming evidence that the average IQ scores of people of different colour, and of different socioeconomic classes, are very different. The issue they raise can be stated quite simply: does the low IQ in some racial groups, or in some lower socioeconomic classes, have a genetic or an environmental basis? Thus, we are examining an example of the classic nature (i.e. genes) versus nurture (i.e. environment) debate. In the following discussion we will concentrate on racial differences, because the arguments apply equally to socioeconomic class differences and, in any case, there is frequently a strong association between race and socioeconomic class.

How do we define intelligence? It is highly questionable whether IQ scores give an unbiased and total assessment of intelligence because some things, such as musical skills, are not correlated with IQ. However, IQ tests do evaluate a large range of skills, and the scores correlate reasonably well with the scholastic success of Caucasians, and

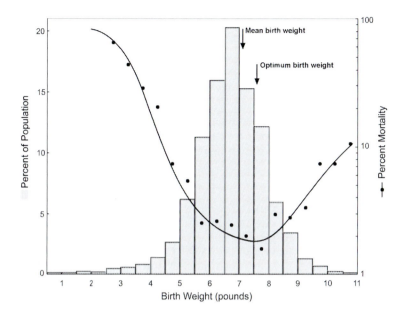

Fig. 12.7 Stabilizing selection for human birth weight (histogram). Early mortality, shown by the points around a fitted curve, is lowest near the mean birth weight. (From *The Genetics of Human Populations*, by L. L. Cavalli-Sforza and W. F. Bodmer © 1971 by W. H. Freeman and Company. Used with permission.)

so they may serve an educational purpose. The form of the present IQ tests was developed soon after 1900 by Alfred Binet, a French psychologist, to identify schoolchildren who would be likely to have difficulty at school. The Binet test was revised in 1916 at Stanford University, and subsequently revised again in 1937 and 1960. It is the standard IQ test in North America.

Interestingly, the 1916 Stanford–Binet test indicated that boys had higher IQs than girls. This was interpreted as a bias favouring males, because of their different experiences, rather than any innate tendency for males to be more intelligent than females. The test was revised to exclude questions where one sex or the other performed better, and so present tests give almost identical IQ distributions for males and females. It is interesting that there has been no successful attempt to eliminate questions where there are different scores for other different racial, cultural or socioeconomic groups.

The test involves answering a large number of questions. The answers are scored and the scores are summed for each individual. These scores are transformed into an IQ test score for each individual by a process of standardization, in which the mean for a large population has a value of 100 and the standard deviation for the population is 15. Thus, the population has a normal distribution of IQs, such that 67% of the population has IQ scores between 85 and 115, 95% of the population has IQ scores between 70 and 130, and 99% of the population has IQ scores between 55 and 145. Naturally, different tests are given to children of different ages. The results of different tests over short time intervals are similar, but the correlation between tests declines as the time interval increases. Some studies have shown that individual IQs vary little between the ages of 2 and 18, but other studies show that they vary over this time period. For example, one study of Swedish schoolchildren showed that the IQs of students tested at 12 years of age increased by an average of 11 points at the end of high school, if they had been subjected to a demanding curriculum. Thus, IQ scores are not perfectly stable with age, and can be increased with appropriate schooling.

There have been many studies to determine the heritability of IQ scores to assess the genetic and non-genetic aspects of this measure. However, there are problems if one uses the parent–offspring regression technique (see Fig. 12.4) because relatives reared together cannot provide data that discriminate between genetic transmission of the trait and environmental transmission from parent to child. These estimates of heritability are likely to be too high because 'good' genes and 'good' environments are likely to be highly correlated with one another. Better estimates can be made by using the technique of estimating the correlations between monozygotic twins that have been reared apart.[2] There are four such studies providing estimates of 0.86 (Cyril Burt), 0.77 (J. Shields), 0.73 (Juel-Nielsen), and 0.69 (Newman, Freeman and Holzinger). These give a combined estimate of 0.81, which is where the widely quoted estimate of 80% for the heritability of IQ has been derived. However, we now know that Burt's data are fraudulent (he made up most of his data) and Shield's data are less than ideal because over two-thirds of his sample were raised by close relatives. The remaining two estimates are based on small sample sizes, and so their combined estimate of 0.71 is rather uncertain. Finally, studies based on the results of adopted children have provided estimates of between 0.45 and 0.65. Thus, the claim that IQ is 80% heritable is certainly an inflated estimate, and more reasonable estimates would be somewhere in the range of 45% to 70%, or even lower (Feldman 1992). However, as we will see, the precise range of heritability estimates for IQ does not impair our ability to evaluate whether the differences between groups have a genetic or an environmental basis.

Numerous studies have shown that the average IQ of blacks in the USA is 10 to 20 points (average 15 points) below that of US whites (Fig. 12.8). If we ignore the question of how the authors of these studies defined 'white' and 'black' people, this represents a considerable difference between the two groups, equivalent to one standard deviation of the distribution of white IQs. Similarly, the average IQ of people in lower socioeconomic classes is below that of people in higher economic classes.

How do we explain these differences? A group comprising mainly psychologists, called hereditarians, argues that the difference between groups is largely genetic in origin. In their view, one's IQ is mainly innate, and no amount of environmental change will

---

[2] Monozygotic twins may be defined as: two individuals that develop by the division and separation of a single fertilized egg into two genetically identical parts (i.e. identical twins).

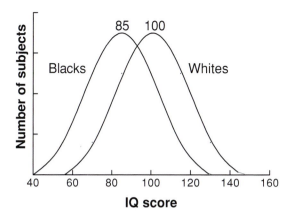

Fig. 12.8 The difference in IQ between idealized samples from blacks and whites in the United States. The mean IQ is shown above the curves for each of the two groups.

eradicate the difference between groups. In case you think that this is merely a racist argument for the genetic superiority of Caucasians, you should be aware that at least one hereditarian, William Rushton of the University of Western Ontario, shows that the average IQ of people of Asian origin is higher than that of Caucasians. On the other hand, many biologists have argued that the differences are mainly due to environmental factors, together with cultural biases in the IQ test questions that favour whites.

The hereditarians' main argument is that the difference in IQ between the two racial groups is mostly genetic in origin, because IQ has a high heritability in both blacks and whites. In other words, hereditarians believe that IQ is mainly genetically determined (as much as 80%), and so this must be the reason for the difference between the two groups. This is a fallacious argument as the following 'thought experiments' make clear.

Imagine we have a population of dogs which vary greatly in size, and may be black, grey or white (the black and white alleles are codominant). Note that this imaginary genetic system for body colour is simply to make it easy to create pure-breeding groups of black or white dogs. Dog size is a polygenic trait with a heritability of 0.8, and there is no association between dog size and colour. In the first experiment we take a group of young white puppies and feed them on a rich diet. At adulthood, these dogs have a body length that is normally distributed with a mean of 100 cm and a standard deviation of 15 cm. The same is true with the offspring of these dogs. We also take a group of young black puppies and feed them on a reduced diet. At adulthood, these dogs have a body length that is also normally distributed, but with a mean of 85 cm and a standard deviation of 15 cm. The same is true for their offspring. The slope of the parent–offspring regression for body length was 0.8 $(= h^2_N)$ in both groups, but the regression line for black dogs was below that of the white dogs. Obviously, we would attribute the difference in size between the two groups of dogs to the difference in their diets, i.e. environmental factors, even though dog size has a high heritability. Thus, even though the variation in dog size *within* each group was mainly due to additive genetic effects (i.e. V_A is 80% of V_P), this was not the reason for the difference *between* the two groups. We can also note that dog size had nothing to do with their colour, even though white dogs were significantly larger than black dogs.

In the second imaginary experiment, we select a group of white dogs for increased size, and simultaneously select a group of black dogs for smaller size. After a few generations of selection we observe that the two groups have diverged in average size. We then take the two groups and grow them in the same area, thereby eliminating potential environmental differences between them. We are not surprised that the white dogs are larger on average than the black dogs, and would attribute this difference to genetic differences in the two lines. As a result of the selective process, we might find that the heritability of dog size was reduced to approximately 0.3 in each of the two lines (see Table 12.3). Thus, even though the variation in dog size within each group was mainly a result of a combination of non-additive genetic effects and environmental effects, the difference between the two groups had a genetic basis.

These imaginary experiments demonstrate that there is no foundation to the hereditarian argument: that if IQ has a high heritability, the differences in IQ scores between different population groups must have a genetic basis. However, even though we have shown that the main hereditarian argument is based on a fallacy, this does not settle the question as to whether the difference in IQ between groups has an environmental or a genetic basis. This requires more direct evidence.

Three types of evidence suggest that most of the difference between groups is a result of environmental factors.

1. Studies that compare the IQ of different races usually have poorly matched samples. The samples not only differ in race, but also differ in socioeconomic status, the type of schooling available to the children, and so on. Thus, differences between groups could be a result of associated environmental differences rather than racial differences. Nichols and Anderson (1973) reduced some of the environmental differences in their study by comparing different ethnic groups of children whose parents had the same occupations, education and income (socioeconomic status). They tested two samples of seven-year-old children of blacks and whites in the United States: one group of high socioeconomic status from Boston, and one group of relatively low socioeconomic status from Baltimore and Philadelphia. The Boston whites and blacks had mean IQs of 104.2 and 100.0, respectively, and the Baltimore–Philadelphia whites and blacks had mean IQs of 95.3 and 91.2, respectively. Thus, the 10 to 20 point difference in IQ between blacks and whites, found in most studies (see above), was effectively reduced to about 4 points simply by stratifying the sample design so that potential racial differences were not confounded by differences arising as a result of socioeconomic factors.

2. If the hereditarian view is correct, children of black and white parents should have IQs intermediate between the two groups, but this is not the case. There was no difference in the average IQ of illegitimate children of black and white American servicemen and German women after the Second World War. Similarly, Tizard (1974) found that mixed-race and white English children who had spent part of their early life in institutions had similar IQ scores, although those of the mixed-race children were marginally higher. Finally, the IQ of children of mixed marriages is reported to correlate more with the IQ of the mother than the father, suggesting that cultural traits transmitted to the child during infancy and early childhood are important, because it is the mother who normally has the major influence on the child at this stage.

3. Evidence for environmental effects transmitted by the adoptive parents is also provided by children adopted soon after birth. The effects are quite general and apply equally to the question of racial differences in IQ as well as differences in IQ related to socioeconomic class. A study by Skodak and Skeels (see Bodmer and Cavelli-Sforza 1976) tested the IQs of 100 children, born to white, unmarried mothers from lower classes, that were adopted into middle-class families. The children's IQs showed a higher correlation with those of the biological mothers than with their adoptive parents, showing a strong genetic effect on IQ. However, the average IQ of the biological mothers was 85 whereas the average for the children was 107. The IQ of the biological fathers was unknown, but it is unlikely that all of the 22 point difference was from that source. Probably the increase in IQ was related mainly to the favourable academic environment offered by the foster homes. Finally, a study of black children adopted by white families in Minnesota showed that they had IQs similar to those of white controls, which suggests that there are no genetic differences in IQ between the races.

From this discussion, we can conclude that the hereditarian argument, which states that differences in IQ between different population groups is mainly a result of genetic differences among groups, is based on a misunderstanding of quantitative genetic theory. The available evidence suggests that most, if not all, of the differences among groups are a result of environmental influences.

What if we had discovered that much of the difference in IQs between groups had a genetic basis? Would the genetic fatalism of the hereditarians, and the belief that group differences in IQ cannot be changed, be justified? The simple answer is no. Consider the case of phenylketonuria, a genetic disease which, among other effects, causes severe mental retardation. At one time there was no treatment for the condition, and in the 1960s it accounted for almost 1% of all severely retarded patients in institutions. Phenylketonuria is a metabolic defect resulting from the absence of an enzyme called phenylalanine hydroxylase, which converts the amino acid phenylalanine to tyrosine. The phenotypic effects of the condition, only expressed in homozygous recessive individuals, are the result of an excess of phenylalanine and its derivatives. The genetic condition can be treated by restricting the dietary intake of phenylalanine. Individuals that are identified soon after birth with the condition, before the classical phenotypic effects are expressed, and who adopt a rigorously controlled diet can live a normal life. Treatment will not reverse the effects of the disease once they have been expressed. Note, however, that phenylketonuria has a close to 100% heritability, and yet an environmental change (of diet) can effectively abolish its effect on IQ.

Finally, my vigorous attack on the hereditarian position of ascribing the differences in average IQ between racial groups to genetic differences may have led some to conclude that there is no genetic basis to IQ and that only the environment is important. However, although appropriate mental stimulation is necessary to develop our IQ to its full potential, some of us will have a higher IQ than others. We cannot all be as clever as Albert Einstein or Madame Curie, our genetic constitution is also important.

12.7 | Summary

When a trait is determined by many gene loci there may be a continuum or a very large number of possible phenotypes. The phenotypic variation of polygenic traits can be partitioned into environmental and genetic components, and the latter further partitioned into additive, dominance and epistatic genetic effects, by suitable breeding experiments.

The response to selection is positively correlated with the proportion of the overall phenotypic variation (V_P) that is determined by the additive genetic effects (V_A). The measure V_A/V_P is called the heritability in the narrow sense of a trait, and when a trait is subjected to intense selection its heritability decreases as inferior alleles are eliminated. This probably explains why traits that are closely related to fitness tend to have low heritabilities, whereas trivial characters tend to have high heritabilities.

The relationship between IQ and race is examined in some detail as an example of the genes versus environment debate. The hereditarian argument that the differences in IQ between groups must have a genetic basis (because the heritability of the trait is high) is shown to be based on a misunderstanding of quantitative genetic theory. The available evidence suggests that most, if not all, of the differences between groups are the result of environmental influences. However, the genetic constitution of individuals has a strong effect on IQ.

12.8 | Problems

1. Two highly inbred lines of mice are crossed and give a variance of 2.5 units in tail length in the F_1 generation. The variance in the F_2 generation is 12.5 units, and the parent–offspring regression for tail length is 0.75.

(a) What is the heritability ($h^2{}_N$) for tail length?

(b) Partition the variance (V_P) of the F_2 generation into the following components: V_E, V_G, V_A and (V_D+V_I).

(c) If the overall average tail length of hybrids is 80 cm, what will be the average tail length of the offspring of parents with tail lengths of 88 and 92 cm? What would your answer be if the average tail length of the parents had been 70 cm?

Chapter 13

Population genetics: summary and synthesis

In the previous seven chapters, we have examined various factors that influence the allelic frequencies in the gene pools of populations. It is easy to become mired in the details and lose sight of the broad, overall picture. The purpose of this chapter is to summarize how genetic variation is developed, maintained and directed in populations, a process which we call microevolution, so that we can develop an overview and general understanding of the interrelationships of the various factors or processes. The scheme that we will be following is summarized in Fig. 13.1.

Evolution can be considered to be a two-step process: first, the production of genetic variation by mutations and genetic recombination and, second, an ordering of that variation by natural selection which may be influenced by processes such as genetic drift and migration.

13.1 | Mutations

Genetic variation is originally created by mutations, which cause changes in the precise sequence of DNA in the chromosomes. Mutation by itself is not an important driving force of evolutionary change because mutations causing the same phenotypic change occur at very low frequencies, somewhere in the order of 1×10^{-5} to 10^{-8} per gamete. It would take many thousands of generations to effect a substantial change in allelic frequency as a result of mutation pressure alone (see Chapter 7). Mutation creates genetic variation in a non-directed fashion, i.e. mutations are not created in relation to their need. For example, mutations conferring resistance to a particular insecticide are just as likely to occur in populations not affected by the pesticide as they are in populations that are being exposed to the pesticide. Most mutations are detrimental and are quickly eliminated by selection, others are neutral (i.e. the mutant form of the allele has the same fitness as the 'normal' form of the allele), and a few mutations are beneficial. However, the chance of a mutation surviving and becoming incorporated into the gene pool is extremely small, even when it is beneficial. Mutations with small phenotypic

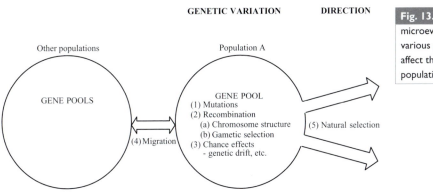

GENETIC VARIATION   DIRECTION

Other populations   Population A

GENE POOLS

GENE POOL
(1) Mutations
(2) Recombination
    (a) Chromosome structure
    (b) Gametic selection
(3) Chance effects
    - genetic drift, etc.

(4) Migration

(5) Natural selection

Fig. 13.1 Schematic diagram of microevolution, showing the various processes or factors that affect the gene frequencies of populations.

effects are more likely to survive than those that have large effects on the organism, because organisms are generally well suited to their surroundings and large changes in their characteristics are likely to be detrimental.

The prevailing neo-Darwinian view is that only the mutations occurring in the germ cells are important in evolution, because they are transmitted from one generation to the next whereas somatic mutations are lost when the individual dies.

Most species maintain a large genetic variability in their populations. Typically, about 5% to 15% of the genes are heterozygous in single individuals, and approximately 20% to 50% of the genes are polymorphic within a population or species (see Chapter 7). It is uncertain how this level of genetic variation is maintained. Some consider that the variation is largely maintained by a balance of selective forces, where some alleles are favoured in some situations and other alleles are favoured in other situations (the balance hypothesis). Others believe that most of the variation is neutral with respect to natural selection, i.e. different alleles of the same gene have the same fitness (the neutral gene hypothesis).

It takes many thousands of generations to develop high levels of genetic diversity in populations because mutation rates, which create the diversity, are so low. If genetic diversity is considerably reduced for any reason, it will require many thousands of generations of mutation to restore it to its original level.

Species with large levels of genetic variation are more likely to adapt to, and tolerate, changes of environment than species with low levels of genetic variation. We should also recognize that abundant species also create an enormous number of mutations each generation (see Chapter 7) and so may also have a better ability than rare species to withstand changes in the environment. However, what is important is the appropriate type of genetic variation, rather than genetic variation *per se*. For example, the American chestnut (*Castanea dentata*) was once one of the dominant trees in the eastern forests of North America, but its lack of resistance to the introduced oriental chestnut blight from China resulted in its total elimination from North America. In contrast, efforts to eradicate or control the

European rabbit (*Oryctolagus cuniculus*) in Australia, by introducing the *Myxoma* virus (which causes a disease called myxomatosis, a form of fibrous skin cancer), failed because of the evolution of resistance. When the virus was first introduced in 1950 there was an epidemic which killed an estimated 99.8% of the rabbits, but a year later only 90% of the rabbits were killed by the virus, and seven years after that, fewer than 30% were killed. The reduction in mortality was a result of a reduced virulence of the virus, as well as an increased immunity to the virus in the rabbits.

13.2 | Genetic recombination

In sexually reproducing organisms, during the process of meiosis and the subsequent production of a zygote from two gametes, there is a recombination of alleles. This occurs every generation. By itself, this does not cause evolution, i.e. change allelic frequencies, as shown by Hardy and Weinberg (see Chapter 6). However, it amplifies genetic variation to produce virtually an infinite variety of different genotypes and phenotypes, such that every individual is genetically unique in most populations (see Chapter 7).

This amplification of genotypic and phenotypic variation is considerably reduced by two factors that are internal to the organism. They are chromosome structure and gametic selection.

13.2.1 Chromosome structure

Different genes do not recombine totally at random because they are linked together structurally to form chromosomes. Genes on the same chromosome tend to move together into the gamete, and the closer they are positioned on the chromosome, the more likely it is that the same combination of alleles of different genes will stay together. There may also be structural changes in the sequence of genes, called inversions, which inhibit crossovers, i.e. prevent the random recombination of alleles of different genes.

There is increasing evidence that genes influencing the same character, or a very favourable combination of genes, are frequently very closely linked and so rarely recombine, or they are protected from recombination by being part of an inversion. A good example of this is provided by the butterfly *Papilio memnon* which occurs in six forms, each of which mimics a different distasteful butterfly (Turner 1984). There are five tightly linked genes that control the shape of the hind wing, the colours of certain patches on the fore and hind wings, and the colour of the abdomen. The alleles of these five genes do not recombine at random but occur in specific sets, or 'supergenes', that are responsible for the appearance of the six different mimics.

Thus, it is possible that the chromosome structure, including the number of chromosomes as well as the sequence of genes on the chromosomes, has evolved to protect favourable groupings of alleles of different genes from recombination to a greater or lesser extent.

13.2.2 Gametic selection

Normally, heterozygous individuals produce two types of gametes with equal frequency. Their alleles recombine at random with the alleles of other genes, except for tightly linked genes, in the formation of the zygote. Sometimes, however, this doesn't happen: there is a bias in favour of one of the alleles such that most of the resulting zygotes only contain one of the alleles. Thus, the heterozygous genotype behaves almost as if it were homozygous for one of the alleles. There are various ways in which this can happen.

One mechanism, called meiotic drive or segregation distortion, occurs during meiosis. When the alleles segregate into different gametes, more than half the gametes contain one of the alleles because the other cells do not develop normally into a gamete. This mechanism may be difficult to distinguish from differential viability. The viability of a gamete may be dependent on the presence or absence of certain alleles, and this creates a bias in the allelic frequencies in the gametes at the time of fertilization. Finally, an allele may affect the swimming speed of the sperm, or the rate at which a pollen tube grows toward the ovum. Such characteristics of the gametes affect their fertilization success, and the offspring may favour one allele rather than another.

In summary, mutation and genetic recombination are responsible for the production of genetic variation but there are internal constraints on the amplification of genetic diversity through sexual recombination. We will now discuss the powerful external forces that limit genetic diversity and perhaps mould it in certain directions.

13.3 Chance effects: genetic drift and inbreeding

In the vast majority of species, the gene pool does not consist of a single group of freely interbreeding individuals. Rather, there is a spatial distribution of organisms such that a species consists of a number of more or less discrete populations. Individuals seldom breed totally at random and tend to restrict the number of possible mating partners. For example, sessile individuals breed more commonly with their neighbours than with distant individuals for obvious reasons. The subdivision of the gene pool into populations and the restriction of mating partners within populations mean that the effective population size of breeding individuals is usually considerably lower than the overall numbers of a species or a population.

Allelic frequencies can change as a result of chance effects, or 'sampling errors', and this change is inversely related to the effective population size. Such changes are trivial in large breeding groups of individuals, but may be large in small breeding groups. Consequently small populations show greater changes in allelic frequencies than larger populations. There is a randomness to the change in allelic frequencies. They may increase or decrease, and the changes for most genes are independent of one another (see Chapter 8). This process, called genetic drift, is a dispersive process in that the allelic frequencies of different populations tend to diverge from one another over time. This leads to spatial variation in allelic frequencies both between and within populations, so that the overall genetic diversity is increased. However, within any breeding unit the change in allelic frequency may lead to the loss of one or more of the alleles, a process called fixation, and so there may be a loss of genetic diversity on a more local scale. This leads to an increase in homozygosity and inbreeding, and the individuals in a breeding unit become genetically more closely related. There are many examples of reduced genetic variation in small populations (see Chapter 8).

If a population is started by a small number of individuals moving to a new area (founder effect), or if a population is reduced to a small size at some point in its history (genetic bottleneck), the chance effects may be extremely large and there can be a considerable reduction in genetic diversity. The consequences of this remain with the population for thousands of generations, because as we have seen (section 13.1) the development and incorporation of new genetic variation into the gene pool is a very slow process.

Chance effects can increase the overall genetic diversity among populations, but decrease genetic variation within populations. These effects are strongly modified by both migration and selection.

13.4 | Migration: gene flow

The tendency for genetic drift to cause spatial heterogeneity in the gene pool is counteracted by migration. Indeed, spatial variation in allelic frequencies, however it is caused, is reduced or limited by gene flow through the process of migration. It is important to remember that the only migrants of importance are those that breed with the receiving populations. Obviously, if an individual moves from one population to another but does not breed, it ultimately has no effect on the local gene pool. The effect of migration on receiving populations depends on how different the migrant genotypes are from the mean of the population and also on the migration rate. Where migration rates are high the populations become more uniform, but in regions where the migration rates are very low there may be sudden changes in the characteristics of neighbouring populations (see Chapter 9). Thus, migration is a key factor influencing the geographical variation of species.

13.5 | Natural selection

The genetic variability that is created by mutation and enhanced by genetic recombination, and subsequently influenced by genetic drift and migration, is subjected to natural selection which directs changes

(a)

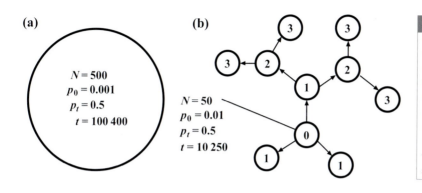

$N = 500$
$p_0 = 0.001$
$p_t = 0.5$
$t = 100\,400$

(b)

$N = 50$
$p_0 = 0.01$
$p_t = 0.5$
$t = 10\,250$

Fig. 13.2 Number of generations (t) required to increase the frequency of a single favourable recessive allele from its initial frequency (p_0) to a final frequency (p_t) of 0.5, where the selection pressure (s) is 0.01. (a) In a randomly mating population of 500 individuals, and (b) in a population that is subdivided into ten subpopulations of 50 individuals.

in the gene pool such that populations become more suited to their local environments. Selection acts in a mechanical way, such that genotypes[1] leaving the most breeding descendants tend to increase in frequency, whereas genotypes leaving fewer breeding descendants tend to decrease in frequency. Genotypic frequencies do not always change in response to natural selection, however, because as our theory and examples have shown in Chapters 10 to 12, it is possible for natural selection to be operating without any resulting change in the allelic or genotypic frequencies (e.g. heterozygote superiority in zygotic selection, and stabilizing selection in polygenic systems). Thus, selection can serve to maintain gene frequencies at some point as well as to change them.

The spread of favoured recessive alleles in populations is extremely slow when they occur at low frequencies (see Table 10.5). For example, imagine a single favourable mutation occurring in a population of 500 individuals. Its starting frequency is $1/(2 \times 500) = 0.001$, and it would take 90 150 generations to increase its frequency to 0.01 at a selection pressure (s) of 0.01. If selection remained constant, it would take an additional 10 250 generations, or a total of 100 400 generations from the original mutation, to reach a frequency of 0.5, at which point it would start to become the most common allele in the population. This is illustrated in Fig. 13.2a.

If the population were subdivided into ten subpopulations of 50 individuals (see Fig. 13.2b), the starting frequency of a favourable mutation in one of the subpopulations would be $1/(2 \times 50) = 0.01$, and it would only require 10 250 generations to increase to a frequency of 0.5 in that subpopulation (Table 10.5). However, while the allele was increasing in frequency, there would be migration between subpopulations (from population 0 to neighbouring populations 1, and then to their neighbouring populations 2, and so on, as shown in Fig. 13.2b). It would only require two to four steps before the favourable gene was transferred to every subpopulation. At a migration rate of

[1] Here we are using the term genotype only to refer to that of a specific character or trait, and so we are only considering a single gene or a relatively small number of genes that affect the specified trait. Selection will operate on the different alleles to change their frequencies and hence the frequencies of the genotypes (see section 3.1).

one individual per subpopulation per generation (i.e. $1/50 = 0.02$) this would only require a few hundred generations before the favourable allele was introduced to all subpopulations. Thus, all subpopulations would reach a frequency of 0.5 for the favourable allele in less than 11 000 generations after the favourable mutation, or about ten times faster than a single breeding unit of the same size (Fig. 13.2a). We can see that if a population is subdivided into smaller breeding units, a combination of selection and migration can increase the speed at which favourable mutations are incorporated into the population, compared to the action of selection on a single large freely breeding population. Clearly, the structure of populations can have an important effect on their evolution.

Selection acts to make populations more suited to their local environments, and so we expect there to be geographical variation in species because environments vary geographically. However, unlike the geographical variation induced by genetic drift, in which there are random changes in allelic frequencies, the allelic frequencies determined by natural selection are directed according to the local environments. Thus, we expect patterns in the characteristics of populations determined by natural selection that are quite different from those determined by genetic drift. For example, if a species relies on camouflage to avoid predation we expect there to be a 'fit' between body colour and the predominant colour of its environment. A good example of this is provided by the peppered moth (*Biston betularia*), which was discussed at length in Chapter 11. Such species tend to be darker in areas where the background colour is dark, and lighter where the background colour is light. This suggests that selection has a stronger effect than genetic drift, and this conclusion is supported by the available theory (see Chapter 8).

It is important to realize that the way in which a population adapts to changes in the environment depends chiefly upon the characteristics that it already possesses. Populations are betrayed by their ancestry. For example, imagine a plant adapting to a more arid environment in which the dry season becomes progressively longer. This situation could develop because either the climate changes over the long term (a temporal change in environment) or the plant may be invading more arid environments (a spatial change in environment). If the plant evades the rigours of the dry season by losing its leaves and becoming dormant, it will probably evolve longer periods of dormancy and perhaps show a more rapid growth pattern during the wet season. However, if the plant retains its leaves during the dry season and reduces evaporation by having narrow leaves with a thick cuticle, it may evolve even narrower leaves with thicker cuticles. It will not switch from one strategy to the other. Similarly, if the number of predators on a species increases, or if the predators become more efficient at finding and killing the species, natural selection will favour an improvement in pre-existing traits. Thus, species that escape predation by running away may become faster and more agile, those that rely on camouflage to escape detection may become even

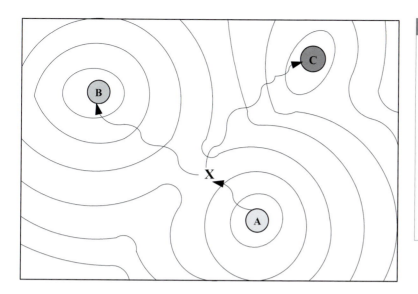

Fig. 13.3 The adaptive landscape model with a multidimensional field of gene combinations (shown in two dimensions), with fitness contours and three peaks (A, B and C). A population on peak A cannot cross the valley (i.e. decrease its fitness) to reach peaks of higher fitness, B and C, unless there is a chance change in gene frequencies (founder effect or genetic drift) which takes it to the valley X. From that point, natural selection can drive the population to any one of the three peaks.

more cryptic, those that depend on being distasteful to avoid being eaten may become even more unpalatable, and so on.

True novelty, then, is rare in evolution. Natural selection tends to be conservative because it creates change in a step-by-step manner, rather than by sudden leaps. Sewall Wright proposed an *adaptive landscape model*, in which genetic drift interacts with natural selection to allow sudden changes in genotype. He envisioned a multidimensional genetic landscape where there are local peaks in fitness corresponding to particular complexes of alleles (Fig. 13.3). The peaks may have different heights, i.e. different levels of fitness. It would not be possible for natural selection by itself to move a population from one peak to another because it would have to cross a genetic region of lower fitness. Sewall Wright envisioned that small populations could make this shift because of chance changes in allelic frequencies. Perhaps a few individuals move to establish a population elsewhere, or a population is reduced to a small number of individuals. Whatever the reason for the small population size, if the population is sufficiently small there can be new combinations of alleles occurring by chance and perhaps one of these combinations might be at the base of another peak in the genetic landscape. If so, natural selection will modify the allelic frequencies to move the population up the new adaptive peak until it reaches the top. If the population has a higher level of fitness than previously it may expand and perhaps replace the parent population through a process of gene flow and selection.

13.6 | Summary

We have considered how the effects of mutation, chance events, migration and selection are integrated to change gene frequencies both within populations and between populations of a species. Such evolutionary changes are frequently referred to as microevolution. The power and the speed at which this level of evolution can occur are particularly well illustrated by the evolution of resistance to drugs in bacteria, to insecticides in insects, and to herbicides in many plants. However, such evolutionary responses are by no means assured and species or populations can face extinction as a result. On the other hand, where the environment fluctuates around a long-term mean, the characteristics of populations may well remain stable, with only minor fluctuations, because of stabilizing selection. Such microevolutionary changes allow populations and species to modify their characteristics in response to changes in the environment.

This synthesis of population genetics and Darwin's evolutionary theories is known as the Modern Synthesis, and one of its tenets is that microevolutionary changes accumulate over vast geological time spans and result in macroevolutionary differences among organisms, i.e. the major differences distinguishing higher taxa. Not everyone subscribes to this position. Most geneticists believe that microevolution can explain macroevolution, but there are many palaeontologists who oppose this point of view and who believe that speciation and major phyletic changes involve different processes. We will not pursue this controversy in this book, and instead will return to the topic of population ecology in the next section.

Part IV

Demography

In Chapters 4 and 5, we examined different models of population growth where the structure of the population, in terms of age or size, was constant or unimportant and so could be ignored. However, we are well aware that such factors as sex and age have profound effects on the chances of an individual dying, or producing offspring, and so we need to incorporate some of these factors into our growth models. These vital statistics of populations are called demographics, and the study of these statistics is called demography.

First, the pattern of mortality in relation to age is examined and quantified in Chapter 14. These age-specific death rates are combined with the age-specific birth rates in the following chapter to calculate the exponential growth rates of populations. Some populations with more complex growth characteristics cannot be modelled by the basic equations, and so matrix models of population growth are also introduced because they can be used to describe the growth of any population. Finally, Chapter 16 considers how the pattern of age-specific birth and death rates might have evolved by natural selection, followed by a brief review of the evolution of life-history traits of organisms.

Chapter 14

Life tables and age-specific death rates

This chapter considers how an individual's chance of dying is influenced by its age and sex. After a preliminary discussion about age-specific death rates, we will review the various ways of constructing life tables, which tabulate the information on age-specific death rates in an orderly way, and finally we will compare some of the life tables of different species of mammals and birds.

14.1 Age-specific death rates

We can develop our understanding of age-specific death rates by considering the work of Peter and Rosemary Grant on the large cactus (ground) finch (*Geospiza conirostris*), in the Galápagos archipelago. During the period 1978–83 they marked 1244 nestlings and followed their subsequent survival year by year. The nestlings could not be sexed, and they made the reasonable assumption that half were male and half were female. Only 27 of the 622 female nestlings survived for one year, 20 for two years, 13 for three years, and so on, until all the females were dead by seven years of age (see Table 14.1 for full data set). If we plot the number of survivors versus age (Fig. 14.1) we obtain the shape of the survivorship curve.

The heavy early mortality obscures the shape of the curve beyond the first year of age. We can deal with this problem by plotting the number of survivors on a logarithmic scale (Fig. 14.2). Plotting the data this way has an added advantage because the slope of the graph gives us a measure of the age-specific death rates, i.e. the steepness of the curve is directly related to the mortality rate. Thus, we can see that the mortality rate is highest during the first year of life, declines to its lowest rate between one and two years of age, and thereafter generally increases with age.

The age-specific death rates, or mortality rates (q_x), are calculated directly from the census information (Table 14.1) as follows. Only 27 of 622 female nestlings (age 0) survived for one year, and so 595 females died during the first year of life. The mortality rate is $595/622 = 0.957$ for this period, which shows that approximately 96% of the females

Table 14.1 Life table for the large cactus (ground) finch (*Geospiza conirostris*) on Genovesa Island for females of known age, banded as nestlings and known to have fledged in the years 1978–83

Age interval (years) (x)	Number at start of interval (S_x)	Number dying in interval (D_x)	Probability of survival from birth (l_x)	Fraction dying in interval (d_x)	Probability of dying in interval (q_x)	Mean expectation of life (e_x)
0–1	(622)	595	1.000	0.957	0.957	0.61
1–2	27	7	0.043	0.011	0.259	2.06
2–3	20	7	0.032	0.011	0.350	1.60
3–4	13	7	0.021	0.011	0.538	1.19
4–5	6	4	0.010	0.006	0.667	1.00
5–6	2	1	0.003	0.002	0.500	1.00
6–7	1	1	0.002	0.002	1.000	0.50
7–8	0	–	0	–	–	–
	$\Sigma = 622$			$\Sigma = 1.000$		

Source: From Table 3.2 of Grant and Grant (1989).

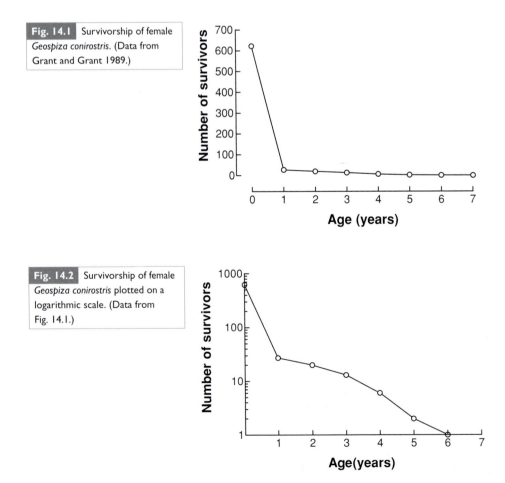

Fig. 14.1 Survivorship of female *Geospiza conirostris*. (Data from Grant and Grant 1989.)

Fig. 14.2 Survivorship of female *Geospiza conirostris* plotted on a logarithmic scale. (Data from Fig. 14.1.)

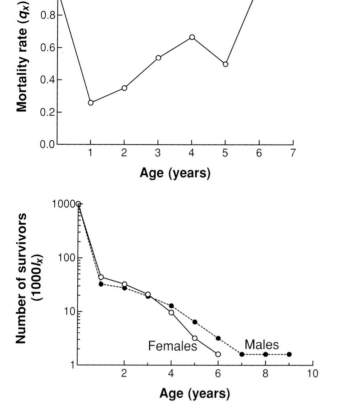

Fig. 14.4 Survivorship of male and female *Geospiza conirostris* that were banded as nestlings during the period 1978–83. (Data from Table 3.2 in Grant and Grant 1989.)

die before they are one year old. Similarly, only 20 of the 27 one-year-old females survived to two years of age, and so 7 died during that period. The mortality rate for females in their second year of life (i.e. aged one to two years) is $7/27 = 0.259$. When the mortality rates are plotted against age (Fig. 14.3), it may be seen that the mortality rate is U-shaped with age, and conforms to our assessment of mortality rates from the semi-logarithmic plot of the survivorship curve (Fig. 14.2).

To facilitate the comparison of different survivorship curves, they are started with the same number of individuals. We do this by converting the number of survivors at each age to an l_x series, which is the probability at birth of surviving to a particular age. This is done by dividing the number of survivors at each age by the number of individuals at birth (i.e. aged 0), and the resulting series will start at 1.0 at birth and decline with age (Table 14.1). Frequently, the l_x series is multiplied by 100 or 1000, converting the series to $100l_x$ or $1000l_x$ so that the number of survivors appears as whole, rather than fractional, numbers at each age.

Male and female survivorship are compared (Fig. 14.4), noting that males can be distinguished from females once they are one year old. Females survived better than the males during their first year of life, but once they reached one year of age males had lower mortality rates than females (Fig. 14.4). The net effect was that males survived

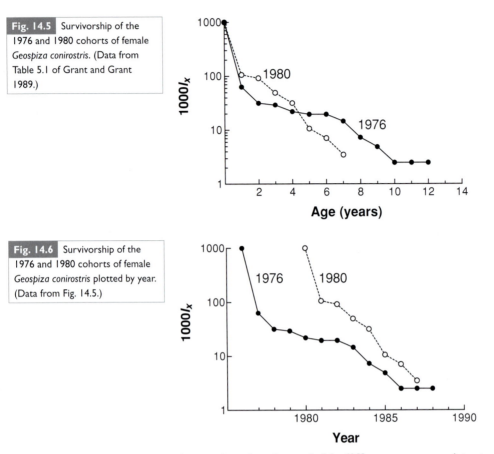

Fig. 14.5 Survivorship of the 1976 and 1980 cohorts of female *Geospiza conirostris*. (Data from Table 5.1 of Grant and Grant 1989.)

Fig. 14.6 Survivorship of the 1976 and 1980 cohorts of female *Geospiza conirostris* plotted by year. (Data from Fig. 14.5.)

better than females and this difference was consistent when the cohorts of different years were compared (Grant and Grant 1989). This is unusual, because females survive better than males in most species.

The survival of cohorts born in different years can be very different. For example, the 1980 cohort of females seem to have a much shorter lifespan than the 1976 cohort (Fig. 14.5). However, if we compare the survivorship of the two cohorts by year rather than age (Fig. 14.6) we see that the survivorship curves are similar in shape. When Fig. 14.6 is compared to the yearly environmental conditions we can separate the age-specific mortality effects from the effects of a fluctuating environment. There was a heavy mortality in both cohorts during the first year of life, and this seemed to be quite consistent across all cohorts (Grant and Grant 1989). The mortality rate during the second year of life was higher for the 1976 cohort than the 1980 cohort because there was a drought in 1977 and the availability of food was reduced, whereas conditions were favourable in 1981. During the period 1982–6, both cohorts showed a similar increase in mortality rates which was thought to be related to the increasing density of birds (which reached peak densities in 1983) and also to the El Niño event of 1982–3 and the following severe drought of 1984–5 (Grant and Grant 1989). When we make this type of comparison, we can see that the difference in survivorship of the two cohorts was almost

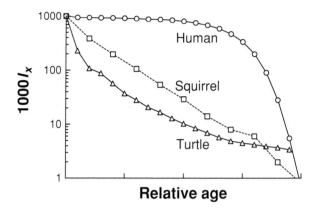

certainly related to differences in the environmental conditions that they experienced.

14.1.1 Types of survivorship curves

Survivorship curves, i.e. l_x series, are often arranged into three main types, and when the l_x series is plotted on a logarithmic scale, the three types have the following characteristics:

Type I The slope of the survivorship curve increases with age, i.e. age-specific mortality rates increase with age. A good example of this is provided by human populations in 'developed' countries (Fig. 14.7).

Type II The slope of the survivorship curve is constant, and so age-specific mortality rates are constant. An example is shown by Belding's ground squirrel (*Spermophilus beldingi*) (Fig. 14.7).

Type III The slope of the survivorship curve decreases with age, i.e. age-specific mortality rates decrease with age. An example is provided by the snapping turtle (*Chelydra serpentina*) (Fig. 14.7). More extreme examples are provided by many long-lived trees that produce a prolific number of seeds.

Few species have survivorship curves that conform exactly to these 'ideal' types. For example, the survivorship curve of the large cactus finch (*Geospiza conirostris*) shows a heavy juvenile mortality rate (Type III) but the adult mortality rate generally increases with age (Type I). We will discuss these 'ideal' survivorship curves again in Chapter 15.

14.2 | Constructing life tables

Death rates vary with both the sex and age of an individual, and they are also affected by the environment. We keep track of these statistics in a very orderly way, but demographers are optimistic people and so rather than talking of death tables they develop *life tables*, and use *survivorship* data rather than age-specific death rates in growth models. To see how life tables are developed we will initially consider the example of one of Darwin's finches from the Galápagos archipelago that we have discussed already (Table 14.1).

1. The first column is an age interval (x), the duration of which will depend on the organism being studied. Usually the time intervals are of equal duration, but occasionally some of the oldest-aged organisms are grouped together and the interval may be indicated as, for example, >15 years. Frequently the age interval is only indicated by the start of the interval, i.e. 0, 1, 2, 3, etc.

2. The second column shows the number of survivors (S_x) at the start of the age interval. In our example the first number is in parentheses because the precise number of nestling females is uncertain. A total of 1244 nestlings was banded but they were impossible to sex at this stage. It was assumed that half were male and half female. The survivorship of the females was followed until they had all died by the end of their seventh year of age. Note that it is common for there to be some uncertainty about the number of individuals in the first age class. For example, we may estimate the number of eggs laid by a fish by counting the number of eggs in adult females and assuming that all are laid.

3. The third column shows the number of individuals dying (D_x) within each age class. This is easy to compute if the number of survivors at the start of each age class is known. The number dying in the first age class is $622 - 27 = 595$; the number dying in the second age class is $27 - 20 = 7$, and so on. Symbolically, this is calculated as $D_x = S_x - S_{x+1}$. We can check our arithmetic by summing the total dying in all age classes. This should equal the number alive at the start of the first age class.

4. To make it easier to compare life tables with very different starting numbers, the number of survivors is converted to a probability of survival series, l_x, by dividing the number of survivors, S_x, at each age by the number alive at the start of the first age class. Thus, $l_0 = 622/622$ or 1.0, $l_1 = 27/622$ or 0.043, $l_2 = 20/622$ or 0.032, and so on. Some demographers calculate $100l_x$ or $1000l_x$ series so that one starts with 100 or 1000 individuals and the following number of survivors will appear as whole rather than fractional numbers.

5. The d_x series is calculated in exactly the same way as the D_x series (column 3) by using the data in column 4. Symbolically, this is calculated as $d_x = l_x - l_{x+1}$, and so $d_0 = 1.0 - 0.043$ or 0.957, $d_1 = 0.043 - 0.032$ or 0.011, and so on. Some of the values in Table 14.1 appear to be incorrect because of rounding errors.

6. The sixth column computes the probability of dying, or the mortality rate (q_x), during each age interval. This is calculated by either D_x/S_x or d_x/l_x. Thus, $q_0 = 595/622$ or 0.957, $q_1 = 7/27$ or 0.259, and so on.

7. Finally, the mean life expectancy (e_x) is calculated for different ages in the last column. This is estimated by summing the number of survivors in age class (x) and older age classes, and dividing this

sum by the number of survivors in age class (x). This estimate assumes that all individuals alive at the start of an age class survive to the end of that age class and then die. The correction is simple, we subtract half of the value of the age interval (x) because we assume that mortality occurs evenly throughout each age interval. Symbolically, this may be stated as $e_x = ((S_x + S_{x+1} + S_{x+2} \ldots S_n)/S_x) - 0.5x$, where S_n is the number in the oldest age class. Thus, $E_0 = [(622 + 27 + 20 + 13 + 6 + 2 + 1)/622] - 0.5$, or 0.61 years, $E_1 = [(27 + 20 + 13 + 6 + 2 + 1)/27] - 0.5$, or 2.06 years, $E_2 = [(20 + 13 + 6 + 2 + 1)/20] - 0.5$, or 1.6 years, and so on. It may surprise you that the mean expectation of life can increase with age. This happens when there is a sharp decrease in mortality rates.

The development of a life table to tabulate information on age-specific death rates is a simple exercise, provided we have either the initial survivorship data (i.e. S_x series) or ages at death (i.e. D_x series). We will now look at the different ways of obtaining this information and developing life tables. Some have rather restrictive assumptions, and the different types of life tables are applied to different situations.

14.2.1 Cohort (horizontal or generation) life tables
In this type of life table the survival of a known group of organisms, called a cohort, is followed from birth to the time when they are all dead. The method is typically applied to plants and sessile animals that are not very long-lived, because they are relatively easy to keep track of and resample during their life. It is difficult to apply to animals which disperse, because dispersal may be confused with mortality. Cohort life tables were used to construct the survivorship curves for Belding's ground squirrel (Fig. 14.7) and for *Geospiza conirostris* (Figs. 14.5 and 14.6). However, the example that we have just considered (Table 14.1) is a composite cohort life table, because the cohorts of different years have been combined to give an average life table for the group. Cohort life tables can be applied to populations at any phase of population growth, i.e. the populations could be increasing or decreasing, or be stationary in size.

14.2.2 Static (stationary or time-specific) life tables
It may be impractical to construct a cohort life table for organisms that are very long-lived, such as elephants and many species of trees, or for highly mobile animals such as many ungulates. Instead, information is collected at a single point in time, which is considered to be representative of the population over a much longer time period. Life tables are constructed using three types of information.

1. Time-specific or vertical life tables
This method avoids the time problem caused by long-lived species by estimating the survival of individuals of known age during a single time interval. Age-specific death rates are calculated independently

Table 14.2 Time-specific life table data for the human female population of Canada in 1980

Age class (years)	Number in each age class	Deaths in each age class in 1980	Annual mortality rate $(1000q_x)$	Survivorship $(1000l_x)$	Number dying in 1980 $(1000d_x)$
0–1	173 400	1 651	9.52	1000	9.52
1–4	685 900	340	0.5	990.5	0.49
5–9	876 600	218	0.25	988.5	0.25
10–14	980 300	234	0.24	987.3	0.24
15–19	1 164 100	568	0.49	986.1	0.48
20–24	1 136 100	619	0.54	983.7	0.54
25–29	1 029 300	578	0.56	981.0	0.55
30–34	933 000	662	0.71	978.3	0.69
35–39	739 200	818	1.11	974.8	1.08
40–44	627 000	1 039	1.66	969.4	1.61
45–49	622 400	1 664	2.67	961.4	2.57
50–54	615 100	2574	4.18	948.5	3.97
55–59	596 000	3 878	6.51	928.7	6.04
60–64	481 200	4 853	10.09	898.5	9.06
65–69	423 400	6 803	16.07	853.2	13.71
70–74	325 600	8 421	25.86	784.6	20.29
75–79	235 100	10 029	42.66	683.2	29.14
80–84	149 300	10 824	72.50	537.4	38.96
85 and above	119 200	18 085	151.72	342.6	51.98

Source: Data from Statistics Canada (1982), cited from Krebs (1985).

for each age-class for the same period of time, hence the time-specific label, and the estimates are combined to develop the full life table. The life table for Caucasians males (Fig. 14.7) was developed using this method, and a partial life table for the female population of Canada in 1980 is developed to illustrate the application of this method (Table 14.2).

Each age group was counted in 1980, and a tally was made of the number of deaths in the same age groups. Note that the method depends on reliably estimating the age of all individuals, as well as the timing of their deaths. The annual mortality rates (q_x) during 1980 were estimated by dividing the number of deaths by the number of females in each age group (e.g. for age class 0–1, $q_x = 1651/173\,400$ or 0.00952). These values were multiplied by 1000 to obtain a $1000q_x$ series (e.g. for age class 0–1, $1000q_x = 0.00952 \times 1000$ or 9.52). The $1000d_x$ series was calculated using the relationship $1000d_x = 1000q_x \times 1000l_x/1000$ (e.g. for age class 40–44, $1000d_x = 1.66 \times 969.4/1000$ or 1.61). The initial $1000l_x$ value is 1000, and other values were calculated by taking the $1000l_x$ value of the previous age class and subtracting from it the $1000d_x$ value multiplied by the number of years in the previous age class (the $1000d_x$ values are annual estimates because it is the annual mortality rate that has been estimated). For example, to calculate the $1000l_x$ for age class 75–9, we use the $1000l_x$ value of the

Table 14.3 Life table for Dall mountain sheep (*Ovis dalli*) in Mount McKinley (now Denali) National Park, Alaska

Age class (years) (x)	Number dying in age class (D_x)	Number surviving at start of age class (S_x)	Probability of survival from birth (l_x)	Number dying in age class (d_x)	Mortality rate (q_x)	Mean expectation of life (e_x)
0–1	121	608	1.000	0.199	0.199	7.1
1–2	7	487	0.801	0.012	0.014	7.7
2–3	8	480	0.789	0.013	0.017	6.8
3–4	7	472	0.776	0.012	0.015	5.9
4–5	18	465	0.765	0.030	0.039	5.0
5–6	28	447	0.735	0.046	0.063	4.2
6–7	29	419	0.689	0.048	0.069	3.4
7–8	42	390	0.641	0.069	0.108	2.6
8–9	80	348	0.572	0.132	0.230	1.9
9–10	114	268	0.441	0.188	0.425	1.3
10–11	95	154	0.253	0.156	0.617	0.9
11–12	55	59	0.097	0.090	0.932	0.6
12–13	2	4	0.007	0.003	0.500	1.0
13–14	2	2	0.003	0.003	1.000	0.5
14–15	0	0	0.000	0.000	–	–

Source: Data from Murie (1944), as used by Deevey (1947).

previous age class (784.6), and subtract from it the number dying each year in the previous age class (20.29) multiplied by 5 (the number of years in that age class). This gives a value of 784.6 − (20.29 × 5) or 683.2. In this manner, the complete life table is constructed.

2. Stationary life tables based on the ages at death within a population

This method was first applied by Edward Deevey (1947), who used Olaus Murie's (1944) data on Dall mountain sheep (*Ovis dalli*) in Mount McKinley (now Denali) National Park in Alaska. Murie collected 608 skulls and estimated their age from the size of their horns. Consequently, he could estimate the age of death of 608 animals (see D_x column of Table 14.3). Deevey used this information to construct a life table based on the following reasoning. All 608 animals must have been alive at birth, and so this would be the starting number in the S_x column. The 121 animals dying in the first year of life would reduce the number of survivors to 487 at age 1, and similarly the seven animals dying in the second year of life would reduce the number of survivors to 480 at age 2, and so on. Deevey reconstructed the survivorship (S_x) series in this way and was then able to calculate the remainder of the life table in the usual way. The pattern of survivorship and age-specific mortality rates is illustrated in Figs. 14.8 and 14.9.

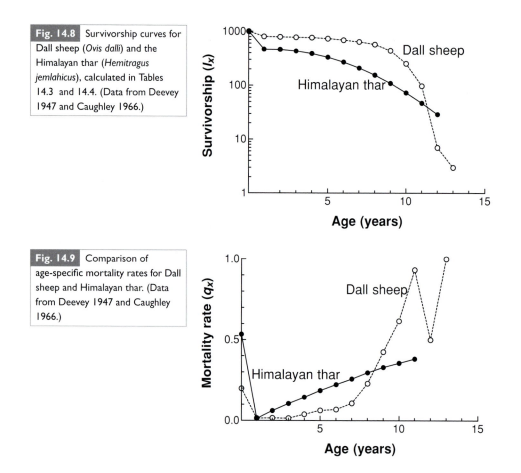

Fig. 14.8 Survivorship curves for Dall sheep (*Ovis dalli*) and the Himalayan thar (*Hemitragus jemlahicus*), calculated in Tables 14.3 and 14.4. (Data from Deevey 1947 and Caughley 1966.)

Fig. 14.9 Comparison of age-specific mortality rates for Dall sheep and Himalayan thar. (Data from Deevey 1947 and Caughley 1966.)

This type of life table is based on some very restrictive assumptions. We must be able to age the skulls accurately, and we must also assume that the survival of the skulls shows no bias with age. For example, if the skulls of animals dying during their first year of life are destroyed (e.g. by weathering, by predators, or by scavengers) more rapidly than the skulls of older animals they would be under-represented in our sample and our estimates of the age-specific death rates would be inaccurate. We also assume that the population is stationary in size (hence the name, stationary life table), so that births exactly balance the deaths. If the population were increasing in size, the younger age classes would be over-represented in our sample; if the population were declining in size the older age classes would be over-represented in our sample; and if the population had first increased and then decreased prior to our sampling, the intermediate age classes would be over-represented in our sample. It is possible to correct population increase or decrease (see Caughley 1977), but this assumes that the population is either increasing or decreasing exponentially and that a stable age structure has developed. For a long-lived species like the Dall sheep, this would require a constant rate of population growth for at least two decades which seems most unlikely. It is obvious that one needs to be very careful when applying this method, and one requires a great deal of information about the

Table 14.4 Partial life table for female Himalayan thar (*Hemitragus jemlahicus*) in New Zealand, constructed from the age structure of the population

Age class (years) (x)	Frequency in sample	Adjusted frequency (S_x)	Probability of survival from birth (l_x)	Number dying in age class (d_x)	Mortality rate (q_x)
0–1	–	205[a]	1.000	0.533	0.533
1–2	94	95.83	0.467	0.006	0.013
2–3	97	94.43	0.461	0.028	0.061
3–4	107	88.69	0.433	0.046	0.106
4–5	68	79.41	0.387	0.056	0.145
5–6	70	67.81	0.331	0.062	0.187
6–7	47	55.20	0.269	0.600	0.223
7–8	37	42.85	0.209	0.054	0.258
8–9	35	31.71	0.155	0.046	0.297
9–10	24	22.37	0.109	0.036	0.330
10–11	16	15.04	0.073	0.026	0.356
11–12	11	9.64	0.047	0.018	0.382
12–13	6	5.90	0.029		
Older	<5				

[a] Calculated from adjusted frequencies and m_x values.
Source: From Caughley (1966).

population to be sure that the basic assumptions are not violated too severely.

3. Stationary life tables based on the age structure of the population

If the population is not changing in size, i.e. is stationary, births balance the deaths and the age structure of the population is the same as the survivorship (S_x) series. It is assumed that individuals can be aged accurately, and that an unbiased sample of the population can be obtained. If the population is increasing or decreasing exponentially and has attained a stable age distribution, it is possible to derive the stationary age distribution (see Caughley 1977), but these conditions seem unlikely to be true for long-lived populations as we have already noted. It should be clear that however we determine the age structure of the population, even if it means killing a sample from the population, the ages represent the survivorship (S_x) series. There have been instances where an investigator has assumed that the age structure represents the ages at death, i.e. the D_x series, because the animals were killed by the sampling method (see Caughley 1966).

An example of this type of life table is shown in Table 14.4 for an ungulate, the Himalayan thar (*Hemitragus jemlahicus*), in New Zealand. Caughley (1966) obtained samples of the population, made by hunters, and the animals were aged by the growth rings on their horns. He made various checks to confirm that sampling was random and that the data were consistent with a stationary population. Caughley had to deal with one problem that is common when applying this method: the observed frequency of females in some age classes is larger than the frequency in younger age classes. Note that the number of females appears to increase between one and three years of age, and then again between four and five years of age (Table 14.4). There are two logical explanations for such patterns: the increases may be a result of sampling error, or they may be real because of fluctuations in population size. For example, if the population had declined dramatically in size during the three- to four-year period prior to taking the sample, we would expect there to be more three- to four-year-old females than younger-aged animals. However, Caughley found no evidence for any changes in population size during this period and explained the fluctuations on the basis of sampling error. Caughley fitted a polynomial function to the observed frequencies to ensure that the numbers either declined or stayed the same from one age to the next. This procedure provided the adjusted frequencies in Table 14.4, and the number of newborns was estimated from fecundity data (see Chapter 15). The life table could then be constructed in the usual way. The pattern of survivorship and the age-specific mortality rates are shown in Figs. 14.8 and 14.9.

14.3 | Comparison of life tables

The shape of the survivorship curve can vary considerably (section 14.1.1). However, if we compare the survivorship curves of humans (Fig. 14.7), and Dall sheep and the Himalayan thar (Fig. 14.8), we may see that they are similar in general shape, although the last two species exhibit heavier early mortality. The similarity of the general shape of these survivorship curves is remarkable, given the uncertainties in the construction of the life tables of the sheep and thar because of the very restrictive assumptions on which they are based (see section 14.2.2).

Perhaps the pattern of the age-specific mortality rates with age is more informative, and this is shown for Dall sheep and the Himalayan thar in Fig. 14.9. Their mortality rates are U-shaped with age, being high at birth, then declining to a minimum at about the time of puberty, and thereafter generally increasing with age. You may remember that similar U-shaped curves were observed for the large cactus finch (Fig. 14.3) and for Canadian human females (Table 14.2). Caughley has proposed that these age-specific mortality curves of mammals are typically U-shaped, and we will discuss how this shape may have evolved in Chapter 16.

14.4 | Constructing life tables using a spreadsheet

The development of a life table from the appropriate S_x or D_x series is a simple exercise, but is somewhat tedious when there is a large number of age classes. We can perform the calculations very efficiently using a spreadsheet, and in Chapter 15 we will extend the table to include age-specific reproductive rates and to calculate the growth rate of age-structured populations. The method of calculating life tables from either survivorship (S_x) data or age at death (D_x) data is outlined in Appendix 14.1.

The two life tables that you have calculated in your spreadsheet may be used to examine most types of life table data by simply substituting either the S_x or D_x series in the appropriate columns. We will go on to examine age-specific reproductive data in the next chapter so that we can calculate the growth rates of age-structured populations.

Appendix 14.1 Constructing life tables using a spreadsheet

1. Title your spreadsheet **Life Tables**; in A3 type **A. Based on survivorship (cohort or stationary)**; and in columns A to G of row 4 type the following headings: **Age, No. alive, No. dying, l_x, d_x, q_x,** and **e_x**. You may wish to centre these headings.
2. Enter **0** (zero) in cell A5, and the sequence of ages **1** to **15** in cells A6 to A20. Then in column B (cells B5 to B20) enter the survivorship series from the second column of Table 14.4. You will need to enter two extra zeros to complete the column. This provides us with our starting information for the life table.
3. We calculate the D_x series in column C as follows: Enter = **B5–B6** in C5 and copy C5 to cells C6 to C20. In C21 type = **@SUM(C5..C20)** or use the Σ function on the toolbar to do the same function. The sum should equal the starting number in cell B5.
4. Calculate:
   (a) the l_x series by typing = **B5/$B$5** in D5, and copying D5 to cells D6 to D20. Check to see that you have the same values as those in Table 14.4.
   (b) the d_x series by typing = **D5–D6** in E5, and copying E5 to cells E6 to E20.
   (c) the q_x series by typing = **E5/D5** in F5, and copying F5 to cells F6 to F20.
   (d) the e_x series by typing = **@SUM(D5..$D$20)/D5-0.5** in G5, and copying G5 to cells G6 to G20. Our life table is now complete.
5. Now type: **B. Based on age at death (stationary)** in A28, and then copy the block A4..G21 and paste to A29. The life table has been replicated and we will modify it as follows:
   (a) Copy the D_x series (column 2) of Table 14.3 into column C (cells C30..C45).
   (b) Enter = **C46** in cell B30 (the starting value in the survivorship series equals the total number of deaths), then type = **B30–C30** in B31, and copy B31 to cells B32 to B45. You will have to do this a few cells at a time.

(c) Click on cell D30. Change the formula B30/$B$5 to **B30/$B$30**, and copy D30 to cells D31 to D45.

(d) Click on cell G30 and change $D$20 in the formula to **$D$45**, and then copy the revised formula to cells G31 to G45. The second life table is now complete.

6. Make two graphs, one showing the l_x series versus age, and the other of the q_x series versus age. They should resemble Figs. 14.8 and 14.9.

7. Save your spreadsheet.

Chapter 15

Age-specific reproduction and population growth rates

Conceptually, it is a simple matter to estimate age-specific birth rates. The total number of live offspring produced by samples of females in different age classes is documented, and then the age specific birth rates (B_x) are calculated by dividing the total number of live offspring produced by the sample of females in each age class by the sample size of females in that age class. Thus, if a sample of 30 two-year-old females gave birth to 120 live offspring during the course of the year, the age-specific birth rates of females in age class 2–3 would be 120/30, or 4.0. In practice, however, it may be difficult to estimate the number of live births. For example, some species of fish lay more than 1 000 000 eggs per female, and it may be extremely difficult to assess what proportion of the eggs are fertilized, i.e. are viable, under natural conditions. Other animals are secretive, and so one cannot observe the number of live births directly. In these cases, a sample of the population may be collected to measure the proportion of the population that is reproductively active in each class and to count the number of eggs, or embryos, or placental scars per female so that age-specific birth rates may be calculated. However, the problem of determining the viability of the offspring at birth still remains.

15.1 Calculating population growth rates from age-specific birth and death rates

One might anticipate that population growth rates would be difficult to calculate from age-specific mortality and birth rates. In practice, however, there are some simple ways of doing this, although some of the calculations may be somewhat tedious. Conventionally, we simplify the problem by calculating the growth rate of the female segment of the population. In effect we assume that the growth rate of the males will be the same, and in most cases this is appropriate because there is a characteristic sex ratio for the population (which may change with age).

Table 15.1 Age-specific survival (l_x) and live female births per female of age x (m_x) for Uinta ground squirrels (*Spermophilus armatus*) in a lawn habitat in Utah, before and after the approximate halving of population density. The population growth parameters are also calculated (see text)

Age (years) (x) (1)	Pre-reduction				Post-reduction			
	l_x (2)	m_x (3)	$l_x m_x$ (2) × (3)	$x\, l_x m_x$ (1) × (2) × (3)	l_x (2)	m_x (3)	$l_x m_x$ (2) × (3)	$x\, l_x m_x$ (1) × (2) × (3)
0	1.000	0.00	0.000	0.000	1.000	0.00	0.000	0.000
0.75	0.292	1.96	0.572	0.429	0.359	1.75	0.628	0.471
1.75	0.128	2.73	0.349	0.612	0.190	2.76	0.524	0.918
2.75	0.041	2.73	0.112	0.308	0.089	2.76	0.246	0.676
3.75	0.013	2.73	0.035	0.133	0.041	2.76	0.113	0.424
4.75	0.000	–	–	–	0.019	2.76	0.052	0.249
5.75					0.009	2.76	0.025	0.142
6.75					0.000			
			$\Sigma = R_0 = 1.069$	$\Sigma = 1.482$			$\Sigma = R_0 = 1.589$	$\Sigma = 2.881$
			$T = 1.386$				$T = 1.813$	
			$r_c = 0.048$				$r_c = 0.255$	
			$r_m = 0.049$				$r_m = 0.282$	

Source: Data from Slade and Balph (1974).

In order to calculate the growth rate of females, we need to calculate the number of live *female* births per female for each age class (m_x) rather than the age-specific birth rates (B_x) as calculated in the introduction. In most cases we assume a 50:50 sex ratio at birth, and so the m_x values are half the B_x values. Thus, in our example above, the m_x value would be 2.0.

To illustrate how population growth rates (r) are calculated from age-specific data, we will examine a study on the Uinta ground squirrel (*Spermophilus armatus*) by Slade and Balph (1974). They captured and marked every individual in the study area and observed their activity from observation towers. During the first few years of the study (1964–8), the population was left undisturbed and data were collected on the age-specific birth and death rates. Then the population density was approximately halved during the period 1968–71, and the effects of this reduction on the population's vital statistics were monitored. Some of their results are presented in Table 15.1, where the method of combining the information on birth and death rates to calculate population growth rates is outlined.

The production of new females for each age class is calculated by multiplying the survivorship (l_x) by the fecundity (m_x). In effect, this details the average production of female offspring for each age class during a female's life. The sum of the $l_x m_x$ series estimates the net reproductive rate, R_0, for the population, which is the average production of female offspring per female during her lifetime. Prior to the reduction of population density, the average female entering the population produced 1.069 female offspring before she died, whereas after the population density was halved, a female replaced herself with 1.589 female offspring before she died, a substantial increase (Table 15.1).

The net reproductive rate (R_0) is a measure of the multiplication rate, λ, per generation (see Chapter 4). It should be obvious that where $R_0 = 1.0$, the population is just replacing itself and is neither increasing nor decreasing, i.e. is stationary; where $R_0 > 1$ the population is increasing in size; and where $R_0 < 1$ the population is decreasing in size. In order to calculate a growth rate, r, per unit time we need to be able to estimate the generation time. There are two basic methods of calculating population growth rates from demographic data, which we will now describe.

15.1.1 The capacity for increase, r_c

The first, and simplest method can be developed in the following way. In Chapter 4 we showed that for populations with constant growth rates, r, the population size at time $t(N_t)$ is predicted by the following equation (Eqn 4.4):

$$N_t = N_0 e^{rt} \qquad \text{(Exp. 15.1)}$$

After one generation, where $t = T$ (the generation time) Exp. 15.1 becomes:

$$N_T = N_0 e^{rT} \qquad \text{(Exp. 15.2)}$$

Rearranging Exp. 15.2 and taking the logarithm of both sides we obtain:

$$\ln\left(\frac{N_T}{N_0}\right) = rT \qquad \text{(Exp. 15.3)}$$

But $N_T/N_0 = R_0$ and so substituting this in Exp. 15.3 and rearranging gives:

$$r_c = \frac{\ln(R_0)}{T} \qquad \text{(Eqn 15.1)}$$

where r_c is the capacity for increase, and $R_0 = \Sigma l_x m_x$. If we can estimate the generation time (T), then we can calculate the value of r_c. One method of doing this is to calculate the average age at which the females produce their offspring (i.e. the mean age of the $l_x m_x$ series). For example, if the $l_x m_x$ values for a population were 2 for one-year-old females, 4 for two-year-old females and 2 for three-year-old females, and were zero for all other ages, it would be obvious that the mean generation time based on this method would be 2 years. When the production of offspring is not so symmetrically distributed around a mean age, the mean age is calculated by weighting the production of offspring by the age at which they are produced (i.e. sum the $x l_x m_x$ series), and dividing that value by the number of offspring produced (i.e. the sum of the $l_x m_x$ series). Symbolically, this is represented by the following equation:

$$T = \frac{\Sigma x l_x m_x}{\Sigma l_x m_x}$$

(Eqn 15.2)

This estimates an average parental age at which all the offspring are born, and is equivalent to what would happen if all of the offspring were born to females at that age. You can check that this equation gives the correct estimates of the generation times for our example above, and for the populations in Table 15.1.

The r_c values for the Uinta ground squirrel population, before and after reduction in density, are given in Table 15.1. We can estimate the multiplication rates per year (λ) by taking the exponents of these estimates. The multiplication rate was 1.049 for the pre-reduction population and 1.29 for the post-reduction population. Obviously, as our estimates of R_0 above showed, the pre-reduction population was almost stationary because a multiplication rate of 5% per year is very low. Slade and Balph suspected that excess individuals emigrated to the surrounding habitat types because these had negative growth rates (i.e. were decreasing). Once the population density was halved, however, the population responded by dramatically increasing the multiplication rate to 29% a year, and this was achieved by a marked increase in survivorship and longevity, and not by an increase in age-specific birth rates (Table 15.1).

15.1.2 The intrinsic rate of natural increase, r_m, and the Euler equation

The second, and more accurate, method for estimating the growth rates of age-structured populations makes use of the Euler equation, which was first developed in the eighteenth century by the Swiss mathematician Leonhard Euler in his analysis of human demography, and was independently derived by Alfred Lotka, at the beginning of the twentieth century, who showed the equation's utility for demographers. The basic equation is as follows:

$$1 = \int_0^\infty e^{-r_m x} l_x m_x \delta x$$

(Eqn 15.3)

and its equivalent discrete form is given by:

$$1 = \sum_0^\infty e^{-r_m x} l_x m_x$$

(Eqn 15.4)

The reasoning behind this development of Eqn 15.4 may be followed if we consider the worked example in Table 15.2. In this example, the population growth rate (r_m) is judged to be approximately 0.1. Our first step is to calculate the number of individuals that would have been born at previous time steps if the population growth rate (r_m) was 0.1 (see column 2). For the previous times 1, 2, . . . , x, this is equal to $e^{-0.1}$, $e^{-0.2}$, . . . , e^{-rx}, which is equivalent to $1/\lambda$, $1/\lambda^2$, . . . , $1/\lambda^x$, and readers should confirm this for themselves if they are not convinced. Essentially, this develops a series of births in succeeding time steps, that increase exponentially from 0.6703 to 1.0, at a growth

Table 15.2 A numerical example to illustrate the development of the Euler equation shown in Box 15.1. The population growth rate (r_m) is 0.1, and the survivorship (l_x) and fecundity (m_x) series are as shown.

(1) Time (x) previous to time 0 (t_0)	(2) Number of individuals born at time x	l_x	(3) Number of individuals surviving to time 0	m_x	(4) Number of offspring born to surviving individuals at time 0
0	1.0	1.0	$l_0 = 1.0$	0	0
1	$e^{-0.1} = 0.9048$	0.8	(2) × 0.8 = 0.7238	0.5	(3) × 0.5 = 0.3619
2	$e^{-0.2} = 0.8187$	0.6	(2) × 0.6 = 0.4912	1.0	(3) × 1.0 = 0.4912
3	$e^{-0.3} = 0.7408$	0.4	(2) × 0.4 = 0.2963	0.4	(3) × 0.4 = 0.1185
4	$e^{-0.4} = 0.6703$	0.2	(2) × 0.2 = 0.1341	0.21	(3) × 0.21 = 0.0282
5	0	0	0	0	0
					$\Sigma = 0.9998$

rate of 0.1. Our next step is to develop the age structure of the population (see column 3). Of the 0.9048 individuals born in the previous time step, only 80% survive to the present time (0), and so the proportion in age class 1 is $0.9048 \times 0.8 = 0.7238$. Thus, the population age structure is given by the series in column 2 (which assumes exponential growth at a rate of 0.1 per time step) multiplied by the l_x series (which corrects for the survivorship of the different aged individuals). Our final step is to calculate the overall production of offspring at time 0, by multiplying the age structure of the population in column 3 by the m_x series, and then summing the resulting series in column 4. The total of 0.9998 is sufficiently close to 1.0 (the number of individuals born at time 0 in column 2) to assume that the population growth rate (r_m) is 0.1.

It may be apparent that the form of the Euler equation is unusual. If we insert the correct value of r_m into the equation, as we did in the example shown in Table 15.2, and do the necessary calculations, we find that the summation of the values for the different age classes is equal to 1.0. However, it is r_m that we are trying to calculate, and so in practice we have to insert trial values for r_m until we hit on the correct one. The procedure of how to do this will be explained later (section 15.2).

15.1.3 Comparison of r_c and r_m

Most authorities consider that r_c is simply an approximation for r_m, but there is a precise relationship between the two estimates that has been elucidated by Laughlin (1965). If there is no overlapping of generations, such as seen in annual plants and many insects, $r_c = r_m$. However, where there is overlapping of generations and the population has a stable age distribution (see section 15.3.2), the true rate of population growth is given by r_m and r_c is an underestimate. This is because for a population with a stable age distribution, the generation time (T) is overestimated by Eqn 15.2. The difference between r_m and r_c becomes greater as the growth rate (r) increases. We can see this in our example of the Uinta ground squirrel (Table 15.1). The pre-reduction value of r_c (0.048) is only about 2% lower than the value of r_m (0.049), whereas for the post-reduction population, r_c (0.255) is approximately 10% lower than the r_m value (0.282).

It should be emphasized that populations will only grow at a rate of r_m when they have attained a stable age distribution (the age distribution when all age classes are increasing in number at the same rate). If a population with overlapping generations is introduced into a new area and increases in number, or if a population has been stationary for a time and then starts to increase in number, the rate of increase during the initial phase will be closer to r_c than r_m. This is because it takes time for the population to attain a stable age distribution.

15.2 Calculating age-structured population growth rates using spreadsheets

The calculation of r_c and r_m is quite simple using a spreadsheet program. For the purposes of this exercise, we will modify the pre-reduction demographic statistics for the Uinta ground squirrel (Table 15.1) so that breeding occurs at yearly intervals from birth. It will be important to have equal-spaced age classes when we extend the spreadsheet in section 15.4. The modified demographic statistics for our spreadsheet are as follows:

Age	l_x	m_x
0	1.000	0
1	0.292	1.96
2	0.128	2.73
3	0.041	2.73
4	0.013	2.73
5	0.000	–

The development of the spreadsheet is described in Appendix 15.1. It is a simple matter to extend the spreadsheet to include more age classes, and preparing spreadsheets reduces much of the tedium of calculating population growth rates from age-specific birth and death rates.

15.3 Matrix models

During the 1940s, matrix models[1] were independently developed for age-structured populations by Bernardelli, Lewis, and Leslie (see

---

[1] These matrix models use matrix algebra to calculate and analyse population demographics (see Searle 1966).

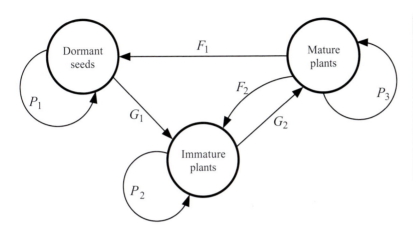

Fig. 15.1 Hypothetical life cycle of a plant with three life stages. The probability of remaining in a particular stage is indicated by the P values; the probability of developing or growing from one stage to the next is indicated by the G values; and sexual reproduction to produce seeds is indicated by F_1 and vegetative reproduction is indicated by F_2.

Caswell 2001). These matrix models were seldom used by ecologists until the 1970s, but are now commonly used to analyse the demographics of populations. Our purpose here is not to worry about matrix algebra *per se*, but to show why these models are important.

So far, we have used the age-specific birth and death rates to calculate the growth rate of a population. For many organisms this is an appropriate approach, but for other organisms it is not. For example, many insects go through a series of developmental stages (egg, larva, pupa and adult) that vary in duration according to food availability, temperature and moisture. In some plants and fish, the capacity for sexual reproduction may be more influenced by size and developmental stage than by chronological age. Thus, an immature, intermediate-sized plant or fish may be a fast-growing juvenile or a stunted 'adult'. Finally, some organisms reproduce both sexually and asexually, and these two types of reproduction may produce offspring at different life stages (e.g. seeds and semi-independent shoots). In cases such as these, it may be difficult or impossible to calculate the growth rate of the population using the more conventional Euler equation, but it is relatively simple to develop a stage or size-classified matrix model.

If we consider the life cycle of the plant that is illustrated in Fig. 15.1, we can note the following. In one time period, a proportion (P_1) of the seeds may remain dormant, a proportion (G_1) of the seeds germinate to develop into immature plants, and the remaining seeds die. Similarly, a proportion (P_2) of the immature plants may remain in an immature state, a proportion (G_2) develops into mature plants, and the remainder die. Finally, a proportion (P_3) of the mature plants survives to the next time period, and may either reproduce sexually to produce seeds (F_1) or reproduce asexually to produce immature plants (F_2). To define how individuals in this population move from one state to another, we develop a transition matrix that is shown in Table 15.3.

A careful comparison of Table 15.3 and Fig. 15.1 reveals that the probability of moving from one stage to another is fully described by this simple matrix. Later we will show how such a matrix can be solved to obtain r_m, and any of the other growth statistics that may be required. Before we do this, however, we will see how to apply the

Table 15.3 Transition matrix defining the movement of individuals from one stage to another for the hypothetical plant population illustrated in Fig. 15.1

		From stage:		
		Seeds	Immature	Mature plant
To stage:	Seeds	P_1	0	F_1
	Immature	G_1	P_2	F_2
	Mature plant	0	G_2	P_3

matrix model to the age-structured populations that were considered in sections 15.1 and 15.2.

15.3.1 A matrix model of age-structured population growth

The model consists of a *transition* or *population projection matrix* [A] which defines how the population moves from one age class to another (see above). Matrix [A] is often referred to as a *Leslie matrix* (after one of the originators of the method), and is a $k \times k$ square matrix where k is equal to the number of age classes in the population. We will consider a simple case of a population with just three age classes to see how the matrix is defined. The model takes the form:

$$n(t+1) = [A] \times n(t) \qquad \text{(Eqn 15.5)}$$

This is a symbolic way of saying that the number (n) in each age class at time $t + 1$ is equal to the transition matrix [A] pre-multiplying the number in each age class at time t (the previous time step). We can expand this equation to show the form of the matrix for age-structured populations where there are three age classes:

$$\begin{bmatrix} n_1 \\ n_2 \\ n_3 \end{bmatrix}(t+1) = \begin{bmatrix} F_1 & F_2 & F_3 \\ P_1 & 0 & 0 \\ 0 & P_2 & 0 \end{bmatrix} \begin{bmatrix} n_1 \\ n_2 \\ n_3 \end{bmatrix}(t) \qquad \text{(Eqn 15.6)}$$

where n_1, n_2 and n_3 are the numbers in the three age classes at times t and $t + 1$; F_1, F_2 and F_3 are the fertility coefficients for the three age classes; and P_1 and P_2 are the probabilities of surviving from age class 1 to 2 and age class 2 to 3, respectively.

Before we show how the F_i and P_i parameters are estimated from the life-table information we need to see how the numbers in each age class are calculated by Eqns 15.5 and 15.6. The numbers in each age class at time $t + 1$ are related to the numbers in each age class at time t according to the parameters in the transition matrix [A]. The values are calculated following the rules of matrix algebra, which need not concern us here, and for Eqn 15.6 they are:

$$n_1(t + 1) = F_1 n_1(t) + F_2 n_2(t) + F_3 n_3(t)$$
$$n_2(t + 1) = P_1 n_1(t) + 0 \times n_2(t) + 0 \times n_3(t)$$
$$n_3(t + 1) = 0 \times n_1(t) + P_2 n_2(t) + 0 \times n_3(t)$$

Table 15.4 Age-specific survival probabilities (P_i) and fertilities (F_i) for the Leslie matrix, calculated from the modified life table information for the Uinta ground squirrel in section 15.2 (see text)

Age (x)	l_x	m_x	Age class (i)	$P_i = l_i/l_{i-1}$	$F_i = m_i P_i$
0	1.000	0			
			1	$0.292/1.000 = 0.292$	$1.96 \times 0.292 = 0.572$
1	0.292	1.96			
			2	$0.128/0.292 = 0.438$	$2.73 \times 0.438 = 1.197$
2	0.128	2.73			
			3	$0.041/0.128 = 0.320$	$2.73 \times 0.320 = 0.874$
3	0.041	2.73			
			4	$0.013/0.041 = 0.317$	$2.73 \times 0.317 = 0.866$
4	0.013	2.73			
			5	$0/0.013 = 0$	$0 \times 0 = 0$
5	0	0			

Thus, at time $t + 1$: n_1 is equal to the sum of the offspring produced by all the age classes during the previous time step t; n_2 is equal to n_1 at the previous time step multiplied by the probability of survival from the first to the second age class; and n_3 is equal to n_2 at the previous time step multiplied by the probability of survival from the second to the third age class. You will note that there is no $P_3 n_3(t)$ term in the equation, and this is because none of these individuals survives to time $t + 1$. It should also be obvious that it is easy to expand the matrix to include more age groups.

The parameters in the Leslie matrix are estimated differently for different situations (see Caswell 2001), and we will only consider the easiest situation to understand, which is for seasonal breeders that are censused immediately after the birth of the young.

Birth-pulse populations with post-breeding census

Imagine studying a population that breeds just once a year and that is censused for survival (l_x) and fertility (m_x) statistics just after the birth of the young. The modified Uinta ground squirrel data (see section 15.2) correspond to this situation, and the survival probabilities (P_i) and fertilities (F_i) are calculated in Table 15.4.

Survival (l_x) and fertility (m_x) were assessed at six points of time (ages of 0 to 5 years), and so there are five age classes (i). The age classes in the matrix model correspond to the intervals between the census times. The probability of survival from one age class to the next (P_i) is simply the l_x value at the start of the age class divided into the l_x value at the start of the following age class. Thus:

$$P_i = \frac{l_i}{l_{i-1}} \qquad \text{(Eqn 15.7)}$$

Females produce their young at the end of an age class, because this is a post-breeding census. The Leslie matrix, however, calculates the number of young by multiplying the fertility by the number of females at the start of the age class. We correct for this by multiplying

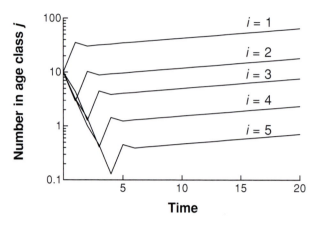

the m_x values by the probability of survival (P_i) during the time interval when we calculate the fertility coefficients (F_i):

$$F_i = m_i P_i \qquad \text{(Eqn 15.8)}$$

The resulting transition or Leslie matrix may be constructed from Table 15.3 as follows:

$$A = \begin{bmatrix} 0.572 & 1.197 & 0.874 & 0.866 & 0 \\ 0.292 & 0 & 0 & 0 & 0 \\ 0 & 0.438 & 0 & 0 & 0 \\ 0 & 0 & 0.320 & 0 & 0 \\ 0 & 0 & 0 & 0.317 & 0 \end{bmatrix}$$

This information may be used to simulate the growth of the population using the matrix model.

15.3.2 Simulating the matrix model of population growth

The procedure for simulating this form of population growth is described in Appendix 15.2, using the parameters calculated in Table 15.4 and the transition matrix we have just derived. We can make the following observations about this form of growth.

A graph of the numbers in each age class over time (Fig. 15.2) shows that after some initial fluctuations, they all grow at the same exponential rate. At this point, a stable age distribution has developed (see step 6 in Appendix 15.2), and the growth rate, r, has stabilized at the value of r_m that is calculated by the Euler equation.

Now if we return to our initial example of a hypothetical plant, imagine that we were able to obtain the following set of estimates for the various parameters in the transition matrix described in Table 15.3.

	Seeds	Immature	Mature
Seeds	$P_1 = 0.01$	0	$F_1 = 25$
Immature	$G_1 = 0.1$	$P_2 = 0.2$	$F_2 = 0.05$
Mature	0	$G_2 = 0.3$	$P_3 = 0.4$

The estimates are annual ones, and so we see that only 1% of the seeds survive from one year to the next whereas 10% germinate. Of the resulting immature plants, 20% remain in that condition from one year to the next and 30% develop into mature plants. The mature plants have an annual survival rate of 40%, produce an average of 25 seeds each, and about 5% produce immature plants by layering. From this information it would be difficult to guess if the population were increasing or decreasing, and we cannot apply the Euler equation to this set of data. However, we can easily calculate the population growth rate by following the matrix method (see steps 7 to 9 in Appendix 15.2). What we find is that the population has a potential growth rate of approximately 13% per year ($\lambda = 1.1325$) and $r_m = 0.124$. If we subsequently found that the plant had a relatively stable population size we would need to refine some of our estimates. Indeed, we could do a sensitivity analysis to determine which of the parameters had the largest effect on population growth. For example, if the germination rate were actually between 6% and 7%, instead of 10%, we would find that the population showed a slight increase in number when $G_1 = 0.07$ but a slow decrease in number when $G_1 = 0.06$. Obviously, this would be a crucial parameter to measure as accurately as possible.

The matrix model can be used to calculate not only population growth rates, such as λ and r_m, but also the stable age distribution, and the reproductive value (see Chapter 16). Readers who are interested in finding out more about matrix models are referred to Caswell (2001) and Gotelli (1995).

15.4 Summary

This chapter has concentrated on the mechanics of calculating growth rates for populations where the birth and death rates vary with age. There are three basic methods. The first is a simple modification of the exponential growth from Chapter 4, and it calculates the capacity for increase, which is a reasonably accurate measure of the growth rate of slowly growing populations. The second method is more accurate when a growing population achieves a stable age distribution, and is based on the Euler equation. Finally, the third method is a matrix model that is extremely flexible and can be used to calculate the growth of any population, even those with unusual characteristics that cannot be analysed by the first two methods.

In the next chapter we will explore the patterns in the age-specific birth and death rates, and also the growth rates of different species, to try and understand the evolutionary forces that shape these parameters and other life-history characteristics of organisms.

15.5 Problems

1. The following pattern of mortality was observed in a fictitious mammal. Of the newborn females, half survived for one year, 10% survived for two

years, 3.75% survived for three years, 1.5% survived for four years, and none survived for five years. Breeding occurred once a year, and immediately following the breeding season the age-specific reproductive rates were determined from the fresh placental scars of females of known age. One-year-old females had an average of 2.8 placental scars per female, two-year-old females had an average of 4.0 placental scars per female, and older females had an average of 4.8 placental scars per female. There was a 50:50 sex ratio at birth.

(a) Calculate the values of r_c and r_m for this population.

(b) Determine the transition or Leslie matrix for this population.

(c) Suppose a population with an excess of males was started with 10 one-year-old females and 20 two-year-old females just prior to breeding. Calculate the number of females in each age class over the next three years.

Appendix 15.1 Calculating growth rates for age-structured populations

1. Title your spreadsheet: **Calculating growth rates for age-structured populations** in A1.

2. Type **trial r_m** = in E3, then in row 5 of columns A to G type the following headings:

   Age (x) l_x m_x $l_x m_x$ $x l_x m_x$ e^{-rx} $e^{-rx} l_x m_x$

3. In columns A to C enter the demographic statistics from the table in section 15.2. Then enter the appropriate formulas to calculate $l_x m_x$ and $x l_x m_x$ in columns D and E. For example, D6 is = **B6*C6** and E6 is = **A6*D6**.

4. Type: **Sum** in E13 and G13, and R_0 =, **T** =, and r_c = in C14 to C16.

5. Enter the formula = **@SUM(D6..D11)** in D14, and copy to cells E14 and G14. In the latter case an error message will appear because column G has not been completed. Exit this message, because a total will be calculated when you complete step 6. The formulas will automatically adjust to the correct summations. Also enter the formula = **E14/D14** in D15, and the formula = **@LN(D14)/D15** in D16. If you have done everything correctly, you will have estimated $R_0 = 1.06918$, $T = 1.635\,786$, and $r_c = 0.040\,893$.

6. Now calculate r_m by first entering a trial value in F3 of 0.041 (a value a little higher than r_c). Enter the appropriate formulas in columns F and G. For example in column F, F6 is = **1/@EXP($F$3*A6)** and G6 is = **F6*D6**. If everything is done correctly, the value of the sum in cell G14 = 1.000356.

7. Now adjust the trial value of r_m in F3 to try and make G14 = 1.0 exactly, or to whatever level of accuracy is deemed sufficient. To reduce the value of G14 you increase the value of r_m in F3. Thus, if we make F3 = 0.0411, G14 = 1.000195; if F3 = 0.0412, G14 = 1.000034; and if F3 is 0.0413, G14 = 0.999873. Clearly, r_m is between 0.0412 and 0.0413.

8. Save your spreadsheet because we will extend it to include a matrix projection of population growth.

Appendix 15.2 Simulation of the matrix model

1. Open your spreadsheet for age-structured population growth (developed in Appendix 15.1).
2. First calculate the parameters for the matrix model. Enter the headings: **For Matrix Model** in H4, and P_i and F_i in H5 and I5. Then enter the formula: = **B7/B6** in H7 and copy to cells H8 to H11, and = **C7*H7** in I7 and copy to cells I8 to I11. These equations correspond to Eqns 15.7 and 15.8. The calculated values for each age class should correspond to those in Table 15.3.
3. To simulate the numbers in each age class:
   (a) Enter the following headings: In C19 type **Number in age class (i)**; in G19 type **Total**; in A20 type **Time (t)**; in cells B20 to F20 type i = 1, i = 2 . . . i = 5; and in cells G20 to I20 type **Nt, lambda,** and **r**.
   (b) Then enter times of **0** to **20** in cells A21 to A41, and initialize the starting number in each age class by entering the value of **1** in cells B21 to F21.
   (c) Enter the formula: = **B21*$I$7+C21*$I$8+D21*$I$9+E21*$I$10** in B22. This calculates the number of newborns entering age class 1 by summing the production of offspring produced by each age class during the previous time step. Then enter the formulas: = **B21*$H$7** in C22, = **C21*$H$8** in D22, = **D21*$H$9** in E22, and = **E21*$H$10** in F22. Finally, copy the formulas in row 22 to rows 23 to 41. This calculates the number in each age class for 20 time steps.
4. In G21 calculate the total population size by using the formula = **SUM(B21 . . F21)** and copy this to cells G22 to G41. Then calculate the multiplication rate, λ, for each time step by typing the formula = **G22/G21** in H22 and copying it to cells H23 to H41. The rate of increase (r) is calculated for each time step using the formula = **LN(H22)** in I22 and copying it to cells I23 to I41. You will see that both λ and r stabilize at values of 1.042083 and 0.041221, respectively (assuming you have done everything correctly). If you insert this r value in cell F3 you will see that this gives us the exact r_m value because the sum of the $e^{-rx}l_x m_x$ values is exactly equal to 1 (in G14).
5. Now graph the results by clicking the Chart button and create a line chart with the x-series as A21 to A41, and five y-series of B21 . . B41, C21 . . C41, . . . , F21 . . F41 to show the numbers in each age class. Plot the y-values on a logarithmic scale. In **Quattro Pro** right-click your chart on the notebook sheet, left-click Edit, position pointer (arrow) on y-axis and double click,

select Log scale, and finally click OK. In **Excel** left-click your chart, double-click the *y*-axis, click Scale, then click logarithmic scale, and finally click OK. Your graph should resemble Fig. 15.2, where each age class eventually increases at the same rate.

6. Calculate the proportion in each age class by typing the formula = **B21/$G21** in K21 and then copying this to rows 21 to 41 of columns K to O. You will see that the proportions stabilize and remain constant over time.

7. We can now consider a more complex transition matrix, such as the one that we developed for a hypothetical plant. In B44 enter **Transition Matrix for hypothetical plant**, and in cells B45 to D45 enter **Seed Immature Mature**, and then enter the same three labels in cells A 46 to A48. Then enter the following values for the transition matrix: **0.01** in B46 (= P_1), **0** in C46, **25** in D46 (= F_1), **0.1** in B47 (= G_1), **0.2** in C47 (= P_2), **0.05** in D47 (= F_2), **0** in B48, **0.3** in C48 (= G_2), and finally **0.4** in D48 (= P_3).

8. Next, in columns A to D of row 50 enter the following headings: **Time (t)**, **Seed**, **Immature**, **Mature**, and then in rows 49 and 50 of column F **Mature lambda**, and finally **r_m** in G50. Then enter times of 0 to 50 in rows 51 to 101 of column A, starting numbers of 1 in B51 to D51, and enter the following formulae: = **B51*$B$46+C51*$C$46+ D51*$D$46** in B52, = **B51*$B$47+C51*$C$47+D51*$D$47** in C52, and = **B51*$B$48+C51*$C$48+D51*$D$48** in D52. These formulae do the matrix calculations. Copy cells B52, C52 and D52 to all cells up to B101, C101 and D101. In F52 type = **D52/D51** to calculate λ, and then = **LN(F52)** in G52 to calculate *r*. Copy F52 and G52 to all cells up to F101 and G101.

9. You will see that λ stabilizes at 1.132542, and *r* stabilizes at 0.124465. You can graph the results by following the instructions in step 5, and you can also calculate the proportion in each state by following the instructions in step 6. You can also see the effect of changing some of the values in the transition matrix, for example, by progressively lowering the germination rate in cell B47 to 0.06.

10. When you have finished, close and exit your spreadsheet.

Chapter 16

Evolution of life histories

If different phenotypes have different age-specific birth and death rates, their growth rates, and hence their fitness (see Chapter 10) will vary. Thus, natural selection shapes both the survivorship (l_x) and fecundity (m_x) curves, and we will look at this particular aspect of evolution in this chapter. However, the life-history characteristics of organisms also include such traits as body size, size of the offspring at birth, the degree of parental care provided to the young, and so on, and consequently our review will also consider some of these life-history traits.

A simplistic view of natural selection would suggest that all organisms should adopt an ideal life history in which they live as long as possible, start to reproduce at an early age, reproduce frequently, and produce a vast number of offspring which have a high rate of survival. However, even a cursory look at the life-history traits of different organisms shows that this is not the case in nature. Consider the following three examples of large, long-lived organisms.

Adult blue whales (*Balaenoptera musculus*) are about 27 metres long, weigh about 150 tonnes, and may live for about 80 years. After a gestation period of about one year, females normally produce a single, well-developed offspring that weighs as much as an adult elephant. The young calves suckle for about a year, and are provided with considerable parental care and protection during their early life. Their survival is quite high. Females begin breeding during their teenage years and produce calves at intervals of about four years, although in the last few decades this interval has been approximately halved in response to the severe reduction of population size in this species.

The American elm (*Ulmus americana*) may reach a height of 38 metres, weigh more than 100 tonnes, and live for well over 100 years. Large trees produce several hundreds of thousands of seeds each year, so that an individual tree may produce several million seeds during the course of its life. The seeds are small, weighing much less than 1 gram, and their survival as well as the survival of any seedlings is extremely poor. Their poor survival may explain why the adults produce so many seeds each year, because survival to the stage of a mature tree is dictated to a large extent by the appearance of openings in the forest by the falling of mature canopy trees. Such events occur infrequently, consequently an individual's chance of replacement is improved if it produces many seeds over a great many years.

The Chinese species of bamboo, *Phyllostachys bambusoides*, lives for about 120 years without reproducing, and then all populations flower, set a prolific amount of seed, and die within one year. Like the elm, their seeds are small and have a low survival rate. Remarkably, transplanted stocks of this species in Japan, England, the United States and Russia reproduce at the same time as the native species in China. The generation cycle seems to be genetically programmed and is not apparently influenced by local environmental conditions.

These three examples of large, long-lived organisms show considerable variation in their age-specific reproductive rates. The blue whale produces one offspring every four years, the American elm produces thousands of offspring each year, and the bamboo reproduces prolifically only at the end of its life. Clearly, if we had considered all types of organisms, we could have shown a much wider array of life-history traits. We might ask, why don't these life histories converge in their characteristics and conform to the ideal life history noted at the beginning of this chapter? One possibility is that organisms have a finite amount of energy at their disposal, and energy used for one purpose, such as growth, repair or maintenance, cannot be used for another purpose, such as reproduction. Consequently, there are trade-offs between different life-history traits. For example, the number and sizes of offspring are frequently inversely correlated, and selection may favour one or other of these traits, but not both simultaneously. In orchids, selection has favoured an increase in the number of seeds, with some species producing as many as 1 billion (10^9). This has been achieved at the expense of size, because each seed is about the size of a fungal spore. In contrast, in the coconut palm (*Cocos nucifera*), selection has favoured increased seed size at the expense of seed number. They produce only a few nuts weighing several kilograms each year. We will be examining some of these dichotomies in life-history traits to try to understand how they may be adaptive in different situations or environments.

16.1 | Evolution of age-specific death rates

It is not obvious how the shape of the survivorship (l_x) curve can be shaped by natural selection. We have seen in Chapters 10 to 12 that the survival of an individual may depend on its genotype or phenotype, but why its chances of survival should necessarily be related to age is not obvious. To understand why this might be so, we must first digress to consider the reproductive values of individuals at different ages.

16.1.1 Reproductive value

How much does one individual contribute in terms of the number of individuals in the next generation? It is intuitively obvious that a young female, just entering her period of breeding, will be likely to contribute more to population growth than a female near the end of her reproductive life, because we not only consider the immediate production of offspring but also include the offspring that a female may produce later in life. Consequently, a young female will probably produce more offspring during the course of her life than a very old female. We measure this contribution of individuals to the future growth of the population by means of the reproductive value (v_x), where x represents the age of the individual. The reproductive value is defined as the relative number of female offspring that remain to be born to each female of age x, and how it contributes to the number of individuals in the next generation (Fisher 1930).

The reproductive value of an individual of age $x(v_x)$ is estimated relative to the reproductive value of a newborn (v_0) by the following formula:

$$\frac{v_x}{v_0} = \frac{\sum_{y=x}^{\infty} e^{-ry} l_y m_y}{e^{-rx} l_x} \qquad \text{(Eqn 16.1)}$$

For the moment we will not explain the form of this equation because this can be made more obvious when we consider a specific example. However, what is being summed is the number of offspring that will be produced by a female from the age of x to the end of her life (denoted by the infinity sign). The term y is used to label all the ages the female passes through from x till she dies. By convention, v_0 is made equal to 1.0, and so Eqn 16.1 is equal to v_x.

In order to understand this equation we will consider a specific example of red deer (*Cervus elaphus*) on the island of Rhum in Western Scotland (Lowe 1969). The basic data and calculation of reproductive values for this population are presented in Table 16.1.

Lowe developed a static life stable by reconstructing the age structure of females from age one onwards, based on their ages at death in the population (see section 14.2.2). The relative number of survivors in each age class was calculated by setting the number of one-year-olds (S_1) to 1000. The number of newborn females that these females would produce was calculated from the age-specific fertility (m_x) data, and theoretically a one-year-old female would produce exactly 1316.142 female offspring during the course of her life. This is the value of S_0. The l_x series was calculated from the S_x series in the usual manner (Chapter 14). This method of constructing the life table assumes a stationary population, and so we should not be surprised that $\Sigma l_x m_x = 1.0$ (i.e. $R_0 = 1$, and $r = 0$).

In this example, the $e^{-rx} l_x m_x$ series is the same as the $l_x m_x$ series, and the $e^{-rx} l_x$ series is the same as the l_x series (Table 16.1). This is because we have a stationary population $(r = 0)$, and so $e^{-rx} = e^0$, or 1.0. Thus, for static populations the e^{-rx} terms in Eqn 16.1 disappear,

Table 16.1 Demographic data for female red deer on Rhum in 1957

Age (x)	S_x	l_x	m_x	$l_x m_x$	$e^{-rx} l_x m_x$	$e^{-rx} l_x$	v_x	q_x
0	1316.142[a]	1.000	0	0	0	1.000	1.000	0.240
1	1000	0.760	0	0	0	0.760	1.316	0.137
2	863	0.656	0	0	0	0.656	1.525	0.098
3	778	0.591	0.311	0.184	0.184	0.591	1.692	0.108
4	694	0.527	0.278	0.147	0.147	0.527	1.548	0.121
5	610	0.463	0.302	0.140	0.140	0.463	1.445	0.138
6	526	0.400	0.400	0.160	0.160	0.400	1.325	0.160
7	442	0.336	0.476	0.160	0.160	0.336	1.101	0.192
8	357	0.271	0.358	0.097	0.097	0.271	0.774	0.493
9	181	0.138	0.447	0.061	0.061	0.138	0.820	0.674
10	59	0.045	0.289	0.013	0.013	0.045	1.145	0.136
11	51	0.039	0.283	0.011	0.011	0.039	0.990	0.176
12	42	0.032	0.285	0.009	0.009	0.032	0.858	0.190
13	34	0.026	0.283	0.007	0.007	0.026	0.708	0.265
14	25	0.019	0.282	0.005	0.005	0.019	0.578	0.320
15	17	0.013	0.285	0.004	0.004	0.013	0.435	0.471
16	9	0.009	0.284	0.002	0.002	0.009	0.284	1.000
17	0	0	0	0	0	0		

$$\sum = 1.000$$

[a]Calculated from $\sum S_x m_x$ from age 1 onwards.
Source: Data from Lowe (1969).

and the reproductive value (v_x) is equal to the production of female offspring by a female over the remainder of her life, divided by the l_x value. For static populations, then, Eqn 16.1 can be simplified to:

$$v_x = \frac{\sum_{y=x}^{\infty} l_y m_y}{l_x} \qquad \text{(Eqn 16.2)}$$

The reproductive value at birth (v_0) is 1.0, whereas for three-year-old females v_x is $1/0.591 = 1.692$ (Table 16.1). On average both of these females produce the same number of offspring, but the three-year-old female has a higher reproductive value than at birth because she has survived the pre-reproductive period (only 0.591 of the females at birth will do so) and so is more likely to produce offspring.

The reproductive value of a female increases from birth until she reaches puberty at three years of age, after which the reproductive value generally declines with age (Fig. 16.1). There is generally an inverse relationship between reproductive values and age-specific mortality rates, and this is particularly evident with the peculiar kink in both curves for eight- and nine-year-old females. Lowe (1969) attributed the marked increase in the mortality rate of these females to 'highly selective age specific mortality factors'. However, there are other possible explanations. This is a static life table for the deer in 1957, and possibly events eight and nine years prior to 1957 could have produced the apparent increase in age-specific mortality. For

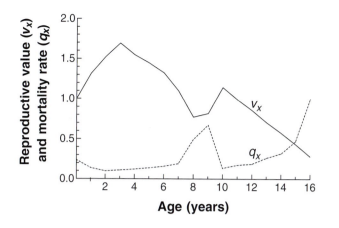

Fig. 16.1 Reproductive value and mortality rate in relation to age for female red deer (*Cervus elaphus*) on the island of Rhum. (Data from Table 16.1 and Lowe 1969.)

example, if reproduction were poor in 1948 and 1949, or if there was a high mortality of newborns in those two years, there would be fewer females entering the population. The result would be an apparent increase in the age-specific mortality rate of eight- and nine-year-old females, because of a violation of the basic assumptions on which the life table is constructed. Now the issue here is not the exact shape of the q_x curve, although one suspects that it does not really have a sudden kink in the middle. What is important is that there is a relationship between the shape of the v_x and q_x curves, and we will return to this point in section 16.1.2.

For populations that are either increasing or decreasing in size, we need to calculate reproductive values using Eqn 16.1 rather than Eqn 16.2. In populations that are increasing in size, offspring that are born later will contribute less to the gene pool and to future population growth than offspring currently being born, because they will be entering a larger breeding population. These offspring are discounted by a factor of e^{-ry}, where r is the growth rate of the population and y is how far in the future the offspring will be born. Similarly, in a declining population, offspring born at a future date are worth relatively more than the current offspring, because they are entering a population that will be smaller. The value of these offspring will also be augmented by a factor of e^{-ry}, which is equivalent to e^{ry} because the value of r is negative in this case. The calculations are somewhat tedious, but are simple to do using a spreadsheet. This could be done by modifying the spreadsheet described in Appendix 15.1.

In conclusion, reproductive values vary with age. The effect of natural selection is greatest when it operates on ages with high reproductive values, because selection against these individuals has a large effect on the growth rate and, therefore, the fitness of the population. Where possible, selection should favour shifting mortality from ages with high reproductive values to those with lower reproductive values.

16.1.2   Evolution of death rates

In Chapter 14, it was noted that in some mammals the mortality is high just after birth, decreases to a minimum around the age of

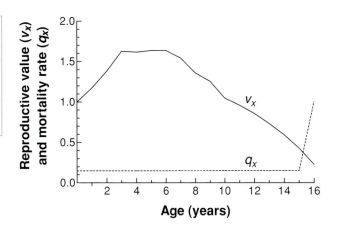

Fig. 16.2 Reproductive value of female red deer (*Cervus elaphus*) if the mortality rate remained constant with age ($q_x = 0.15$) except for the last age class when all die, and the age-specific fertility values (m_x) are the same as those in Table 16.1 (see text).

puberty, and thereafter steadily increases with age. Fisher (1930) noted an inverse relationship between age-specific mortality rates and reproductive values in humans, and suggested that the U-shaped mortality curve with age was moulded by natural selection, according to the magnitude of the reproductive value. To examine why this might be so, consider a fictitious example based on the data for red deer (section 16.1.1). Imagine that the mortality rate is constant with respect to age, except for the oldest age class where all the individuals die. In this case, the reproductive values increase from birth to the age of puberty, remain almost constant for a few years as the increase in fertility with age approximately compensates for mortality, and then steadily decline after six years of age (Fig. 16.2). How might this dome-shaped curve of reproductive value influence the mortality rate?

Consider the part of the curve to the right of its peak. Detrimental traits expressed at ages with peak reproductive values have a very large effect on fitness. Natural selection should favour a delay in the expression of such deleterious traits, because mortality would be transferred to those with lower reproductive values, and so the overall fitness of the population would increase. The same is true at all ages where the reproductive value declines with increasing age. Thus, modifier genes delaying the expression of deleterious genes would have a selective advantage over those advancing their expression. It is theorized that 'late' modifier genes accumulate in the population, and lead to increasing mortality rates with age after the age of peak reproductive value. Analogous arguments can be applied to beneficial genetic traits, but in this case there should be an accumulation of modifier genes that advance the expression of such characters to earlier ages.

Reproductive values increase with age in the part of the curve to the left of the peak values. There is no advantage to delaying the effects of deleterious traits for these young females, unless they can be delayed until after the age of peak reproductive value. Why should mortality rates decrease from birth to puberty or, conversely, why should the mortality rates increase toward the time of birth? There are two obvious reasons why the mortality rate should be high soon after birth. First, the change from living as an embryo in an amniotic sac inside of the mother to being a free-living individual may not be successfully accomplished (e.g. young with a problem that impairs their locomotion could live successfully as an embryo, but have a high risk of death after birth). Second, if the mother dies while she is still nursing, her young are also likely to die. In the latter case, the dependency of the young on the mother for food decreases as they age, because weaning does not take place at an instant of time but is a gradual process. The effect of both of these causes of mortality is to have a declining risk of mortality as the young grow older. Thus, the decrease in mortality rates with age prior to puberty is likely to have very different causes than the increase in mortality rates after puberty in mammals.

It is difficult to understand the evolution of age-specific death rates. More recent theoretical studies by Hamilton (1966) and Charlesworth (1980) have cast doubt on Fisher's theoretical relationship between natural selection and reproductive values. These developments are beyond the scope of this book and readers interested in this topic are referred to Rose (1991). The point of this discussion, however, is to show that survivorship curves, or age-specific mortality rates, can be subjected to natural selection.

16.2 | Evolution of age-specific fertility

There are three aspects of reproductive rates that we will consider. First, should litter sizes be small or large? Second, should an organism breed once (semelparity) or repeatedly (iteroparity)? And third, should an organism start to reproduce early or later in life?

16.2.1 Number of offspring

How many offspring should an organism produce during one breeding event? In our introduction to this chapter we saw that there is an enormous range of possibilities, from a single offspring in the blue whale to about 1 billion (10^9) seeds in some orchids. Individuals that produce the largest number of descendants have the greatest fitness, and so we might expect that all organisms should produce many offspring. Consequently, we need to explain why some species produce so few offspring.

David Lack, a British ornithologist, proposed that 'The number of eggs in the clutch has been evolved to correspond with that from which, on the average, the most young are raised' (Lack 1968, p. 5). This has become known as Lack's hypothesis, and it has also been applied to other animals that provide parental care to their young. In birds where the young remain in the nest, Lack proposed that the limit is set by the amount of food which the parents can bring for their young, and he tested his hypothesis in a classical study on Swiss starlings (*Sturnus vulgaris*). In many ways, birds are ideal to test this hypothesis. It is relatively easy to count the number of eggs a bird

Table 16.2 Post-fledgling survival in relation to brood size for Swiss starlings (*Sturnus vulgaris*) banded as young

Brood size (1)	Number of broods (2)	Number of eggs (1) × (2) = (3)	Recovered young >3 months after fledging			
			Number (4)	Percentage recovered (4) × 100/(3)	Average number per brood (4)/(2)	Relative fitness[a]
1	65	65	0	0	0	0
2	164	328	6	1.83	0.0366	0.34
3	426	1 278	26	2.03	0.0610	0.57
4	989	3 956	82	2.07	0.0829	0.77
5	1 235	6 175	128	2.07	0.1036	0.96
6	526	3 156	53	1.68	0.1008	0.94
7	93	651	10	1.54	0.1075	1.00
8	15	120	1	0.83	0.0667	0.62
9	2	18	0	0	0	0
10	1	10	0	0	0	0
Total	3 516	15 757	306			

[a]Relative fitness in terms of the average number of recovered young per brood.
Source: Data from Lack (1948).

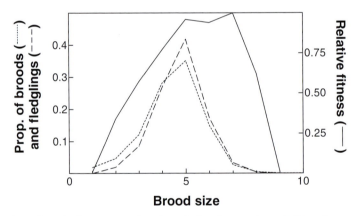

Fig. 16.3 Proportions of broods and young recovered more than three months after fledging in relation to brood size for Swiss starlings (*Sturnus vulgaris*). The relative fitness is defined in terms of the average number of young recovered per brood. (Data from Lack 1948.)

lays, band the young that hatch in the nest, and then to recapture the young after fledging to estimate their relative survival in relation to clutch size. Some of Lack's data on Swiss starlings are presented in Table 16.2 and Fig. 16.3.

Lack studied more than 3500 broods, which were approximately normally distributed around a clutch size of 5, with a mean of 4.5, assuming a 1:1 correspondence between clutch and brood size. More than 15 000 chicks that were produced from these clutches and 306 were recaptured three months or more after fledging. The recovered young were also approximately normally distributed around a clutch size of 5, with a mean of 4.75 at this stage. Thus, a large clutch size did not necessarily result in more young being produced. For example, the production of offspring per brood was similar for those with clutches of 3 and 8 eggs (Table 16.2). The failure of large broods to produce

Table 16.3 Nestling weights in grams of 15-day-old starlings in relation to brood size

Brood of 2		Brood of 5		Brood of 7	
Mean	Range	Mean	Range	Mean	Range
88.0	87.5–88.5	77.6	72.5–83.0	71.4	66.0–77.0

Source: Data from Lack (1948).

more offspring was probably related to the undernourishment of the young (Table 16.3).

According to Lack's hypothesis the most common clutch size of 5 should produce the most offspring per brood, but we can see (Fig. 16.3) that on average, a clutch size of 7 produced the most number of recovered young, closely followed by a clutch size of 5 and then 6. These results suggest that the optimum clutch size, based on the production of surviving young per brood, should be slightly larger than is observed. Thus, these data do not appear to support Lack's hypothesis unequivocally. It is interesting to note, however, that Lack ensured the support of his hypothesis by combining the data for clutch sizes of 7 and 8, thereby reducing their fitness to less than that calculated for a clutch size of 5.

The testing of Lack's hypothesis is not as simple as it may seem. In Lack's study of Swiss starlings, fewer than 2% of the young were recovered and this small sample size means that we cannot reject or accept Lack's hypothesis with any degree of confidence. This is not a criticism of Lack's study; rather it is a statement that most ecological studies do not provide ideal data. Another way of testing Lack's hypothesis is to add eggs or chicks to normal-sized broods and see if they can be successfully raised. Such studies have produced mixed results. Some species seem incapable of successfully raising enlarged broods, whereas other species do appear to be successful in rearing enlarged broods that are bigger than the most common clutch size. The question is, why haven't these latter species evolved to increase their clutch size?

There are many possible answers to this question but we will consider just two of them. First, clutch size is not solely determined by the genotype but also by environmental factors (Chapter 12). Hypothetically, for example, the genotype for a clutch size of 5 in the Swiss starling might result in an actual clutch size of 3–7 eggs depending on the environmental variance (V_E). Other genotypes might display similar variation, so there could be considerable overlap in the phenotypic expression of different genotypes for clutch size. In this situation we would have to calculate the number of offspring produced by the frequency distribution of clutches resulting from each genotype (e.g. clutches of 1–5 eggs for the three-egg genotype, clutches of 2–6 eggs for the four-egg genotype, and so on) in order to determine the production of each genotype. Mountford (1968) has shown that it is possible for a clutch size of 5 to be selected for, even

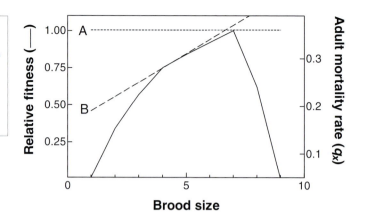

Fig. 16.4 Predicting the optimal brood size from a combination of adult mortality and the production of offspring (equivalent to fitness) from a single brood. The optimum brood size lies at the intersection of the adult mortality and relative fitness curves (see text).

though it does not fledge the largest number of young, if the number of offspring produced by the frequency distribution of eggs resulting from this genotype is greater than that produced by the frequency distribution of clutches of other genotypes. In this case it would be virtually impossible to test Lack's hypothesis.

A second explanation considers the lifetime production of young by females with different clutch sizes. If adult mortality increases with clutch size, it may be advantageous to produce a lower clutch size if the lifetime reproductive success is increased. For example, suppose a female that raises six young survives on average for four breeding seasons, for a lifetime production of 24 young, whereas a female that raises five young survives on average for five breeding seasons, for a lifetime production of 25 young. Obviously, the latter strategy should be favoured by natural selection. The general analysis of this is shown in Fig. 16.4. The optimum brood size is determined by the highest point of intersection of the functions for relative fitness and adult mortality. Where there is no relationship between adult mortality and brood size (A), the mortality curve will intersect the curve of relative fitness at its peak, and will support Lack's hypothesis. However, if the adult mortality rate increases with brood size (B), the intersection of the two curves is to the left of the peak of the relative fitness curve, and so a lower brood size is favoured. Unfortunately, it is difficult to relate adult mortality to brood size, and so there are few studies of this relationship in birds. The mortality rate of adult female blue tits (*Parus caeruleus*) does increase with brood size (Nur 1984), and so this second explanation is a plausible reason why some bird species seem to lay smaller clutches than the optimum indicated by the production of a single brood.

If we consider the lifetime production of offspring by females, it is obvious that we need to consider both the frequency of reproduction as well as litter size.

16.2.2 Frequency of reproduction: annual and perennial strategies

The issue of whether an organism should breed once or repeatedly was first examined by Lamont Cole (1954), who compared the growth rates of annual and perennial plant populations. For an annual plant, the number of individuals (N_A) at time $t + 1$ is equal to the number of individuals in the previous year (time t) multiplied by the number of seeds they produced (B_A), assuming that they all germinate, which is equivalent to the following expression:

$$N_A(t + 1) = B_A N_A(t) \qquad \text{(Exp. 16.1)}$$

The multiplication rate of the annual is:

$$\lambda_A = \frac{N_A(t + 1)}{N_A(t)} = B_A \qquad \text{(Exp. 16.2)}$$

Similarly, for a perennial plant with a seed production of B_P and an adult survival rate of s_A, the number of individuals (N_P) at time $t + 1$ is given by:

$$N_P(t + 1) = B_P N_P(t) + s_A N_P(t) \qquad \text{(Exp. 16.3)}$$

And the multiplication rate of the perennial is:

$$\lambda_P = \frac{N_P(t + 1)}{N_P(t)} = B_P + s_A \qquad \text{(Exp. 16.4)}$$

If the annual and the perennial have the same multiplication rate (i.e. $\lambda_A = \lambda_P$) or fitness, we can see from Exps. 16.2 and 16.4 that:

$$B_A = B_P + s_A \qquad \text{(Exp. 16.5)}$$

If $s_A = 1$ we have an immortal perennial, and so s_A is less than 1 in the real world. Thus, an annual will have a higher growth rate than a perennial, or will be equivalent to an immortal perennial, if it produces just one more seed than the perennial. Cole reasoned that it would require far less energy to produce one more seed than to produce the structures necessary for the plant to survive from year to year, i.e. to be a perennial. So he asked, why aren't all plants annuals?

This question became known as Cole's paradox, and it was almost 20 years before it was solved by Eric Charnov and William Schaffer (1973). Their solution is very simple. Expression 16.5 assumes that all of the seeds produced by annuals and perennials survive. If we include seedling or juvenile survival rates (s_j), Exp. 16.5 is modified to:

$$s_j B_A = s_j B_P + s_A \qquad \text{(Exp. 16.6)}$$

And if we divide through by s_j, Exp. 16.6 becomes:

$$B_A = B_P + \frac{s_A}{s_j} \qquad \text{(Exp. 16.7)}$$

Expression 16.7 predicts that an annual has to produce s_A/s_j more offspring than a perennial to match its growth rate. Now it is easier to see how an annual strategy might be favoured in some circumstances and a perennial strategy favoured in other circumstances. For example, if the ratio s_A/s_j is large, because juvenile survival is poor compared to adult survival, the perennial strategy may be favoured, whereas if juvenile survival is high an annual strategy may be favoured. This is only true when juvenile survival is the same in both the annual and perennial species, which may be a reasonable assumption when an organism reaches an evolutionary watershed where it might adopt an annual or a perennial strategy. However, if we make the assumption that the juvenile survival of annuals (s_{jA}) is lower than that of a perennial (s_{jP}), because they have a larger number of offspring, Exp. 16.7 becomes modified to:

$$B_A = \frac{s_{jP}}{s_{jA}} B_P + \frac{s_A}{s_j} \qquad \text{(Exp. 16.8)}$$

Now the situation is more complicated. If a species can increase the ratio of s_{jP}/s_{jA} by investing more in each offspring, a perennial strategy may be favoured, but if a species can sufficiently increase the production of offspring (B_A) an annual strategy will be favoured. What is obvious from Exps. 16.7 and 16.8 is that annual species should produce more offspring than perennials in a single breeding event, and the difference may be particularly large if the juvenile survival rate is much lower in annuals compared to perennials.

16.2.3 Generation times: when to start breeding

The growth rate and fitness of an organism depends on how many offspring it successfully produces. It also depends on the age at which offspring are produced, because an individual that produces offspring early in its life has a higher growth rate than an individual that produces its offspring later in life, even though the two individuals may produce the same number of offspring. In the last chapter we saw that the rate of increase (r) may be predicted by the simple equation:

$$r = \frac{\ln(R_0)}{T} \qquad \text{(Eqn 15.1)}$$

The replacement rate (R_0) is determined by the age-specific pattern of survival (l_x) and fertility (m_x), and T is the generation time. If we take the logarithm of both sides of this equation and plot the known values of r, R_0 and T for different organisms we obtain a graph similar to Fig. 16.5.

This graph demonstrates that generation time (T) generally has a much larger influence on the growth rate (r), and therefore fitness, than the replacement rate (R_0). For example, if we hold the generation time constant and increase the replacement rate from 2 to 100 000 we can see that there is only about a tenfold increase in the rate of increase (r). However, if we hold the replacement rate constant, a similar 50 000-fold increase in the generation time would reduce the rate of increase by a factor of 50 000, because r and T are inversely related (see Eqn 15.1). Thus, it would seem obvious that to maximize its fitness, an organism should breed as soon as possible rather than delay its breeding until later in life. Many organisms don't follow this obvious solution, however, and so we must examine the types of advantages that may be gained by having a long generation time.

First, our conclusion that extremely large changes in the replacement rate (R_0) only produce relatively small changes in the intrinsic rate of natural increase (r) is only valid for replacement rates of 2 or

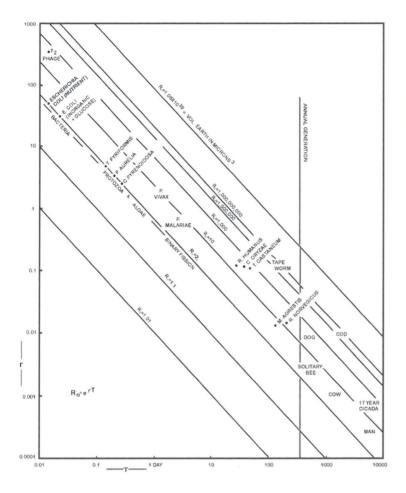

Fig. 16.5 Relationship between generation time (T), the replacement rate (R_0), and the intrinsic rate of natural increase (r). (From Smith, F. E. 1954, In Boell, E. J. (ed.) *Dynamics of Growth Processes*. Copyright © 1954, renewed 1982. Reprinted by permission of Princeton University Press.)

more. It is not valid for organisms with replacement rates between 1 and 2. For example, suppose an organism was able to increase its R_0 value from 1.1 to 1.2 by small increases in fertility or survivorship. The intrinsic rate of natural increase would increase from 0.0953 to 0.1853, i.e. by a factor of 1.9. Thus, in evolutionary terms, it might pay organisms with low rates of increase to expend energy on improving survival and increasing litter size or the number of breeding attempts, rather than to expend energy on rapid growth and development to enable them to breed at an earlier age.

Second, generation time increases with the increase in body size (Fig. 16.6), and there may be many advantages associated with larger body size. For example, larger organisms may have fewer predators, they are typically better able to withstand changes in the physical environment, and they have better powers of movement than smaller organisms. Consequently, they may be better able to exploit certain environments that are too harsh for small-sized organisms. Thus, there may be selection pressures against reducing the generation time if it results in a reduction of body size.

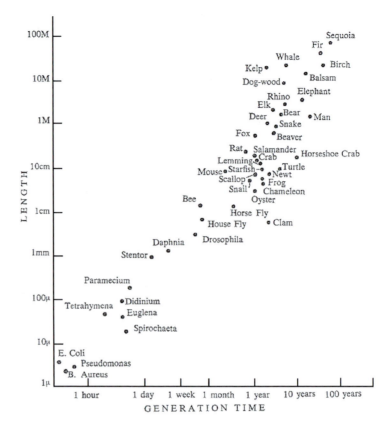

Fig. 16.6 Relationship between body length (i.e. size) and generation time for a wide variety of organisms. (From Bonner, J. T. 1965, *Size and Cycle*. Copyright © 1965. Reprinted by permission of Princeton University Press.)

We have observed that there is a wide range of generation times and that larger organisms have longer generation times than smaller organisms. However, the rate of population growth is inversely related to generation size and so we can conclude that large organisms will typically have lower population growth rates than smaller organisms. Our next step is to consider the life-history characteristics of organisms in a holistic way, rather than by considering each character in isolation, in an effort to understand how organisms may be suited to different environments and ways of life.

16.3 | Life-history strategies: *r*- and *K*-selection

Robert MacArthur and Edward O. Wilson (1967) proposed that the population density, in relation to the density that can be sustained by the environment (*K*), may be an important selective force on life-history traits. They imagined that some populations are maintained at low population densities for much of their history (because of catastrophic mortality from events like fire, frosts, drought and habitat disturbance) and so their population growth is generally not limited by lack of resources. The best strategy for such populations is to maximize their rate of increase (*r*) by producing large numbers of

Table 16.4 Correlates of *r*- and *K*-selected populations

Condition	*r*-selection	*K*-selection
1. Climate or physical conditions	Variable and/or unpredictable; uncertain	Fairly constant and/or predictable; more certain
2. Mortality	Often catastrophic, non-directed, density independent	More directed, density dependent
Survivorship	Often Type III (see Chapter 14)	Usually Types I & II (Chapter 14)
3. Population size	Highly variable in time; usually well below carrying capacity; unsaturated communities; recolonization each year	Fairly constant in time; at or near carrying capacity; saturated communities; recolonization not necessary
Intra- and interspecific competition	Variable, often lax	Usually keen
4. Colonizing ability	Large	Small
5. Selection favours	High r_{max}	Greater competitive ability
	Rapid development	Slower development
	Early reproduction (short generation time)	Delayed reproduction (long generation time)
	Small body size	Large body size
	Semelparity (single reproduction)	Iteroparity (repeated reproduction)
	Short lifespan, usually less than one year	Long lifespan, usually more than one year

Source: After Pianka (1970) and Wilson (1975).

offspring at an early age, and so they can be considered to be *r*-selected. In contrast, *K*-selected populations are able to maintain their population densities near to the carrying capacity (*K*), and their offspring face strong competition for the available resources. In these circumstances, selection favours investing energy into fewer offspring in order to increase their chance of survival. Their analysis was extended by Eric Pianka (1970) and he proposed a larger suite of life-history traits that are characteristic of the two strategies (Table 16.4).

The concept of *r*- and *K*-selection should not be taken too literally, but it can be a useful way to bring some sort of order to the enormous diversity that exists in the life histories of organisms. For example, if we compare the life-history traits of multimammate rats and red deer we can gain some appreciation of their life-history strategies based on the correlates listed in Table 16.4.

I have studied the multimammate rat (*Mastomys natalensis*) in western Uganda. It lives in grassland areas and the populations can vary considerably in density. These small mammals weight about 50 g and may live for as long as a year, but most die within six months of birth. During the rains when food is abundant they will breed repeatedly, but they stop breeding during the dry season. Thus, their population density is related to rainfall. Females produce an average of 12–13 young at intervals of three to four weeks. The young disperse after weaning, and they may start to breed within four to six weeks of birth during the rainy season. Populations can rapidly increase in number under favourable conditions. During the dry season the numbers decline as food becomes scarce, but this is an opportunistic species that migrates into burnt grassland areas vacated by other species. They are the dominant species for the first two months after a fire, but they are not good competitors, and their numbers decline as the grass regrows and other small mammals invade the area. It may be seen that these rodents have many of the features of r-selected species described in Table 16.4.

In contrast, red deer have much more stable populations, and so there is little point in having a high population growth rate. These large animals (adults weigh 100–200 kg or more, depending on the subspecies) live for 15–20 years and females do not start breeding until they are three years of age (see Table 16.1). They breed repeatedly but produce on the average fewer than one young per year (see m_x values in Table 16.1). The young are provided with considerable parental care. The life-history features of this species fit the pattern described for K-selected species in Table 16.4.

We should recognize that organisms do not always fit so neatly into the r- or K-selected categories because the selective forces that shape their life-history traits are not just of two types, i.e. either favouring high population growth rates with a high turnover rate of the population, or favouring low population growth rates with a low turnover rate of the population. For example, we noted in the introduction that elm trees are large, long-lived, and breed repeatedly (K-selected traits) but they also produce vast numbers of small seeds (r-selected traits). This particular set of life-history traits makes sense when one considers the life cycle of the elm and many other trees. Mature individuals in the canopy of forest or woodland need to be large in order to compete for light and space. The population may remain remarkably constant in size for many decades because the death of large canopy trees is infrequent. Individuals may die if they succumb to attacks by pathogens, but frequently their death is the result of disturbances by strong winds or fires which are irregular in occurrence. In any case, the ability of seedlings to become established and grow into large individuals depends on the death of mature individuals which create gaps in the canopy. These occurrences are infrequent and unpredictable. It makes no sense for such trees to produce few, very large seeds, because seedlings, whether small or large, cannot compete with canopy trees until the latter are removed. It is better to produce large numbers of small seeds that can be dispersed widely, and which may be at the right place at the right time to take advantage of gaps created in the canopy by the falling of large trees. Thus, part of the life cycle has K-selected traits, and part has r-selected traits.

There are other unusual combinations of life-history traits. For example, the periodic cicadas (*Magicicada*) live in the ground for 13 or 17 years and then entire populations emerge at the same time to reproduce. Similarly, the bamboos live for many years (for about 120 years in the case of *Phyllostachys bambusoides*) before the entire population flowers, set seeds, and dies. What is striking about these species is that they have long generation times, and yet they are semelparous (breed once), and the populations are highly synchronized in their life cycle. It has been suggested that the long generation time allows individuals to grow to a large size before breeding, which enables them to produce more offspring. The unusual degree of synchrony, where the entire population reproduces at the same time, allows a population to swamp the ability of predators to cause catastrophic mortality at a critical stage of the life cycle. The critical stage is the adult in the case of cicadas, and the seed in the case of the bamboos. Several other hypotheses, however, have been suggested to account for these unusual combinations of life-history traits (see Karban 1997 and Yoshimura 1997).

A different set of selection pressures may account for a similar grouping of characteristics in the Pacific sockeye salmon (*Oncorhynchus nerka*). Between the ages of three and seven years, individuals migrate from the streams and rivers where they grew up to the oceans where they feed and grow rapidly in size. At the age of seven years they return to their birth place, breed, and die. Again, we have an unusual combination of semelparity with large size and long generation time. In this case, however, there may be selection for large size, and consequently delayed reproduction, because the cost of migrating upstream is high, and larger fish can swim faster than smaller fish. Larger fish also produce more offspring.

It is claimed that comparisons and interpretations of this sort are rather trivial, and in some respects they are. Many ecologists are very critical of the concept of *r*- and *K*-selection (see Roff 1992 and Stearns 1992 for reviews) and its popularity has waxed and waned over the years. There is little doubt that it does not represent reality, because the life-history characteristics of most organisms do not fit neatly on the *r*–*K* continuum. Indeed, considering the extraordinary diversity of life forms it would be remarkable if their life-history traits could be explained so simply. In addition, attempts to confirm the theory experimentally, by keeping laboratory populations of protozoa (Luckinbill 1979) and fruit flies (Taylor and Condra 1980) in uncrowded conditions to select for *r*-selected traits, or in crowded conditions to select for *K*-selected traits, were not always successful. Even so, as we have already noted, it can be a helpful way to look at life-history traits provided that we do not take our analyses too literally.

16.4 Summary

There is considerable variation in the life-history characteristics of organisms, and the question is how they may have been shaped by natural selection. The contribution that an individual makes to the future growth of a population, i.e. its reproductive value, varies with age, and it has been suggested that natural selection will favour traits that reduce the death rates of individuals with high reproductive values, even at the expense of increasing the death rate of those with lower reproductive values. This premise is explored to explain how the shape of the mortality curve with age might have evolved in mammals.

Reproductive rates are examined from three perspectives. First, how many offspring should be produced at each breeding event? The evolution of clutch size in birds is considered to see if they correspond with that from which, on average, the most young are raised (Lack's hypothesis). A brief review shows that both juvenile and adult mortality in relation to clutch size are important determinants of clutch size. Second, should an organism breed once or repeatedly? A theoretical analysis shows that the juvenile survival is important in 'deciding' which strategy to follow, but annual species should produce more offspring than perennial species. Third, should an organism breed at an early age or delay its breeding? A review of the evidence suggests that organisms that produce large numbers of offspring should breed as early as possible, whereas those that produce few offspring should delay breeding if they grow to a larger size and become more competitive.

In reviewing the various aspects of reproductive rates, a general pattern of various traits becomes apparent, which are usually referred to as life-history strategies. One such scheme, the r- and K-selection concept, is briefly considered. Although it does not represent reality, it can be a helpful way to look at the enormous diversity that exists in the life histories of organisms.

Part V

Interactions between species, and the behaviour of individuals

In this last section of the book, we consider two different aspects of population biology. First, we examine some aspects of the interactions between different species. There are many ways in which species interact – symbiosis, commensalism, competition, predation, etc. – but we will only consider competition (Chapter 17) and predation (Chapter 18) because of space limitations. These two types of interactions have a very powerful effect on what Darwin termed 'the struggle for existence'. Thus, it is likely that these two processes apply powerful selective forces on the characteristics of organisms. It will also be observed that in many cases, the behaviour of individuals plays an important role in these interactions.

Behaviour is considered in Chapters 19 and 20, and we return to some of the issues that Darwin raised in the fourth and seventh chapters of his book, *The Origin of Species*. After discussing the genetic basis of behaviour at the start of Chapter 19, the problem of altruistic behaviour is considered. In this type of behaviour, some individuals appear to reduce their fitness to help other individuals, and the most extreme example of this is the existence of sterile castes in insects. This type of behaviour appears contrary to the theory of natural selection, which states that only those traits that improve the fitness of an individual can evolve in populations. Hamilton's resolution of this difficulty to the theory of natural selection is briefly described, and the chapter concludes with a description of game theory models which analyse the presence of different behaviours in populations. Chapter 20 looks at sexual selection, which Darwin introduced as a type of selection that differed from natural selection, and goes on to consider the various mating systems of animals. This completes our Darwinian view of population biology.

Chapter 17

Interspecific competition and amensalism

The word 'competition' is used in everyday language, and so we all have a feeling for what it means. We tend to think of competition as an active process in which individuals are striving for a common goal, and trying to outdo each other so that there are winners and losers. In the biological world, individual organisms struggle to obtain the resources necessary for living, such as water, light and food, and we can think of this struggle as involving both intraspecific and interspecific competition. Darwin talked of these processes in terms of the 'struggle for existence' in the development of his theory of natural selection.

17.1 Defining competition

How do we define competition so that we can study the process in a rigorous way? Many ecologists prefer an operational definition that gives us a way of measuring whether competition is occurring or not. Following this logic, I will modify the definition of Emlen (1973) and define competition as follows: *Competition occurs when two or more individuals or species experience depressed fitness (reduced r or K) attributable to their mutual presence in an area.* Thus, in simple terms, competition is defined in terms of a mutual inhibition of growth. We have informally used this definition to define and measure intraspecific competition in Chapter 5 (section 5.1), and we will see that it is easy to extend the logistic growth model to include interspecific competition.

There is also a one-sided interaction between species termed *amensalism*, where there is a negative effect on one species but no effect on the other species. A favourite example of this type of interaction is allelopathy between plants, where toxic metabolites produced by one species inhibit the growth of the other species but there are no reciprocal negative effects. Nevertheless, the production of the toxic metabolites undoubtedly costs the producers something, although this may be extremely difficult to measure, and so amensalism is best characterized as a form of one-sided competition.

In theory, there is a clear distinction between interspecific competition and amensalism. In interspecific competition both species inhibit each other's growth, whereas in amensalism only one species has its growth inhibited by the other. In practice, however, it may be difficult to discriminate between cases of highly asymmetrical competition and amensalism because of our limited ability to detect low levels of inhibition. There are many cases where one species is much more affected than the other and where it is extremely difficult to detect any measurable negative effects on the stronger competitor. These cases of asymmetrical competition will appear to be amensal. Similarly, we may also have difficulty detecting interspecific competition when it is weak, and in these cases might conclude that there is no interspecific competition between two or more species. Bearing these difficulties in mind, Connell looked at 98 reciprocal tests of competition between pairs of species, where the response of the addition or removal of individuals of each species on the abundance of the other was noted. No interaction was observed for 44 pairs of species, there were reciprocal negative effects for 21 pairs, but only one species appeared to be inhibited in 33 pairs of species (Connell 1983). It would appear that amensalism is the most common form of competition, although many of 33 one-sided interactions were probably very asymmetrical forms of competition. Similarly, even though competition was not detected between 44 pairs of species it might be more prudent to conclude that the effects of interspecific competition in these cases were insignificant compared to other factors influencing the growth of these populations.

17.2 | Types of competition

Interspecific competition can be broadly categorized into two types, *exploitation* and *interference*, following a scheme first proposed by Park (1954).

Exploitation competition (also called *resource competition* and *scramble competition*) occurs when there is a utilization of common resources, such as light, nutrients, water, nest sites and food, by different individuals or species. Space is also an important resource for sessile organisms, primarily terrestrial plants, and aquatic, mainly marine, organisms. Utilization of a resource by one individual or species prevents its utilization by another, and if the resource is in limited supply, the consequent reduction in its availability leads to a reduction in the r or K of other individuals or species. There are two things to note about this form of competition. First, it is an indirect effect because the inhibitory or competitive effects result purely from the reduced availability of a resource. Second, the resource must be limiting if competition is to occur. For example, most terrestrial organisms utilize oxygen, but this resource is not limiting in the terrestrial environment and so there is no competition between organisms for this resource.

Interference competition (also called *contest competition*) occurs when organisms impede the access of others to a resource, even if the resource is not in short supply. Interference usually involves chemical or behavioural interactions between organisms prior to the utilization of a resource. Note that this type of competition involves a direct effect of an organism on its competitors. Where resources are spatially fixed, resources may be defended by territorial behaviour, which denies access to the resources to conspecifics and sometimes other species. Where the territories of different species overlap, there may be behavioural interactions which lead to the reallocation of resources, such as a cheetah giving up its prey if confronted by a leopard or lion. Similarly, some species produce chemical growth inhibitors, which reduce the growth rates of other species and so inhibit their ability to exploit resources. Flour beetles condition their food with chemicals, and the growth of competitors is inhibited when they ingest the food. In this case there is a complex interweaving of both the exploitation and interference forms of competition, and their effects are not easily separated.

Competition can be a difficult interaction to study, because species can affect each other's growth in so many ways. This is illustrated by the following two examples.

Dung beetles (mostly Scarabaeidae) use the excrement of large vertebrates as food for themselves and their offspring. Different species exploit the patches of dung in different ways. Some species rapidly remove dung and roll it away to bury (the rollers); other species remove dung from the underside of the pat and bury it in their tunnels constructed beneath the dung (the tunnellers); and a third group of species live and breed in the dung patch (the dwellers) (Doube 1991). There may be intense intraspecific and interspecific competition between dung beetles (Hanski and Cambefort 1991) because dung may be a very ephemeral resource. Anderson and Coe (1974) counted 16 000 dung beetles arriving at a 1.5-kg pile of elephant dung in East Africa, and all of the dung was buried by tunnellers or taken away by rollers in two hours! In these situations, there is intense exploitation competition, and I have observed a similar situation in rollers utilizing buffalo dung in Meru National Park, Kenya (Fig. 17.1 top).

On one occasion I awoke at dawn to find several buffalo pats on our lawn, where a herd of buffalo had been feeding overnight. Soon dung beetles began arriving from all directions, attracted by the smell of the excrement, and within two hours all of the dung had been removed, largely by rollers (Fig. 17.1 bottom). The activity of the rollers was frantic, and the intense exploitation of the dung meant that those that arrived early obtained dung, and those that arrived later usually got none. There was also interference competition, as late arrivals tried to steal from those who had a ball of dung. It was not clear to me what factors determined the success of these fights. In some

Fig. 17.1 Fresh buffalo dung (top) in which two dung beetles are starting to make their dung balls, and a roller (bottom) taking its dung ball away to be buried. (Photographs by the author.)

cases the results of the fights were farcical. Two individuals would be fighting over a ball of dung, and while they were so occupied a third individual would arrive and steal it, leaving the two combatants fighting over nothing. Normally, however, one of the combatants would win, and Heinrich and Bartholomew (1979) have shown that in *Kheper laevistriatus* the winners are larger and have a higher body temperature, which allows them to move faster and overcome their opponent. In a similar way, size is also important in interspecific competition between rollers (Hanski and Cambefort 1991). However, very small balls of dung are not worth stealing by large species of rollers, and so interspecific interference only occurs between species that are not too dissimilar in size.

Competition between plants can be much more subtle. Many plants produce chemical substances that inhibit the germination and growth of other plants (Whittaker 1970). This phenomenon, called *allelopathy*, may be categorized as a form of interference competition or amensalism. McPherson and Muller (1969) have studied allelopathy in chamise (*Adenostoma fasciculatum*) in the hard chaparral[1] of California. There was almost no herbaceous undergrowth in the chamise stands studied by McPherson and Muller, and they showed that this was a result of chemical inhibition. Chamise produces a water-soluble material which accumulates on the surface of their leaves during dry periods. When it rains, this substance is washed off, and is carried to the soil where it inhibits the growth and germination of many plants, including its own species. The chaparral is susceptible to fire, which not only destroys the source of the chemical inhibitor but also appears to break it down in the soil. Following a fire there is a rapid germination of plants, and a rich herbaceous layer is formed. Gradually, however, as the chaparral shrubs regenerate or grow, the allelopathic mechanisms reassert themselves. The growth and germination of new plants are inhibited, and the herbaceous plants decline in abundance. Allelopathy appears, therefore, to have a major effect on the structure of this plant community.

What generalizations can we make from these two examples? First, the competitive interactions may be highly visible and obvious, as was the case in dung beetles. The exploitation of dung may be so rapid that it is easy to demonstrate a limitation of the resource. If females don't obtain dung, they cannot lay their eggs and the birth rate is reduced. However, if the density of dung beetles was low, it would be more difficult to show a limitation of the resource and a reduction in the growth rate (r). The intensity of competition may be increased either by increasing the density of beetles, if the resource stays constant, or by decreasing the amount of dung, if the number of beetles stays constant. Thus, it is the population density per unit of resource that is important when determining the intensity of competition.

Second, the competitive process may be extremely subtle, as in the case of allelopathy. It took many careful experiments to show how chamise inhibited the germination and growth of other species, even though the inhibition was almost total. Thus, it may be easier to study the effect of competition, i.e. the inhibition of growth of one species by another, rather than the mechanism involved. This is why we have defined competition in terms of its effects.

Third, competition between individuals and species is often extremely asymmetrical, and may vary through time. For example, we can see an inhibition of herbaceous plants by chamise, but the inhibition of chamise by herbaceous plants may be non-existent in old chaparral stands and extremely difficult to show in chaparral stands after a fire. In the latter situation, herbaceous plants might

---

[1] Chaparral is a vegetation type of evergreen, small-leaved shrubs, that occurs in Mediterranean climates.

slow the regeneration and growth of chamise by their utilization of light, water and soil nutrients, but I suspect that the effects would be relatively small and difficult to show.

17.3 | The Lotka–Volterra model of interspecific competition

In the mid-1920s, a simple mathematical model of interspecific competition was independently derived by Alfred James Lotka, a physical chemist in the United States who was interested in modelling biological processes, and Vito Volterra, an Italian mathematician. Volterra had been asked to model the process by his daughter, Luisa, an ecologist, and her fiancé, Umberto d'Ancona, who was a marine biologist. The model is now called the Lotka–Volterra competition model. The model is a simple extension of the logistic growth model (Chapter 5) for a pair of species, which are designated as N_1 and N_2. When the two species are growing independently, their population growth is reduced by intraspecific competition as follows:

$$\frac{\delta N_1}{\delta t} = r_1 N_1 \left(\frac{K_1 - N_1}{K_1} \right) \qquad \text{(Exp. 17.1)}$$

$$\frac{\delta N_2}{\delta t} = r_2 N_2 \left(\frac{K_2 - N_2}{K_2} \right) \qquad \text{(Exp. 17.2)}$$

These equations are simple modifications of Eqn 5.2a. When the two species grow together the growth rate of each species is further reduced by the presence of the other, i.e. by interspecific competition. Lotka and Volterra modified the above two expressions as follows:

$$\frac{\delta N_1}{\delta t} = r_1 N_1 \left(\frac{K_1 - N_1 - \alpha N_2}{K_1} \right) \qquad \text{(Eqn 17.1)}$$

$$\frac{\delta N_2}{\delta t} = r_2 N_2 \left(\frac{K_2 - N_2 - \beta N_1}{K_2} \right) \qquad \text{(Eqn 17.2)}$$

We are familiar with most of the terms in this pair of equations. The carrying capacities of the two species are denoted by K_1 and K_2, the rates of population increases are denoted by r_1 and r_2, and the densities of the two species are denoted by N_1 and N_2. The coefficients α and β (called *competition coefficients*) are new to us, and as they are a key feature of the model we need to understand what they represent. In simple terms, α is a coefficient to make the individuals of species 2 equivalent to individuals of species 1, in terms of their effect on the population growth of species 1. For example, if each individual of species 2 had the same effect as 2.5 individuals of species 1 on the growth of species 1, α would equal 2.5. Similar reasoning shows that β is a coefficient to make the individuals of species 1 equivalent to individuals of species 2, in terms of their effect on the

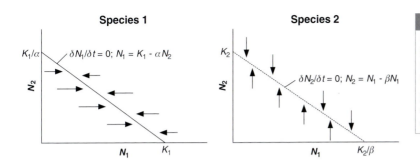

Species 1

K_1/α

$\delta N_1/\delta t = 0; N_1 = K_1 - \alpha N_2$

N_2

N_1 K_1

Species 2

K_2

$\delta N_2/\delta t = 0; N_2 = N_1 - \beta N_1$

N_2

N_1 K_2/β

Fig. 17.2 Graphical representation of the zero isoclines of two species in the Lotka-Volterra competition model. The arrows show the direction of population growth for each species at various combination densities of the two species.

population growth of species 2. We can express these relationships as follows:

$$\alpha = \frac{\text{effect of one unit of sp. 2 on the growth of sp. 1}}{\text{effect of one unit of sp. 1 on the growth of sp. 1}} \quad \text{(Exp. 17.3)}$$

$$\beta = \frac{\text{effect of one unit of sp. 1 on the growth of sp. 2}}{\text{effect of one unit of sp. 2 on the growth of sp. 2}} \quad \text{(Exp. 17.4)}$$

Normally the units are individuals, in which case the competition coefficients are a measure of the relative importance *per individual* of interspecific and intraspecific competition. However, in some cases the species are measured by biomass or volume, and we would use these measures to compare the effects of competition.

To determine the outcome of competition between the two species, Eqns 17.1 and 17.2 must be solved simultaneously. We do this by determining the equilibrium population densities when the two species reach their combined saturation densities and there is no further growth, i.e. when $\delta N_1/\delta t$ and $\delta N_2/\delta t = 0$. This occurs when the numerator of the terms in parentheses in Eqns 17.1 and 17.2 equal zero.

Thus, when $\delta N_1/\delta t = 0$, $K_1 - N_1 - \alpha N_2 = 0$, and this may be rearranged to show us that at equilibrium:

$$N_1 = K_1 - \alpha N_2 \quad \text{(Eqn 17.3)}$$

Similarly,

$$N_2 = K_2 - \beta N_1 \quad \text{(Eqn 17.4)}$$

Equations 17.3 and 17.4 can be represented graphically (Fig. 17.2) as zero isoclines,[2] which represent the densities of the two species when there is no further population growth. The graphs and equations make intuitive sense. If species 2 is not present, species 1 will grow to its carrying capacity, K_1, but its equilibrium density is reduced as species 2 (N_2) increases in density. We can see from Eqn 17.3 that N_1 will decline to zero when $\alpha N_2 = K_1$, and so this occurs when $N_2 = K_1/\alpha$. Similar reasoning shows us that species 2 will grow to K_2 in the absence of species 1 (i.e. $N_1 = 0$), and will decline to zero when

---

[2] A zero isocline represents a set of conditions where there is no growth, i.e. $r = 0$, which in the case of interspecific competition occurs when a species is at its saturation density.

Table 17.1 Growth parameters for *Saccharomyces cerevisiae* and *Schizosaccharomyces kephir* when cultured under aerobic and anaerobic conditions

	K	r	Competition coefficient	Relative alcohol production
Aerobic conditions				
Saccharomyces (sp. 1)	9.80	0.287 69	$\alpha = 1.25$	1.25
Schizosaccharomyces (sp. 2)	6.9	0.189 39	$\beta = 0.85$	0.80
Anaerobic conditions				
Saccharomyces (sp. 1)	6.25	0.215 29	$\alpha = 3.05$	2.08
Schizosaccharomyces (sp. 2)	3.0	0.043 75	$\beta = 0.40$	0.48

Source: 1932 data from Gause (1934).

$N_1 = K_2/\beta$. In addition, each species can increase in density when the combined densities of the two species occur to the left of its zero isocline, but will decline in density when the combined densities of the two species occur to the right of its zero isocline (Fig. 17.2).

17.3.1 Five cases of competition

The equilibrium densities have been determined separately for each species, but the equilibrium density of species 1 depends on the equilibrium density of species 2, and vice versa. To understand the combined dynamics of the two species we combine the two graphs, and discover that there are five possible combinations of the two isoclines, which represent five possible outcomes of competition as predicted by the Lotka–Volterra equations.

Cases 1 and 2: Competitive dominance, and elimination of one species by another

The great Russian biologist Gause used the approach of Lotka and Volterra to investigate competition between two species of yeasts, *Saccharomyces cerevisiae* and *Schizosaccharomyces kephir* (= *S. pombe*), in the early 1930s. First, he grew the two species separately and fitted a logistic growth curve to estimate the r and K values for each species (see Chapter 5). Then the two species were grown together, and he estimated the competition coefficients, α and β, by the way in which the growth curves were modified. He did this for cultures grown in anaerobic and aerobic conditions and obtained the following results given in Table 17.1.

If we use these data to predict the outcome of competition (Fig. 17.3), under aerobic conditions the model predicts that *Saccharomyces* will eliminate *Schizosaccharomyces*, because it has the higher growth characteristics (r and K values) and the competition coefficients of the two species are similar. Under anaerobic conditions, however, it is predicted that *Schizosaccharomyces* will eliminate *Saccharomyces*, because its increased competitive ability (α is much greater than β) more than compensates for its inferior growth characteristics (r and K values). In each case, the zero isocline of one species lies to

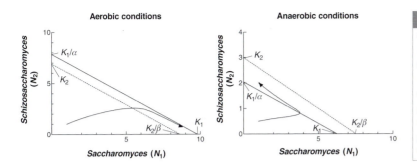

Fig. 17.3 The outcome of competition between *Saccharomyces cerevisiae* (solid line) and *Schizosaccharomyces kephir* (dotted line) grown under aerobic and anaerobic conditions, as predicted by the Lotka–Volterra model. Arrows show the predicted growth of the two species. (Data from Gause 1934.)

the right of the other (Fig. 17.3) and so it can continue to increase in density at the expense of the other species and should eventually eliminate it. In fact, however, neither species was eliminated because the two species went into a resting stage as they approached their combined saturation densities.

Now my objective is not to show that the Lotka–Volterra model is useless. I could have selected an example that supports the prediction of the model. We can make, however, the following observations from Gause's work. First, if you tried to predict the outcome of competition from the data in Table 17.1, without drawing the zero isoclines, I suspect that you would guess incorrectly. Most people expect *Saccharomyces* to win under both sets of conditions because it consistently has the higher r and K values, although others expect *Schizosaccharomyces* to win because it always has the higher competition coefficient. The model predictions, therefore, are not always very obvious. Second, a change in conditions can alter the outcome of competition, and so one species may be a superior competitor to another under some conditions but be an inferior competitor under other conditions. Finally, Gause's work on yeast is interesting because it is one of the few cases where the process of competition has been quantified. Gause grew his yeast with an excess of sugar, and so this should not have been limiting to growth. However, growth was inhibited by the increasing concentration of alcohol, and Gause showed that under aerobic conditions both species were inhibited to the same degree by alcohol. He calculated the relative production of alcohol per unit volume of the two species and showed that they corresponded to the competition coefficients of the two species when grown under aerobic conditions (Table 17.1). Gause concluded that competition between the two species grown in aerobic conditions is entirely regulated by their relative alcohol production. The competitive interaction appears to be more complex under anaerobic conditions. *Saccharomyces* appears to inhibit *Schizosaccharomyces* purely by the production of alcohol (the competition coefficient of 0.4 is approximately equal to its relative alcohol production of 0.48 – see Table 17.1), but *Schizosaccharomyces* produces 2.08 times as much alcohol per unit volume than *Saccharomyces* but inhibits the growth of the latter species 3.05 times as much. Gause postulated that other products, such as carbon dioxide, were also involved in the competitive process.

Table 17.2 Percentage of cultures where *Tribolium confusum* eliminated *T. castaneum* when cultured at different temperatures and relative humidity

Temperature	Relative humidity	
	30%	70%
24 °C	100%	71%
29 °C	87%	14%
34 °C	90%	0%

Source: Data from Park (1962).

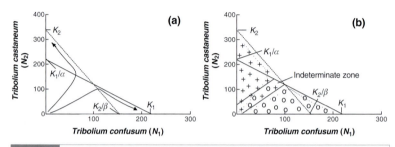

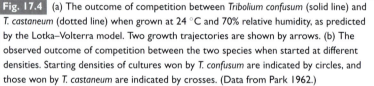

Fig. 17.4 (a) The outcome of competition between *Tribolium confusum* (solid line) and *T. castaneum* (dotted line) when grown at 24 °C and 70% relative humidity, as predicted by the Lotka–Volterra model. Two growth trajectories are shown by arrows. (b) The observed outcome of competition between the two species when started at different densities. Starting densities of cultures won by *T. confusum* are indicated by circles, and those won by *T. castaneum* are indicated by crosses. (Data from Park 1962.)

Case 3: Either species can eliminate the other when grown in the same conditions

Competition between different species of flour beetles has been extensively studied by Park, Mertz, Dawson, and others. They are ideal experimental animals, because they are small, about 4–5 mm in length as adults, and can complete their entire life cycle in small containers of flour. They can be counted by sieving the flour, and it is possible to do well-replicated experiments by keeping several containers in controlled environment chambers. In one such series of experiments, Park (1962) studied the growth of single and mixed species populations of *Tribolium confusum* and *T. castaneum* at different temperatures and humidity (Table 17.2). *Tribolium confusum* always eliminated *T. castaneum* at 24 °C and 30% relative humidity (Case 1), whereas at 34 °C and 70% relative humidity *T. castaneum* always eliminated *T. confusum* (Case 2). However, at intermediate temperatures and humidity either species can eliminate the other, although *T. confusum* wins more frequently at lower humidity and temperatures and *T. castaneum* wins more frequently at higher humidity and temperatures (Table 17.2).

If we consider the interaction at 24 °C and 70% relative humidity, the carrying capacity of *T. confusum* (K_1) was 220 and of *T. castaneum* (K_2) was 340, and the competition coefficients were $\alpha = 1$ and $\beta = 2.2$,

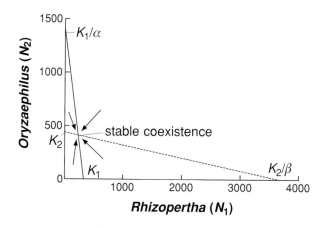

Fig. 17.5 Outcome of competition between *Rhizopertha* (solid line) and *Oryzaephilus* (dotted line), as predicted by the Lotka–Volterra model. Arrows show the predicted growth of the two species from different combinations of their densities. (Data from Crombie 1945.)

enabling us to draw the zero isoclines for this interaction (Fig. 17.4a). It may be seen that the model predicts that either species can win depending on their initial densities and relative rates of increase.

Park grew cultures starting with different combinations of densities of the two species (Fig. 17.5) and showed that a species would always eliminate the other if the starting densities were weighted in its favour. However, there was a region of intermediate densities, which he called an indeterminate zone, where it was not possible to predict with certainty the winning species. In this region, stochastic (chance) events probably determined which species increased faster than the other, so that it would overwhelm and eventually eliminate the other species.

The process of competition between these two species is complex. There is the exploitation of the flour by the two species, but this is affected by the production of growth inhibitors by each species, which is difficult to quantify. There are also predation and cannibalism of eggs and pupae by the larvae and adults. Each species prefers to eat the eggs and pupae of the other species, and it is likely that this mutual predation dominates the competitive interaction. Park considered that this mutual predation was a type of interference competition.

The Lotka–Volterra model correctly predicts the outcome of competition between these two species. Noting the conditions for Case 3 from the intercepts of the two isoclines (Fig. 17.6), we see that $K_1 > K_2/\beta$ and so $\beta > K_2/K_1$, and that $K_2 > K_1/\alpha$ and so $\alpha > K_1/K_2$. Interspecific competition is usually stronger than intraspecific competition in Case 3.

Case 4: Coexistence of the two species at a stable equilibrium density

Two species will coexist in stable equilibrium when each species inhibits its own growth more than it inhibits the growth of the other species, i.e. intraspecific competition is stronger than interspecific competition in both species. An example of this type of competition is provided by the flour beetles *Oryzaephilus* and *Rhizopertha*, when they are grown in cracked wheat (Crombie 1945).

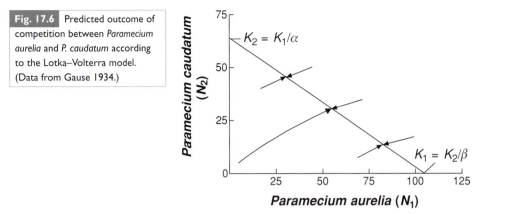

In one set of experiments, the carrying capacities were 330 for *Rhizopertha* (K_1) and 440 for *Oryzaephilus* (K_2), and the competition coefficients were $\alpha = 0.235$ and $\beta = 0.12$. The predicted outcome of competition between these two species is shown in Fig. 17.6, and this reflects what is observed. Apparently, the larvae of *Rhizopertha* live, feed and pupate inside the cracks in the grains of wheat, whereas the larvae of *Oryzaephilus* live and feed on the surface of the grain. The adults of both species live and feed on the surface of the grain. The difference in feeding habits of the larvae, and probably a reduced level of predation by *Oryzaephilus* on the eggs and pupae of *Rhizopertha*, allows the two species to coexist in stable equilibrium. The importance of reducing pupal predation has been demonstrated in competition between *Tribolium confusum* and *Oryzaephilus*. *Tribolium* always eliminated *Oryzaephilus* in flour cultures, but when the flour was 'seeded' with capillary tubes there was stable coexistence of the two species. The smaller species, *Oryzaephilus*, could pupate in the capillary tubes and so was protected from predation.

The conditions for Case 4 may be inferred from the intercepts of the zero isoclines. We see that $K_1 < K_2/\beta$ and so $\beta < K_2/K_1$, and $K_2 < K_1/\alpha$ and so $\alpha < K_1/K_2$. Normally, the effects of intraspecific competition are greater than those of interspecific competition.

Case 5: Coexistence at a range of equilibrium densities

When $\alpha = K_1/K_2$ and $\beta = K_2/K_1$ the zero isoclines of the two species are coincidental (Fig. 17.6), and the model predicts that the two species can coexist at a range of densities, depending on their initial densities and relative growth rates. Many consider that this case is impossible, but we will consider one example because it reveals a fundamental flaw in the basic Lotka–Volterra model.

Gause (1934) examined competition between *Paramecium aurelia* and *P. caudatum* which appears to conform to this situation (Table 17.3). Although the Lotka–Volterra model predicts that the two species will coexist, *P. caudatum* was eliminated from the mixed species cultures by about day 16. The main reason for the displacement of *P. caudatum*

Table 17.3 Growth parameters for *Paramecium aurelia* and *P. caudatum* cultivated separately and together in buffered medium with a 'half-loop' concentration of bacteria

Parameter	*Paramecium aurelia*	*Paramecium caudatum*
Carrying capacity	$K_1 = 105$	$K_2 = 64$
Intrinsic rate of increase	$r_1 = 1.1244$	$r_2 = 0.7944$
Competition coefficient	$\alpha = 1.64$	$\beta = 0.61$

Source: Data from Gause (1934).

by *P. aurelia* is related to the daily sampling of the cultures to estimate their densities. To quote from Gause (1934):

> The biomass of every species was decreased by 1/10 daily. Were the species similar in their properties, each one of them would again increase by 1/10, and there would not be any alteration in the relative quantities of the two species. However, as one species grows quicker than another, it succeeds not only in regaining what it has lost but also in seizing part of the food resources of the other species. Therefore, every elementary movement of the population leads to a diminution in the biomass of the slowly growing species, and produces its entire disappearance after a certain time.

Gause's observation makes a great deal of sense. Populations are reduced by predation and various forms of disturbance, and their ability to recover from these reductions undoubtedly influences the outcome of competition between species. However, the Lotka–Volterra model only uses the carrying capacities (K) and the competition coefficients (α and β) to predict the outcome of competition, so it would be useful to modify the model so that the growth rates (r) can also influence the outcome.

17.3.2 Complicating the model: introducing a removal factor

Slobodkin (1961) modified the basic Lotka–Volterra model by including a non-selective removal factor (m), and showed that the relative growth rates of the two species may be important in determining the outcome of competition. He modified Eqns 17.1 and 17.2 by removing a proportion (m) of each population at each time step, and obtained following pair of equations:

$$\frac{\delta N_1}{\delta t} = r_1 N_1 \left(\frac{K_1 - N_1 - \alpha N_2}{K_1} \right) - m N_1 \qquad \text{(Eqn 17.5)}$$

$$\frac{\delta N_2}{\delta t} = r_2 N_2 \left(\frac{K_2 - N_2 - \beta N_1}{K_2} \right) - m N_2 \qquad \text{(Eqn 17.6)}$$

If the removal factor is selective, such as a predator eating more of one species than the other, we can still make it conform to our model by making the appropriate reduction to the growth rate, r,

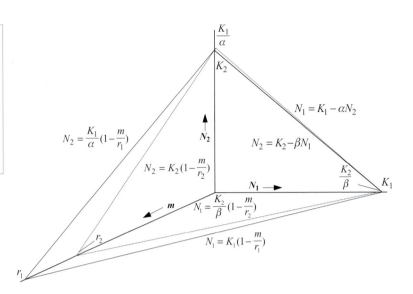

Fig. 17.7 Competition between two species with a removal rate (m). The zero isoclines for species 1 are shown as solid lines and their equations and intercepts are shown on the outside of the figure; those for species 2 are shown as dotted lines with their equations and intercepts on the inside of the figure. See text for interpretation.

of the species with the higher removal rate. We now have a three-dimensional model in which the numbers of species 1 (N_1) and species 2 (N_1) vary according to the removal rate (m) as well as the competitive interaction between the two species (Fig. 17.7). We determine the outcome of competition in exactly the same way as for the simple Lotka–Volterra model, by calculating the equilibrium conditions when $\delta N_1/\delta t$ and $\delta N_2/\delta t = 0$. When, $\delta N_1/\delta t = 0$ Eqn 17.5 can be rearranged as:

$$N_1 = K_1 \left(1 - \frac{m}{r_1}\right) - \alpha N_2 \qquad \text{(Exp. 17.5)}$$

Three zero isoclines can then be derived from this expression as follows: when $m = 0$, $N_1 = K_1 - \alpha N_2$, which conforms to the simple Lotka–Volterra model; when $N_2 = 0$, $N_1 = K_1(1 - m/r_1)$; and when $N_1 = 0$, $N_2 = (K_1/\alpha)(1 - m/r_1)$. Similarly, the intercepts on the three axes are derived as follows: when N_2 and $m = 0$, $N_1 = K_1$; when N_1 and $m = 0$, $N_2 = K_1/\alpha$; and when N_1 and $N_2 = 0$, $m = r_1$ (see Fig. 17.7). The zero isoclines and intercepts for species 2 are derived in the same way. The three isoclines for each species define the edges of their isoplanes, which are described by Exp. 17.5 and the analogous expression for species 2.

The model is illustrated for Case 5 where species 1 has the higher growth rate (Fig. 17.7). When there is no removal factor operating ($m = 0$) the model reverts to the basic Lotka–Volterra model, as shown on the back panel of the graph. However, when there is a removal factor operating (i.e. $m > 0$) the zero isoplane of species 1 lies outside of that of species 2, and so the model predicts that species 2 will be eliminated. Thus, Slobodkin's modification of the model neatly explains Gause's observations for *P. aurelia* and *P. caudatum* because *P. aurelia* has the higher growth rate (see Table 17.3).

The inclusion of a removal factor in Case 5 changes the outcome of competition to favour the species with the highest growth rate (r) so that it excludes the other species. The same is true for Cases 3

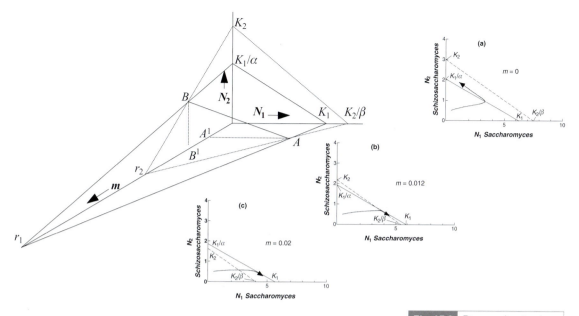

Fig. 17.8 Diagram showing the relationship between interspecific competition between species 1 (solid lines) and species 2 (dotted lines), the intrinsic rate of natural increase (*r*), and a non-specific removal factor (*m*). The zero isoclines are shown at different removal rates in figures (a), (b) and (c) to the right. See text for discussion.

and 4 but only at high removal rates. At low removal rates the cases remain unchanged, although the relative density of the species with the higher growth rate, or the proportion of times it wins the competitive encounter increases as the removal rate increases. For Cases 1 and 2, where one species or the other always wins the competitive interaction, the inclusion of a removal factor can lead to interesting outcomes if the inferior competitor has the higher rate of increase. This is illustrated for Case 2, where species 2 wins in the absence of a removal factor (Fig. 17.8). A careful examination of the figure reveals that at removal rates less than A^1 the outcome of the interaction remains unchanged because the zero isoplane of species 2 lies beyond that of species 1 (Fig. 17.8a). At removal rates higher than B^1 species 1 wins because of its higher growth rate (Fig. 17.8c). At removal rates between A^1 and B^1, however, the two zero isoplanes intersect along the locus AB and so the two species are in equilibrium where the superior competitive ability of species 2 is balanced by the superior growth rate of species 1. The question is whether the equilibrium is stable, as in Case 4, or unstable, as in Case 3. The situation corresponds to an unstable equilibrium, as shown in Fig. 17.8b where the intersection of the zero isoclines corresponds to Fig. 17.4a. Thus, at intermediate removal rates either species can win the interaction, and the winner depends on the initial densities. Whether the equilibrium is stable or unstable depends on the relative slopes of the two zero isoclines in the absence of a removal factor.

Slobodkin (1961) provided experimental verification of the prediction that a non-specific removal factor can promote coexistence of two species when there is competitive exclusion in the absence of a removal factor. He performed experiments on green hydra (*Hydra viridissima*) and brown hydra (*H. littoralis*). In the absence of a removal factor brown hydra were invariably eliminated by the green because the latter had a supplemental energy source from their symbiotic green algae. However, if a fixed percentage of newborn animals of each species was removed, the two populations stabilized and coexisted for the duration of the experiment. Similarly, he noted that the azuki bean weevil (*Callusobruchus chinensis*) always eliminated the southern cowpea weevil (*C. quadrimaculatus*) when the two were maintained on azuki beans, but if a parasitic wasp (*Neocatolaccus mamezophagus*) is added to the cultures, both species coexisted indefinitely (Utida 1953). The wasp shows no preference between the two weevils.

We can make the following general conclusions from the Lotka–Volterra model and its modification by Slobodkin. Two species will probably coexist if interspecific competition is low relative to intraspecific competition, whereas if interspecific competition is high relative to intraspecific competition one species will be eliminated by the other. These general predictions may be modified by the relative carrying capacities of the two species. The introduction of a removal factor, such as predation or physical disturbances such as wave or ice scouring, can either promote or reduce the likelihood of coexistence depending on the balance of competitive ability and rates of population increase. At low dilution rates the ability of a species to maintain itself against its competitors is highly dependent on its competitive ability, but as the removal rate increases the competitive interactions become progressively less important and it is the population growth rate (r) that becomes more important. At intermediate removal rates, the competitive advantage of one species may be balanced by the higher growth rate of the other species and coexistence may be possible. Thus, the selection pressures on the various characteristics of the population will probably vary in different environments. Similar conclusions were reached when we considered the evolution of life histories in Chapter 16 (see Table 16.4).

To help you better understand these attempts to model competition we will now proceed to simulate competitive interactions using Slobodkin's modification of the Lotka–Volterra model.

17.4 | Simulating competition between two species

The procedure for making a spreadsheet simulation of Slobodkin's modification of the basic Lotka–Volterra competition model is outlined in Appendix 17.1. In this simulation, the zero isoclines are computed according to the dilution rate (m), and so they will change in relation to m as shown on the right-hand side of Fig. 17.8. When you have completed the first simulation, do the following exercises:

1. Using the anaerobic data from Table 17.1 with $m = 0$ gives us a situation which corresponds to Case 2, where species 2 wins (*Schizosaccharomyces* in this case). However, we see that $r_1 > r_2$ and so the outcome of competition should swing in favour of species 1 when there is a removal rate operating. For example, set $m = 0.02$ (cell B7) and see that species 1 wins the interaction. So far what we are observing is analogous to what is illustrated in Fig. 17.8,

where the superior competitor wins at low removal rates and the species with the highest intrinsic rate of natural increase wins at high removal rates. The question is, what happens at intermediate removal rates? Progressively change m from 0.012 to 0.014 and note that at the lower value species 2 wins, and at the higher value species 1 wins (you may wish to simulate this over more time increments). We can see from the intersection of the zero isoclines that in the intermediate region it corresponds to Case 3.

2. Work through the various data sets in section 17.2.1 to see how the model deals with the various cases. You should obtain graphs that correspond to those presented in Figs. 17.3 to 16.6. You will have to enter your own r values for those cases where none is provided. You can also vary m to see the effect of the removal rate on the various competitive interactions.

17.5 The utility of the Lotka–Volterra competition model

The utility of a model may be judged in two ways. It may help us understand a system or process, and it may have a predictive capability. Ideally, it does both of these things. On this basis we can ask whether the basic Lotka–Volterra competition model and Slobodkin's modification of it are useful or not.

There is no simple answer to this question. Some authors consider the model to be successful in broad terms in spite of its limitations (e.g. Begon and Mortimer 1986). If we consider the qualitative predictions of the basic and modified model (see the end of section 17.2.2 for details) we see that they make intuitive sense, and it is helpful to understand that the outcome of competition between two species depends not only on their characteristics but also on external mortality factors. However, the models assume that the individuals of a species are all equivalent, and the carrying capacities and competition coefficients are also constant, which is extremely restrictive. For these reasons, the models are best applied to unicellular organisms and adult insects, which vary little in size, growing under controlled conditions. Thus, our choice of examples in section 17.2.1 was no accident. In most of these cases the model predicted the outcome of competition quite accurately, but not in the case of yeast because the cells entered a resting phase and stopped growing. The assumptions of the model also imply that the inhibitory effects of both intraspecific and interspecific competition are linear functions of density (i.e. the zero isoclines are straight lines). This was shown not to be the case in competition between two species of *Drosophila* (Ayala *et al.* 1973). The authors of this study were able to modify the basic model to produce appropriately curved isoclines which predicted the outcome of competition exactly. We should note that the basic Lotka–Volterra model made the correct qualitative prediction of coexistence in the experiments of Ayala *et al.* (1973), but the modified equations were necessary to estimate the equilibrium densities of the two species.

The main criticism of the basic or modified model, however, is that it has limited predictive capabilities when applied to real ecosystems (Keddy 1989). Environments vary both spatially and over time, and so carrying capacities and competition coefficients will also vary. In addition, in many cases the body size or age class structure of the population can also have a profound influence on its competitive ability, and this can also vary considerably over time. These variations of environmental conditions and population structure mean that prediction of a stable coexistence at a fixed set of densities is unlikely, although they may still coexist. Similarly, one species may tend to eliminate another species in one set of environmental conditions, but the reverse may occur in a different set of environmental conditions, with the result that the two species may oscillate in density as the environment fluctuates. Obviously, things are a lot more complicated in the real world. Nevertheless, the basic model was successfully fitted to field observations of great tits (*Parus major*) and blue tits (*P. caeruleus*) to explain their coexistence (Dhondt 1977), and was also applied to the field experiment of Brown and Davidson (1977) to examine possible competition between ants and rodents in the desert of Arizona.

The last example points to another problem of the Lotka–Volterra model. The basic model deals with the interaction between a pair of species, and so Brown and Davidson (1977) simply grouped all ants and all rodents to use the model in their analysis of competition between these two taxa. However, if we wish to analyse the competition between many species in real ecosystems we need to measure the competitive effects between each pair of species. For example, in a community of 10 species a total of $10^2 - 10 = 90$ competition coefficients and 10 carrying capacities would have to be determined to use the model. Clearly, it can only be applied to very simple systems.

We have not exhausted the complications and difficulties of applying the model to multiple species, but the case has been made, the Lotka–Volterra model has a limited ability to analyse competition in the majority of communities or ecosystems and so we will use a different approach in the next section. Nevertheless, the model is useful in showing that the outcome of competition between species is related to the balance of intraspecific and interspecific competition, the carrying capacities of the species and the reduction of population densities by external factors such as predation and disturbance.

17.6 Interspecific competition and community structure

Interspecific competition between pairs of species results in one species eliminating the other, or both species coexisting at reduced

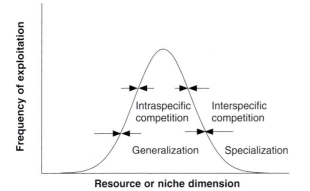

Frequency of exploitation

Intraspecific competition

Interspecific competition

Generalization

Specialization

Resource or niche dimension

Fig. 17.9 Hypothetical exploitation curve of a population with respect to one niche dimension. The niche may represent a resource, such as food, or an environmental gradient, such as moisture. The shape of the curve is determined by selective forces that promote either greater specialization or generalization. (After Root 1967.)

densities. Consequently, when we consider communities of organisms that potentially compete for a common set of resources we can anticipate that their competitive interactions might be important in determining the structure of the community.

17.6.1 The ecological niche

The subject of how communities of organisms exploit a common set of resources is intertwined with niche theory. This is a vast subject and will only be dealt with superficially here. For those who would like to delve more into the subject of the niche I recommend that you read Pianka (1988) and Whittaker and Levin (1975). For our purpose we can consider that an organism's niche is defined by where it lives, which can be progressively described in terms of its regional, habitat and microhabitat distribution, and also the resources it requires, which can be described in terms of what, where, and how it acquires those resources.

An organism is only adapted to exploit part of the environment and its niche is made up of many dimensions, what it eats, where it nests or lays its eggs, the environmental conditions it tolerates, and so on. This exploitation can be plotted as an exploitation curve (Fig. 17.9), which reflects the variation in resource use by the population. Some of this variation occurs within an individual, and some occurs between different individuals. The shape of the curve is determined by the interaction of many selective forces. Intraspecific competition selects to broaden the niche of a population so that it becomes more generalized as population density increases, but this tendency is usually opposed by interspecific competition, which tends to select for a more efficient utilization of the resources through the evolution of specializations. Similarly, a generalist strategy is favoured if resources are scarce, whereas the opposite is true if resources are abundant.

17.6.2 Niche evolution and community structure

Let us consider what might happen when two similar species compete for a common set of resources in the same area or habitat. Imagine that the two species are insectivorous birds that overlap considerably

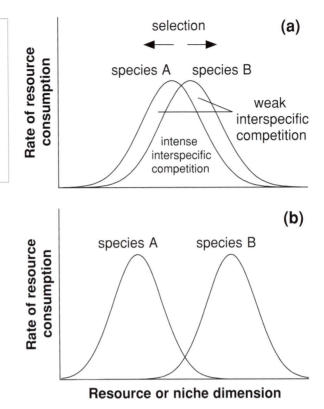

Fig. 17.10 (a) Species A and B exhibit strong interspecific competition because they overlap considerably in their use of a common resource such as food. Natural selection may promote a divergence in their resource requirements (b) resulting in the reduction of interspecific competition and allowing for the coexistence of the two species.

in the sizes of insects they are adapted to catch and eat. If the effects of interspecific competition are stronger than those of intraspecific competition, the Lotka–Volterra theory predicts that one species will eliminate the other. However, a different outcome of the competitive interaction is also possible over the course of many generations of interaction. Let the resource or niche dimension in Fig. 17.10a represent the range of sizes of the insect food available. Both species eat a range of different-sized insects, with species A eating smaller-sized insects on average than species B. If the between-individual variation in diet has a genetic basis, natural selection may occur. Individuals of species A that eat smaller insects than average will face less competition and so will tend to increase in frequency in the population, and similarly individuals of species B that eat larger insects than average will increase in frequency. Thus, the two species will tend to diverge in their characteristics so that their resource requirements overlap less. If interspecific competition becomes less than intraspecific competition, the two species can coexist (Fig. 17.10b). The way in which this divergence occurs depends on the availability of the different sizes of insects. If there were few larger-sized insects available, species B would not shift in that direction and so most of the shift in resource use would have to occur in species A. The selection pressure also depends on the relative abundance of the two species. For example, if species B was attempting to invade an area inhabited by species A its abundance would probably be less and so

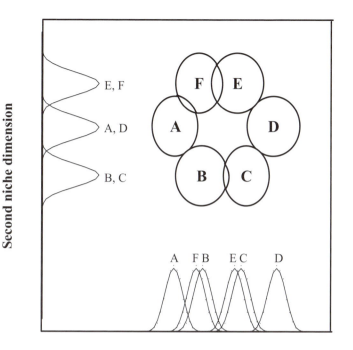

Fig. 17.11 Hypothetical niches of six species (A–F) viewed in two dimensions. Although there may be considerable overlap of niches in either of the single dimensions (represented by bell-shaped curves), there is minimal overlap when both niche dimensions are considered. See text for discussion.

the selection on species B would be stronger than the selection of B on species A. In this case it would be species B that would shift its resource use.

We can envision similar processes leading to a series of bird species that are specialized to feed on different size classes of insects. The degree of specialization that is possible will depend on the availability of resources. If insects are very abundant, it may be possible to specialize on a narrow size class, but if they are more scarce the feeding niche would have to be broader in order to obtain sufficient resources to sustain the population. However, we have only considered one way in which the birds can diversify their feeding niches. They can also diversify their feeding niches by feeding in different places. For example, we might have birds feeding on much the same sizes of insects, but one species may be searching through leaf litter to find the insects concealed there, another may only take insects on the wing, and yet another may glean insects from the foliage of trees. Thus, the feeding niches may overlap considerably in one dimension, such as food size, but be separated on another dimension, such as food location. This packing of species is illustrated in two dimensions in Fig. 17.11, where the first niche dimension represents food size and the second niche dimension represents feeding location. All of these methods of feeding require specific adaptations of beak morphology, flying ability, and other aspects of behaviour. If these feeding specializations are largely driven by the need to avoid or reduce interspecific competition, we can see that interspecific competition has considerable evolutionary consequences.

Table 17.4 | The niche relations among eight species of *Ducula* and *Ptilinopus* fruit pigeons in New Guinea lowland rain forest

Species	Body mass (g)	Ratio of body mass to body mass of next species in guild	Fruit size consumed (mm)				Feeding location	
			7	20	30	40	Branch size	Branch location
Ducula pinon	802				×	×	Large	Central
		1.35						
D. zoeae	592				×	×		
		1.43						
D. rufigaster	414			×	×			
		1.63						
Ptilinopus perlatus	245			×	×			
		1.50						
P. ornatus	163		×	×				
		1.33						
P. superbus	123		×	×				
		1.62						
P. pulchellus	76		×					
		1.55						
P. nanus	49		×				Small	Peripheral

Source: After Diamond (1973).

A good example of niche separation in relation to feeding habits is provided by Jared Diamond's work on a fruit-eating guild of pigeons in New Guinea (Table 17.4). The eight species of coexisting pigeons form a graded size sequence over a 16-fold range in body mass, and the larger species feed on larger fruits than the smaller species. A particular fruit tree may attract up to four consecutive members of the guild, but the smaller species feed on the peripheral, smaller branches and so there is some spatial separation of feeding location (Table 17.4).

Each species weighs approximately 1.5 (range 1.33 − 1.65) times the next pigeon in the sequence, and this represents an unusually tight packing of species in relation to food resources or, expressed in another way, an unusually narrow set of niches. More typically, where food is less abundant and there are fewer competing species, the size ratios are approximately 2 or even higher, indicating that the food niches are broader than those of the New Guinea fruit pigeons. Diamond (1973) calculated the size ratios in several guilds of birds in New Guinea and found they were never less than 1.33 or greater than 2.73. Species with similar habits with a weight ratio of less than 1.33 are too similar to coexist and must segregate spatially. For example, the cuckoo-shrikes *Coracina tenuirostris* and *C. papuensis* occur in different habitats on New Guinea where their average weights are

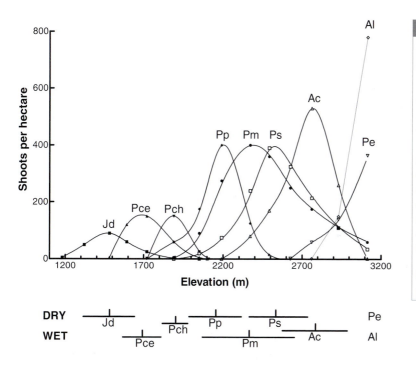

Fig. 17.12 Distribution of coniferous trees in relation to elevation (shown as continuous distributions on graph) and moisture (shown below graph as the mean and one standard deviation) on north-facing slopes in the Santa Catalina and Pinaleño Mountains, Arizona. The tree species are indicated by genus and species initials: *Juniperus deppeana, Pinus cembroides, P. chihuahuana, P. ponderosa, Pseudotsuga menziesii, Pinus strombiformis, Abies concolor, A. lasiocarpa, Picea engelmanni.* (From Whittaker, Lenin, and Root 1973, *American Naturalist,* University of Chicago Press, with permission.)

73 g and 74 g respectively, but they often coexist in the same tree on New Britain, where their respective weights are 61 g and 101 g. If the weight ratio exceeds 2.73 a medium-sized bird with a weight ratio of about 1.65 can invade and coexist with both the large and small species, so that there would be a sequence of three rather than two species. The regularity of the size sequences in these guilds of birds strongly suggests that the organization of these communities is not random, and it also fits with the predictions of niche theory that were first developed by Hutchinson (1959). He noted that if a linear measure, such as bill length, is used to grade the feeding niches of a guild, the ratios of consecutive species usually range between 1.1 and 1.4 and average 1.26, and these measures correspond to the cube root of the body mass comparisons.

Such regularities in the distribution of species may also be observed along habitat gradients. A good example is provided by the study of Whittaker *et al.* (1973) on coniferous trees in relation to an altitude and a moisture gradient (Fig. 17.12). The various species form a broadly overlapping sequence in relation to altitude, and their peaks in abundance are approximately evenly spaced. This in itself indicates that the structure of these tree communities is not haphazard or random, but what is particularly interesting is that where species overlap in their altitudinal distribution, they separate in relation to a moisture gradient with some species occurring in drier areas and others occurring in more moist areas (Fig. 17.12). Once again these observations are in accordance with our niche theory, with the niches of the different tree species being distinct from each other when viewed along two habitat gradients.

17.6.3 Including the effects of predation

Community structure may also be influenced by predation or other factors that reduce the abundance of species because this reduces interspecific competition (see section 17.3.2). Darwin was well aware of this fact and noted the following in the chapter on 'The struggle for existence' in *The Origin of Species*:

> If turf which has long been mown, and the case would be the same with turf closely browsed by quadrupeds, be let to grow, the more vigorous plants gradually kill the less vigorous, though fully grown plants; thus out of twenty species growing on a little plot of mown turf (three feet by four) nine species perished, from the other species being allowed to grow up freely.

Later in the same chapter Darwin noted that cattle grazing prevented the successful invasion by Scots fir into an area of heath in the south of England. In one square yard of the heath he counted 32 little trees that had been browsed by cattle and prevented from growing into mature plants. Parts of the heath had been enclosed, eliminating the grazing effects of cattle, within the last ten years of his study. The fir trees were growing so thickly and profusely in the enclosed areas that not all would survive due to intraspecific competition. Thus, predation can affect community structure directly and not just by the reduction of interspecific competition.

The effects of grazing were rigorously studied by Tansley and Adamson in the 1920s (see Harper 1977), who placed enclosures to exclude grazing by rabbits on an area of very diverse chalk grassland. Within six years the diverse grassland community changed to a much more uniform grassland dominated by *Bromus erectus* (called *Zerna erecta* by Tansley and Adamson). In a later study, Hope-Simpson showed that when rabbits were excluded for longer periods, the vegetation slowly changed still further to become dominated by shrubs. These experiments predicted the changes that were to occur some decades later when myxomatosis decimated the British rabbit population in the years following 1954. Grazing is a complicated process (Harper 1977) and the effects will vary according to the type of vegetation, the type of grazer, and the intensity and selectiveness of grazing. For example, cattle feed on taller vegetation by rolling their tongues around the plant and pulling, and may uproot the plant if it is not well rooted. Their feeding tends to be less selective than grazers like horses and rabbits that essentially clip the vegetation with their teeth. Nevertheless, grazing can completely change the structure of the vegetation community by preventing taller species from overshadowing and crowding out shorter plants. If grazing is at intermediate rates it may lead to an increase in floral diversity, but if it is absent or if it is very intense there may be a reduction of species diversity.

The effects of predation on community structure have also been convincingly demonstrated for an invertebrate community inhabiting the rocky intertidal sea coast area in Washington State in North America (Paine 1966, 1974). The community mainly consists of sessile or sedentary species, including chitons, limpets, mussels (*Mytilus*), whelks (*Thais*), goose-necked and acorn barnacles, and the starfish (*Pisaster*). *Thais* preyed on *Mytilus* and acorn barnacles, but *Pisaster* preyed on all species in the community. If *Pisaster* was selectively removed from the community, the number of species decreased from 15 to eight because *Mytilus* increased in abundance and slowly crowded out many of the other species. It appears that the top predator reduced the competition for space in this intertidal community in much the same way as grazers prevent taller species from overshadowing and crowding out smaller species in grassland. As we will see in the next chapter, top predators frequently select the most abundant prey species, switching from one species to another as they vary in density, and this also can lead to a greater diversity of prey species coexisting in a community. The effects of predator–prey interactions and the interspecific competition effects between prey species are inextricably intertwined in terms of their impacts on community structure.

17.7 | Summary

Where there is interspecific competition each species reduces the growth potential of the other(s) and so there is a mutual reduction of fitness. If the inhibition of growth is completely one-sided, the interaction is called amensalism.

Competition occurs either indirectly through species exploiting resources, which are in short supply, required by other species, or directly by species interfering with other species and reducing their access to resources.

The Lotka–Volterra model of interspecific competition predicts that species can coexist if the effect of interspecific competition is much lower than intraspecific competition, but if the reverse is true, or if one species is a much better competitor than the other, coexistence is not possible and only one species will survive the interaction.

If there are removal factors operating, which keep the species below their carrying capacities, the rates of population growth influence the outcome of competition. At high removal rates, the species with the higher growth rate will win, whatever the relative competitive abilities of the two species, but at intermediate removal rates there may be coexistence if the superior competitive ability of one species is balanced by the higher growth rate of the other species.

Competition may be important in determining the structure of communities. There are regular patterns in the distribution of species with similar habits living in the same general area, such that they are subtly adapted to live in different microhabitats or tend to require slightly different resources. These differences in ways of life are called niches, and we believe that they have evolved largely as a result of intra- and interspecific competition and predation pressures. The niches represent a series of adaptations and so an organism's biochemical, physiological, morphological and behavioural attributes have evolved to 'fit' its niche. For example, birds feeding on different-sized insects in different ways (in mid-air, in leaf litter, gleaned off surfaces, etc.) differ in the size and shapes of their beaks, flying ability or agility, and other aspects of their behaviour. If we look for evidence of continuing direct competition between the various species we will find that it is likely to be low relative to intraspecific competition because of the separation of niches. Indeed the separation of niches may be such that it is difficult to demonstrate interspecific competition in many cases. Nevertheless, we consider that the ghosts of interspecific competition linger on (Connell 1980) and are reflected to some degree by the patterns of niches and the structures of communities that presently exist.

17.8 | Problems

1. Brown and Davidson (1977) examined the possible competition for seeds between rodents and ants in a desert in Arizona by means of a field experiment. In unmanipulated areas (i.e. controls) there was an average of 318 ant colonies and 122 rodents per plot. In two plots, where the rodents were trapped out and then excluded by mesh fences, the average number of ant colonies increased by 71% to 543, and in two other plots, where the ants were killed with insecticide, the mean number of rodents increased by 18% to 144. In two other plots where both ants and rodents were excluded the seed biomass increased by 24% to 5.12 kg from 4.13 kg on the control plots.
   (a) Do these results confirm that ants and rodents are competing for seeds? Are there alternative explanations for these results?
   (b) Assuming that there is interspecific competition, calculate the approximate interspecific competition coefficients for the two species.
2. Competition was studied between two species of protozoa. When grown separately, the carrying capacities were 70 individuals per ml for *Paramecium caudatum* and 11 individuals per ml for *Stylonychia mytilus*. When grown together the inhibitory effect of *Stylonychia* on *Paramecium* (α) was 5.5, and for *Paramecium* on *Stylonychia* (β) was 0.12.
   (a) The two species coexisted. Is this outcome of competition predicted by the Lotka–Volterra model?
   (b) When grown under slightly different conditions, the carrying capacity of *Stylonychia* increased to 20 individuals per ml and the inhibitory effect of *Paramecium* on *Stylonychia* (β) increased to 0.2. Otherwise, the characteristics of the two species did not change. Predict the outcome of competition using the Lotka–Volterra model.
   (c) The actual outcome of competition in part (b) was that *Paramecium* eliminated *Stylonychia*. Account for this observation, given that the intrinsic rates of natural increase per day (r) were 1.1 for *Paramecium* and 0.26 for *Stylonychia*, and that the cultures were monitored by removing one-tenth of the culture on a daily basis.

Appendix 17.1 Simulating interspecific competition

1. Enter a title for your spreadsheet in A1, and then in rows 3 to 7 of column A type: **SPECIES 1**; $r_1=$; $K_1=$; **Alpha**=; **m**=; and in rows 3 to 6 of column D type: **SPECIES 2**; $r_2=$; $K_2=$; **Beta**=. Then

enter the values from Table 17.1 (Anaerobic conditions) in the appropriate places in columns B and E. Your value for m is 0 (zero).

2. In columns A to E of row 9 type the following headings: **Time** (t); **N$_1$**; **delta N$_1$**; **N$_2$**; and **delta N$_2$**. To start with, we program the spreadsheet to draw the zero isoclines, and you may wish to re-mind yourself of this by typing **These/ rows draw/ the zero/ iso-clines/ and reset** in rows 10–14 of column A (the breaks between rows are indicated by / marks. Then enter=**$B$5*(1-$B$7/$B$4)** (= K$_1$) in B10 and **0** (zero) in D10; **0** (zero) in B11 and =**($B$5/$B$6)*** **(1-$B$7/$B$4)** in D11; **0** (zero) in B12 and =**$E$5*(1-$B$7/$E$4)** in D12; =**($E$5/$E$6)*** **(1-$B$7/$E$4)** in B13 and **0** (zero) in D13; and finally **0** (zero) in both B14 and D14. These zero isoclines are calcu-lated in relation to the removal rate, m.

3. (a) Enter **0** (zero) in A15, then enter =**A15+1** in A16 and copy to cells A17–A50 to obtain a time series of 0–35.

   (b) Enter **1** as starting values in cells B15 and D15, then enter =**B15+D15** in B16 and=**D15+E15** in 16, and copy cells B16 and D16 to B17–50 and D17–50.

   (c) Then enter =**($B$4*B15/$B$5)*($B$5-B15-$B$6*D15)-$B$7*B15** in C15, and =**($E$4*D15/$E$5)*($E$5-D15-E 6*B15)-$B$7*D15** in E15. These equations represent Eqns 17.5 and 17.6. Copy cells C15 and E15 to cells C16–50 and E16–50.

4. You have now completed the simulation for 35 time steps. If more time steps are required, the values in row 40 can be copied for as many rows as you wish. Now make two graphs of the simulation. First make an x–y plot where the x-series is B10 . . B50, and the y-series is D10 . . 50. You will obtain a graph similar to the right-hand graph of Fig. 17.4. Label the axes as N1 and N2. Second, make a graph of population size versus time, and so the x-axis is A15 . . A50, and the 1st series B15 . . B50 and the 2nd series is D15 . . D50.

5. Follow the exercises as laid out in the text. When you have finished, save and exit the spreadsheet.

Chapter 18

Predation

We typically think of predators as animals that kill and eat other animals, such as lions eating zebra, or spiders eating flies. These are *true predators* that consume prey animals to obtain food for their own survival and reproduction. However, there are other types of predators that have some but not all of the features of true predators. These include *parasitoids*, which are hymenopterans or dipterans that are free-living in the adult stage, but whose larvae live in or on other arthropods (usually insects), doing little harm at first but eventually consuming and killing the host just prior to pupation. There are also plant and animal *parasites* that live in an obligatory relationship with another species, and harm their hosts, but usually do not kill it. Then there are animals that eat plants, the *herbivores*. Seed-eating herbivores act like true predators, because they consume all of their 'prey'. Others act rather like parasites, because they live in close association with the plant and derive their nourishment from it (e.g. aphids). However, the majority of herbivores only consume a part of the plant, and their detrimental effects can be very variable. Partial or complete defoliation of a plant may have a large effect on the plant's fitness, by reducing its growth rate and seed production, and possibly leaving the plant more vulnerable to attack by plant pathogens. For some pasture plants, however, a moderate amount of grazing may have beneficial effects, by preventing the invasion of taller plants that would overshadow and eliminate the shorter pasture plants.

Although the four categories above are distinct, they have many features in common and so we will be using the words predation and predator in a general sense. Generally, predator and prey populations influence each other's growth, and so their growth is coupled in some way. There have been many attempts to model the growth of predator and prey populations, and we will examine some of them in this chapter.

18.1 | The Lotka–Volterra model of predation

In addition to modelling interspecific competition, Alfred Lotka and Vito Volterra also independently modelled the growth of predator and prey populations in the mid-1920s. They argued that the growth of the prey (H) and predator (P) populations could be described by the following pair of equations:

$$\frac{\delta H}{\delta t} = rH - aHP \qquad \text{(Eqn 18.1)}$$

$$\frac{\delta P}{\delta t} = cHP - dP \qquad \text{(Eqn 18.2)}$$

where r is the intrinsic rate of natural increase of the prey, H is the number of prey, P is the number of predators, a being the attack rate of the predators, c is the conversion rate or efficiency of converting prey biomass into predator offspring, and d is the death rate of the predators.

When we examine these equations, we soon see that they include some peculiar features or assumptions.

1. The prey population (Eqn 18.1) grows exponentially in the absence of predation (i.e. when $aHP = 0$, $\delta H/\delta t = rH$). It would seem more reasonable to describe the growth of the prey population in the absence of predation by the sigmoid growth equation.
2. The number of deaths due to predation (aHP) is a constant fraction of the product of predator and prey densities, and so would be the same if there were 100 prey and 1 predator or 100 predators and 1 prey. It is as if the predators and prey move about at random, in which case their encounter rate would be the product of their densities, and a constant fraction (a) of these encounters results in predation. We will see later that the form of this function varies according to such factors as the hunger or degree of satiation of a predator.
3. The rate of increase of the predator (Eqn 18.2) is directly linked to the efficiency of converting prey biomass into predator offspring (note that cHP is proportional to aHP), and so there are no other limits to predator growth, such as territoriality (i.e. space).
4. The death rate (d) of the predator is also constant, and it would seem more reasonable to make it a function of the amount of food eaten.

Both Lotka and Volterra were probably aware of many of these shortcomings, but they deliberately developed these equations to obtain a desired result. To determine the outcome of their predation model, we follow the approach used to analyse their competition model. First, we derive the zero isoclines, i.e. the equilibrium population sizes when the predator and prey populations are not changing in size. For the prey population, when $\delta H/\delta t = 0$, $aHP = rH$, which simplifies to:

$$P = r/a \qquad \text{(Exp. 18.1)}$$

Thus, the number of predators (P) required to hold the prey population in equilibrium is related to the growth rate of the prey and the attack rate of the predator rather than prey density, which

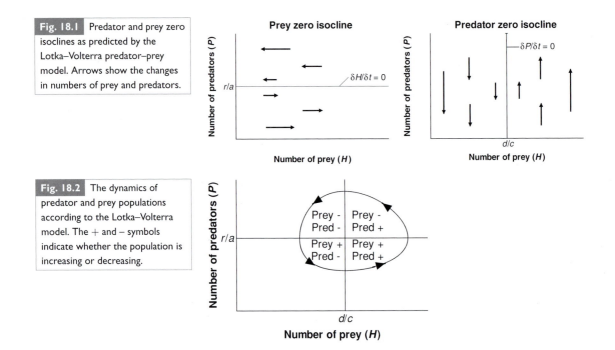

Fig. 18.1 Predator and prey zero isoclines as predicted by the Lotka–Volterra predator–prey model. Arrows show the changes in numbers of prey and predators.

Fig. 18.2 The dynamics of predator and prey populations according to the Lotka–Volterra model. The + and − symbols indicate whether the population is increasing or decreasing.

seems unrealistic. If the number of predators is greater than r/a the prey population will decrease in size, and if the number of predators is less than r/a the prey population will increase in size (Fig. 18.1).

Similarly, for the predators $\delta P/\delta t = 0$ when $cHP = dP$, which simplifies to:

$$H = d/c \qquad \text{(Exp. 18.2)}$$

Thus, the predator population is held in equilibrium by a fixed number of prey, irrespective of predator density, which also seems unrealistic. If the number of prey is greater than d/c the predator population will increase in size, and if the number of prey is less than d/c the predator population will decrease in size (Fig. 18.1).

The two zero isoclines intersect at right angles when the two graphs are superimposed (Fig. 18.2), and the model predicts that there will be sustained oscillations in the numbers of prey and predators (Fig.18.3). The predator oscillations lag one-quarter of a cycle behind the prey, so that the change in predator numbers at any time reflects the change in prey numbers in the preceding quarter of the cycle (Fig. 18.2).

Lotka and Volterra concluded that these oscillations were a direct consequence of the interaction between the two species. However, in view of the rather strange assumptions of the model, there is good reason to believe that they constructed it in a form that would give rise to sustained oscillations. We are not sure why they did this, but perhaps they were aware of the sustained oscillations in lynx (*Felis lynx*) and snowshoe hare (*Lepus americanus*) populations

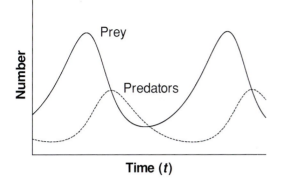

Fig. 18.3 Sustained oscillations of predator (solid line) and prey (dotted line) populations according the Lotka–Volterra model.

that occurred in Canada, revealed by the Hudson Bay records of pelts of these animals from the 1820s onwards (Elton and Nicholson 1942).

We will simulate the Lotka–Volterra predation model to show these oscillations, and to illustrate another peculiar feature of the model.

18.2 | Simulating the Lotka–Volterra predation model

If you follow the procedure for simulating the model, as outlined in Appendix 18.1, the resulting graphs do not resemble Figs. 18.2 and 18.3. This is because we converted the differential Eqns 18.1 and 18.2, which are for infinitesimally small time steps, into difference equations with a time step of one unit. This was done for our other simulations in previous chapters, and our approximations have been acceptable, but this time we find that the model is very sensitive to time lags. There is an exponential function (rH) in Eqn 18.1, which results in the explosive increase of the prey. The impact of predators on prey numbers occurs after too long of a time increment (i.e. there is a long time lag), and so the predator–prey oscillations increase in amplitude extremely rapidly. Do the following exercises to make the simulation resemble the Lotka–Volterra model more closely, and to explore some of the features of the model.

1. The differential equations can be better approximated by making smaller time increments for our calculations, and this is done by reducing the value of the time step (δt) in cell E3. For example, change the value of E3 from 1 to 0.1, which is equivalent to taking 10 time steps to calculate each step in our original simulation. When you do this, you obtain a series of oscillations which increase in amplitude, but more slowly than in our initial simulation. Now decrease the value of the time step (E3) to 0.01, which is equivalent to taking 100 time steps to calculate each time step in our initial

simulation. You will see that in this case you obtain sustained oscillations that are very nearly stable. If we further decreased the value of the time step (δt), we could approximate the differential equations even more closely, but we would require many more time steps to see the results.

2. Now vary your starting values in cells B10 and C10 and see that there is a unique oscillation associated with each pair of starting values. If we set the values of H and P to the values given in cells F10 and G10, there are no oscillations. Now increase these starting values by one to obtain small oscillations. The oscillations increase in amplitude the greater the difference between the starting values and the values in F10 and G10. Thus, the Lotka–Volterra model predicts that the amplitude of the oscillations in predator and prey numbers is determined by the initial numbers of the predator and prey.

3. What happens if a non-specific mortality factor, such as a pesticide, increases the mortality rate of both the predator and prey populations? In this case, the value of r decreases in Eqn 18.1 and the value of d increases in Eqn 18.2. To explore this situation, first set the value of B10 to 50 and the value of C10 to 10. Check the oscillation in numbers of both the predator and prey populations, and note that the prey zero isocline (P in cell F10) has a value of 20, and the predator zero isocline (H) has a value of 40, assuming that you are using the last set of parameters in exercise 1. Now decrease the value of r from 0.5 to 0.45, then 0.4, and finally to 0.2 (in cell E4) and at the same time increase the value of d from 0.6 to 0.66, then 0.72, and finally to 0.96 (in cell E7). This simulates an increase in the mortality rate of both populations. In response, the prey zero isocline declines in value and the predator zero isocline increases in value, and the net effect is that the average size of the prey population increases and the average size of the predator population decreases. Thus, the model predicts that if the growth rate of the prey population is reduced there is a corresponding decrease in the size of the predator population, whereas if the death rate of the predator is increased there will be an increase in the average size of the prey population.

18.3 | Laboratory experiments

Gause (1934) was inspired by the theoretical work of Lotka and Volterra on the interactions between species. He tested the predictions of their predator–prey model, just as he had tested the predictions of their model for interspecific competition. He used two ciliate protozoans; *Paramecium caudatum* as the prey and a suctorian *Didinium nasutum* as the predator (Fig. 18.4).

In the first experiment (Fig. 18.4a), Gause introduced a few *Paramecium* into an oat medium, which contained bacteria on which the *Paramecium* fed, and two days later introduced a few *Didinium* which

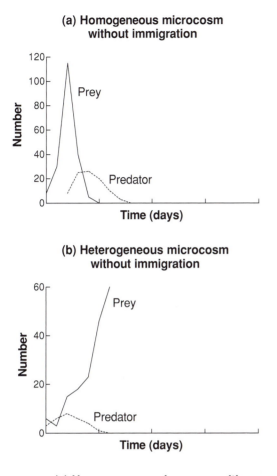

(a) Homogeneous microcosm without immigration

Prey

Predator

Number

Time (days)

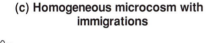

(b) Heterogeneous microcosm without immigration

Prey

Predator

Number

Time (days)

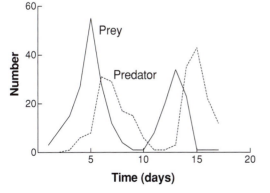

(c) Homogeneous microcosm with immigrations

Prey

Predator

Number

Time (days)

Fig. 18.4 A schematic representation of the results of Gause's experiments in the interaction between *Paramecium caudatum* (prey) and *Didinium nasutum* (predator). (Data from Gause 1934.)

fed on the *Paramecium*. The results were always the same, and appeared to be independent of the size of the microcosm. The *Paramecium* rapidly increased in numbers at first, but once *Didinium* was introduced and began to increase in number, the *Paramecium* were quickly devoured. Eventually all the *Paramecium* were eaten, and then the *Didinium* starved and perished. The best that one may claim is a single oscillation in numbers of the predator and prey. Gause concluded that there was no innate periodic oscillation in numbers of *Paramecium* and *Didinium* in this simple system.

Gause then introduced a prey refuge for the *Paramecium*, in the form of a sediment that *Paramecium* could enter and not the *Didinium* (Fig. 18.4b). The *Didinium* rapidly consumed all of the *Paramecium* swimming in the medium, but could not eat those in the sediment. The predators starved for lack of food, after which the *Paramecium* emerged from the sediment and took over the whole of the microcosm. Again, there was no series of oscillations.

Finally, Gause established a simple microcosm, in which one *Paramecium* and one *Didinium* were introduced every third day. This was to simulate immigration from other populations of these species. In this situation there were sustained oscillations in the numbers of predators and prey (Fig. 18.4c).

Gause (1934) concluded that the oscillation of predator and prey was not an innate characteristic of the interaction between the two species, but depended on movement of prey and predators from one part of the system to another. He envisioned that predators and prey 'played' a gigantic game of hide-and-seek in the real world. A local patch of prey would build up its numbers before being discovered by a predator population which would rapidly decimate the prey population and might even exterminate it. Before this happened, however, the prey population would have dispersed emigrants to start new populations elsewhere, and they in turn would build up their numbers before being discovered by the predator. Thus, one can think of local oscillations, which may be very extreme and might result in the local extermination of both prey and predator, but if the species were sufficiently widespread, the interaction between the two species could persist and overall the numbers of the two species would vary much less.

Huffaker (1958) and Huffaker *et al.* (1963) conducted a classical series of experiments with a prey mite, *Eotetranychus sexmaculatus*, which feeds on the skins of oranges, and a predator mite, *Typhlodromus occidentalis*. Trays of oranges, with various portions of their surface areas exposed, were presented as food for the prey mites and the predatory mites were introduced to feed on the prey mites. In simple systems the results were similar to those observed by Gause for ciliate protozoa. There was a single oscillation where either the prey and the predatory mites became extinct (similar to Fig. 18.4a), or a few prey mites survived and eventually recovered their population size (similar to Fig. 18.4b). The lack of persistence of the predator–prey system was not altered by simply increasing the size of the system. If the prey was given a dispersal advantage over the predator, by providing launching platforms from which they could disperse on silken strands (the predatory mites cannot disperse using this method), the predator–prey system persisted for longer periods. For example, a 120-orange 'universe' persisted for more than seven months, during which time there were three classical predator–prey oscillations (Huffaker 1958), and a 252-orange 'universe' persisted for 490 days and was only terminated because a viral disease reduced the prey mites to a level that was insufficient to maintain the predatory mite population. Thus, Huffaker's results tend to support the Gause's conclusions. The experimental 'universe' was populated by several subpopulations which were out of phase with one another. Provided the prey could disperse faster than the predator, the overall population could be maintained, even though individual subpopulations became extinct as a result of predation.

Similar results were also obtained by Pimental (1961), Pimental *et al.* (1963) and Pimental and Stone (1968) using the housefly (*Musca domestica*) as prey, and a hymenopteran parasite, *Nasonia vitripennis*, as the predator. *Nasonia* feeds on body fluids from both the adult and pupal stages of the prey, which is frequently killed by these attacks. A 'universe' was constructed, consisting of a number of interconnected chambers in which subpopulations of *Musca* and *Nasonia* could develop, and from which they could disperse to other chambers. The host–parasite oscillations became more sustained the larger and more complex they made the experimental system. If they provided a dispersal advantage to the prey, by placing baffles between chambers which slowed the movement of *Nasonia* but not *Musca*, the system also persisted longer. Interestingly, as the experiment progressed, the prey (*Musca*) became increasingly resistant to parasitism by *Nasonia*, and the latter became less virulent.

These experiments tended to support Gause's conclusions that predator–prey oscillations are not an innate feature of their interaction but are a result of the spatial distribution of prey populations and the relative powers of dispersal of the predator and prey. Imagine several subpopulations of prey increasing in size. Sooner or later they are discovered by predators that build up their subpopulations in response, and which eventually cause a decrease in size of the prey subpopulations, i.e. an oscillation. The predators may exterminate the prey subpopulation before dispersing to find other prey subpopulations, or they may disperse when the prey subpopulation reaches a size when it is no longer profitable to hunt them. Meanwhile, some of the prey will have dispersed to start new subpopulations, and so there is a game of hide-and-seek with the predator one step behind the prey.

While this may happen in some predator–prey systems, it is certainly not universal. In some cases, there are regular oscillations of predator and prey. For example, the parasitoid wasp *Heterospilus prosopidis* and the bean weevil (*Callusobruchus chinensis*) (its host) oscillated for six years in a small experimental system (Utida 1957). In other cases, the predator and prey appear to have little effect on each other's density. For example, tawny owls (*Strix aluco*) feed on wood mice (*Apodemus sylvaticus*) and bank voles (*Clethrionomys glareolus*). Large changes in prey density appear to have no effect on the density of the owls, although their breeding is affected (Southern 1970). Clearly, what is

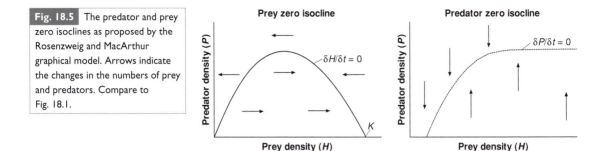

Fig. 18.5 The predator and prey zero isoclines as proposed by the Rosenzweig and MacArthur graphical model. Arrows indicate the changes in the numbers of prey and predators. Compare to Fig. 18.1.

needed is an approach that will allow us to model a wide variety of predator–prey interactions to allow for, and explain, these different outcomes. One such model is the graphical model of Rosenzweig and MacArthur (1963). This model is of immediate appeal to most students because there are no mathematical equations; rather it makes arguments for the shape of the predator and prey zero isoclines on logical grounds, and then infers the outcome of different predator–prey interactions.

18.4 The Rosenzweig and MacArthur graphical model of predation

You will recall that the Lotka–Volterra model predicts that the prey zero isocline is a horizontal line (Fig. 18.1). Rosenzweig and MacArthur (1963), however, argued that the prey zero isocline should be dome-shaped (Fig. 18.5) based on the following line of reasoning. If the prey population was growing according to the logistic equation, the predator population would have to consume the increase in the prey population, as predicted by Eqn 5.2, to hold the population in check. This increase of the prey population has a parabolic shape in relation to prey density (Fig. 5.2), and so this should be the shape of the prey zero isocline. Thus, the largest number of predators could be sustained at half the carrying capacity ($K/2$) of the prey population, and higher and lower prey densities could sustain fewer predators. Even if prey population growth is not exactly logistic, it is likely that the largest increase in size occurs at intermediate densities, and so the prey zero isocline would still be dome-shaped.

Similarly, the predator zero isocline is unlikely to be a vertical straight line, as predicted by the Lotka–Volterra model, because a fixed number of prey cannot keep a predator population at equilibrium at all predator densities. Rosenzweig and MacArthur argued that the predator zero isocline would slope up and to the right to reach the carrying capacity of the predator (Fig. 18.5). They reasoned that there would be a minimum prey density required to support a predator population (the intercept on the prey axis), and increasing competition between predators as their density increases would require a

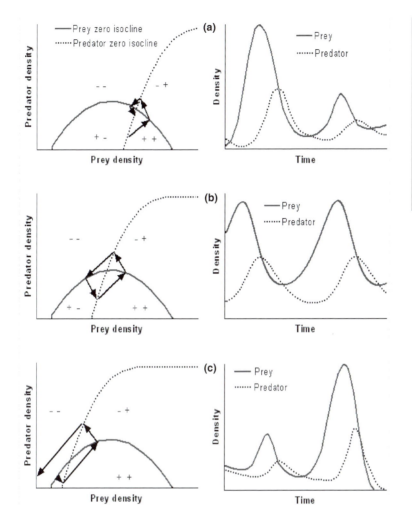

Fig. 18.6 Predator–prey interactions according to the Rosenzweig and MacArthur graphical predation model. The predator exploits the prey population at high (a), intermediate (b) and low (c) population densities (see text). The + and − symbols indicate whether the populations are increasing or decreasing, and the first symbol refers to the prey and the second to the predator population.

greater prey density to sustain them. The steepness of the curve would depend on the intensity of the competition between predators. The carrying capacity of the predator is usually set by something other than prey density, such as the availability of nest sites.

When the zero isoclines of the Rosenzweig and MacArthur model are combined there are different outcomes, depending on how they intersect one another (Fig. 18.6). There are three types of predator–prey oscillations predicted by the graphical model. If the predator doesn't exploit the prey until the prey is near its carrying capacity, there will be damped oscillations (Fig. 18.6a), reaching a stable equilibrium at the intersection of the two zero isoclines. If the predator exploits the prey at intermediate prey densities and the two zero isoclines intersect at the peak of the prey zero isocline, there are sustained oscillations (Fig. 18.6b) similar to those predicted by the Lotka–Volterra model. Finally, if the predator can exploit the prey population at very low prey densities, the oscillations increase in amplitude and

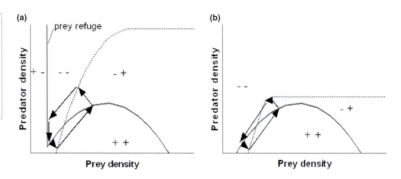

Fig. 18.7 Limiting the amplitude of oscillations (a) by the provision of a prey refuge where the prey are protected from predation, or (b) by limiting the carrying capacity of the predator. Symbols as explained in Fig. 18.6.

ultimately result in the extinction of either the predator or both the prey and predator (Fig. 18.6c).

Unstable interactions of the predator and prey can be stabilized either by providing the prey with a refuge where they are protected from predation, or by reducing the carrying capacity of the predator (Fig. 18.7). It may be seen that these changes to the system serve to impose a limit on the amplitude of the predator–prey oscillations, and so the systems may be sustained indefinitely.

18.5 | The functional response of predators

So far we have focused on trying to explain the coupled oscillations of predator and prey numbers that are frequently, but not always, observed. We can think of this as a preliminary look at the numerical response of the predator to changes in prey density, as well as the response of the prey to changes in predator density. The predator–prey interaction can also be studied in terms of the functional responses of the predator to changes in prey density, first described by Solomon (1949), and to changes in predator density. The functional responses determine how the number of prey attacked per predator changes in relation to both prey density and predator density. These functional responses are influenced by the characteristics of both the predator and the prey and have been investigated in detail by Crawford Holling (1959a, 1959b, 1961, 1963, 1964, 1965, 1966), whose terminology will be followed here.

18.5.1 Functional responses of predators to changes in prey density

This type of functional response examines how the number of prey eaten per predator changes in response to changes in prey density. There are a variety of possible responses of this sort, and Holling has classified them into four types (Fig. 18.8), which we will discuss in turn to identify the particular components (i.e. predator and prey characteristics) that determine the form of these relationships.

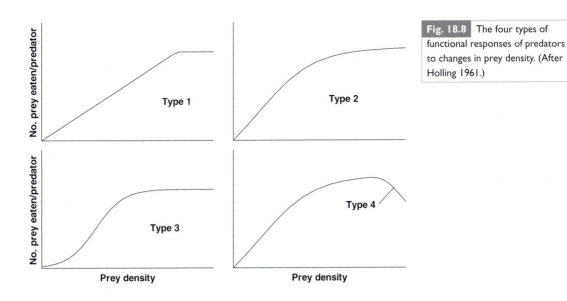

Fig. 18.8 The four types of functional responses of predators to changes in prey density. (After Holling 1961.)

The Type 1 response

The number of prey attacked or eaten per predator increases linearly as the prey density increases, and then abruptly levels off at some upper limit (Fig. 18.8). This is a form of response that is typical of filter feeders. At low prey densities, the number of prey eaten by a predator is determined by the filtering rate, the exposure time (i.e. time spent feeding) and the prey density. If the filtering rate and time exposed remain constant, the number eaten will double if the prey density doubles because it is just as easy to filter two prey items as it is to filter one. However, as the prey density increases, at some point the ingestion rate reaches its maximum capacity and the response abruptly levels off, presumably by alteration of the filtering rate. Holling considered the time required to ingest the food to be equivalent to a component called 'handling time', which in this case only exerts its effect at high prey densities. Holling concluded that there were three basic components which determined the form of the functional response: the exposure time (the duration of feeding activities) and the searching rate (i.e. the filtering rate in this case), which operated at low prey densities, and at higher prey densities there was the sudden addition of the third component of handling time.

The Type 2 response

As the prey density increases, the number of prey attacked per predator increases at a slower and slower rate until it eventually levels off (Fig. 18.8). This is a very common form of functional response, which is also determined by three basic components; the exposure time, the searching rate and the handling time. The first two components are defined in a similar way as in the Type 1 response. The handling time, however, includes the time to pursue, subdue and eat each prey item individually, as well as the time the predator takes to prepare itself to look for more prey. As prey density increases, more prey is consumed, and more of the exposure time is taken up by the handling time, until at high prey densities the predator spends all of its time handling prey (i.e. number of prey eaten × handling time = the exposure time). This description is accurate for an insatiable predator, and has been observed for the belostomatid bug *Lethocerus* attacking tadpole larvae. In most cases, however, the function will level off below this theoretical limit because the predator becomes satiated. Holling added a fourth component, hunger, to account for this, and proposed that this component could be included by making the handling time a function of hunger. As the predator becomes more and more satiated, the handling time becomes longer, because the predator takes longer to consume the prey and prepare itself to look for more prey. The result is that the curve will level off below that of an insatiable predator, but the general form of the response is not altered.

The Type 3 response

This response resembles a sigmoid growth curve, where the number of prey attacked per predator increases at an increasing rate at low prey densities, but at a decreasing rate at higher densities until it levels off (Fig. 18.8). The last part of the curve, where the slope is decreasing, is explained in the same way as the Type 2 response. The first part of the curve, where the slope is increasing, is explained by changes in the behaviour of the predator which increase their efficiency of attacking the prey. There are several aspects of predator behaviour that may change, and we will consider these in turn.

First, there may be a change in behaviour which Holling has called the stimulation of searching by prey discovery. When a predator discovers a particular prey item, it frequently changes its behaviour to search actively for that type of prey. For example, in a cage where there are twigs on the floor, captive birds pay little attention to the floor after an initial exploration of the cage environment. If geometrid caterpillars, which resemble twigs, are placed on the floor of the cage, on discovering this prey item the birds will immediately start to search through the twigs looking for further prey. At low prey densities they may lose interest because their search is not rewarded, but as the prey density increases they discover further prey items before they lose interest, and so this activity is reinforced. This activity may also include the development of a systematic search pattern, so that the predators become more effective in searching through an area. In addition, the predators may also develop a search image where they become better at locating camouflaged or concealed prey. The net effect of these changes in behaviour is that the searching rate, and the ability to locate prey, increase as the prey density increases.

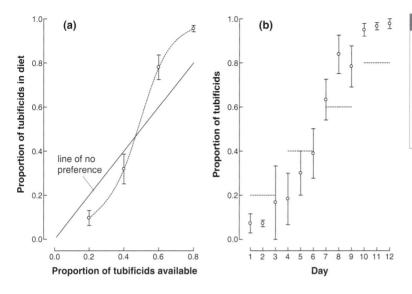

Fig. 18.9 (a) Predator switching by guppies given a choice of feeding on fruit flies or tubificid worms; and (b) showing the speed at which the switch occurs when the proportion of tubificids increases from 0.2 to 0.8 at three-day intervals. (From Murdoch and Oaten 1975, with permission.)

Second, with practice the predator becomes better at capturing and subduing its prey. Thus, the more a particular prey item is attacked and eaten, the more efficient and successful the predator becomes at eating that type of prey. As a consequence, the proportion of successful attacks increases, thereby increasing the attack rate, and the handling time decreases, which leaves more time to search for further prey. Again, these changes in behaviour are related to changes in prey density.

Finally, as the density of the prey increases, it may pay a predator to switch from a less abundant prey type to the more abundant prey type. This is known as predator switching and will also result in a Type 3 response. In order to switch from one type of prey to another, the predator may have to learn a new set of search, attack and subduing skills like those we have just discussed. The switch in prey preference is shown for guppies (*Poecilia reticulata*) given a choice of fruit flies (*Drosophila*) and tubificid worms as prey (Fig. 18.9).

The Type 4 response

The first part of the curve may correspond to any of the previous types of functional responses, and so we are solely concerned with the reduction of the number of prey attacked or eaten that is sometimes observed at high prey densities (Fig. 18.8). There are four possible reasons for this reduction. First, in the case of filter feeders with a Type 1 functional response, the filtering mechanism may be swamped and become clogged at extremely high prey densities. Consequently, the predator may spend time cleaning and freeing its filtering apparatus and so spend less time feeding. Second, predators may become confused, or less able to focus on an individual prey item, when there are many prey to choose from. For example, when goldfish (*Carassius auratus*) try to attack an individual *Daphnia* in dense swarms, they

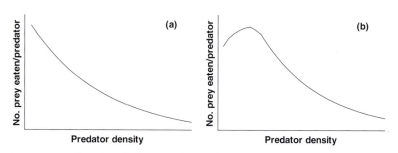

Fig. 18.10 Functional responses of predators to changes in predator density, showing the effects of competition between predators (a) and with the added effect of co-operation between predators or group stimulation of predators (b).

become confused and distracted by other *Daphnia* that enter their line of vision, and eat less prey than when fewer *Daphnia* are present. Similarly, one of the functions of fish schooling is to make it more difficult for predators to single out individuals for attack. Third, some prey may co-operate or share the load of looking out for potential predators and warning others of their presence. For example, large herds of ungulates are less vulnerable to attack by lion than small groups because they are more likely to detect the predator and take appropriate evasive action. Finally, large numbers of prey may intimidate or even be able to defend themselves against attack by some predators. For example, buffalo (*Synceros caffer*) have been known to drive off and even kill a lion (*Panthera leo*) that is trying to attack them.

18.5.2 Functional response of predators to changes in predator density

A second type of functional response concerns how the number of prey eaten per predator changes in response to changes in predator density. Holling identified two such responses (Fig. 18.10) which we will discuss in turn.

Competition for food increases as the density of the predators increases and results in a decrease in the number of prey eaten or attacked per predator (Fig. 18.10a). There are two components of this competition: exploitation and interference (see section 17.2). Exploitation means that prey consumed by one predator are unavailable to another, and similarly parasites and parasitoids find less unexploited prey to attack as the predator density increases. Interference competition can have stronger effects and include such activities as predators fighting for the same prey item, or predators establishing feeding territories to defend rich sources of food. Such behaviour reduces the time available for searching for prey with the result that fewer prey are eaten as the density of the predator increases.

There are some cases in which the number of prey eaten per predator increases at low predator densities, but then decreases once the predator density increases beyond a certain density because of the increasing competition between predators (Fig. 18.10b). The initial increase probably occurs in most of the social carnivores that hunt prey which are difficult to capture and kill. For example, the adult females in a pride of lions co-operate with one another when they hunt large ungulates. They may attack the same prey individual from different directions so that the prey is less able to defend itself, and in some cases a lion may steer potential prey towards an area where other members of her pride are lying in ambush. In this way, a large pride will be more successful than a small pride when attacking animals like buffalo, wildebeest or kudu. Wolves also co-operate when hunting for caribou, moose and elk, by taking turns at leading when tracking their prey through snow in winter, thereby reducing individual fatigue, and by attacking the prey from different directions when they finally corner them.

The initial increase in the rate of predation may also be a result of group stimulation. For example, a bird feeding on small invertebrates on the seashore, or on worms in an area of lawn, may be observed by other birds which are then attracted to feed in the same area. What this does is to increase a predator's area of perception, because the predator may not only detect prey directly but may detect prey by observing the behaviour of other predators. An extreme example of this effect is provided by vultures (Accipitridae) which change their flight to a very characteristic circling pattern when they detect a dead or dying animal. This attracts other vultures which circle in a cluster which is visible for very long distances. In the case of a dead elephant a few hundred vultures may gather before descending to feed. One may ask why the vultures display this behaviour and why an individual doesn't discretely fly down and feed on the dead animal. There are two reasons for this. Some species of vultures are unable to open up a carcass to feed, and so they attract a species that will do this for them. However, there is also safety in numbers, because once a vulture has gorged itself on meat it is unable to fly until the meal is digested and becomes vulnerable to attack by other predators.

18.6 Predation and evolution: prey characteristics that reduce the risk of predation

Predators tend to select prey types that are easy to catch and subdue, and avoid prey types that are distasteful or noxious in some way. Thus, predation acts as a powerful selective force on the characteristics of prey, which have responded by evolving a whole variety of ways to reduce the risk of predation. Predation, however, is only one of a whole range of selective forces operating on prey populations. Selection balances the risks and benefits of the different selective pressures, which may oppose each other at times. For example, prey may have to increase the risk of predation in order to feed themselves and not starve to death. Consequently, we need to keep this sort of balance in mind and avoid looking at prey characteristics from the single perspective of reducing the risk of predation. It is easy to reach false conclusions, and so where possible it is important to test if the characteristic really does reduce the risk of predation. The following review is not exhaustive, and the various defence mechanisms could have been grouped in other ways.

1. **Hiding.** Some prey avoid detection by living in holes or crevices. Some may live all of their life concealed in this way, but others may need to emerge from their hiding place in order to feed. Examples include many small mammals that live in burrows in the ground, fish that live in crevices in coral reefs, shellfishes that live in sediment and insects that live under the bark of trees. Of course, these animals may live in such places for reasons other than avoiding predation. For example, insects may be feeding on the living cambium layer that lies immediately beneath the bark, and small mammals can create a warm microclimate in their burrows, which reduces the amount of energy they need to consume in order to keep a constant body temperature. Concealment does not provide total protection against predation, because some predators are adapted to search out these types of prey. For example, the body-shapes of snakes and weasels allow them to enter the burrow systems of small mammals and attack the prey there, and the beaks of some birds are adapted to allow them to search through sediments for shellfish, or to penetrate bark to discover the insects hiding there. However, this method of concealment does reduce the potential range of predators to which the prey are exposed.

2. **Camouflage.** Prey may hide in another way, by using camouflage to avoid detection. It is a very effective method, as the following experience demonstrates. I was carefully scouring the ground looking for signs of small mammals in Kenya when I almost stepped on a black-faced sandgrouse (*Eremialector decoratus*) incubating its eggs (Fig. 18.11). It took off at the last second, thoroughly scaring this potential predator, who had no idea of its presence. The disruptive

Fig. 18.11 Black-faced sandgrouse on nest. Inset: a pair of sandgrouse showing disruptive coloration. (Photographs by the author.)

Fig. 18.12 Selection of background colour by 12 white moths in Merrit, British Columbia. Eleven of the 12 moths chose the white stripe on the bright red van. (Photograph by Vanessa Bourhis, with permission.)

coloration of this bird helps to break up its body outline so that it blends with its surroundings, and its concealment is aided by keeping perfectly still.

The evolution of camouflage was briefly considered in Chapter 3, and the strong selection pressure on body colour in the peppered moth (*Biston betularia*) as a result of bird predation was documented in Chapter 11. In this last example, we noted that birds selected the most conspicuous individuals as they rested on the trunks of trees, with the result that in polluted areas most of the moths were black, whereas in non-polluted areas most of the moths were a light, speckled colour. The use of crypsis to avoid detection also requires appropriate behaviour. Prey must select appropriately coloured backgrounds to match their body colour, and may even have to orient themselves so that patterns of markings on the body match the direction of background marks (e.g. horizontal lines on birch bark). One can test to see if prey exhibit this appropriate behaviour by presenting a choice of backgrounds to see which ones are selected. An unintentional experiment of this sort is illustrated in Fig. 18.12. It is also important that cryptic prey remain stationary or move very slowly during daylight, otherwise they become more noticeable to predators. Many cryptic prey space themselves out so that they are more difficult to find. If a predator accidentally discovers a well-camouflaged item of prey, it has less chance of finding another if they are well spaced, compared to the situation where the prey are clumped together.

There is a tendency to concentrate on spectacular examples of camouflage where detection is exceedingly difficult. However, we should recognize that even relatively poor camouflage may reduce the risk of predation, because predators do not have perfect vision and cannot scan all of their surroundings with equal efficiency.

3. **Warning coloration.** Some species appear to advertise their presence with bright body colours. These may be examples of warning coloration, called aposematic coloration, that signal to predators that the organism is toxic, noxious or distasteful. This suggests that distasteful species are more likely to be conspicuously coloured than cryptic species, and indeed in one experiment where different coloured insects were fed to *Cercopithecus* monkeys only 17.8% of 101 cryptic insects were distasteful, whereas 83.9% of aposematic insects were distasteful (Carpenter 1921).

Warning colorations are typically sharply contrasting stripes of yellow and black, blue and red, orange and green, or some other combination of these colours, and are very effective in deterring attacks by many predators. Once a predator is stung by a wasp, or eats a brightly coloured insect that causes it to vomit, it very quickly learns to avoid similarly coloured organisms. Other predators may learn to avoid such noxious prey by observing the reaction of the unlucky predator.

The rapid learning of avoidance of distinctively coloured prey has been demonstrated by feeding birds flour-and-lard 'caterpillars' that are either red or blue in colour. The birds will eat both colours equally, but if quinine is added to the red 'caterpillars' the birds rapidly learn to avoid eating the distasteful red type. Moreover, if the 'caterpillars' are all made half red and half blue, the birds carefully eat the blue half and leave the red half of the 'caterpillar'.

If the warning colorations of different species are similar, the load of educating predators may be shared between them. Predators are also less likely to be confused, and should make fewer errors in selecting palatable prey compared to the situation where they are presented with a wide variety of warning colours. Consequently, it is advantageous for noxious species to resemble each other, at least in general coloration, and this convergence is known as Müllerian mimicry. The similar striping and buzzing of wasps and bees is a well-known Müllerian complex. A predator that has been stung by a wasp will avoid other species of wasps, as well as avoiding similarly coloured bees.

Although aposematic coloration is an effective predator deterrent, there are predators that specialize in eating these noxious types of prey. For example, the bee-eaters of Africa, southern Asia and Australia are a group of birds that eat Hymenoptera, and are insensitive to their stings. Similarly, grosbeaks in North America can eat the monarch butterfly (*Danaus plexippus*), because they are insensitive to the noxious cardiac glycosides they contain, whereas other species of birds will vomit and show other signs of distress if they eat them. Obviously, predators that can break this form of predator defence have little difficulty in finding their prey, and the latter must rely on other predator defences to reduce the risks of predation by these specialists.

Table 18.1 | The results of an experiment on Batesian mimicry. Toads were either first offered stinging honeybees followed by palatable droneflies (experimental group) or only offered droneflies (control group). Both groups were also offered mealworms. The number and percentage eaten, and the number rejected are shown for each food item

	Model (honeybees)		Mimic (droneflies)		Alternative food (mealworms)	
	Eaten	Rejected	Eaten	Rejected	Eaten	Rejected
Experimental toads	36 (45%)	44	26 (43.3%)	34	140	0
Control toads	–	–	110 (75.5%)	30	140	0

Source: From Brower and Brower (1966).

4. **Batesian mimicry.** There is another form of mimicry, called Batesian mimicry, where a palatable species (the mimic) closely resembles a noxious species (the model). This is a case of false advertising. Examples of this form of mimicry include hover flies that mimic wasps, and the classic case of the viceroy butterfly (*Limenitus archippus*) which mimics the unpalatable monarch butterfly. Several experiments have shown that such mimics have a reduced risk of predation because the predators confuse them with noxious species (the models). For example, Brower and Brower (1966) first offered stinging honeybees to a group of toads, and then offered the same experimental group of toads a mimic (droneflies). A control group of toads was only offered the mimic (droneflies). Both groups of toads were also offered an alternative prey type of mealworm. The results clearly show that the mimic is eaten less if the predator had previous experience with the model (Table 18.1).

In Batesian mimicry, the mimic obtains protection from predation at the expense of the model, because if a naive predator first encounters the mimic it may later attack the model believing it to be palatable. Typically, the mimic resembles the model very closely in coloration, form and general habits. If it is not a good mimic, predators will learn how to distinguish it from the model, and there is little point in resembling an unpalatable species if it does not occur at the same time and place as the model. The density of the mimic will also be influenced by that of the model. If a mimic is more abundant than the model, it will receive less protection than if it is less abundant than the model. In one experiment, birds were presented with mimics and models in different proportions. When only 10% of the prey was distasteful (the model), the predation of the mimics was reduced by 20% compared to the controls, where all prey were mimics, but when 40% of the prey was distasteful, the predation of the mimics was reduced by 80%. The degree of protection provided by the model will also depend on how noxious the model is. If a model is extremely noxious, it will protect a large population of mimics because once a predator has experienced the model it will be very reluctant to try eating

Fig. 18.13 The tortoise retreats into its shell when threatened where it is safe from attack by most predators. (Photograph by the author.)

anything that resembles it, but if the model merely tastes somewhat unpleasant a predator may well try eating others to see if they are more pleasant.

5. **Anatomical defences.** Large size makes some animals almost invulnerable to true predators, although not to parasitic attacks. There are no natural predators of adult African elephants (*Loxodonta africana*), other than humans, and it would be a foolhardy lion that would attempt to attack an animal this size. Similarly, the presence of weapons, such as horns, antlers and large canine teeth, can deter a predator from attacking. For example, a colleague of mine observed a leopard (*Panthera pardus*) preparing to attack a feeding adult warthog (*Phacochoerus aethiopicus*) in western Uganda. At the last moment, the warthog became aware of the leopard and turned to face it. The leopard abandoned its attack, presumably because of the risk of severe injury from the canine tusks of the warthog.

Other prey rely on more passive means to deter predators, such as the armour of tortoises (Fig. 18.13), spines in such animals as the sea urchins and the porcupine, and the thorns of plants. Some animals appear to take advantage of the protection afforded by the thorns of plants, to live in an area which cannot be penetrated by certain types of predators (Fig. 18.14).

6. **Behavioural defences: vigilance.** So far we have considered a variety of ways in which prey can reduce the likelihood of attack. However, once a predator initiates an attack, the prey can reduce the success of the attack, and evade capture in a variety of ways. One common response is to take evasive action by running, flying or swimming away. To do this, prey must be vigilant, using their senses to detect a predator early in its attack so that they have sufficient time to escape. We might expect vigilance to be related to predation pressure. It makes sense that vigilance would be low where there is little risk of predation, compared to situations where the

Fig. 18.14 The lesser bushbaby (*Galago senegalensis*) is protected from attack by raptors by living in thorny *Acacia* thickets. (Photograph by the author.)

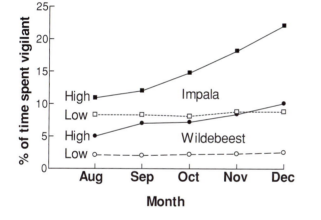

Fig. 18.15 Vigilance of impala and wildebeest in low and high predator conditions three to five months after the reintroduction of lion and cheetah which created the high predator condition. (Data from Hunter and Skinner 1998.)

risk of predation is high, because the time spent in being vigilant might be more profitably employed in feeding or other activities. Luke Hunter studied the relationship between predation pressure and vigilance in two African ungulates, impala (*Aepyceros melampus*) and wildebeest (*Connochaetes gnou*), in the Phinda Resource Reserve in northern KwaZulu–Natal, South Africa. The Reserve was established in 1990, and predation pressure was low because lion and cheetah (*Acinomyx jubatus*) had been absent from the area for at least four decades, and other large predators had been kept at very low levels by hunting. In 1992, lions were reintroduced in March and cheetah were reintroduced in May into half of the Reserve. Hunter monitored the vigilance of the ungulates from August to December in both halves of the Reserve, and observed that vigilance approximately doubled during this time in the area where lion and cheetah had been reintroduced, but remained constant in the other half of the Reserve where these predators were absent (Fig. 18.15).

We might also expect the vigilance of individual animals to be related to herd or group size, because as the size of the group increases overall vigilance can be maintained even though each individual spends less time scanning for predators. Hunter noted a negative correlation between individual vigilance behaviour and group size for impala and wildebeest at both predation levels. However, group size was not the reason for the difference in vigilance between high and low predation levels (Fig. 18.15) because group size was very similar in both areas. We might also expect that animals on the edge of the herd would be more vigilant than those near the centre of the herd, because they would be more likely to fall victim to a predator. Again, this was shown to be the case (Hunter and Skinner 1998), with animals at the front of the herd showing the highest degree of vigilance.

Although Hunter showed that individual vigilance increased as the predation pressure increased, as the group size became smaller, and as individuals were closer to the edge of the herd, it still remains to be proven that these changes in vigilance lead to a reduction in the success of attacks by predators. Kenward (1978) conducted an experiment on pigeons to show the effects of group size and overall vigilance on predation success by goshawks (*Accipiter gentilis*). He released a hungry, trained goshawk at a set distance from wild flocks of woodpigeons (*Columba palumbus*). As expected, the larger the flock, the sooner the pigeons detected the goshawk and took flight, reducing the probability of the goshawk making a successful attack. Thus, the risk of predation was reduced by increased group size, because of an overall increase in vigilance.

7. **Behavioural defences: alarm calls.** Many animals that live in groups give an alarm call when they detect a predator, to alert the other members of the group. This raises two questions: wouldn't the individual's chance of escape be better if it didn't warn other members of the group, and why draw attention to yourself, particularly to a predator, by giving an alarm call? These questions can be answered by considering the example of Belding's ground squirrel, which gives specific alarm calls to identify different types of predators. What follows applies to aerial predators and not to ground predators. When an individual sees a hawk approaching, it gives the hawk alarm call as it escapes, and all the other members of the colony sprint for the nearest burrow. If an individual had not alerted other members of the colony as it escaped, it would have become more obvious to an aerial predator as the only moving target compared to the situation where all members of the colony madly dashed for cover. Thus, giving an alarm call actually helps to disguise the caller, as it joins the mass confusion of rushing to a burrow. In fact, Sherman (1985) has shown that callers are less likely to be captured by a predator than non-callers, presumably because they have a head start on the non-callers. Obviously, it pays to be vigilant.

8. **Behavioural defences: group living.** Living in groups also may also reduce an individual's chance of being attacked. We saw in section 18.5.1 that although the number of prey attacked per predator generally increases with prey density, the *probability* of an individual being attacked only increases with prey density in part of the Type 3 response (i.e. where the slope of the curve is increasing with prey density). In all other cases, the chance of an individual being attacked declines as the prey density increases, and this is also true in the Type 3 functional response beyond a certain prey density. We can think of this as a dilution effect, where the capacity of a predator is swamped by the large number of prey. We saw in Chapter 16 that the highly synchronized reproduction of bamboos and certain cicadas has been proposed as a predator-swamping mechanism.

   Animals may aggregate for purely selfish reasons, in what Hamilton has called the 'selfish herd'. The selfish herd principle is where an individual improves its own survival at the expense of other members of the group. Such aggregations may be quite temporary in order to improve an individual's chance of survival at a critical stage in an organism's life. For example, Adélie penguins (*Pygoscelis adeliae*) have to 'run the gauntlet' of leopard seals (*Hydrurga leptonyx*) when they leave the ice to go out to sea to feed. The leopard seals tend to swim close to the edge of the ice, and so the penguins typically gather in groups at the edge of the ice and then jump en masse into the water when they swim to their feeding grounds. The leopard seals can only eat a few penguins in such a short time, and so most members of the group escape. To conform to the selfish herd principle, an individual should try to be in the centre of the group of penguins entering the water because the first and last individuals presumably have a lower chance of survival. Similarly, in herds of African ungulates one might expect individuals to avoid being at the edge of a herd where the risk of predation by large carnivores is greatest.

9. **Behavioural defences: mimicking the behaviour of a noxious species.** There are cases where the prey may suddenly mimic a noxious species if the predator gets very close, which may so startle the predator that it abandons it attack, giving the prey time to escape. I have observed this type of behaviour in a plated lizard (*Gerrhosaurus* sp.) in Zimbabwe. Normally, if the lizard is approached, it will run away and escape long before you get very close to it. However, if you surprise the lizard it wriggles just like a snake, causing one to step back in alarm, at which point it rapidly runs away. I was repeatedly fooled by one individual in this way, and found it very difficult not to recoil in alarm.

10. **Behavioural defences: attacking the predator.** Even when a predator successfully captures its prey it may not necessarily eat it. Some prey use chemical deterrents when attacked. For example, the bombardier beetle (*Brachinus* sp.) sprays a boiling mixture of hydroquinones and hydrogen peroxide at predators. Similarly, the

skunk (Mustelidae) emits a very powerful odour which has much the same effect as teargas. Other prey may try to fight off an attack by a predator using whatever weapons they may have, such as teeth, horns, antlers and hooves. Whilst many such attempts are futile, the scars on some survivors show that this method of last resort is occasionally successful.

11. **Behavioural defences: diverting the attack**. Some prey escape being consumed by misdirecting predators so that they attack a non-vital part of the body. Some fish and butterflies have false eyes or heads at the tail end of the body, and if this part of the animal is attacked it gives the prey a chance to escape. Some lizards use their tail as a decoy. It may be brightly coloured to attract attention, and the tail may break off and wriggle on the ground when the animal is attacked. This attracts the predator's attention very effectively, giving the animal time to escape.

As this brief survey shows, prey have evolved a wide range of methods to reduce the risk of being eaten by predators. At the same time, predators have evolving ways of increasing their chances of catching and eating their prey, but that is another story. Thus, there is a co-evolution of predator and prey, where each improvement in predator avoidance by the prey leads to enhanced prey-capture skills by the predator.

18.7 | Summary

The numerical responses of the predator–prey interaction was modelled independently by Lotka and Volterra, and their model showed that there would be sustained oscillations in the numbers of predators and prey. This prediction was tested by several researchers on different experimental systems, and they found that sustained oscillations would only occur if there were several subpopulations of prey whose powers of dispersal were greater than that of the predator. Prey populations increase when predators are absent or at a low level, but as the predator population increases it reduces the prey to the point of extinction forcing the predator to move elsewhere for food. Before this happens, however, some of the prey migrate to start a new population which will increase in density until it is found by the predator and the cycle starts again.

A review of predator–prey systems in nature, however, shows that not all of these systems oscillate, and those that do oscillate may have stable, damped, or unstable oscillations. The Rosenzweig and MacArthur graphical model provides a more versatile analysis of a wide range of numerical responses of predator–prey interactions, and reveals that prey refuges and low carrying capacities of predators help stabilize this response.

The predator–prey interaction can also be analysed in terms of the number of prey eaten per predator (the functional response), and how this relates to both predator and prey densities. This functional response of predators to their prey is very variable, and is related to the behaviour of both predators and their prey.

Predation exerts a powerful selective force on the characteristics of their prey, and a survey is made of the wide range of ways in which prey attempt to reduce the risk of being eaten.

Appendix 18.1 Simulating the Lotka–Volterra predation model

1. Title your spreadsheet in cell A1. Then in cells A3 to A7 type the following: **time step (dt) =** in A3, **rate of increase of prey (r) =** in A4, **attack rate of predators (a) =** in A5, **conversion rate of prey to predators (c) =** in A6, and **death rate of predators (d) =** in A7. Then enter the following values for these parameters in cells E3 to E7: **1** (one) in E3, **0.5** in E4, **0.025** in E5, **0.015** in E6, and **0.6** in E6.
2. In row 9 of columns A to G enter the following titles: **Time (t)** in A9, **Prey (H)** in B9, **Pred (P)** in C9, **delta H** in D9, **delta P** in E9, **P =** r/a in F9 (the prey zero isocline), and **H = d/c** in G9 (the predator zero isocline).
3. Now set up the spreadsheet as follows:
   (a) Enter 0 (zero) in A10, and the formula = A8+$E$3 in A11. This creates a counter for a series of time steps.
   (b) Enter a starting value of **40** in B10, and the formula = B9+D9 in B11.
   (c) Enter a starting value of **40** in C10, and the formula = C9+E9 in C11.
   (d) Enter the formula = ($E$3*B9-($E$4*B9*C9))*$E$3 in D10 and copy to D11. This simulates Eqn 18.1 multiplied by a time step, and the following step (e) simulates Eqn 18.2 multiplied by a time step.
   (e) Enter the formula = ($E$5*B9*C9 − ($E$6*C9))*$E$3 in E10 and copy to E11.
   (f) Enter the formula = $E$3/$E$4 in F10. This calculates the prey zero isocline (P) from Exp. 18.2 and the following step (g) calculates the predator zero isocline (H) using Exp. 18.4.
   (g) Enter the formula = $E$6/$E$5 in G10.
   (h) Copy row 11 (columns A–E) to rows 12 to 2010 to calculate 2000 time steps.
4. Now make two graphs. The first of the number of predators (y-series = C10..C2010) versus the number of prey (x-series = B10..B2010), similar to Fig. 18.2; and the second of the number of prey (1st y-series = B10..B2010) and predators (2nd y-series = C10..C2010) versus time (x-series = A10..A2010), similar to Fig. 18.3.
5. The graphs do not look like Figs. 18.2 and 18.3. To see why, read section 18.2 and complete the exercises as outlined. When you have finished, save and exit your spreadsheet.

Chapter 19

Animal behaviour, natural selection and altruistic traits

In chapter six of *The Origin of Species*, Darwin showed that behavioural traits are evolutionary adaptations that have evolved by means of natural selection in just the same way as morphological and physiological traits. For this to be true, two conditions are necessary. First, variation in behaviour must be related to differences in survival or reproductive success, and second there must be a genetic basis to this variation in behaviour, at least in part.

It is not difficult to see that variation in behaviour can influence survival and reproductive success. For example, the success of lions in catching and eating animals like wildebeest (*Connochaetes* spp.) or zebra (*Equus* spp.) depends partly on their ability to stalk and get sufficiently close to the herd so that they are able to catch and bring down an animal when they make their final attack. If their hunting technique is good, they may be successful, but if they have a poor hunting technique they will probably see their intended prey escape before they can reach them and will go hungry as a consequence. On the other hand, the flight response of wildebeest and zebra depends on their ability to detect the lions before they attack, and this requires constant vigilance as we saw in Chapter 18. The least vigilant individuals, and those that are slow to respond when predators are detected, are the ones that are most likely to be killed in an attack. We can imagine that high levels of vigilance are adaptive in areas where there are high levels of predation, but may be disadvantageous in areas of very low predation, because animals with lower levels of vigilance may eat more and have better energy reserves to withstand periods of drought, or may produce more offspring on average. Thus, the survival value of behaviour may depend on the environment in the same way that the cryptic colour of *Biston betularia* depends on the background colour of the environment (Chapter 11). The question is, however, whether this variation in behaviour between individuals has any genetic basis.

19.1 | The genetic basis of behaviour

Variation in behaviour, both within and between populations, can be subjected to genetic analysis in exactly the same way as morphological and physiological traits. In some cases, there are more or less discrete classes in the pattern of behaviour, which suggests that the behaviour is coded for by one or two genes. For example, individual *Drosophila melanogaster* larvae move different distances when they are feeding, and it has been possible to create genetically uniform strains that either move a lot (the 'rovers') or a little (the 'sitters'). When adults of these two strains were crossed, the larvae of the F_1 generation were all rovers. When the adults of the F_1 generation were crossed, the larvae of the F_2 generation occurred in a 3:1 ratio of rovers to sitters (de Belle and Sokolowski 1987). These results are exactly what is expected for a simple Mendelian trait where the sitter phenotype is recessive to the rover phenotype.

The hygienic cleaning behaviour of honeybees provides a more complex example of genetic control of a behavioural trait. There is a bacterial disease, called American foulbrood, that infects the larvae and kills the pupae of the European honeybee (*Apis mellifera*). One strain of honeybees, called Brown, developed a resistance to this disease, because the worker bees uncapped the cells containing dead pupae and removed their bodies. This behaviour prevented the spread of this infection in the colony. Walter Rothenbuhler investigated the genetic basis of this behaviour by crossing hygienic bee colonies of the Brown strain, with unhygienic colonies of the Vanscoy strain. This was done by artificial insemination of the queens. His results are very clear (Fig. 19.1). When he crossed the hygienic Brown strain with an unhygienic strain, the resulting colonies were all unhygienic,

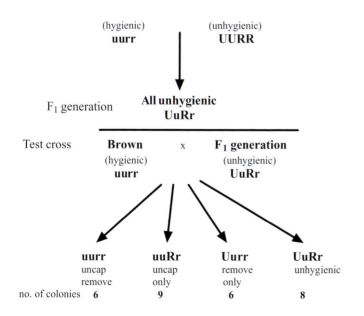

Fig. 19.1 Genetic analysis of hygienic behaviour in honeybees. Uncapping (u) is recessive to non-uncapping behaviour, and removal behaviour (r) is recessive to the non-removal of dead larvae. (After Rothenbuhler 1964.)

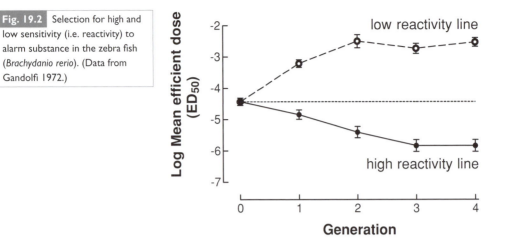

Fig. 19.2 Selection for high and low sensitivity (i.e. reactivity) to alarm substance in the zebra fish (*Brachydanio rerio*). (Data from Gandolfi 1972.)

which suggests that hygienic behaviour is recessive to unhygienic behaviour. When he performed a test cross by backcrossing the F_1 generation with the Brown strain, he produced four types of colonies in a $1:1:1:1$ ratio (Fig. 19.1). The $1:1:1:1$ ratio was very approximate because he only produced a total of 29 colonies. Approximately one-quarter of the colonies were hygienic, because they uncapped and removed the dead pupae, another quarter of the colonies would uncap the infected cells but would not remove the dead pupae, another quarter would remove the dead pupae if the infected cells were uncapped for them, and the final quarter of the colonies would neither uncap, nor remove, dead pupae and so were unhygienic. These results are exactly what one would expect if the hygienic behaviour was controlled by two unlinked genes, one for uncapping behaviour, and the other for removal behaviour.

In many instances, however, the variation in behaviour is of a more continuous nature because there are not discrete classes of behaviour. Such behaviours are more likely to be polygenic traits which can be modified by appropriate selection experiments (see Chapter 12). An example of selection on a behavioural trait of this type is provided by the flight response of zebra fish (*Brachydanio rerio*) to a specific alarm substance (Gandolfi 1972). The latter is a chemical, contained in deep epidermal cells of many fish, which is released if the skin is broken, such as when the fish is attacked by a predator. Several species of fish exhibit a fright reaction to this chemical, and flee the area to avoid danger. The sensitivity to this alarm substance varies in the population, with some individuals showing a response to very low concentrations of the substance and others only responding to higher concentrations. In four generations of selection, Gandolfi developed two lines, which were either highly sensitive to the alarm substance (high reactivity line) or only showed a response at concentrations more than 1000-fold higher (Fig. 19.2)

The genetic basis of behaviour has been documented in thousands of similar examples of genetic analysis. Some people are troubled by the idea that behaviour is controlled to some extent by genes. This is particularly true for human behaviour because there is a fear that such information will be misunderstood and misused. The idea that behaviours are solely determined by genes is called *genetic determinism*, and this idea has been used to argue for the genetic superiority of certain races, social classes, and the male gender. Recall the issue of race and IQ, which we discussed in Chapter 12. We saw that the hereditarians believe that there are differences in IQ between races that are determined by genetic differences, and so cannot be altered. One can then use this line of reasoning to justify providing inferior education to certain 'inferior' races. This was done with devastating effects by the Nationalist government in South Africa during the apartheid years, and so the fears are well justified.

Can we say that behaviour is solely genetically determined when we show a genetic basis to the variation in the pattern of behaviour? The simple answer is no. Genes may influence behaviour, but so does the environment. For example, the movements of the rover and sitter larval phenotypes of *Drosophila* are not fixed. If we lowered the temperature, or put them in a medium which was more difficult to move through, they would probably move less. Indeed, it is possible that there are environmental conditions where the two phenotypes would behave in the same way. Similarly, the hygienic behaviour of honeybees is only expressed if the hive is infected by a disease that kills the larvae. Otherwise there is no need to uncap and remove pupae. Clearly, then, behaviour is the result of a complex interaction between genetic and environmental factors. Our main purpose, however, for demonstrating a genetic basis to the variation of behavioural traits is to show that they can evolve through the process of natural selection.

19.2 Behaviours that appear contrary to the theory of natural selection

One of the difficulties to the theory of natural selection that Darwin noted (in chapter six of *The Origin of Species*) is the presence of sterile castes in the social insects (bees, wasps, ants and termites). How can natural selection favour the evolution of individuals that leave no offspring? Darwin had no solution to this problem, but he believed it had something to do with selection at the level of the family (all the individuals in a nest), rather than at the individual level. He was on the right track, but it would take just more than 100 years before the problem of sterile castes, an extreme form of altruism, was eventually solved. By altruism, we mean an action or behaviour performed by an individual which benefits another individual at some apparent cost to the fitness of the altruist. I say apparent cost, because as we will see there are different ways of measuring the fitness of an individual.

Table 19.1 Coefficients of relatedness (r) between relatives.

Relationship	r	Relationship	r
Parent–offspring	0.5	Full siblings	0.5
Grandparent–grandchild	0.25	Half-siblings	0.25
Uncle/aunt–niece/nephew	0.25	Cousin–cousin	0.125

19.2.1 The evolution of altruistic behaviour

How do we account for behaviours where someone risks their life to save someone else? To begin with, consider one of the many versions of an apocryphal story about J. B. S. Haldane. He is drinking a beer in a pub when he is asked by a friend if he would risk his life to save someone from drowning. Haldane makes some calculations on the back of an envelope, and then declares: 'If I had a one in ten chance of drowning but saved the life of my child I would save five copies of genes for this behaviour for each loss of my genes. I would save fewer copies of such genes in more distant relatives, but the trait could evolve in small groups of closely related people.' Whatever the truth of this story, Haldane did write an article in the *New Biologist* making similar statements in 1953.

Haldane's argument is rather simple, and is key to our understanding of the evolution of altruistic behaviour. First, we need to know how we are genetically related to different relatives. This is given by the coefficient of relatedness (r), which is the probability of two individuals possessing the same rare allele by inheriting it from a recent common ancestor. For example, if I inherited this rare allele from one of my parents, I would have a 50% chance of passing it on to any one of my children because I am heterozygous for the trait and only half of my germ cells carry the trait. My children would also have a 50% chance of passing on this allele to their children, and so the coefficient of relatedness between me and my grandchildren is $0.5 \times 0.5 = 0.25$. Similarly, my brothers and sisters would have a 50% chance of inheriting this allele from our common parents, and so the coefficient of relatedness between me and my full siblings is 0.5. Like me, they have a 50% chance of passing the allele on to their children, and so the coefficient of relatedness between me and my nieces and nephews is $0.5 \times 0.5 = 0.25$. Various coefficients of relatedness between relatives are given in Table 19.1.

Now imagine that the rare allele is for an altruistic behaviour, such as risking my life to save a relative. If I saved one of my offspring and died doing so, the frequency of the altruistic trait would decline because the probability of my child carrying the trait is only 0.5. If I saved two of my offspring and died doing so, the frequency of the altruistic trait would not change because the frequency of alleles in the next generation is given by $r \times 2$, which is 0.5×2, or 1.0. Continuing the argument, if I saved three of my children and died doing so, the frequency of the altruistic trait would increase, because there would be $r \times 3$, which is 0.5×3, or 1.5 copies of the allele on average in the next generation. However, to be strictly accurate in our calculations, we should calculate both the probability of my dying in the attempt of saving my children, and the probability of my saving the life of the child. Thus, as Haldane calculated, if I had a one chance in ten of dying but was always successful in saving my children, it would pay to try to save even one child, because there would be five such altruistic alleles saved in the children for each one lost in the parent. To summarize, the altruist should be willing to risk his or her life if the number of genes that are identical by descent (see section 8.5.1) is expected to increase in future generations as a result of his or her actions.

We used the measure of identity by descent to calculate the coefficient of inbreeding in section 8.5.1, and may wonder how the two coefficients are related. In fact, the contribution of a single ancestor to the coefficient of inbreeding to one of its descendants is exactly half the coefficient of relatedness between them. For example, in section 8.5.1 we calculated the coefficient of inbreeding between one grandparent and its grandchild to be 0.125, and we see that the coefficient of relatedness between them is 0.25 (Table 19.1). Inbreeding, however, increases the proportion of alleles identical by descent, and this increases the likelihood of evolving altruistic behaviour, which is one reason why Haldane concluded it could evolve in small groups of closely related people.

In the example described above, I improved my direct fitness by saving my offspring, which increased the frequency of the altruistic trait, although it does not seem so purely altruistic any longer. However, I can make exactly the same argument if I save the lives of my brothers and sisters, because I have the same coefficient of relatedness with them as I have with my children. Thus, I can increase the frequency of an altruistic trait in a population not only by leaving more direct descendants, but also by helping my kin to leave more descendants.

The act of saving a child from drowning is instinctive, rather than a calculated action where one computes the chances of increasing the number of genes identical by descent in the population. Haldane observed that the genes for altruistic behaviour could only have a chance of spreading in the population if the person risking their life was closely related to the drowning child, which only occurs in small human populations where there is inbreeding.

W. D. Hamilton (1964) developed Haldane's idea more formally to show the conditions under which an altruistic trait can evolve. He showed that the overall fitness of an individual, which he termed *inclusive fitness*, is the sum of the *direct fitness* by producing one's own offspring, and *indirect fitness*, where relatives produce additional offspring as a result of being helped by the individual's actions. The inclusive fitness of an individual is calculated as follows:

$$\text{Direct fitness} = N_1 \times r = f_D \qquad \text{(Exp. 19.1)}$$
$$\text{Indirect fitness} = (N_2 \times r) + (N_3 \times r) \ldots \text{etc.} = f_I \qquad \text{(Exp. 19.2)}$$
$$\text{Inclusive fitness} = f_D + f_I \qquad \text{(Exp. 19.3)}$$

Table 19.2 | Calculation of indirect fitness (f_I), direct fitness (f_D), and inclusive fitness for the first two years of life for male pied kingfishers exhibiting different behaviours

| Behaviour in first year | First year | | | Second year | | | | | Inclusive fitness |
	N_H	r	f_i	N_O	r	s	m	f_d	$f_i + f_d$
Primary helper	$1.8 \times 0.32 = 0.58$			$2.5 \times 0.5 \times 0.54 \times 0.60 = 0.41$					0.99
Secondary helper	$1.3 \times 0.00 = 0.00$			$2.5 \times 0.5 \times 0.74 \times 0.91 = 0.84$					0.84
Delayer	$0.0 \times 0.00 = 0.00$			$2.5 \times 0.5 \times 0.70 \times 0.33 = 0.29$					0.29

Symbols: N_H, number of extra young produced by helped parents; N_o, number of offspring; r, coefficient of relatedness between the male and N_H or N_o; s, probability of surviving from year 1 to year 2; m, probability of finding a mate in year 2.
Source: From Reyer (1984).

where N_1 is the number of direct offspring, N_2, N_3, etc. are the numbers of additional offspring produced by relatives because of the individual's help, and r is the coefficient of relatedness between the individual and the various offspring. This latter measure is necessary to express the various offspring in identical genetic units, so that they can be simply added together. Obviously, helping a distant relative produce additional offspring is less valuable to me, in terms of the survival of my genes, than if I produced my own offspring.

We can use Hamilton's concept of inclusive fitness to study why altruistic behaviours might occur in a population, and this is best illustrated using a specific example. The pied kingfisher (*Ceryle rudis*) in Africa is a colonial nester, and males outnumber females, so many cannot obtain a mate. Only about 5% of the yearling males obtain a mate, and the remainder adopt one of three strategies. Some become primary helpers, and provide considerable help to their mothers by bringing food to her and her nestlings, as well as by attacking predatory snakes and mongooses. Other males become secondary helpers of unrelated, or distantly related, nesting pairs, but they provide much less help than the primary helpers. The remaining excess males, called delayers, provide no help to nesting pairs and simply wait until the next year to try to obtain a mate. Thus, there appears to be two levels of altruistic behaviour, one providing considerable help to close relatives, and one providing less help to non-relatives or very distant relatives. In addition, there is a more selfish type of behaviour on the part of the delayers. The survivors of these non-breeding yearling males then try to breed in their second year. The benefits and costs of these three strategies were measured by Heinz-Ulrich Reyer (1984), and his results are presented in Table 19.2.

The number of extra young produced (N_H) by parents with primary or secondary helpers was determined by comparing these categories with parents who had no helpers. The average coefficient of relatedness between the primary helpers and the extra young they help to produce was 0.32, because in some cases the young were full siblings

Table 19.3 Direct, indirect and inclusive fitness for male pied kingfishers during the first two years of life

Status	Year	Gain in fitness		
		Direct (f_D)	Indirect (f_I)	Inclusive ($f_D + f_I$)
First-year breeder	1	0.96	0	0.96
	2	0.80	0	0.80
	Total	1.76	0	1.76
Primary helper	1	0	0.45	0.45
	2	0.42	0.20	0.62
	Total	0.42	0.65	1.09
Secondary helper	1	0	0.04	0.04
	2	0.87	0.01	0.88
	Total	0.87	0.05	0.92
Delayer	1	0	0	0
	2	0.30	0	0.30
	Total	0.30	0	0.30

Source: From Reyer (1990).

($r = 0.5$) and in others one of the original parents had died before the second brood and so the young were half-siblings ($r = 0.25$). Reyer initially estimated that the secondary helpers gained no indirect fitness in their first year, because he thought they were unrelated to the extra young they helped raise, i.e. $r = 0$. He subsequently modified this value to <0.05, because some of the secondary helpers helped distant relatives, but even so, their indirect fitness is considerably lower than that of the primary helpers. Table 19.2 also suggests that males not breeding in their first year only increase their overall fitness by breeding in their second year. This is not the case, as some of the helpers continued to help in their second year. Reyer (1990) calculated a more complete set of estimates for the various strategies adopted by yearling males, which are presented in Table 19.3.

We can now begin to understand the breeding strategies of male pied kingfishers. Breeders have the highest fitness (Table 19.3), but only a very small percentage of males (approximately 4.7%) can adopt this strategy in their first year because there aren't enough females. If breeding becomes possible, because of the appearance of an unmated female after the breeding season has started or because a breeding male dies, then helper males immediately give up their helper status and try to become breeders. Reyer observed helpers switching to breeders three times during his study.

The direct fitness of both primary and secondary helpers was higher than that of the delayers, because the latter have a much lower probability of finding a mate. Thus, it pays directly to display this apparently altruistic behaviour. Overall, however, the direct fitness of primary helpers is only about half that of secondary helpers, because they have a lower survival rate and a lower probability of finding a mate (Table 19.2). Secondary helpers probably have a higher survival rate because they provide much less help to the parents, and they have a higher probability of finding a mate because many of them breed with the female they helped in the previous year. Primary helpers do not mate with the female they help because she is their mother, and they appear to avoid incestuous matings. The reduction in direct fitness of primary helpers relative to secondary helpers is more than offset by the gain in indirect fitness, with the result that the inclusive fitness of primary helpers is marginally higher than that of the secondary helpers.

Reyer's study is interesting because it shows that behaviour that appears to be altruistic can become established in a population under certain conditions. If only a small proportion of the population can breed directly, it may pay the non-breeders to enhance the breeding potential of those that breed, because their inclusive fitness is higher than those that do not help (the delayers). Of particular interest, however, is the observation that the reduction in direct fitness of primary helpers, relative to secondary helpers, is more than offset by the gain in indirect fitness. We can take this last observation a step further. If an individual's direct fitness is decreased to zero, because of a gene for sterility, but this reduction is more than offset by a resulting gain in indirect fitness, the gene for sterility would increase in the population! This concept provided the key to begin to explain the evolution of sterile castes in insects.

19.2.2   The evolution of sterile castes in insects

Many insects are eusocial, where different types of individuals, called castes, co-operate to produce offspring. A colony may consist of a single queen that produces all the offspring for the group, some males that may mate with a new queen but do no work, and various sterile castes of females. The latter may gather food to feed other members of the colony, they may tend and raise the young, or act as guards or soldiers to protect the colony. Clearly, the sterile castes have no direct fitness, because they do not produce offspring directly, but they can have an indirect fitness by helping to raise the queen's offspring. What factors allow this system to evolve?

One factor that is important is the coefficient of relatedness (r) between the sterile females and the offspring they help raise. The latter are their sisters because they have all been produced by the same queen. Normally, full siblings have an r value of 0.5 (Table 19.1), but in the Hymenoptera (ants, bees and wasps) the males are haploid and the females are diploid. If the female mates with a single male, her female offspring (i.e. sisters) will have a coefficient of relatedness of 0.75, because they will all receive the same set of genes from the father (100%) and on average will share 50% of their genes from the mother. In the Hymenoptera, sisters are more closely related to each other ($r = 0.75$) than they are to their offspring ($r = 0.5$). Thus, a female can increase her inclusive fitness more by helping a fertile sister produce additional offspring than she can by producing her own offspring! Perhaps this is the reason why eusociality is so common

Fig. 19.3 Male Defassa
waterbuck (*Kobus defassa*) can use
their horns as lethal weapons.
(Photograph by the author.)

in the Hymenoptera compared to other groups of animals that have
more conventional methods of sex determination.

We have considered an ideal case where the queen has mated
with a single male. Frequently, however, the queen mates with several males and so the coefficient of relatedness may be much lower
than 0.75. Indeed, in the termites and the naked mole rat (*Hetero-
cephalus glaber*), which are also eusocial, the males and females are
both diploid and so the coefficient of relatedness between full siblings will only average 0.5. Clearly, there are other factors that are
also involved in the evolution of sterile castes. Readers who are interested in this topic are referred to Alcock (1998) who provides a very
nice overview.

So far we have considered altruistic behaviour in terms of actively
helping other members of the population. We will now consider behaviours where individuals limit the harm they do to others in the
population, even though at first sight it may seem that such restraint
would not be to their benefit.

19.2.3 Limiting aggressive behaviour

The evolution of ritualized, non-injurious behaviour in many animal
contests puzzled biologists for a long time. Animals may be defending
an extremely valuable resource, such as a rich feeding territory or a
breeding territory, and yet contests for the resource seldom escalate to
all out conflict. If we look at the weaponry of some animals (Fig. 19.3)
it is clear that they could use it to injure their opponents, sometimes
with lethal consequences. Typically, however, they appear to practice
restraint, and merely push and grapple with their opponent in a trial

of strength (Fig. 19.4). At the end of an encounter, the loser retreats and the winner either watches it leave or chases it off. There are frequent opportunities for the victor to deliver a *coup de grâce*, but this is seldom if ever taken.

Until the 1960s, the accepted argument for this type of behaviour was that it was 'for the good of the species'. Essentially, this was a non-Darwinian, group selection argument, which stated that it is advantageous to the group or species to limit fighting and the chance of severe injury. In the early 1970s, George Price and John Maynard Smith collaborated to show that it could also be advantageous to the individual to practice restraint, and so this type of behaviour could be explained in a manner that is consistent with Darwin's theory of natural selection.

Maynard Smith and Price (1973) developed a general model of animal contest behaviour that involved game theory. Game theory is a branch of mathematics that analyses the decisions made by two or more individuals, where the outcomes depend on what individuals and their opponents choose to do. For those people who are not familiar with this mathematical approach the results seem rather artificial at first. For this reason I will slowly develop the model and endeavour to explain the purpose of the exercise at each step.

The basic Hawk–Dove model

This model considers that a population of individuals will adopt one of two behavioural strategies when trying to claim a valuable

Table 19.4 Pay-off matrix for the basic Hawk–Dove game where B is the benefit to the victor of a contest, C is the cost of injury from fighting, and D is the cost of the aggressive displays of doves

		Against	
		Hawk	Dove
Pay-off to	Hawk	$a = \dfrac{(B-C)}{2}$	$b = B$
	Dove	$c = 0$	$d = \dfrac{B}{2} - D$

resource. An individual may make an aggressive display towards an opponent to try and drive it away, but if attacked will retreat and flee without injury (Dove strategy). Or it may attack an opponent, even at the risk of a serious injury (Hawk strategy). We assume that there is a genetic basis to the individual's behaviour. The model assigns costs and benefits to the various contests between individuals. Let $B =$ the benefit to the victor (i.e. the value of the food or mating opportunities acquired), let $C =$ the cost of injury from fighting, and let $D =$ the cost of the aggressive display made by doves. We can now calculate a pay-off matrix for all the combinations of encounters between Hawks and Doves (Table 19.4).

What happens when a Hawk attacks a Hawk? If we assume that they are evenly matched and so will win half of the time, the average pay-off (a) for each encounter is half of the benefits less the cost of injury, i.e. $(B - C)/2$. If a Hawk meets a Dove it always wins, and so the Hawk obtains all of the benefits (B) at no cost for its pay-off (b) while the Dove obtains nothing as its pay-off (c) in these encounters. Finally, when two evenly matched Doves meet, each will win half of the time, and so the average pay-off (d) is half of the benefits ($B/2$), less the cost of displaying (D). Note the difference in pay-off calculations for encounters between Hawks (a) and between Doves (d). In encounters between Hawks, only the loser risks injury and so the average cost of injury (C) is halved, whereas both Doves display in encounters between Doves.

Now that we have determined the pay-offs for the various encounters we can assign various values to B, C and D and look at the overall results. Although these values will be somewhat arbitrary, we will see that there is some logic to their relative value. We will look at a couple of examples to show what we mean.

Example 19.1 When the cost of injury (C) is low relative to the benefit (B)

In this example let $B = 50$, $C = 25$ and $D = 10$. Note that $C < B$, and that $D < C$. When we use Table 19.4 to calculate the pay-off matrix we obtain the following:

		Against	
		Hawk	Dove
Pay-off to	Hawk	12.5	50
	Dove	0	15

Even though a population composed purely of Doves has a greater average pay-off or fitness (15) than a population composed purely of Hawks (12.5), a population of Doves cannot withstand an invasion by Hawks because the latter will receive a pay-off of 50 because it always wins. Moreover, a Dove cannot invade a population of Hawks because it will always lose in an encounter with a Hawk (pay-off = 0). Thus, in this set of circumstances it pays to be a Hawk, and selection would favour the Hawk strategy, which is called an evolutionarily stable strategy or ESS.

If this was the case, the population would adopt the Hawk strategy (Doves would be selected against), fighting would escalate, and the cost of injury would increase. At some point the cost of injury would exceed the benefits, and we will examine this state of affairs in our next example.

Example 19.2   When the cost of injury (C) exceeds the benefits (B)
In this example let $B = 50$ (as before), $C = 100$ and $D = 10$. When we calculate the payoff matrix using Table 19.4, we obtain the following:

		Against	
		Hawk	Dove
Pay-off to	Hawk	−25	50
	Dove	0	15

A population composed purely of Doves can still be invaded by a Hawk, because the average pay-off to the Hawk (50) is greater than the average pay-off between Doves (15). Similarly, a population of Hawks can be invaded by a Dove because even though the average pay-off to the Dove is 0, it is still greater than the average Hawk–Hawk pay-off of −25. This suggests that the population will stabilize at some intermediate frequency of both Hawks and Doves.

To determine the equilibrium frequencies of Hawks and Doves, let the frequency of Hawks equal p and the frequency of Doves equal $1 - p$. We can compute the average pay-off for the Hawks and Doves by multiplying their average pay-off per encounter by the frequency of their opponents. Thus, the average pay-off for Hawks is $-25p + 50(1 - p)$, which reduces to $50 - 75p$, and the average pay-off for Doves is $0p + 15(1 - p)$, which reduces to $15 - 15p$.

At equilibrium, the average pay-off or fitness of the two strategies should be the same, and so the average pay-off for Doves should equal

Table 19.5 Pay-off matrix for the Hawk–Dove–Bourgeois game. The pay-offs a, b, c and d are given in Table 19.4

		Against		
		Hawk	Dove	Bourgeois
Pay-off to	Hawk	a	b	$(a + b)/2$
	Dove	c	d	$(c + d)/2$
	Bourgeois	$(a + c)/2$	$(b + d)/2$	$(b + c)/2$

the average pay-off for Hawks. In this case, $15 - 15p = 50 - 75p$, which reduces to $60p = 35$, and so the frequency of Hawks $(p) = 35/60$ or 7/12. Obviously, the frequency of Doves $(q) = 5/12$.

The equilibrium between the two strategies could be achieved in one of two ways. If the behaviour of individuals is fixed, there should be seven Hawks for every five Doves, but individuals could adopt the Hawk or Dove strategies in a $7:5$ ratio. It seems unlikely that individuals would adopt such different strategies at random; rather they would vary their strategy according to their perceived chance of winning an encounter, or according to the value of the resource they would lose. We will now look at an extension of the Hawk–Dove model that begins to take such factors into account.

The Hawk–Dove–Bourgeois model

In this model individuals adopt one of three strategies. They may adopt the Hawk or Dove strategy that we have already considered, or they may adopt the Bourgeois strategy. In this strategy, the individual acts as a Dove or a Hawk according to the circumstances. For example, it may adopt a Hawk strategy if it perceives that it is bigger and stronger than its opponent, or adopt a Dove strategy if it is smaller and weaker than its opponent. For the moment we will ignore the problem of what it should do if it is equally matched to its opponent. Alternatively, or in addition, it may adopt a Hawk strategy if it is the owner of a resource (e.g. a breeding territory), and a Dove strategy if it is an intruder. For the sake of simplicity, we will assume that it adopts the Hawk strategy half the time and the Dove strategy the other half of the time. Now part of the pay-off matrix conforms to the basic Hawk–Dove model in Table 19.4, and so we can simply add on the interactions with the Bourgeois individuals (Table 19.5).

When a Hawk meets a Bourgeois, half the time the latter is playing a Hawk, in which case its pay-off is a, and half the time it is playing Dove, in which case its pay-off is b. Thus, the average pay-off to the Hawk will be $(a + b)/2$.

When a Dove meets a Bourgeois, half the time the latter is playing a Hawk, in which case the pay-off to the Dove is c, and half the time it is playing a Dove, in which case its pay-off is d. So on average, the pay-off to the Dove will be $(c + d)/2$.

When a Bourgeois meets a Hawk, it adopts the Hawk strategy half the time and receives a pay-off of a, and the other half of the time it adopts a Dove strategy and receives a pay-off of c. On average, then, it receives a pay-off of $(a + c)/2$.

When a Bourgeois meets a Dove, it adopts a Hawk strategy half the time and receives a pay-off of b, and half the time it adopts a Dove strategy and receives a pay-off of d. Consequently, on average it receives a pay-off of $(b + d)/2$.

Finally, when the Bourgeois meets another Bourgeois, half the time it acts as a Hawk and its opponent like a Dove, and so the pay-off is b, and half the time it acts as a Dove and its opponent like a Hawk, and so its pay-off is c. On average, then, the pay-off in these encounters is $(b + c)/2$.

If we use the values for B, C and D in the second example, and apply the Hawk–Dove–Bourgeois pay-off matrix from Table 19.5, we obtain the following:

| | | Against | | |
		Hawk	Dove	Bourgeois
	Hawk	−25	50	12.5
Pay-off to	Dove	0	15	7.5
	Bourgeois	−12.5	32	25

This matrix indicates that Bourgeois is the best behavioural strategy to follow. A population of Bourgeois has an average pay-off (fitness) of 25, whereas a population of Hawks has an average pay-off of −25, and a population of Doves has an average pay-off of 15. A population of Bourgeois cannot be invaded by Hawks because the Hawk will only receive a pay-off of 12.5 compared to the Bourgeois 25, and similarly cannot be invaded by Doves because the latter's pay-off is only 7.5. A population of Hawks, with an average pay-off of −25, can be successfully invaded by both Doves (pay-off = 0) and Bourgeois (pay-off = −12.5). Similarly, a population of Doves, with an average pay-off of 15, can be successfully invaded by both Hawks (pay-off = 50) and Bourgeois (pay-off = 32.5). Thus, Bourgeois is an ESS.

Relating the Hawk–Dove–Bourgeois model to the real world

Territorial disputes between male speckled wood butterflies (*Pararge aegeria*) in England (Davies 1978) may be related to the Hawk–Dove–Bourgeois model. Approximately 60% of the males defend patches of sunlight on the woodland floor, and the remaining males patrol the canopy. When one of the patrolling males enters a territory, the resident male approaches the intruder and the two butterflies perform a spiral flight, lasting three to four seconds, after which the resident returns to the sunspot and the intruder leaves. The resident always wins, as can be shown by removing a male from a territory and replacing it with another male. When the former owner returns to his former territory, he always loses against the new owner. Thus, the owner of a territory always adopts a Hawk strategy and the intruder always adopts a Dove strategy. If two males were introduced to the same territory where there was no owner, each of the males acted as though he were the owner and a protracted spiral flight followed (i.e. both males acting as Bourgeois).

A study of the same species in Sweden revealed that the winner in territorial disputes between males in dense spruce forests was not always the owner of the territory (Wickman and Wicklund 1983). If a male temporarily left his territory unattended, he would frequently regain his territory if it had been taken over by an intruder, unlike the observations of Davies. Why does the behaviour of this species vary? It is suggested that the benefit (B) of holding a territory in England is not very high because sunspots are numerous. The cost (C) of forcing a resident male from a territory is high and so the Bourgeois strategy is favoured. In contrast, there are few sunspots on the forest floor in Sweden and the resource is more valuable (B is high relative to C) and so a Hawk strategy is favoured. The factors that help determine which males win in the disputes over territories are not known, but it is likely that a combination of body size and body temperature are important, as was determined in the contests between dung beetles described in Chapter 17.

As it stands, the Hawk–Dove–Bourgeois model has only a crude resemblance to reality in most cases. Nevertheless, it does point us in the direction of understanding why it may be in an animal's interest not to escalate a contest into an all-out attack. Animals use a number of signals to gauge the strength of an opponent, which may influence their decision whether to escalate a contest or not. For example, body sizes are correlated with the deepness of the croak in frogs, the rate of roaring in male red deer (*Cervus elaphus*) and the loudness and rate of bugling in elk (*C. canadensis*). The sizes of deer antlers and ungulate horns are also related to body size. In some cases, such as the North American bison (*Bison bison*) and African sable antelope (*Hippotragus niger*), males walk parallel to one another as if assessing each other's condition and size. When there is a large discrepancy in size, the smaller individual usually terminates the confrontation at this stage of initial assessment. If the individuals are more evenly matched, the interaction may escalate to a physical contest. In ungulates, this usually takes the form of head-to-head shoving or butting, where the antlers or horns are interlocked. Again, if there is a large discrepancy in strength between the contestants, the weaker individual may break off the match and usually is allowed to escape unscathed. However, when the two individuals are evenly matched, the contests can become violent with a high chance of injury. For example, fighting between red deer stags on the island of Rhum resulted in an estimated 23% of the stags showing some sign of injury during the rut, and up to 6% were permanently injured. Thus, the cost of injury may be very real and very high.

Fig. 19.5 Territorial behaviour and ritualized fighting in topi (*Damaliscus lunatus*). Territorial males stand on termite mounds (top); when they are challenged (centre) the territorial male has the advantage of height; the intruder has been knocked to his knees in the clash of heads (bottom) and retires from the contest. (Photographs by the author.)

In some cases, the owners of territories may have an advantage over intruders, even when they are relatively evenly matched in size and strength. For example, in some areas of East Africa, territorial topi (*Damaliscus lunatus*) stand on termite mounds so that intruders have to approach uphill (Fig. 19.5). As a result, the resident nearly always wins these encounters, and at times it appears as though the intruder expects to be smashed to its knees. Of course, the habit of standing on termite mounds may have additional benefits, such as giving the individual a better vantage point to spot predators.

Why challenge a territorial male if there appears to be a low chance of winning a contest? One possibility is that a male may look big and strong, but may be weak because it is sick, or it may have become injured in a previous fight. Providing a male can initiate a contest and then withdraw, should the resident prove to be bigger and stronger, before it escalates into a full-scale battle, this strategy can be a successful one. This strategy also protects against the evolution of false signals, because sooner or later the signaller has to back up his claim of superior strength. Thus, the evolution of larger weapons, without the necessary strength and size to use them, is doomed to failure.

This brief review of altruism, sterile castes, and limits to aggression shows that it is possible to explain their evolution in ways that are consistent with Darwin's theory of natural selection.

Chapter 20

Sexual selection and mating systems

In addition to his theory of natural selection, Darwin also proposed a theory of sexual selection to account for certain types of sexual dimorphism (Darwin 1859). He was trying to explain the evolution of secondary sexual characteristics, like the tail of the peacock. The huge ornamental tail in this species appears to be maladaptive, in the sense that it increases the chances of the individual being eaten by a predator by making it harder for the males to fly away, and so is not readily explained by the theory of natural selection. Darwin went on to develop his theory of sexual selection more fully in one of his later books, *The Descent of Man and Selection in Relation to Sex* (1871).

In this chapter we will look at the basic reasons for sexual competition, go on to consider sexual selection, and finally make a brief survey of some of the different types of mating systems in animals. In a sense, we are completing a circle. We started this book by looking at Darwin's theory of natural selection, and we will end it by looking at a particular type of selection, namely sexual selection.

20.1 | Sexual conflict and competition

In sexual reproduction, the interests of males and females may conflict with one another. There may also be competition within members of one sex for the reproductive services of the other. The seeds of this conflict and competition lie in the evolution of anisogamy. It is generally assumed that the gametes were all similar in the primitive condition (i.e. isogamy), but gradually two types of gametes evolved (i.e. anisogamy) in most evolutionary lines. Male gametes, or sperm, gradually evolved to become smaller, more mobile, and relatively short-lived. They are energetically relatively cheap to produce and are usually produced in vast numbers. In contrast, the female gametes, or eggs, gradually evolved to be larger, less mobile, and relatively long-lived. They are much more expensive to make and so are usually produced in smaller numbers.

The difference in energetic costs of producing eggs and sperm is believed to form the basis for many of the differences between males

Table 20.1 Sexual selection as a consequence of anisogamy in idealized males and females

Characteristic	Males	Females
1. Gametes	Small, very numerous, cheap to produce	Large, few in number, expensive to make
2. Parental investment	Low	High
3. Potential reproductive rate	High	Low
4. How to maximize individual fitness	Mate with as many females as possible	Select a male of the highest quality
5. Consequences of efforts to maximize fitness	Competition between males for mates, high variation in reproductive rates	Selection among potential mates, low variation in reproductive rates

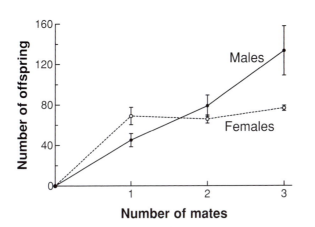

Fig. 20.1 In the fruit fly (*Drosophila melanogaster*) the males increase their reproductive success by increasing the number of matings, but females do not increase their reproductive success by mating with more males. (Data from Bateman 1948.)

and females. The fact that males can produce enormous numbers of sperm means that they can increase their reproductive potential and fitness if they mate with several females. Females, on the other hand, produce relatively few eggs and so it is generally not advantageous for them to mate with many males. Rather, it is to their advantage to be very selective in the choice of their mate. Thus, there is a fundamental difference in the 'ideal' reproductive strategy of males and females. Males will compete to mate with as many females as possible, and if some males are successful it means that other males will be unsuccessful and so there will be a large variation in the reproductive potential of different males. Females should be selective in their choice of mates, choosing those with superior phenotypes and, presumably, superior genotypes. Most females will mate and so there will be less variation in their reproductive potential. There will also be selection pressure on them to care for their progeny to improve the survival of their offspring. This difference in overall strategy of the two sexes is illustrated in Table 20.1.

Bateman (1948) provided evidence for sexual selection in a classic series of experiments on *Drosophila melanogaster*. Males increased their individual fitness by mating with more females, whereas females did not increase their fitness by mating with more males (Fig. 20.1). He

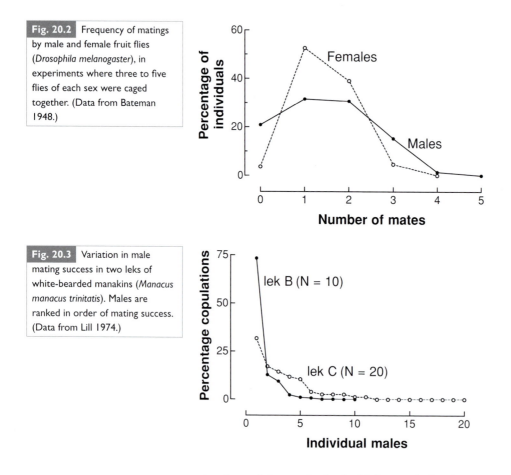

Fig. 20.2 Frequency of matings by male and female fruit flies (*Drosophila melanogaster*), in experiments where three to five flies of each sex were caged together. (Data from Bateman 1948.)

Fig. 20.3 Variation in male mating success in two leks of white-bearded manakins (*Manacus manacus trinitatis*). Males are ranked in order of mating success. (Data from Lill 1974.)

also showed that males had a higher variation in reproductive success than females, as measured by the number of mates (Fig. 20.2). It may be seen that several males were not able to mate whereas other males were able to obtain two, three, or even four different mates, providing convincing evidence of competition between males for mates. In contrast, very few females did not mate, and most mated with only one or two males.

There is convincing evidence that females exercise choice when selecting mates. For example, Lill (1974) studied small, frugivorous birds, called white-bearded manakins (*Manacus manacus trinitatis*), living in primary and secondary tropical forest in the West Indies. Groups of six to 50 males display on areas, called leks, to attract mates. Each male vigorously defends and displays on a small cleared area, 15–90 cm in diameter, that are spaced apart from each other, but otherwise provide no resources for the female. Females can select which male they wish to mate with, and Lill showed that certain males mate frequently and many not at all, particularly on the larger leks (Fig. 20.3).

In summary, the differences in selection pressures in the two sexes lead to a differential allocation of resources with respect to reproduction. Females allocate most of their reproductive effort to producing relatively few, large gametes which receive considerable parental care. Much less effort is put into the mating process. In contrast, males produce enormous numbers of very small gametes and allocate considerable effort to the mating process, competing with other males for access to mates. Much less effort is put into parental care of the offspring.

20.2 | Sexual dimorphism and sexual selection

There are striking morphological differences between the sexes in many species of animals, a phenomenon that is called *sexual dimorphism*. In mammals where the males fight for breeding territories (Chapter 19), males are frequently larger than females, and this size difference reaches an extreme in elephant seals where the males are about three times heavier than females. In contrast, some male spiders have a body mass that is less than one hundredth of the female (Fig. 20.4). We are not certain why this should be the case. It has been suggested that their small size reduces their risk of being eaten by the female, but it has also been suggested that they can increase their fitness by maturing at an earlier age when they are smaller in size. This tendency would be counterbalanced, however, by the fact that males fight each other to breed with the female, and it is usually the largest male that wins these contests.

Many males have weapons which may be absent in the females, for example antlers in deer. In other cases, both sexes may possess weapons but they are emphasized in the males, for example, the canine teeth in some primates and the horns of some ungulates. The sexes may be differentially coloured, and typically it is the male that is the more brightly coloured.

The reason for a particular sexual dimorphism may be uncertain, as we have already noted in some spiders. In other cases, the

Fig. 20.4 Sexual dimorphism of body size in the Saint Andrew's cross spider (*Argiope* sp.). The large female is accompanied by two males. (Photograph by the author.)

advantage of the difference between the sexes is obvious. For example, female fecundity in many insects and fishes is positively correlated with body size and, as a result, the females are larger than the males. In this case, the sexual dimorphism is explained by natural selection. However, in many cases sexual dimorphism may be a result of *sexual selection*, which is defined as differential reproduction as a result of variation in the ability to obtain mates. This may occur in two different ways:

1. Same-sex contests. Individuals of one sex compete or fight with one another for mating opportunities. This favours the evolution of traits that are likely to improve an individual's success in a confrontation, such as large size, increased strength, weapons, and specific threat signals. This is called *intrasexual selection*.
2. Mate preference by the opposite sex. Traits of one sex are selected for by the mating preferences of the other sex. This favours the evolution of conspicuous colours, exotic structures like enlarged tail feathers, and behavioural displays, including vocal calls, that provide information about the quality of a mate. This is called *intersexual selection*.

In most cases (see Table 20.1), the same-sex contests are between males, and it is female choice or preference that selects the traits of the males. However, as we will see, there are cases of so-called *sex role reversal* where the opposite is true, because it is the male who provides parental care for the young, rather than the female.

20.2.1 Same-sex contests: intrasexual selection

In the European common toad (*Bufo bufo*), there is strong evidence for intrasexual selection of body size in the males. Breeding occurs over a period of a few days, and males outnumber the females. Consequently, there is considerable competition among the males to clasp the females from behind in a mating position called amplexus, until the female spawns. Most females are intercepted by males before they reach the ponds, and at this stage there is little size selection of the males (Fig. 20.5). However, by the time the females spawn, two to four days after reaching the water, most of the females mate with larger males (Fig. 20.5), which suggests that the smaller males have been displaced by their larger rivals. This was convincingly demonstrated by a simple experiment where a female was placed in a bucket with both a large and a small male. In 41 replicates of this experiment, 18 large and 23 of the small males were in amplexus after a period of five minutes. However, 24 hours later, 10 of the 23 small males had been displaced by the larger male, whereas none of the 18 larger males had been displaced by their smaller rivals (Halliday 1993). This shows that larger males have a better chance than small males of successfully mating with a female.

One might predict that male toads would be larger than the females because of this intrasexual selection, but the opposite is the case. Presumably, the selection for larger body size in females is

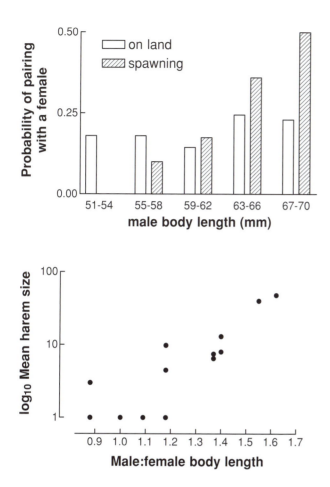

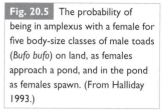

Fig. 20.5 The probability of being in amplexus with a female for five body-size classes of male toads (*Bufo bufo*) on land, as females approach a pond, and in the pond as females spawn. (From Halliday 1993.)

Fig. 20.6 Harem size in pinnipeds is positively correlated with sexual dimorphism of body size. (From Alexander et al. 1979, with permission.)

stronger than in the males, and it is suggested that larger females are selected by natural selection because they produce more offspring than smaller females.

Frequently, however, intrasexual selection for larger body size results in the males being larger than the females. For example, variation in the degree of sexual dimorphism of different species of seals and other pinnipeds is correlated with the size of their harem (Fig. 20.6). Species where the two sexes are similar in size tend to be monogamous, but as the size of the harem increases the males become increasingly larger than the females. It appears as though males that increase their investment in fighting ability are rewarded with increased chances of mating.

Mature males may also have weapons, such as horns in beetles, reptiles, and ungulates (Fig. 19.3), tusks in anurans and certain mammals, and spurs in some arthropods and birds. These weapons may be reduced or absent in the females, suggesting that they may have been emphasized by sexual selection. Horns and antlers are certainly used by male ungulates when fighting for breeding territories (see 19.2.3), and removal of antlers in male reindeer (*Rangifer tarandus*) and red deer reduces their fighting ability and dominance status and

Table 20.2 Mating success in long-tailed widowbirds subjected to different tail treatments (see text). The mean number of active nests (± standard deviation) per territory is given for nine males in each of the four treatments, before and after treatment. The difference in number of active nests showed that males with elongated tails attracted significantly more females than those with shorter tails

	Shortened	Control I	Control II	Elongated
Before treatment	1.33±1.118	1.56±1.130	1.44±2.068	1.67±1.500
After treatment	0.44±0.727	0.89±1.054	0.44±1.014	1.89±1.764
Difference	−0.89	−0.67	−1.00	0.22

Source: Data from Andersson (1982).

so presumably affects their mating success. Thus, there is evidence for intrasexual selection for these weapons. The issue is complicated, however, because the size of the weapons is usually strongly correlated with body size, and so they may also be used as signals of potential strength and condition to male rivals. It is also possible that females use these signals as a basis for mate choice, although this remains to be shown (Andersson 1994).

20.2.2 Mate preference by the opposite sex: intersexual selection

Typically, mate choice is made by the female (Table 20.1), and Darwin suggested that this type of selection could account for the ornamental plumage of birds. One of the first field tests of this hypothesis was by Andersson (1982) who studied the long-tailed widowbird (*Euplectes progne*). The males of this species are remarkable in that their tail is often more than half a metre long, and they are highly conspicuous as they fly over their breeding territories. The females are inconspicuous, and nest within the male territories. Andersson tested the effects of tail length on the ability of males to attract females. Early in the breeding season he mapped the territories of 36 males, and assigned them at random to one of four treatment groups. He counted the number of active female nests within each territory, and they were similar in all four groups (Table 20.2). In one group (short) the tails were cut to about 14 cm in length, and the removed feathers were glued to the tail feathers of another group of males (long), thereby elongating their tails by 20–30 cm. There were two control groups. One control (control I) had the tail feathers cut and glued back on to restore the original length, the other group (control II) was only marked to identify them. After this treatment, the males with elongated tail feathers attracted significantly more females than the other treatments (Table 20.2), which supports Darwin's theory of female choice.

If males with longer tails attract more females, why don't the males have even longer tails? It is suggested that the advantage of obtaining more mates by growing a longer tail is counterbalanced by the cost, perhaps by increased predation because males with longer tails fly more slowly. Thus, the intersexual selection for increased tail length is probably opposed by natural selection.

In some pipefishes, the females transfer the eggs to males, which brood the embryos on their ventral body surface and supply nutrients to the offspring. Females can produce broods more rapidly than the males can raise them, and so males are likely to be the limiting resource in terms of female reproduction. On this basis we can expect a reversal of sex roles, with the males showing a stronger selection of females as mates compared to the selection of males by females.

Mate selection has been studied in two species of pipefish, *Syngnathus typhle* and *Nerophis ophidion* (Berglund *et al.* 1986, Rosenqvist 1990). In *S. typhle*, female fecundity increases with body size, and males have a brood pouch and so larger males can carry more offspring. There is no sexual dimorphism of body size, but both sexes prefer larger mates with females showing the strongest preference (Fig. 20.7). In *N. ophidion*, males have no special brood pouch but carry the offspring on their ventral side. There is no correlation between male body size and brood size, but female fecundity increases with body size. Interestingly, females are larger than the males and males prefer females of larger body size. When female body size was held constant, males preferred females with large ornamental skin folds, which may be an indicator of their dominance ranking, and they also preferred females with the largest area of blue nuptial colours, which is a reliable indicator of female fecundity (Fig. 20.7).

In pipefish, males do not appear to invest more energy than females in the offspring, although the cost to the males in terms of reduced growth and increased mortality has not been taken into account in making these estimates. Even so, the difference in reproductive rates between the sexes, where the females can produce young almost twice as fast as the males can care for them, seems to explain adequately the basis of sexual selection in these two species.

20.2.3 Combined effects of intra- and intersexual selection

The effects of intra- and intersexual selection may augment each other. A good example of this is seen in the northern elephant seal (*Mirounga angustirostris*), which has the largest harem size in the

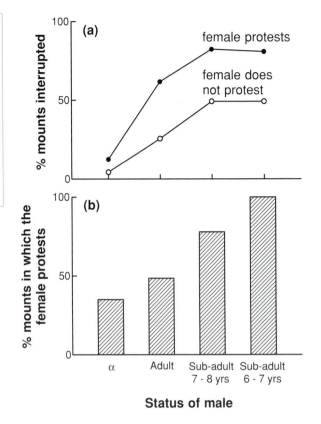

Fig. 20.8 (a) The influence of female behaviour on the mating success of male northern elephant seals (*Mirounga angustirostris*) of different rank, and (b) the probability that females will protest when mounted by males of different rank. (Reprinted from Halliday 1978, *Behavioural Ecology: An Evolutionary Approach* (eds. J. R. Krebs and N. B. Davies), pp. 180–213, with permission of Blackwell Publishing.)

pinnipeds, with as many 50 individuals in a harem (see Fig. 20.6). Females leave the sea once a year to give birth on the beach, and also to mate. Because suitable beaches are scarce, it is possible for males to control a harem of females provided they are sufficiently strong to fight off other males. The fights between males are very violent, and only the largest and strongest are able to form a harem. These alpha males, comprising less than 10% of the males, fertilize nearly 90% of the females. Other males are able to mate, but at a much lower frequency, and their mating attempts are often interrupted by a more dominant male. Clearly, there is strong intrasexual selection for increased body size in males, but there is also intersexual selection because females protest more frequently if a male of lower dominance and size attempts to mate with them (Fig. 20.8b). These protests attract the attention of higher-ranking males of greater body size, and the frequency of interrupted mating attempts also increases (Fig. 20.8a).

20.2.4 Sexual selection versus natural selection

Although we have treated sexual selection as though it is distinct from natural selection, the two processes are not fundamentally different. Natural selection increases fitness by improving survival and the number of offspring produced, whereas sexual selection increases fitness by increasing mating success and, presumably, the production of more offspring. In addition, sexual selection always acts differentially on the two sexes, whereas natural selection may operate equally on males and females, although not necessarily so.

When we considered sexual selection on tail length in the long-tailed widowbird, it was postulated that natural selection countered the effects of sexual selection and prevented the runaway selection for longer and longer tails in the males. This brings us to the question of why certain traits should be exaggerated by sexual selection. In some cases one can see the utility of the selection. Traits like body size and breeding coloration may be correlated with the fecundity of a mating partner. But what is the utility of extremely long tails in male widowbirds or the huge fantail of the peacock (*Pavo* spp.)? There are various hypotheses to account for such traits. One hypothesis is that males with emphasized traits may provide direct benefits to the female or her offspring. Perhaps such males may be able to hold a superior territory in terms of size or quality, or may provide superior parental care. This hypothesis may be able to account for some cases of sexual selection where there is a pair bond between the males and females for part or all of the breeding season, but in many cases (e.g. lek mating systems) the male has no further contact with the female after mating. In this case any benefits must be indirect. One hypothesis of indirect benefits is that the traits are arbitrary in nature. Once females begin to prefer males in which certain traits are emphasized, there will be runaway selection provided the traits are heritable. Selection drives the system to emphasize the traits more and more, providing female choice remains constant, because females prefer breeding with males with the most emphasized traits and will produce sons with similar characteristics who have an increased chance of mating. Once the female choice, i.e. the emphasized trait, carries an ecological cost, the effects of sexual selection will be counterbalanced by natural selection and the traits may stabilize at some intermediate value. Another hypothesis of indirect benefits postulates that the emphasized traits are indicators of genetic quality. The emphasized traits are linked to, or are expressed in the presence of, other genes which have a direct positive effect on fitness. In other words, males with such traits have 'good genes' which will be passed on to the offspring. We will not deal here with the evidence supporting the different hypotheses. Interested readers are referred to excellent discussions of this topic by Alcock (1998), Andersson (1994), Cronin (1991) and Futuyma (1998).

20.3 | Animal mating systems

There are many mating systems in animals. Some, like the cnidarians (hydroid polyps, corals and jellyfish), release their gametes into the water, and fertilization occurs more or less at random. I say more or less at random, because some sperm may swim faster than others and so will be more likely to fertilize the eggs, and it is possible that eggs may even be selective when it comes to fertilization by different sperm. Nevertheless, males can effectively mate with many females and similarly females can mate with many males. Other animals practice *monogamy*, in which males and females have a single mating partner. However, this too may vary. A pair of swans (*Cygnus olor*) may breed together for 15 years, and less than 1% of the pairs break up each year. They have a lifelong pair bond. House martins (*Delichon urbica*), however, while monogamous during the raising of a single brood, will mate again at random, and so the break up of pairs is close to 100%. They practice serial monogamy, which produces much the same effect as polygamy in terms of their offspring. Polygamy may be of two types: *polygyny*, in which several females mate with a single male, and *polyandry*, in which several males mate with a single female. Here too there is variation because some polygamous species establish pair bonds during the breeding season and others do not. The mating system within a species is not necessarily constant. For example, individuals of the common dunnock or hedge sparrow (*Prunella modularis*) may practice monogamy, polygyny or polyandry all within the same population! Thus, it is not easy to have a nice tidy classification of mating systems.

The purpose of this section is to examine three basic types of mating systems: polygyny, polyandry and monogamy, to see if we can understand their determinants. We can expect polygyny where males invest little and the females invest a lot in raising the progeny, and polyandry when the males invest more in parental care than the females, and there may be monogamy where the parental investment of the two sexes is more equal (see section 20.1).

20.3.1 Polygyny

Polygyny occurs in a variety of ways. In *female defence polygyny*, the males monopolize a group of females directly, and attack other males that try to mate with their harems. In *resource defence polygyny*, the males defend territories that contain resources for the females. Males with the richest territories, in terms of resources, attract the most females. Finally, in *lek polygyny*, the males establish small territories that contain no resources for the female other than the breeding male. Males display on their territories, and females select their mate. The advantage to successful males is obvious in these three types of polygyny, but it is less obvious why females might choose to share a male with other females. We will examine this problem as we briefly discuss each of these types of polygyny.

Female defence polygyny

When females in breeding condition occur in defensible clusters, males compete for these clusters. We have already considered the example of the elephant seal in section 20.2.3. Females cluster on suitable beaches, and provide an opportunity for males to establish territories and prevent other males from mating with the females,

Fig. 20.9 Male impala (*Aepyceros melampus*) and harem. (Photograph by the author.)

with variable degrees of success. The size of the harem is directly related to the size of the male and his fighting ability.

In some species of ungulates the females occur in large herds, perhaps as a defence against predation (see Chapter 18). This also presents an opportunity for males to monopolize a group of females and maintain a harem. This is seen in species like impala (Fig. 20.9) and red deer. The male's success in this breeding strategy depends not only on his ability to compete with rival males, but also on his ability to control the movement of the females. From the female's perspective, the advantage to polygyny stems from the advantages of group living, in terms of increased survivorship for herself and her offspring. She is also assured of mating with a male of high genetic quality, because only the strongest males are able to maintain such a harem.

In some cases, the females seem to have little choice in the matter. The male marine isopod *Paragnathia formica* digs a burrow, into which he drags a large number of females that he captures. He sits at the entrance to the burrow and can prevent the females from leaving and can also prevent rival males from entering.

Resource defence polygyny

Male red-winged blackbirds (*Agelaius phoeniceus*) establish territories in the spring, typically in areas of emergent vegetation in wetlands. Males that have the largest territories, containing the most suitable vegetation for nesting, attract the most females. Non-territorial males do not breed. Experienced males tend to have better territories and provide more food to the offspring than other males (Searcy 1979). In this case there is a pair bond between the male and the females for the duration of the breeding season.

Where the females live on the male territories and the male provides some degree of parental care (e.g. red-winged blackbirds), why would a female choose polygyny rather than monogamy? Presumably the answer to this question will depend on the degree to which a female's fitness is reduced by sharing the male with other females (C), compared to the reduction in fitness by moving to mate with a lone male on a lower-quality territory (PT, the polygyny threshold). This is the basis of the simple polygyny threshold model of Orians (1969), who proposed that if PT is greater than C, the female should choose polygyny. The model assumes that females can accurately assess the costs and benefits of the various choices and that the males (and females) are not being deceitful.

It is not easy to test the polygyny threshold model because it is difficult to identify and measure the critical resources (i.e. PT and C), to measure female fitness, and to identify the true mating choices faced by females. For these reasons many experimental tests of the model are difficult to interpret and do not always support the model. Contrary to expectations, there seems to be no cost (C) to females in polygynous relationships in some populations of the red-winged blackbird (Searcy and Yasukawa 1989). Presumably the polygynous males are able to compensate, by providing additional resources to the females. In contrast, studies of the pied flycatcher (*Ficedula hypoleuca*) have shown that there is a cost to second females in polygynous relationships, because females in monogamous relationships have a higher fitness than females in polygynous relationships (Alatalo *et al*. 1981, Alatalo and Lundberg 1984).

If females in monogamous relationships have higher fitness, why do females enter polygynous relationships? One obvious reason is that unmated males may be unavailable. However, in the case of the pied flycatcher, Alatalo and his co-workers have suggested that the females are deceived by the males. In this species, males maintain territories that contain a tree with a nest hole for the female. Polygynous males have more than one breeding territory which may be several hundred metres apart in the forest. It is suggested that females do not know that a male already has a mate, and the secondary female settles down and breeds only to receive little help from her mate. There is conflicting evidence about whether the secondary female knows about the primary female (see Andersson 1994). Whatever the case, polygynous males have a higher fitness than monogamous males, because the combined fitness of his females is greater than the fitness of single females. Thus, polygynous males achieve their advantage at the expense of both mates, but sometimes it is the male that is being deceived.

Recent studies using genetic fingerprinting to reveal the parentage of offspring of similar species to those just discussed are revealing a much more complicated story (K. Wiebe, pers. comm.). There are cases of polygyny and monogamy as expected, but there are also many cases where either part or all of the offspring are related to the female but not the male (i.e. the female is deceiving the male), cases where some of the offspring are not related to either parent (i.e. both parents are deceived by another female), and a few cases of polyandry where a female lays eggs in two nests and leaves most of the cost of raising her offspring to two different males. Clearly, there appears to be a complex of mating strategies operating which will require detailed studies to decipher.

In some species there is no pair bond between the sexes. For example, male topi (*Damaliscus lunatus*) (Fig. 19.5) establish territories, and in some areas they select areas of grass that are unusually green which probably gives an indication of the richness of grazing. Females tend to visit males on greener territories (Balmford *et al.* 1992), and so the owners of these territories have more chances of mating. The females, however, do not spend large amounts of time feeding on the male territories, and so this type of polygyny is not very different from lek polygyny.

Lek polygyny

In some cases the males do not defend or control either resources or females. Instead, males in breeding condition come together in groups called leks where they defend a very small territory. The territories simply provide a site where the males can display, and mate with any females that visit them. After copulation, the female departs and has no further contact with the male. In many cases, there is a strong selection of the males by females (Fig. 20.3) and so leks have been extensively studied to try and identify the basis for this selection.

In a lek system where the male does not provide any parental care, what is the advantage to the female? One advantage is that she can select her mate and may be able to use various traits as indicators of male quality. For example, in Jackson's widowbird (*Euplectes jacksoni*, a close relative of the long-tailed widowbird, discussed in section 20.2.2, which practices resource-based polygyny), the males form leks and dance around displaying themselves. Females select males that jump more frequently, and who have the longest tails. In most cases, however, it is not clear why the females choose to mate with so few males on a lek. It has been suggested that females copy each other, and that certain dominant males are able to provide more protection from harassment from undesirable males than other males.

What is the advantage of the lek system for males, particularly in those species where few males do most of the mating? It has been suggested that larger aggregates of males attract more females than smaller aggregates of males, and so the chances of obtaining a mate might be increased. Although larger leks attract more females in the Uganda kob (*Kobus kob*) (Deutsch 1994), the chances of obtaining a mate are not increased because the relationship is a linear one and so the number of females per male remains constant with lek size. However, the chances of dominant males obtaining matings might be increased. In one species of birds, the ruff (*Philomachus pugnax*), mating success does increase with lek size, up to a point, but then remains constant with further increases in lek size (Widemo and Owens 1995).

The highly skewed mating success of individual males (Fig. 20.3) is probably not as great as it appears, because lek composition does not remain constant over time. In the case of the Uganda kob, a male can only remain as part of the lek for a few days before it must leave and build up its strength for another session. This turnover of individuals means that the variation in the lifetime reproductive success of the males is probably much smaller than the variation that is observed over a single breeding season.

20.3.2 Polyandry

In this rare mating system, females have a long-term mating relationship with more than one male, because the males provide much of the parental care. We saw one example of this in certain pipefish (section 20.2.2), and it represents a reversal of roles from the more common polygynous mating systems.

Another example of this type of breeding system is found in the American jacana or lily trotter (*Jacana spinosa*), which live on lily-covered lakes. Each female defends a large territory within which are several smaller male territories. Each male defends a floating nest and raises the young. The female mates with all of the males, lays her eggs in each nest, and defends her harem of males from other females. The females are much larger than the males, and are dominant over them.

In this type of breeding system the advantages to the female are obvious. She is emancipated from incubating the eggs and providing direct care for the young, and so she has a much higher reproductive potential than would otherwise be the case. The advantages to the male of this mating system are less obvious. He might be raising offspring that he has fathered, but he is undoubtedly also raising young fathered by other males because the female mates with all of the males in her harem. The male has no way of discriminating between eggs he may have fertilized and those that have been fertilized by other males. Consequently, selection will favour a male caring for a clutch of eggs, which may contain some eggs fertilized by himself, and not disrupting the breeding effort of other males who may be raising young that he has fathered. The male has little opportunity to mate with other females because he is dominated by his mate, and abandoning the nest would expose it to the risk of predation, which is particularly high in this species.

20.3.3 Monogamy

Until recently, it was estimated that 90% of birds were monogamous and that this type of mating system was more common among birds than any other group of animals. It was proposed that this is because both the eggs and the chicks of most species require considerable parental care. Eggs need to be incubated and protected from predation, and the chicks need to be fed and kept warm and protected. Males that help the female provide parental care may produce more offspring than those that do not. Thus, birds seemed to fit the general model in which similar parental investment in the offspring selects for monogamy.

Since the development of DNA fingerprinting, by which it is possible to determine the parentage of young, the common perception of monogamous birds co-operating to raise their offspring has had to be revised. In several supposedly monogamous species, both males and females may mate with other individuals. For example, it has been estimated that about 30% of the offspring of swallows are not the progeny of the ostensible father. Such high levels of bastard offspring (to use the vernacular to describe the offspring that are unrelated to the 'father'), resulting from extra-pair copulations, are common in birds that live in colonies, such as seabirds, swallows, bee-eaters, herons and sparrows (Birkhead and Møller 1992). Apparently, the close proximity of these birds' nests provides considerable opportunity for extra-pair copulations. This mating with neighbouring females might have been predicted for males, because if a male can induce more than one female to raise his offspring he can improve his fitness, as indicated in Table 20.1. However, careful study has shown that this sort of behaviour is not just the result of certain males forcing themselves on other females, the females also practise deceit. To investigate the factors affecting female mating patterns, researchers have performed plastic surgery on the males to make them either more or less physically attractive to the females. For example, if the tail fork of male swallows is made asymmetrical, they are less attractive to females, and if the tail fork is made slightly longer and more symmetrical such males are highly attractive to females. Such research has shown that females are more likely to mate with another male if their partner is subordinate, younger, and is physically unattractive. These females choose to have extra-pair copulations with males that are dominant, older, and more physically attractive. It appears that females may be attempting to select mates of higher quality, even though they are in what is assumed to be a monogamous relationship.

In mammals only the female feeds the young, both during gestation and during the period of lactation after birth. Any male care, in terms of protecting young from predators, transporting young, or providing food is trivial by comparison. So the argument that both parents should have more or less equal investment in the raising of their offspring cannot be used to explain the existence of monogamy in about 5% of mammalian species.

A phylogenetic analysis of the evolution of monogamy in mammals (Komers and Brotherton 1997) suggests that it occurs when females are solitary and have small, exclusive ranges, which allows males to monopolize them. It is in the interest of males to mate and guard a single female, rather than risk enlarging their territories to include two or more females, because the incidence of male intruders would be much higher. He can, therefore, have a higher degree of confidence of his paternity of the offspring, and avoids the risk of raising offspring fathered by an intruding male. An example of a monogamous mammal is the dik-dik (*Madoqua kirki*) (Fig. 20.10).

20.4 | Conclusions

An individual's abilities to attract mating partners, to breed successfully and to produce and raise offspring are obviously vital

Fig. 20.10 Monogamous dik-dik, *Madoqua kirki*, on their common territory (above) and a territorial dispute between two neighbouring males (below). (Photographs by the author.)

components of its fitness. In this brief review of the behaviour of reproduction we have seen that the interests of males and females, in terms of individual fitness, frequently do not coincide. Typically, the males seek to mate with as many females as possible to maximize their fitness, whereas females try to obtain mates of high quality and try to obtain the exclusive attention of the male in order to maximize their fitness. When the male provides most or all of the parental care of the offspring, the roles are reversed. Both of these mating strategies are not as pure as was once thought, because genetic fingerprinting has shown that supposedly polygynous species, for example, also include individuals practicing polyandry. There are numerous cases of apparent monogamy where both sexes co-operate extensively in raising their young, but even here genetic analysis has shown that both parents can practise deceit on the other in order to increase their individual fitness. Thus, our understanding of mating strategies is rapidly being revised. Finally, sexual selection tends to be emphasized in species that are mainly polygynous and polyandrous, and so these species tend to be more sexually dimorphic than species that are mainly monogamous.

Chapter 21

Epilogue

We have come to the end of a journey during which we have introduced the four main areas of population biology. By now you will be realizing that a full understanding of the subject requires a grasp of the basic principles of evolution, population genetics, population ecology and behavioural ecology. A true synthesis of these areas is demanding because there are so many connections to be made as we shift between genetics, ecology and behaviour, and then try to make sense of it all from a Darwinian perspective. Nevertheless, it is important to attempt some form of synthesis because we will obtain a much more complete understanding of whatever process or phenomenon we are studying. Consider the following two examples.

First, the interaction between predators and their prey. There are numerous models of the growth of predator and prey populations that try to explain how predators affect the numbers and growth of their prey populations, and vice versa. Although these models help us to understand something about this type of interaction, a lot of questions remain. Why do some predators switch from eating one type of prey to another, and why can one predator limit the numbers of its prey but another cannot? Answers to these types of questions requires knowledge of an array of different factors. For example, the behaviour of both predators and their prey affect who is eaten and at what rates; the rates of energy acquisition versus energy expenditure may vary for different prey items, and predators may vary their diet accordingly; and genetic variation amongst the prey may make some more susceptible to predation than others. In summary, as we look at the system from different perspectives we obtain a much better picture of the system as a whole.

Second, an integrated approach is also important in the study of small populations. We may have a good theoretical understanding of the genetics of small populations, including genetic drift, inbreeding, gene flow or migration between populations, and the effects of selection, but this does not explain why the populations are small. Are there ecological factors, such as fragmentation of suitable habitat or the presence of superior competitors that keep the numbers low, or are there behavioural factors, such as social structure, that limit the size of the breeding population? Until we integrate these different perspectives of the biology of these types of populations, our understanding of the system as a whole will be very limited.

This book makes many connections between the different areas of population biology and achieves a modest level of integration of the subject, but a true synthesis has not been realized. There are two reasons for this. First, this is an introduction to the subject and one needs to know the basics of all areas before a more effective synthesis can be made. Second, it also reflects the present way that we investigate this area of biology. Most studies still look at things from one or two perspectives, because of the constraints of time and the expertise of the individual. In future, I hope there will be many more integrated group studies that look at populations from several perspectives simultaneously. I believe that our approach will have to change if we are going to make much more headway in our understanding of the biology of populations.

There are many other interesting topics in population biology, not covered in this text, that can be explored. For example, the subject of island biogeography is well introduced by Wilson and Bossert (1971) and Gotelli (1995), metapopulation biology is covered by Hanski (1999), and many areas of behavioural ecology are superbly introduced by Krebs and Davies (1993). I urge you to continue your journey to explore these other topics in population biology, as well as to explore to a greater depth the areas we have already covered. You will gain new insights about nature during your endeavours. Remember that the basic principles you have learned are not just things that we read about in books, but we can see them operating in the world around us if we take the time to look. So perhaps as you rake up the seeds from a neighbour's elm tree or swat mosquitoes as you laze on the verandah you can think of 'overproduction of offspring', or as you combat weeds in the garden you can reflect on the powers of dispersal and the competitive ability of different plants. For deeper understanding, talk to those who are doing research in the area of populations, your professors and their graduate students, to find out what they are studying and how they are changing our understanding of the subject. As you learn more about population biology, the more you will come to realize the truth that 'There is a grandeur in this view of life . . .' (Darwin 1859).

Glossary

This glossary attempts to help the reader by explaining what I mean by many of the more specialist words used throughout the text. Note that these meanings are used in the context of population biology and so may have somewhat different meanings when used elsewhere. In addition, some of the terms are explained more fully in the text.

abiotic Non-living. Usually applied to the physical and chemical features of an organism's environment.

adaptation Any change in feature of an organism that enables it to survive and reproduce in its environment better than if it lacked the feature.

adaptive landscape A graph of the average fitness of a population in relation to genotypic frequency. Peaks on the landscape correspond to genotypic frequencies with a high average fitness, valleys to genotypic frequencies with low average fitness.

additive effect The effect of an allele on a character when it measures half the phenotypic difference between homozygotes for that allele compared to homozygotes for a different allele; i.e. heterozygotes are exactly midway between the phenotypic scores of the two homozygotes.

additive genetic variance The part of the genetic variance in a character that is attributable to the additive effects of alleles.

allele One of the alternative forms of a gene with a DNA sequence that differs from other forms of that gene. Normally, alleles are recognized by their phenotypic effects.

allelic frequency The occurrence of a specified allele in a population relative to all alleles at that gene locus. Expressed as a proportion (between 0 and 1) or a percentage (between 0 and 100).

allozyme One of several forms of an enzyme coded for by different alleles at a gene locus.

altruism Behaviour that decreases the chances of survival or reproduction of an individual (i.e. decreases its fitness) while increasing those of another individual of the same species.

amensalism An interaction between two organisms or species in which one adversely affects the second but the second has no effect on the first. For example, some plants produce chemicals that inhibit the growth of other plants adjacent to them.

aposematic Coloration or markings that serve to warn would-be predators that the individual is poisonous, foul-tasting or dangerous, for example, the yellow and black stripes on a wasp or bee.

artificial selection Selection by humans of a chosen trait in a captive population, usually of a domesticated species. It differs from **natural selection** in that fitness (i.e. whether it is selected to breed the next generation) is defined in terms of the chosen trait, rather than determined by the entire genotype.

assortative mating The tendency to mate with others of like phenotype or genotype, for example, tall individuals preferentially mating with tall individuals. This will increase the proportion of homozygous individuals in the population. See **disassortative mating**.

autosome A chromosome other than a sex chromosome.

bacteriophage A virus that is parasitic within a bacterium; each phage is specific to one type of bacterium.

balance theory The theory that most genetic variation is maintained in the population by a balance of selective forces, with the result that most evolution is directed by natural selection. See **neutral theory**.

Batesian mimicry The resemblance of a palatable animal (the mimic) to a noxious animal (the model) that is avoided by predators because of its warning coloration. For example, hover flies mimic noxious wasps.

biotic Living. Usually applied to the influences of other organisms (as prey, competitors, predators or pathogens) as part of an organism's environment.

blending inheritance An early erroneous theory that assumed that hereditary substances from parents merged in their offspring. Compare to **Mendelian inheritance** or **particulate inheritance**.

bottleneck A severe, but short-lived, reduction in population size. The genetic variation in the population is severely reduced by **genetic drift** when the size of the population is small.

carrying capacity The maximum population size of a species that can be sustained indefinitely by a given habitat or area. Symbol K.

catastrophism The theory that changes in the earth's crust have resulted chiefly from sudden violent events some thousands of years ago, and that there is little change occurring at present. Compare to **uniformitarianism**.

character A trait, feature or property of an organism.

chromosome A structure in the cell nucleus that carries the genetic material (DNA) bound to various proteins. The genes or alleles are arranged in a sequence along the structure, and the position of each gene is called a locus.

cline A gradient in the mean value of a trait or in the allelic frequency in a population over a geographic transect. For example, the salt tolerance of a species may decline as one moves upstream from the mouth of an estuary.

codominance The situation in which both alleles of a gene are fully expressed in the phenotype. For example, pink flowers may be the phenotype of a plant with one allele for red flowers and the other allele for white flowers.

coefficient of relatedness The probability of two individuals possessing the same rare allele by inheriting it from a recent common ancestor. In general, it is the proportion of alleles among two individuals that are **identical by descent**.

coevolution The joint evolution of two or more interacting species where each evolves in response to selection imposed by the other(s). For example, the beak in seed-eating birds may be thickened to crack the hard seed coat of seeds. This selects for seeds with harder seed coats, which in turn selects for birds with even thicker bills.

cohort A group of individuals born at the same time in a population.

cohort life table A life table constructed by monitoring the survival or death of a cohort of individuals. Compare with **static life table**.

competition An interaction between individuals of the same or different species whereby resources used by one are unavailable to others, which results in a mutual depression of fitness (reduced growth rate or carrying capacity).

Darwinism Darwin's two theories of evolution: that all species are derived from other species and so have a common ancestor; and that the main mechanism of evolutionary change is natural selection.

deme A local population, usually small, in which the individuals breed randomly with each other.

demography A study of the processes that change the size of a population, i.e. birth, death and dispersal.

density dependence The tendency for the growth rate of the population to be affected by population density. Typically, the death rate of the population increases, or the birth rate decreases, as the density of the population increases.

deterministic There is a fixed outcome that can be predicted exactly from a given set of initial conditions. Compare with **stochastic**.

diploid Having two sets of chromosomes and genes, one from the mother and one from the father. Compare with **haploid** and **polyploid**.

disassortative mating The tendency to mate with a different phenotype or genotype. For example, some plants with long styles preferentially mate with plants with short styles. This mating tendency increases the proportion of heterozygous individuals in the population. See **assortative mating**.

dispersal The movement of individuals from one locality to another.

DNA Deoxyribonucleic acid; the molecule that controls inheritance.

dominance In genetics, the extent to which an allele produces the same phenotype when it is heterozygous compared to when it is homozygous. An allele (A) is said to be (completely) dominant if the phenotype of the heterozygotes (Aa) is the same of the homozygotes (AA). Dominance is incomplete if the heterozygous phenotype is close to, rather than identical with, the homozygote of the dominant type. Compare with **codominance** and **recessive**.

electrophoresis The movement of charged particles in a fluid or gel under the influence of an electric field. In studies of genetic variation in populations, the technique has been used to distinguish between different proteins (and therefore alleles) which differ in motility because the molecules vary in size and electric charge.

environment The complex of external abiotic and biotic factors that may affect the function or activity of a population, organism or part of an organism such as a gene. Note that the environment of a gene will probably include other genes within the organism.

epistasis The interaction between two or more gene loci on the phenotype or fitness such that the joint effect of the genes differs from the sum of the effects of each gene locus taken separately.

equilibrium An unchanging condition, e.g. of population size or genetic composition. See **stable equilibrium**, **unstable equilibrium** and **neutral equilibrium**.

evolution The change in a lineage of populations between generations. The change is normally documented by a change in genotypic or phenotypic frequencies.

evolutionarily stable strategy (ESS) Usually a heritable behaviour which, if adopted by most of the population, cannot be improved upon by any other strategy and so will become established by natural selection.

exploitation Competition where the use of resources by individuals reduces the level of the resources and causes adverse effects on other individuals (competitors) using those resources. The resources must be limiting if competition is to occur.

exponential growth The growth of a population where the individual, or per capita, rate of increase remains constant. The time it takes a population to double in size remains constant, whatever the size of the population.

fecundity The number of gametes, fertilized eggs, seeds or live offspring produced by an individual.

fitness The average reproductive success of an entity from one generation to the next, in which the entity may be an allele or genotype (where the genotype is for a specific trait). Frequently the fitness is expressed as a relative fitness where the average contribution of the allele or genotype to the next generation is compared with that of another allele or genotype (normally the superior type).

fixation The process by which an allele becomes fixed in the population when it becomes the only allele of a gene, i.e. achieves a frequency of 1 or 100% in the population.

founder effect The loss of genetic variation when a new isolated population is formed by a very small number of individuals from a larger population.

frequency-dependent selection Selection where the fitness of a genotype or phenotype depends on its frequency in the population.

functional response The relationship between a predator's consumption rate of prey (i.e. the number of prey eaten per predator) and either prey density or predator density.

gene A functional unit of heredity, which in this book may be considered to be a sequence of nucleotides in the DNA molecule coding for either part or all of a protein, residing at a particular locus on a chromosome.

gene flow The movement of alleles into the gene pool of a population from one or more other populations. For this to happen, there must be immigration of individuals from other populations, and these individuals must successfully breed with the resident population.

genetic drift Random changes in the frequencies of alleles or genotypes within a population due to sampling error in the gametes.

genome The complete set of genes or genetic material in a cell or organism.

genotype The set of genes of an individual organism represents its overall genotype, but more frequently the term is used to denote the genetic composition at a specified gene locus or group of loci.

gradualism The proposal that large changes in a phenotype are the result of the accumulation of many small changes.

group selection The differential survival of whole populations as a result of differences among them of one or more characteristics.

guild A group of species that exploit a type of environmental resources in a similar way.

habitat The place where an organism lives.

haploid A cell (usually a gamete) or organism with only one set of genes or chromosomes, and so there is only one allele at each gene locus.

Hardy–Weinberg ratio The ratio of genotypic frequencies in a randomly mating population where there is no mutation, selection or drift operating. The Hardy–Weinberg ratio for a gene with two alleles (A and a, with a frequencies of p and q) and three genotypes (AA, Aa, and aa) is p^2 AA: $2pq$ Aa: q^2 aa. The ratio is a neutral equilibrium and may be changed by the action of mutation, selection and drift.

herbivore An animal that consumes plants. Some consume the entire plant (e.g. seed-eaters and grazers of phytoplankton) and act like true predators, others act like parasites in the way that they obtain their nourishment from a plant (e.g. aphids), but most herbivores attack a large number of plants and only consume part of the plant without killing it.

heritability The proportion of the variance among individuals in a trait that is attributable to differences in genotype.

heterogametic The sex with two different **sex chromosomes**. In mammals, this is the male sex which has sex chromosomes XY. See **homogametic**.

heterozygote An individual with two different alleles at a gene locus.

heterozygote superiority The situation is which, at a gene locus, the heterozygote has a higher fitness than either homozygote. Also called heterozygote advantage.

homogametic The sex with two of the same kind of **sex chromosomes**. In mammals, this is the female sex which has sex chromosomes XX. See **heterogametic**.

homozygote An individual with two copies of the same allele at a gene locus.

identical by descent Two or more copies of an allele are identical by descent if they have been derived from a single copy of the allele in a common ancestor.

inbreeding Relatives interbreed more frequently than if mates were chosen at random in a population.

inclusive fitness The fitness of a gene or genotype measured by the number of copies of genes identical by descent that are passed on to the next generation both directly by an individual as well as indirectly by its relatives as a result of the individual's actions. Thus, if an individual has two offspring on average, and by the provisioning of extra food helps a sibling produce one additional offspring on average, it will have an inclusive fitness of 1.25 (a direct fitness of 1.0, because each of its two offspring share half of its genes with its parent, and an indirect fitness of 0.25, because the additional offspring produced by its sibling have half of its genes in common with the one parent which in turn has half of its genes in common with its sibling). See **kin selection**.

interference Competition between organisms where one prevents another's use of resources contained in the area. This is typically achieved by behavioural and chemical interactions.

intrinsic rate of natural increase The per capita rate of increase of a population with a stable age distribution when there is no inhibition of growth by intraspecific competition.

isocline A line on a graph along which the population has the same rate of growth.

iteroparity A life history where individuals reproduce more than once during their lifetime. Compare with **semelparity**.

kin selection A form of selection in which the fitness of an allele is increased through altruistic acts to relatives (kin), which increases their reproductive success and results in more copies of the allele (which have descended from a common ancestor and so are identical by descent) being passed on to the next generation. See **inclusive fitness**.

K-selection The selection of life-history traits that favour a population of organisms staying close to the carrying capacity in a stable environment. The traits include large size, delayed reproduction, iteroparity, the production of few offspring with much parental care, a long lifespan, and a strong competitive ability. Compare with *r*-selection.

Lamarckism The theory of inheritance proposed by Jean-Baptiste de Lamarck which suggested that changes acquired during an organism's life could be inherited. Commonly referred to as *inheritance of acquired characteristics*.

lek A group of male territories that are vigorously defended for the purpose of sexual display and mating.

life table A table of statistics relating to survival, life expectancy and mortality in relation to age for a specified population.

locus The position on a chromosome occupied by a specific gene.

logistic growth A form of population growth in which the per capita rate of growth decreases linearly with increasing population density. The resulting growth curve is S-shaped and is frequently called a sigmoid growth curve.

macroevolution Evolution on a large scale, where the phenotypic changes are sufficiently great that new genera or higher taxa originate.

mean The average of a number of values; e.g. the mean of 4, 5 and 9 is $(4 + 5 + 9)/3 = 6$.

Mendelian inheritance The mode of inheritance of diploid species, in which heritable information is encoded within genes that are passed unchanged from parent to offspring, except on rare occasions when a mutation occurs. At each gene locus in an individual there are two alleles, one from the father and one from the mother, and these two alleles are usually represented equally in the individuals gametes.

microevolution Usually small evolutionary changes within a population or species.

migration In population genetics is used as a synonym for gene flow among populations; and in other contexts refers to the movement of individuals or whole populations from one area to another and may not involve gene flow.

mimicry Where one species resembles another because it is advantageous to do so. See **Batesian mimicry** and **Müllerian mimicry**.

Modern Synthesis The synthesis of Darwin's theory of natural selection, Mendelian inheritance and population genetics. Also called neo-Darwinism.

modifier gene A gene that modifies the phenotypic expression of genes at one or more loci.

monogamy A mating system where both males and females have a single mating partner.

Müllerian mimicry A type of mimicry where two noxious species evolve the same general pattern of warning coloration. For example, some bees and wasps have a similar yellow and black striping on their bodies.

mutation A random change in the sequence of nucleotides in the DNA molecule. The source of genetic variation.

natural selection The differential survival from one generation to the next of alternative forms of traits or entities, with the result that organisms in the population that are best adapted to the local environment increase in frequency relative to less well-adapted forms generation after generation.

nature versus nurture A debate about whether the phenotype is mainly the result of genetic factors (nature) or environmental effects (nurture). The debate is frequently heated when dealing with behavioural traits, particularly those of humans.

neutral alleles Alleles at the same locus that have the same fitness.

neutral equilibrium An unchanging state or condition, such that if the state is changed to a new position it remains at that point unless subject to some external force.

neutral theory The theory that most genetic variation is neutral with respect to fitness with the result that most evolution at the molecular level occurs by genetic drift. See **balance theory**.

niche Where and how the individuals of a species live. It is defined by location of the habitat where a species lives, and what, where and how it obtains the resources necessary for its survival.

parasite An organism that obtains its nutrients from another organism, causing harm to their host but usually not killing it.

parasitoid An insect whose larval stage lives in or on another animal, initially doing little harm but eventually killing its host. May be regarded as being intermediate between a parasite and a true predator.

parthenogenesis Reproduction without the egg being fertilized, i.e. the asexual reproduction of females.

particulate inheritance The transmission from parent to offspring of discrete units or factors that help determine the characteristics of an organism. Consistent with **Mendelian inheritance**, but contrasts to **blending inheritance**.

phenotype The morphological, physiological, behavioural, biochemical and other properties of an organism resulting from an interaction of the genotype and environment. Typically, a specific subset of characteristics is referred to.

pleiotropy The effect of a gene on two or more unrelated characteristics.

Poisson distribution Frequency distribution for a number of items per unit area or number of events per unit time, when the number occurs at random.

polyandry A system of mating in which a female has more than one male mate.

polygamy A system of mating in which an animal has more than one mate of the opposite sex.

polygenic traits A character whose variation is influenced in whole or in part by the allelic variation at several gene loci.

polygyny A mating system in which males mate with more than one female.

polymorphism The presence in the population of more than one allele at a gene locus. It also refers to phenotypic variation of a trait within a population.

polyploid The presence of more than two entire sets of chromosomes in an individual.

population A group of organisms, that usually reproduce sexually and share a common gene pool. They usually occupy a more or less defined locality, and the individuals interact more with each other than they do with individuals of other populations of the same species.

population genetics The study of the processes that affect gene or allelic frequencies.

preadaptation A feature of an organism that by chance allows an organism to exploit a new niche or environment.

predation The consumption of one living organism (the prey) by another (the predator).

predator An organism that consumes other living organisms. They can be divided into **true predators, herbivores, parasites** and **parasitoids**.

prey An organism that is killed and eaten by a predator.

quantitative trait A character showing continuous variation in a population because it is polygenic.

race In biology, a poorly defined term for a localized set of populations with a phenotype that is distinct from other populations of the species, and is often used in the same sense as subspecies. In humans, the term is often used but is less clear because there is a continuum between the various so-called distinct phenotypes or races.

random mating The probability of mating with individuals of specified genotypes or phenotypes equals the frequency of those genotypes or phenotypes in the population.

recessive An allele (a) is completely recessive to an alternative allele (A) if the phenotype of the heterozygote (Aa) is the same as the homozygote (AA) of the alternative (dominant) allele and different from the homozygote (aa) of the recessive allele. An allele may be partly, rather than completely, recessive: see **codominance, dominance**.

recombination The exchange of DNA between pairs of chromosomes, called crossing over, during cell division in the production of gametes. This process causes a mixing or recombination of alleles so that offspring have a different combination of alleles and traits from their parents.

reproductive rate The number of offspring produced by an individual per unit time (which is defined).

reproductive value The expected relative contribution of an individual to the number of individuals in the next generation of the population, from a specified age of the individual to the end of its life.

r-selection The selection of life-history traits which result in an ability to increase rapidly in numbers. The traits include small size, early reproduction, semelparity, large numbers of offspring, and a short lifespan. Compare with *K*-selection.

resource Something that is consumed or used by an organism, such as food, water and nesting sites.

selection A synonym of natural selection.

selection coefficient The difference between the mean relative fitness of a specified genotype and that of a reference genotype, which is usually the genotype with the highest fitness and given a value of 1.

semelparity A life history where individuals, particularly females, reproduce only once during their lifetime. Compare with iteroparity.

sex chromosome A chromosome that influences sex determination.

sexual reproduction The production of offspring by the fusion of two different gametes containing genetic material, one from the father and one from the mother.

sexual selection The differential production of offspring because of variation in the ability to obtain mates. The selection occurs either through competition between members of one sex, usually the males, for the chance to breed with the other sex, or through members of one sex, usually the females, choosing certain members of the opposite sex.

sigmoid curve An S-shaped curve, e.g. logistic growth curve.

species Members of a group of populations that actually or potentially interbreed with each other under natural conditions This is the biological species concept. In the case of fossils and asexual species, the term is used to denote groups of individuals that look similar, i.e. a phenetic species concept.

stabilizing selection Selection that promotes keeping a trait constant, by selecting against extremes of the phenotype and where an intermediate value of the phenotype has the highest fitness.

stable equilibrium An unchanging state of population size or gene frequency, such that if displaced from that state will return to the equilibrium condition.

standard deviation The square root of the variance.

static life table A life table constructed from the age structure or age at death of individuals in a population determined at a single moment of time. Compare with **cohort life table**.

stochastic Randomly determined; a property having a random probability pattern around some particular value that may be analysed statistically but cannot be determined exactly.

subspecies A group of populations of a species that share distinctive features and live in a different geographical area from other subspecies.

survivorship The probability of a newborn individual living to a particular age.

survivorship curve A plot of survivorship (on the vertical axis) against age (on the horizontal axis). The survivorship is frequently plotted on a logarithmic scale.

territory An area or volume defended by an individual or a group of individuals, from which other individuals, usually of the same species, are excluded.

true predator An animal that kills and consumes other animals (their prey) more or less immediately after attacking them.

uniformitarianism The theory that changes in the earth's crust during geological time have resulted from the action of continuous and relatively uniform natural processes like uplifting, erosion and sedimentation.

unstable equilibrium An unchanging state of population density or allelic frequency, but if the system is disturbed it moves away from the equilibrium value.

variance A measure of variation calculated by the average squared deviation of observations from their arithmetic mean. Symbolized σ^2 or s^2, it is calculated by the formula $[\Sigma(\bar{x} - x_i)^2]/(n-1)$, where $\bar{x}$ is the mean of the observations, x_i is the value of each individual observation, and n is the number of observations.

vestigial A rudimentary or atrophied state of an organ or part of the body, as a result of reduction through evolution from a more elaborate, functional state in an ancestor.

wild type The most common allele in wild populations, assuming there is one. Other alleles of the gene are termed mutations.

zero isocline An isocline along which the rate of population growth is zero.

zygote The cell formed by the union of a male and female gamete through the process of sexual reproduction.

Solutions to problems

CHAPTER 4

1. The λ per year $= 6000/5000 = 1.2$, and so the r_m per year $= \ln(1.2) = 0.18232$ (using Eqn 4.6). The population size after three years can be estimated using either Eqn 4.2 ($N_t = 5000 \times 1.2^3 = 8640$) or Eqn 4.4 ($N_t = 5000 \times e^{0.18232 \times 3} = 8639.96$, or 8640).

2. The λ per century $= 900$ million$/600$ million $= 1.5$, and so the r_m per century $= \ln(1.5) = 0.4055$ (using Eqn 4.6). The r_m per year $= 0.4055/100 = 0.00405$. The λ per year can be calculated, using Eqn 4.5, as $e^{0.00405} = 1.004$, or approximately 0.4% per year.

3. A 15% increase per year $= \lambda$ of 1.15 per year. When the population doubles in size, $N_t/N_0 = 2$. If we rearrange Eqn 4.2, we can see that $2 = \lambda^t$. Taking the logarithm of both sides (i.e. $\ln(2) = \ln(\lambda)t$) we find $0.6931 = 0.14t$, and so $t = 4.96$, or approximately 5 years.

4. First convert the r_m per week to r_m per day so that r_m and t are in the same time units. So, r_m of 0.14 per week is equivalent to $r_m = 0.14/7 = 0.02$ per day. Then use Eqn 4.4 to estimate N_t, setting N_0 to 24, r_m to 0.02, and t to 65. The answer is approximately 88 rats.

5. The multiplication rate (λ) over a four-week period is 5. Using Eqn 4.6 we calculate the r_m per four weeks as $\ln(5) = 1.6094$. The r_m per day is $1.6094/28 = 0.0575$, and we may use Eqn 4.5 to calculate the λ per day ($\lambda = e^{0.0575} = 1.059$).

6. There are two possible answers. If we consider the birth rate $= 36/1000 = 0.036$ and the death rate $= 19/1000 = 0.019$ to represent instantaneous rates, then $r_m = 0.036 - 0.019 = 0.017$ per year. Using this value in Eqn 4.4 and setting $N_0 = 2\,907\,000\,000$ and $t = 1$, we calculate N_t as $2\,956\,841\,452$. The increase in population size is $2\,956\,841\,452 - 2\,907\,000\,000 = 49\,841\,452$. However, if we consider the birth and death rates to represent finite rates then $R_m = 0.017$ per year. From this point of view, we can calculate $\lambda = 1 + R_m = 1.017$ using Exp. 4.8, and so $r_m = \ln(1.017) = 0.01686$. Using this value in Eqn 4.4 gives us an answer of $2\,956\,419\,000$ and so the increase in number $= 49\,419\,000$. Either answer is acceptable.

7. (a) The population increased from $N_0 = 2\,907\,000\,000$ to $N_t = 2\,957\,000\,000$ during a one-year period ($t = 1$). If we use Eqn 4.4, $2\,957\,000\,000 = 2\,907\,000\,000 \times e^r$. To solve for r_m, divide through by $2\,907\,000\,000$ and take the logarithm of both sides of the equation. The answer is $r_m = 0.0171$.

   (b) We know that $r_m = b - d$. Using our answer for r_m in part (a) we may see that $0.0171 = b - 0.019$, and so $b = 0.0171 + 0.019 = 0.0361$.

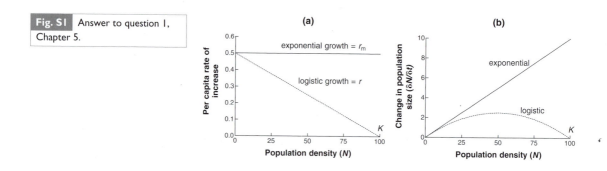

Fig. S1 Answer to question 1, Chapter 5.

CHAPTER 5

1. The relationships are described in Fig. S1. Note that the units on the x and y axes are entirely arbitrary. The per capita rate of increase remains constant in exponential growth but declines linearly with increasing density in logistic growth (Fig. S1a). The change in population size increases proportionately with the increase in population size in exponential growth, but attains a maximum value at half the carrying capacity (i.e. $K/2$) in logistic growth (Fig. S1b).

2. (a) Use Eqn 4.4. Set $N_0 = 5$, $N_t = 1044$ and $t = 28$ days. The answer is 0.1908 per day.

   (b) Again using Eqn 4.4, and setting $N_0 = 5$, $r_m = 0.1908$ and $t = 7 \times 15 = 105$ days, we can solve it for N_t. The answer is approximately 2 509 722 214 individuals!

   (c) Using Eqn 5.4, and setting $K = 2500$, $N_0 = 5$, $N_t = 1044$ and $t = 28$ days, we can solve it for r_m. The answer is 0.21 per day. Note that to estimate r_m you need to know the population size at three points, N_0, N_t and K.

   (d) If the population is growing logistically, the answer in part (c) is the correct value of r_m. Equation 5.4 automatically adjusts for the reduction in r by density dependent effects. Part (a) gives the value of r corresponding to a population density somewhere between 5 and 1044 in Fig. S2. There has already been some suppression of the growth rate during the first month of growth as a result of density-dependent effects.

   (e) Using any of the variants of Eqn 5.2, set $K = 2500$, $N = K/2 = 1250$ (this is where $\delta N/\delta t$ is a maximum) and $r_m = 0.21$, and solve the equation for $\delta N/\delta t$. The answer is 131.25 or approximately 131 individuals per day.

3. (a) 10 days because the doubling time stays constant in exponential growth. (b) First, use Eqn 5.4 and solve it for r_m by setting $t = 10$, $K = 100$, $N_0 = 20$ and $N_t = 40$. The value of r_m is 0.0981 per day. Use Eqn 5.4 again, but set $N_t = 80$ and $r_m = 0.0981$, and solve it for t. The value of t is 28.26 days, which is the time

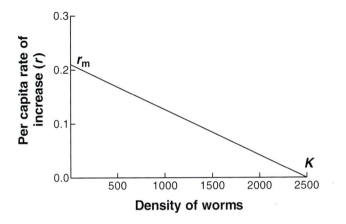

Fig. S2 See question 2(d), Chapter 5.

it takes the population to grow from 20 to 80 individuals. Our final answer is $28.26 - 10 = 18.26$ days.

4. (a) Substitute $K = 5 \times 10^6$, $N_0 = 2 \times 10^3$, $t = 3$ and $r_m = 0.29$ in Eqn 5.3. The answer is 4.77×10^3.

   (b) The maximum sustained yield $(\delta N / \delta t)$ is possible when $N = K/2$. We set $N = K/2$ in Eqn 5.2 and solve it for $\delta N / \delta t$. The maximum sustained yield is approximately 3.6×10^5 cells per ml per hour.

   (c) We can use Eqn 5.4, setting $r_m = 0.29$, $K = 5 \times 10^6$, $N_0 = 2 \times 10^3$ and $N_t = K/2 = 2.5 \times 10^6$. The solution is approximately 27 hours.

CHAPTER 6

1. (a) Using Eqn 6.1, the expected frequency of heterozygotes is $2pq$, which is $2 \times 0.9 \times 0.1 = 0.18$.

   (b) The total proportion of rhesus positive people in the population is $p^2 + 2pq$, which is $0.9^2 + 2 \times 0.9 \times 0.1 = 0.81 + 0.18 = 0.99$. Therefore, the fraction of these people that are heterozygous is $0.18/0.99 = 0.1818$.

2. The expected frequency of the M allele is 0.734, and of the N allele is 0.266. Using the expected Hardy–Weinberg equilibrium frequencies of $p^2 + 2pq + q^2$ and multiplying by the sample size of 203, the expected frequencies are 109.4 MM, 79.3 MN and 14.4 NN. These look very similar to the observed results. One may calculate a χ^2 value of 0.89 for these data (see section 6.4.2), which is not significant. We can conclude, therefore, that the population is in Hardy–Weinberg equilibrium and that mating is random.

3. Using a similar procedure to question 1, the frequency of the B allele is 0.5107, and of the C allele is 0.4893. The expected equilibrium frequencies are 146.6 BB, 280.9 BC and 134.6 CC. These are very different to the observed values and so the milk herd is unlikely to be in Hardy–Weinberg equilibrium. The χ^2 value for

these data is 104.5, which is considerably higher than the value of 3.84 which denotes a significant difference between the observed and expected frequencies. We can see that the observed numbers of homozygous individuals (BB and CC) are less than the expected number. As the young calves were in the expected Hardy–Weinberg proportions this suggests that there is an increased mortality of homozygous individuals as they grow from calf to adult, i.e. a strong selection against homozygous individuals.

4. The expected frequency of recessives in the population is q^2 which is observed to be 1 in 2000 or 0.0005. The frequency of the recessive allele for cystic fibrosis (q) is $\sqrt{(0.0005)} = 0.02236$. The frequency of carriers is $2pq = 2 \times 0.97764 \times 0.02236 = 0.0437$. Taking the reciprocal of this value, we see that the frequency of carriers in the population is 1 in 22.9 or approximately 1 in 23 individuals.

5. The dark-coloured phenotype is made up of two genotypes, CC and Cc, corresponding to frequencies of p^2 and $2pq$ (if the frequency of the C allele is symbolized by p) or $q^2 + 2pq$ (if the frequency of the C allele is symbolized by q). We cannot estimate the frequency of the C allele directly because the dark phenotype is made up of two genotypes, but we can estimate the frequency of the c allele from the proportion of light-coloured individuals in the population because they are homozygous recessive, cc (see section 6.4.1). If 96% of the population is dark, then 4% are light coloured, and this represents a frequency of $4/100 = 0.04$. This represents p^2 or q^2 (see above), and so the frequency of the c allele in the population is $\sqrt{(0.04)} = 0.2$. Therefore, the frequency of the *carbonaria* allele (C) is $1 - 0.2 = 0.8$.

CHAPTER 9

1. Using Eqn 9.3, set $q_t = 0.118$, $q_0 = 0.176$, $q_m = 0$ and $t = 10$. The answer (m) = 0.039.

2. First calculate q_m for each population: for population 1 = (0.5 + 0.8 + 0.9)/3 = 0.7333, for population 2 = (0.2 + 0.8 + 0.9)/3 = 0.6333, for population 3 = (0.2 + 0.5 + 0.9)/3 = 0.5333, and for population 4 = (0.2 + 0.5 + 0.8)/3 = 0.5. Then use a rearranged Eqn 9.2 to calculate the following:

$$\text{When } q_0 = 0.2, q_t = (1 - 0.05)^5(0.2 - 0.7333) + 0.7333 = 0.3206$$
$$q_0 = 0.5, q_t = (1 - 0.05)^5(0.5 - 0.6333) + 0.6333 = 0.5302$$
$$q_0 = 0.8, q_t = (1 - 0.05)^5(0.8 - 0.5333) + 0.5333 = 0.7397$$
$$q_0 = 0.9, q_t = (1 - 0.05)^5(0.9 - 0.5) + 0.5 = 0.8095.$$

3. Use Eqn 9.2 and set $q_t = 0.55$, $q_0 = 0.75$, $q_m = 0.25$ and $m = 0.05$. We obtain: $0.3 = 0.95^t \times 0.5$, which simplifies to $0.95^t = 0.6$. The logarithm of both sides of the equation yields $-0.0513 \times t = -0.5108$, and so $t = 9.96$, or approximately 10 generations.

CHAPTER 11

1. (a) You cannot calculate the relative fitness independently for each genotype. You must account for breeding both within and between genotypes by making the assumption of random mating. Follow the steps laid out in Example 11.3. First, calculate the allelic frequencies from the numbers of the three genotypes in generation 1. Thus:

Frequency of allele $G = [6 + \frac{1}{2}(284)]/1462$, or 0.1012

Similarly, the frequency of allele $B = 0.8988$.

Then, calculate the expected numbers of the three genotypes based on the expected Hardy–Weinberg ratios $(p^2 + 2pq + q^2)$. Thus, $GG = 0.1012^2 \times 1200$, or 12.3, $GB = 2 \times 0.1012 \times 0.8988 \times 1200$, or 218.3, and $BB = 0.8988^2 \times 1200$, or 969.4.

The absolute fitness is calculated from the ratios of Observed/Expected, and the relative fitness and selection coefficients are calculated as follows:

Genotype	Absolute fitness	Relative fitness (W)	Selection (s)
GG	$4/12.3 = 0.3252$	$0.3252/1.1177 = 0.2910$	$1 - 0.2910 = 0.7090 = s_1$
GB	$244/218.3 = 1.1177$	$1.1177/1.1177 = 1$	$1 - 1 = 0$
BB	$952/969.4 = 0.9821$	$0.9821/1.1177 = 0.8787$	$1 - 0.8787 = 0.1213 = s_2$

(b) From Eqn 10.15 $\hat{q} = \dfrac{0.709}{0.709 + 0.1213}$, or 0.8539.

If you are confused as to which selection coefficient is s_1 and which is s_2 in the equation, note that we expect the frequency of the brown allele to be higher than the green allele because selection is less against the brown allele.

2. (a) It is wise to lay out the information as follows:

	carbonaria	typica	
Genotype	CC Cc	cc	
Starting frequency	0.10	$0.90 = q_0^2$	So $q_0 = \sqrt{0.9}$ or 0.9487
Final frequency	0.90	0.10	$q_t = \sqrt{0.1}$ or 0.3162

We can see that the frequency of *typica* is declining and so the frequency of the allele is q and the frequency of the recessive genotype is q^2. The starting and final allelic frequencies are easily calculated as shown. We know that for *typica* $W = 0.67$, and so the selection coefficient against *typica* is $1 - 0.67 = 0.33$.

To calculate the number of generations (t) to effect the change in allelic frequencies we use Eqn 10.11, because the situation conforms to Case C – complete dominance, selection against the recessive. Thus:

$$0.33t = \frac{0.9487 - 0.3162}{0.9487 \times 0.3162} + \ln\left[\frac{0.9487(1 - 0.3162)}{0.3162(1 - 0.9487)}\right]$$

This has a solution of $t = 17.6$, or approximately 18 years.

(b) If the frequency of *carbonaria* is 0.36, then the frequency of *typica* (q^2) is 0.64 in 1924. Thus, the allelic frequency (q) is 0.8 in 1924. The frequency of the *carbonaria* allele when it was first introduced was $1/(2 \times 5000)$, or 0.0001. Thus, the frequency of the *typica* allele would have been 0.9999 at that time. If we substitute these values into Eqn 10.11, we obtain:

$$0.33t = \frac{0.9999 - 0.8}{0.9999 \times 0.8} + \ln\left[\frac{0.9999(1 - 0.8)}{0.8(1 - 0.9999)}\right]$$

The solution is $t = 24.5$ years, and so the *carbonaria* allele was introduced into the population around the turn of the century.

3. **(a)** The information is as follows:

	typica	*carbonaria*	
Genotype	CC Cc	cc	
At start	0.5	$0.5 = p_0^2$ so	$p_0 = \sqrt{0.5}$ or 0.7071 and $q_0 = 0.2929$
10 years later	0.1	0.9	$p_t = \sqrt{0.9}$ or 0.9487 $q_t = 0.0513$

We cannot calculate q directly because the frequency of the dominant *typica* phenotype is $q^2 + 2pq$, which cannot be solved. We can see that the frequency of the *carbonaria* genotype is increasing and the frequency is equal to p^2. Therefore, we calculate p first, and then q ($= 1 - p$).

The situation conforms to Case D – complete dominance, selection against the dominant, and so we need to use Eqn 10.14 to solve for s as follows:

$$10s = \frac{0.2929 - 0.0513}{0.9487 \times 0.7071} + \ln\left[\frac{0.2929(1 - 0.0513)}{0.0513(1 - 0.2929)}\right]$$

With the solution of $s = 0.24$.

(b) We should note that we are provided with the frequency of an allele and not the frequency of a genotype. The frequency of the *carbonaria* allele increases from 0.01 to 0.1, and so the frequency of the *typical* allele decreases from 0.99 ($= q_0$) to 0.9 ($= q_t$).

For Case D we use Eqn 10.14, setting $s = 0.24$. The solution is $t = 385$ years.

For Case C we use Eqn 10.11. The solution is 10.4 years.

One may see that favourable dominant alleles increase much faster than favourable recessive alleles when they are at low frequencies.

(c) The survival rate of *carbonaria* is 0.58, and that of *typica* is 0.48. Taking the ratio of the logarithms of these survival rates (see Example 11.2) gives a relative fitness for *typica* of 0.7422, and so $s = 1 - 0.7422$, or approximately 0.26. We can see that this is very similar to the selection coefficient based on differential predation of the two phenotypes by birds.

4.

Flower colour	Red	Pink	
Genotype	RR Rr	rr	Total
Starting numbers	180	90	270
Numbers after 5 years	227	85	312
Frequency at start	0.67	0.33	$q_0 = \sqrt{0.33}$ or 0.5773
Frequency after 5 years	0.7276	0.2724	$q_t = \sqrt{0.2724}$ or 0.5220

(a) This conforms to Case C – complete dominance, selection against the recessive. Use Eqn 10.11, setting $t = 5$. The solution is $s = 0.0814$.

(b) The equilibrium frequency is zero, because the frequency of the pink allele will continue to decline until it is eliminated.

(c) We can obtain a more accurate direct estimate of allelic frequencies. The frequency of $q_0 = 0.5519$, and $q_t = 0.5224$. We now have a situation conforming to Case B because it is stated that the relative fitness of the heterozygotes is intermediate between those of the two homozygotes. Consequently, we must use Eqn 10.8 to solve for s. The solution is $s = 0.0475$.

5. (a) At the start, $q_0 = 0.5$ (half the alleles of the heterozygous plants), and $q_t = 1/200 = 0.005$ (there is a single chlorophyll-deficient allele in 100×2 alleles). Using Eqn 10.13 we find the solution is 198 generations.

(b) We use Eqn 11.2, and set $u = 4.3 \times 10^{-4}$, and $s = 1$. The solution is $\hat{q} = 0.0207$.

(c)

Phenotype	Normal	Heterozygous	Lethal
Genotype	AA	Aa	aa
Observed numbers	132	52	0
Frequency of A (p) = 0.8587			
Frequency of a (q) = 0.1413			
Expected numbers	135.7	44.7	3.7
Absolute fitness	0.9729	1.1646	0
Relative fitness (W)	0.8354	1	0
Selection coefficient	$s_1 = 0.1646$		$s_2 = 1$

The allelic frequencies are calculated from the observed frequencies of the genotypes. We can then calculate the expected genotypic frequencies, assuming they are in Hardy–Weinberg equilibrium. The absolute fitness of each genotype is then calculated from the ratio of Observed/Expected values.

6. (a)

	Non-Jewish Canadian	Jewish Canadian
$q^2 =$	1/550,000	1/3600
$q =$	1.35×10^{-3}	1.67×10^{-2}
Carriers $(2pq) =$	2.69×10^{-3}	3.28×10^{-2}
$=$	1 in 371	1 in 31

(b) From Eqn 11.2 we can see that $u = \hat{q}$ when $s = 1$. Therefore, we estimate $u = 1.82 \times 10^{-6}$ for non-Jewish Canadians, and $u = 2.74 \times 10^{-4}$ for Jewish Canadians. There is no particular reason why the mutation rates should be so different in the two groups. This illustrates the dangers of using Eqn 11.2 to estimate mutation rates (see section 11.2.4). The increased incidence of Tay–Sachs disease in the Jewish population is probably related to founder effects in Ashkenazi Jews (see Chapter 8).

(c) We use Eqn 10.13, setting q_t and q_0 from the values given in part (a). The solution is 681.6 generations, or 17 040 years. This shows that if the equilibrium frequency of the disadvantageous allele is changed for any reason, it will take a long time to reach the equilibrium predicted from a balance between mutation and selection. This emphasizes why it is inadvisable to use Eqn 11.2 to estimate mutation rates.

CHAPTER 12

1. (a) Heritability is equal to the parent–offspring regression coefficient, i.e. $h^2_N = 0.75$.

(b) The phenotypic variance of the F_1 generation is equal to V_E because all of the individuals are genetically identical ($V_G = 0$). Thus, from Eqn 12.1 $V_E = 2.5$. The overall variance of the F_2 generation is $V_P = 12.5$. Therefore, from Eqn 12.1, $V_G = V_P - V_E$, or $12.5 - 2.5$, or 10.0. From Eqn 12.3, $V_A = 0.75 \times 12.5$, or 9.375. Finally, from Eqn 12.2, $(V_D + V_I) = V_G - V_A$, or $10 - 9.375$, or 0.625.

(c) The overall phenotypic mean of the parental population, Y_P, is 80 cm. The parents selected to breed the next generation have an average tail length, Y_S, of 90 cm. The selection differential is calculated using Eqn 12.4, so $S = 90 - 80$, or 10 cm. The response to selection is predicted from Eqn 12.6, so $R = 10 \times 0.75$, or 7.5 cm. We can now estimate the average tail length of the offspring using a modification of Eqn 12.5 ($Y_R = R + Y_P$) so $Y_R = 7.5 + 80$, or 87.5 cm. If the average tail length of the parents had been 70 cm, we can follow the same steps to show that $S = -10$ cm, $R = -7.5$ cm and $Y_R = 72.5$ cm. Note that there is a regression in the phenotypic scores of the offspring toward the overall mean of the parental population.

CHAPTER 15

1. (a) We obtain the following l_x and m_x series for these data:

Age	l_x	m_x
0	1.0000	0
1	0.5000	1.4
2	0.1000	2.0
3	0.0375	2.4
4	0.0150	2.4
5	0	0

We then calculate $R_0 = 1.026$ (following the procedure in Table 15.1), the generation time $(T) = 1.4756$ (using Eqn 15.2) and $r_c = 0.01739$ (using Eqn 15.1). Equation 15.4 gives a value for r_m of 0.01746. This value is best calculated using your spreadsheet.

(b) Using Eqns 15.7 and 15.8, and following the procedure outlined in Table 15.2 we obtain the following survival probabilities (P_i) and fertility coefficients (F_i):

Age class I	P_i	F_i
1	0.5	0.7
2	0.2	0.4
3	0.375	0.9
4	0.4	0.96
5	0	0

The corresponding Leslie matrix is:

$$\begin{bmatrix} 0.7 & 0.4 & 0.9 & 0.96 & 0 \\ 0.5 & 0 & 0 & 0 & 0 \\ 0 & 0.2 & 0 & 0 & 0 \\ 0 & 0 & 0.375 & 0 & 0 \\ 0 & 0 & 0 & 0.4 & 0 \end{bmatrix}$$

(c) At the start the numbers in each age class are:

$$n_1 = 10$$
$$n_2 = 20$$
$$n_3 = 0$$

$n_4 = 0$

$n_5 = 0$

At time 1, the numbers are calculated as:

$n_1 = 10 \times 0.7 + 20 \times 0.4 + 0 \times 0.9 + 0$
$\times 0.96 + 0 \times 0 = 15$

$n_2 = 10 \times 0.5 = 5$

$n_3 = 20 \times 0.2 = 4$

$n_4 = 0$

$n_5 = 0$

At time 2, the numbers are:

$n_1 = 15 \times 0.7 + 5 \times 0.4 + 4 \times 0.9 + 0$
$\times 0.96 + 0 \times 0 = 16.1$

$n_2 = 15 \times 0.5 = 7.5$

$n_3 = 5 \times 0.2 = 1$

$n_4 = 4 \times 0.375 = 1.5$

$n_5 = 0$

Finally, at time 3, the numbers in each age class are:

$n_1 = 16.1 \times 0.7 + 7.5 \times 0.4 + 1 \times 0.9 + 1.5$
$\times 0.96 + 0 \times 0 = 16.61$

$n_2 = 16.1 \times 0.5 = 8.05$

$n_3 = 7.5 \times 0.2 = 1.5$

$n_4 = 1 \times 0.375 = 0.375$

$n_5 = 1.5 \times 0.4 = 0.6.$

CHAPTER 17

1. (a) The results are consistent with the definition of interspecific competition whereby each species inhibits the growth of the other. The presence of each taxon appears to reduce the abundance of the other, and when both groups are removed there is an increase in the abundance of seeds (the resource being exploited by both groups of animals). However, there are only two replicates of each treatment and control, and so it is possible that the results reflect environmental variability rather than a response to the removal of taxa. If there were more replicates, we would have more confidence in the results, provided they show the same trends.

(b) Let ants be taxon 1 and rodents taxon 2. Then $K_1 = 543$ and $K_2 = 144$, and the equilibrium densities are $N_1 = 318$ and $N_2 = 122$. We can now use Eqns 17.3 and 17.4 to solve for α and β. Thus, $N_1 = K_1 - \alpha N_2$, and so $318 = 543 - \alpha 122$, with the solution $\alpha = 1.84$. Similarly, $N_2 = K_2 - \beta N_1$ and so $122 = 144 - \beta 318$, with the solution $\beta = 0.069$.

2. (a) First, determine the zero isoclines. For *Paramecium* (species 1) the x-intercept is $K_1 = 70$, and the y-intercept is $K_1/\alpha = 70/5.5$, or 12.7. Similarly, for *Stylonychia* the y-intercept is $K_2 = 11$, and the x-intercept is $K_2/\beta = 11/0.12$, or 91.7. Draw a graph of the zero

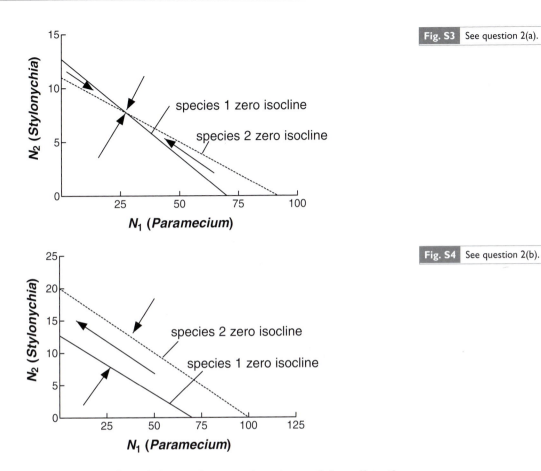

Fig. S3 See question 2(a).

Fig. S4 See question 2(b).

isoclines (Fig. S3). It may be seen that the model predicts the observed coexistence of the two species.

(b) The zero isocline of *Paramecium* (species 1) is unchanged, but for *Stylonychia* (species 2) the *y*-intercept is now 20 and the *x*-intercept is $20/0.2 = 100$. Now when we draw the zero isoclines (Fig. S4) we see that the model predicts that *Stylonychia* will out-compete and eliminate *Paramecium*.

(c) The model predicts that *Stylonychia* wins against *Paramecium*, but the reverse was observed. We note that the superior competitor (*Stylonychia*) has the lower growth rate (*r*), so the situation could resemble that illustrated in Fig. 17.8, where the species with the higher growth rate (*Paramecium*) has the advantage at high removal rates (*m*). This can be confirmed by using your simulation model and substituting the appropriate values for the two species with $m = 0.1$.

References

Adams, J. and Ward, R. H. 1973. Admixture studies and the detection of selection. *Science* 180: 1137–43.

Alatalo, R. V. and Lundberg, A. 1984. Polyterritorial polygyny in the pied flycatcher *Fidecula hypoleuca*: evidence for the deception hypothesis. *Annales Zoologici Fennici* 21: 217–28.

Alatalo, R. V., Carlson, A., Lundberg, A. and Ulfstrand, S. 1981. The conflict between male polygamy and female monogamy: the case of the pied flycatcher *Fidecula hypoleuca*. *American Naturalist* 117: 285–91.

Alcock, J. 1998. *Animal Behaviour* 6th edn, Sinauer Associates, Sunderland, MA.

Alexander, R. D., Hoogland, J. L., Howard, R. D., Noonan, K. M. and Sherman, P. W. 1979. Sexual dimorphism and breeding systems in pinnipeds, ungulates, primates and humans. In: Chagnon, N. A. and Irons, W. (eds.) *Evolutionary Biology and Human Social Behaviour: An Anthropological Perspective*, pp. 402–35. Duxbury Press, North Scituate, MA.

Allison, A. C. 1956. The sickle-cell and haemoglobin C genes in some African populations. *Annals of Human Genetics* 21: 67–89.

Anderson, J. M. and Coe, M. J. 1974. Decomposition of elephant dung in an arid, tropical environment. *Oecologia (Berlin)* 14: 111–25.

Andersson, M. 1982. Female choice selects for extreme tail length in a widowbird. *Nature* 299: 818–20.

　　1994. *Sexual Selection*. Princeton University Press, Princeton, NJ.

Ayala, F. J. and Valentine, J. W. 1979. *Evolving: The Theory and Processes of Organic Evolution*. Benjamin/Cummings, Menlo Park, CA.

Ayala, F. J., Gilpin, M. E. and Ehrenfeld, J. G. 1973. Competition between species: theoretical models and experimental tests. *Theoretical Population Biology* 4: 331–56.

Balmford, A., Rosser, A. M. and Albon, S. D. 1992. Correlates of female choice in resource-defending antelope. *Behavioral Ecology and Sociobiology* 31: 107–14.

Bateman, A. J. 1948. Intra-sexual selection in *Drosophila*. *Heredity* 2: 349–68.

Begon, M. and Mortimer, M. 1986. *Population Ecology: A Unified Study of Animals and Plants*, 2nd edn. Blackwell Scientific Publications, Oxford.

Behé, M. J. 1966. *Darwin's Black Box*. Simon & Schuster, New York.

Berglund, A., Rosenqvist, G. and Svensson, I. 1986. Mate choice, fecundity and sexual dimorphism in two pipefish species (Syngnathidae). *Behavioral Ecology and Sociobiology* 19: 301–7.

Birkhead, T. R. and Møller, A. P. 1992. *Sperm Competition in Birds*. Academic Press, London.

Bishop, J. A. 1972. An experimental study of the cline of industrial melanism in *Biston betularia* (L.) (Lepidoptera) between urban Liverpool and rural North Wales. *Journal of Animal Ecology* 41: 209–43.

Bishop, J. A. and Cook, L. M. 1975. Moths, melanism and clean air. *Scientific American* 232: 90–9.

Bodmer, W. F. and Cavalli-Sforza, L. L. 1976. *Genetics, Evolution, and Man*. W. H. Freeman, San Francisco, CA.

Bonnell, M. J. and Selander, R. K. 1974. Elephant seals: genetic variation and near extinction. *Science* 184: 908–9.

Bonner, J. T. 1965. *Size and Cycle: An Essay on the Structure of Biology*. Princeton University Press, Princeton, NJ.

Bouzat, J. L., Lewin, H. A. and Paige, K. N. 1998. The ghost of genetic diversity past: historical DNA analysis of the greater prairie chicken. *American Naturalist* 152: 1–6.

Bowland, A. E., Bishop, K. S., Taylor, P. J., Lamb, J., Van der Bank, F. H., Van Wyk, E. and York, D. 2001. Estimation and managment of genetic diversity in small populations of plains zebra (*Equus quagga*) in KwaZulu–Natal, South Africa. *Biochemical Systematics and Ecology* 29: 563–83.

Brower, J. V. Z. and Brower, L. P. 1966. Experimental evidence of the effects of mimicry. *American Naturalist* 100: 173–87.

Brown, J. H. and Davidson, D. W. 1977. Competition between seed-eating rodents and ants in desert ecosystems. *Science* 196: 880–2.

Buri, P. 1956. Gene frequency drift in small populations of mutant *Drosophila*. *Evolution* 10: 367-402.

Cairns, J., Overbaugh, J. and Miller, S. 1988. The origin of mutants. *Nature* 335: 142–5.

Carlson, T. 1913. Über Geschwindigkeit und Grösse der Hefevermehrung in Würze. *Biochemische Zeitschrift* 57: 313–34.

Carpenter, G. D. H. 1921. Experiments on the relative edibility of insects, with special reference to their coloration. *Transactions of the Royal Entomological Society of London* 54: 1–105.

Caswell, H. 2001. *Matrix Population Models: Construction, Analysis, and Interpretation*, 2nd edn. Sinauer Associates, Sunderland, MA.

Caughley, G. 1966. Mortality patterns in mammals. *Ecology* 47: 906–18.
    1977. *Analysis of Vertebrate Populations*. Wiley, New York.

Cavalli-Sforza, L. L. and Bodmer, W. F. 1971. *The Genetics of Human Populations*. W. H. Freeman, San Francisco, CA.

Charlesworth, B. 1980. *Evolution in Age-Structured Populations*. Cambridge University Press, Cambridge.

Charnov, E. L. and Schaffer, W. M. 1973. Life-history consequences of natural selection: Cole's result revisited. *American Naturalist* 107: 791–3.

Clarke, C. A. and Sheppard, P. M. 1966. A local survey of the distribution of industrial melanic forms in the moth *Biston betularia* and estimates of the selective values of these in an industrial environment. *Proceedings of the Royal Society of London B* 165: 424–39.

Cole, L. C. 1954. The population consequences of life history phenomena. *Quarterly Review of Biology* 29: 103–37.

Congdon, J. D., Dunham, A. E. and van Lobel Sels, R. C. 1994. Demographics of common snapping turtles (*Chelydra serpentina*): implications for conservation and management of long-lived organisms. *American Zoologist* 34: 397–408.

Connell, J. H. 1980. Diversity and the coevolution of competitors, or the ghost of competition past. *Oikos* 35: 131-8.
    1983. On the prevalence and relative importance of interspecific competition: evidence from field experiments. *American Naturalist* 122: 661–96.

Crombie, A. C. 1945. On competition between different species of graminivorous insects. *Proceedings of the Royal Society of London B* 132: 362–95.

Cronin, H. 1991. *The Ant and the Peacock*. Cambridge University Press, Cambridge.

Crow, J. F. 1986. *Basic Concepts in Population, Quantitative, and Evolutionary Genetics*. W. H. Freeman, New York.

Darwin, C. 1859. *The Origin of Species by Means of Natural Selection, or the Preservation of Favoured Races in the Struggle for Life*. John Murray, London.

1871. *The Descent of Man, and Selection in Relation to Sex*. John Murray, London.

Davies, N. B. 1978. Territorial defence in the Speckled Wood Butterfly (*Pararge aegeria*): the resident always wins. *Animal Behaviour* 26: 138–47.

Dawkins, R. 1986. *The Blind Watchmaker*. Oxford University Press, Oxford.

1996. *Climbing Mount Improbable*. Oxford University Press, Oxford.

de Belle, J. S. and Sokolowski, M. B. 1987. Heredity of *rover/sitter*: alternative foraging strategies of *Drosophila melanogaster* larvae. *Heredity* 59: 73–83.

Deevey, E. S., Jr. 1947. Life tables for natural populations of animals. *Quarterly Review of Biology* 22: 283–314.

Deutsch, J. C. 1994. Uganda kob mating success does not increase on larger leks. *Behavioral Ecology and Sociobiology* 34: 451–9.

Dhondt, A. A. 1977. Interspecific competition between great and blue tit. *Nature* 268: 521–3.

Diamond, J. M. 1973. Distributional ecology of New Guinea birds. *Science* 179: 759–69.

Doube, B. M. 1991. Dung Beetles of Southern Africa. In: Hanski, I. and Cambefort, Y. (eds.) *Dung Beetle Ecology*, pp. 133–55. Princeton University Press, Princeton, NJ.

Dublin, L. I., Lotka, A. F. and Spiegelman, M. 1949. *Length of Life*. Ronald Press, New York.

Dudley, J. W. 1977. 76 generations of selection for oil and protein percentage in maize. In: Pollack, E., Kempthorne, O. and Bailey, T. B. (eds.) *Proceedings of the International Conference on Quantitative Genetics*, pp. 459–73. Iowa State University Press, Ames, IA.

East, E. M. 1916. Studies on size inheritance in *Nicotiana*. *Genetics* 1: 164–76.

Elton, C. and Nicholson, M. 1942. The ten-year cycle in numbers of the lynx in Canada. *Journal of Animal Ecology* 11: 215–44.

Emlen, J. M. 1973. *Ecology: An Evolutionary Approach*. Addison-Wesley, Reading, MA.

Falconer, D. S. and Mackay, T. F. C. 1996. *Introduction to Quantitative Genetics*, 4th edn. Longman, Harlow, UK.

Feldman, M. W. 1992. Heritability: some theoretical ambiguities. In: Keller, E. F. and Lloyd, E. A. (eds.) *Keywords in Evolutionary Biology*, pp. 151–7. Harvard University Press, Cambridge, MA.

Fisher, R. A. 1930. *The Genetical Theory of Natural Selection*. Oxford University Press, London.

Frank, S. A. 1996. Models of parasitic virulence. *Quarterly Review of Biology* 71: 37–78.

Futuyma, D. J. 1982. *Science on Trial: The Case for Evolution*. Pantheon Books, New York.

1998. *Evolutionary Biology*, 3rd edn. Sinauer Associates, Sunderland, MA.

Gandolfi, G. 1972. Selection for high and low reactivity to alarm substance in the zebra fish, *Brachydanio rerio*. *Atti Società Italiana di Scienze Naturali* 113: 28–36.

Gause, G. F. 1934. *The Struggle for Existence*. Williams & Wilkins, Baltimore, MD.

Ghiselin, M. T. 1969. *The Triumph of the Darwinian Method.* University of California Press, Berkeley, CA.

Gotelli, N. J. 1995. *A Primer of Ecology.* Sinauer Associates, Sunderland, MA.

Grant, B. R. and Grant, P. R. 1989. *Evolutionary Dynamics of a Natural Population: The Large Cactus Finch of the Galápagos.* University of Chicago Press, Chicago, IL.

Grobler, J. P. and Van der Bank, F. H. 1993. Genetic variability in South African blue wildebeest (*Connochaetes taurinus*). *Comparative Biochemistry and Physiology B* 106: 755–62.

1994. Allozyme variation in South African impala populations under different management regimes. *South African Journal of Wildlife Research* 24: 89–94.

Hall, B. G. 1983. Evolution of new metabolic functions in laboratory organisms. In: Nei, M. and Koehn, R. K. (eds.) *Evolution of Genes and Proteins*, pp. 234–57. Sinauer Associates, Sunderland, MA.

1990. Spontaneous point-mutations that occur more often when advantageous than when neutral. *Genetics* 126: 5–16.

Halliday, T. R. 1978. Sexual selection and mate choice. In: Krebs, J. R. and Davies, N. B. (eds.) *Behavioural Ecology: An Evolutionary Approach*, pp. 180–213. Blackwell Scientific Publications, Oxford.

1993. Sexual selection and mating systems. In: Skelton, P. (ed.) *Evolution: A Biological and Palaeontological Approach*, pp. 264–306. Addison-Wesley, Wokingham, UK.

Hamilton, W. D. 1964. The evolution of social behaviour. *Journal of Theoretical Biology* 7: 1–52.

1966. The moulding of senescence by natural selection. *Journal of Theoretical Biology* 12: 12–45.

1975. Innate social aptitudes of man: an approach from evolutionary genetics. In: Fox, R. (ed.) *ASA Studies 4: Biosocial Anthropology*, pp. 135–55. Malaby Press, London.

Hanski, I. 1999. *Metapopulation Ecology.* Oxford University Press, Oxford.

Hanski, I. and Cambefort, Y. 1991. Competition in dung beetles. In: Hanski, I. and Cambefort, Y. (eds.) *Dung Beetle Ecology*, pp. 133–55. Princeton University Press, Princeton, NJ.

Harper, J. L. 1977. *Population Biology of Plants.* Academic Press, London.

Hartl, D. L. and Clark, A. G. 1989. *Principles of Population Genetics*, 2nd edn. Sinauer Associates, Sunderland, MA.

Heinrich, B. and Bartholemew, G. A. 1979. Roles of endothermy and size in inter- and intraspecific competition for elephant dung in an African dung beetle, *Scarabaeus laevistratus. Physiological Zoology* 52: 484–96.

Herrnstein, R. J. and Murray, C. 1994. *The Bell Curve.* Simon & Schuster, New York.

Holling, C. S. 1959a. The components of predation as revealed by a study of small mammal predation of the European sawfly. *Canadian Entomologist* 91: 293–320.

1959b. Some characteristics of simple types of predation and parasitism. *Canadian Entomologist* 91: 385–98.

1961. Principles of insect predation. *Annual Review of Entomology* 6: 163–82.

1963. An experimental component analysis of population processes. *Memoirs of the Entomological Society of Canada* 32: 22–32.

1964. The analysis of complex population processes. *Canadian Entomologist* 96: 335–47.

1965. The functional response of predators to prey density and its role in mimicry and population regulation. *Memoirs of the Entomological Society of Canada* 45: 1–60.

1966. The functional response of invertebrate predators to prey density. *Memoirs of the Entomological Society of Canada* 48: 1–87.

Huffaker, C. B. 1958. Experimental studies on predation: dispersion factors and predator–prey oscillations. *Hilgardia* 27: 343–83.

Huffaker, C. B., Shea, K. P. and Herman, S. G. 1963. Experimental studies on predation: complex dispersion and levels of food in acarine predator–prey interactions. *Hilgardia* 34: 305–30.

Hunter, L. T. B. and Skinner, J. D. 1998. Vigilance behaviour in African ungulates: the role of predation pressure. *Behaviour* 135: 195–211.

Hutchinson, G. E. 1959. Homage to Santa Rosalia, or why are there so many kinds of animals? *American Naturalist* 93: 145–59.

Jensen, A. R. 1969. How much can we boost IQ and scholastic achievement? *Harvard Educational Review* 39: 1–123.

Johnson, C. 1976. *Introduction to Natural Selection*. University Park Press, Baltimore, MD.

Karban, R. 1997. Evolution of prolonged development: a life table analysis for periodical cicadas. *American Naturalist* 150: 446–61.

Keddy, P. A. 1989. *Competition*. Chapman & Hall, London.

Kenward, R. E. 1978. Hawks and doves: factors affecting success and selection in goshawk attacks on wild pigeons. *Journal of Animal Ecology* 47: 449–60.

Kettlewell, H. B. D. 1955. Selection experiments on industrial melanism in the Lepidoptera. *Heredity* 9: 323–42.

1956. Further selection experiments on industrial melanism in the Lepidoptera. *Heredity* 10: 287–301.

Komers, P. E. and Brotherton, P. N. M. 1997. Female space use is the best predictor of monogamy in mammals. *Proceedings of the Royal Society of London B* 264: 1261–70.

Krebs, C. J. 1985. *Ecology: The Experimental Analysis of Distribution and Abundance*, 3rd edn. Harper & Row, New York.

1994. *Ecology: The Experimental Analysis of Distribution and Abundance*, 4th edn. Harper & Row, New York.

Krebs, J. R. and Davies, N. B. 1993. *An Introduction to Behavioural Ecology*, 3rd edn. Blackwell Scientific Publications, Oxford.

Lack, D. 1947. *Darwin's Finches*. Cambridge University Press, Cambridge.

1948. Natural selection and family size in the Starling. *Evolution* 2: 95–110.

1967. *The Natural Regulation of Animal Numbers*. Clarendon Press, Oxford.

1968. *Ecological Adaptations for Breeding in Birds*. Methuen, London.

Laughlin, R. 1965. Capacity for increase: a useful population statistic. *Journal of Animal Ecology* 34: 77–91.

Lederberg, J. and Lederberg, E. M. 1952. Replica plating and indirect selection of bacterial mutants. *Journal of Bacteriology* 63: 399–406.

Lees, D. R. 1981. Industrial melanism: genetic adaptation of animals to air pollution. In: Bishop, J. A. and Cook, L. M. (eds.) *Genetic Consequences of Man-Made Change*, pp. 129–76. Academic Press, London.

Lieske, D. J. 1997. Population dynamics of urban merlins. M.Sc. thesis, University of Saskatchewan.

Lill, A. 1974. Sexual behaviour of the lek-forming White-bearded Manakin (*Manacus manacus trinitatis* Hartert). *Zeitschrift für Tierpsychologie* 36: 1–36.

Lowe, V. P. W. 1969. Population dynamics of the red deer (*Cervus elaphus* L.) on Rhum. *Journal of Animal Ecology* 38: 425–57.

Luckinbill, L. S. 1979. Selection of the r/K continuum in experimental populations of protozoa. *American Naturalist* 113: 427–37.

Luria, S. and Delbrück, M. 1943. Mutations of bacteria from virus sensitivity to virus resistance. *Genetics* 28: 491–511.

MacArthur, R. H. and Wilson, E. O. 1967. *The Theory of Island Biogeography.* Princeton University Press, Princeton, NJ.

Majerus, M. E. N. 1998. *Melanism: Evolution in Action.* Oxford University Press, Oxford.

Malthus, T. R. 1826. *An Essay on the Principles of Population, as It Affects the Future Improvement of Society,* 6th edn. John Murray, London.

May, R. M. 1976. Models for single populations. In: May, R. M. (ed.), *Theoretical Ecology: Principles and Applications,* pp. 4–25. Blackwell Scientific Publications, Oxford.

Maynard Smith, J. and Price, G. R. 1973. The logic of animal conflict. *Nature* 246: 15–18.

Mayr, E. 1982. *The Growth of Biological Thought: Diversity, Evolution, and Inheritance.* Harvard University Press, Cambridge, MA.

1997. *This is Biology: The Science of the Living World.* Harvard University Press, Cambridge, MA.

McNeilly, T. 1968. Evolution in closely adjacent plant populations. III. *Agrostis tenuis* on a small copper mine. *Heredity* 23: 99–108.

McPherson, J. K. and Muller, C. H. 1969. Allelopathic effects of *Adenostoma fasciculatum,* "Chamise", in the California chaparral. *Ecological Monographs* 39: 177–98.

Merrell, D. J. 1981. *Ecological Genetics.* Longman, Harlow, UK.

Miller, K. R. 1999. *Finding Darwin's God: A Scientist's Search for Common Ground between God and Evolution.* HarperCollins, New York.

Mørch, E. T. 1941. Chondrodystrophic dwarfs in Denmark. *Opera ex Domo Biologica Hereditariae Humanae Universitatis Hafniensis* 3: 1–200.

Mountford, M. D. 1968. The significance of litter size. *Journal of Animal Ecology* 37: 363–7.

Mourant, A. E., Kopec, A. C. and Domaniewska-Sobczac, K. 1976. *The Distribution of the Human Blood Groups and Other Polymorphisms,* 2nd edn. Oxford University Press, Oxford.

Murdoch, W. W. and Oaten, A. 1975. Predation and population stability. *Advances in Ecological Research* 9: 2–131.

Murie, O. 1944. *The Wolves of Mount McKinley.* US Department of the Interior, Washington, DC.

Naylor, B. G. and Handford, P. 1985. In defence of Darwin's Theory. *BioScience* 35: 478–83.

Nichols, P. L. and Anderson, V. E. 1973. Intellectual performance, race, and socio-economic status. *Social Biology* 20: 367–74.

Nur, N. 1984. Feeding frequencies of nestling blue tits (*Parus caeruleus*): costs, benefits and a model of optimum feeding frequency. *Oecologia* 65: 125–37.

Oliphant, L. W. and Haug, E. 1985. Productivity, population density and rate of increase of an expanding Merlin population. *Raptor Research* 19: 56–9.

Orians, G. H. 1969. On the evolution of mating systems in birds and mammals. *American Naturalist* 103: 589–603.

Paine, R. T. 1966. Food web complexity and species diversity. *American Naturalist* 100: 65–76.

1974. Intertidal community structure: experimental studies on the relationship between a dominant competitor and its principal predator. *Oecologia* 15: 93–120.

Park, T. 1954. Experimental studies of interspecific competition. II. Temperature, humidity, and competition in two species of *Tribolium*. *Physiological Zoology* 27: 177–238.

1962. Beetles, competition, and populations. *Science* 138: 1369–75.

Pearl, R. 1927. The growth of populations. *Quarterly Review of Biology* 2: 532–48.

Pearl, R. and Reed, L. J. 1920. On the rate of growth of the population of the United States since 1790 and its mathematical presentation. *Proceedings of the National Academy of Sciences of the USA* 6: 275–88.

Pianka, E. R. 1970. On *r*- and *K*-selection. *American Naturalist* 104: 592–7.

1988. *Evolutionary Ecology*, 4th Edn. Harper & Row, New York.

Pimental, D. 1961. Animal population regulation by the genetic feedback model. *American Naturalist* 95: 65–79.

Pimental, D. and Stone, F. A. 1968. Evolution and ecology of parasite–host systems. *Canadian Entomology* 100: 655–62.

Pimental, D., Nagel, W. P. and Madden, J. L. 1963. Space–time structure of the environment and the survival of parasite–host systems. *American Naturalist* 97: 141–67.

Ralls, K., Brugger, K. and Ballou, J. 1979. Inbreeding and juvenile mortality in small populations of ungulates. *Science* 206: 1101–3.

Rennie, J. 2002. 15 answers to creationist nonsense. *Scientific American* 287: 78–85.

Reyer, H.-U. 1984. Investment and relatedness: a cost/benefit analysis of breeding and helping in the pied kingfisher. *Animal Behaviour* 32: 1163–78.

1990. Pied kingfishers: ecological causes and reproductive consequences of co-operatice breeding. In: Stacey, P. B. and Koenig, W. D. (eds.) *Cooperative Breeding in Birds: Long-Term Studies of Ecology and Behavior*, pp. 527–57. Cambridge University Press, Cambridge.

Roff, D. A. 1992. *The Evolution of Life Histories*. Chapman & Hall, New York.

Root, R.B. 1967. The niche exploitation pattern of the Blue-grey Gnatcatcher. *Ecological Monographs* 37: 317–50.

Rose, M. R. 1991. *The Evolutionary Biology of Ageing*. Oxford University Press, Oxford.

Rosenqvist, G. 1990. Male mate choice and female–female competition for mates in the pipefish *Nerophis ophidion*. *Animal Behaviour* 39: 1110–16.

Rosenzweig, M. L. and MacArthur, R. H. 1963. Graphical representation and stability conditions of predator–prey interactions. *American Naturalist* 97: 209–23.

Rothenbuhler, W. C. 1964. Behavior genetics of nest cleaning in honey bees. *American Zoologist* 4: 111–23.

Ruse, M. 1982. *Darwinism Defended: A Guide to the Evolution Controversies*. Addison-Wesley, London.

Schlichting, C. D. and Pigliucci, M. 1998. *Phenotypic Evolution: A Reaction Norm Perspective*. Sinauer Associates, Sunderland, MA.

Searcy, W. A. 1979. Female choice of mates: a general model for birds and its application to red-winged blackbirds (*Agelaius phoeniceus*). *American Naturalist* 114: 77–100.

Searcy, W. A. and Yasukawa, K. 1989. Alternative models of territorial polygyny in birds. *American Naturalist* 134: 323–43.

Searle, S. R. 1966. *Matrix Algebra for the Biological Sciences.* Wiley, New York.

Selander, R. K. 1976. Genic variation in natural populations. In: Ayala, F. J. (ed.) *Molecular Evolution,* pp. 21–45. Sinauer Associates, Sunderland, MA.

Sherman, P. W. 1985. Alarm calls of Belding's ground squirrels to aerial predators: nepotism or self-preservation? *Behavioral Ecology and Sociobiology* 17: 313–23.

Sherman, P. W. and Morton, M. L. 1984. Demography of Belding's ground squirrels. *Ecology* 65: 1617–28.

Slade, N. A. and Balph, D. F. 1974. Population ecology of Uinta ground squirrels. *Ecology* 55: 989–1003.

Slobodkin, L. B. 1961. *Growth and Regulation of Animal Populations.* Holt, Reinhart & Winston, New York.

Smith, F. E. 1954. Quantitative aspects of population growth. In: Boell, E. J. (ed.) *Dynamics of Growth Processes,* pp. 277–94. Princeton University Press, Princeton, NJ.

Sniegowski, P. D. and Lenski, R. E. 1995. Mutation and adaptation: the directed mutation controversy in evolutionary perspective. *Annual Review of Ecology and Systematics* 26: 553–78.

Solomon, M. E. 1949. The natural control of animal populations. *Journal of Animal Ecology* 18: 1–35.

Southern, H. N. 1970. The natural control of a population of Tawny Owls (*Strix aluco*). *Journal of Zoology* 162: 197–285.

Spooner, R. L., Mazumder, N. K., Griffin, T. K., Kingwill, R. G., Wijeratne, W. V. S. and Wilson, C. D. 1973. Apparent heterozygote excess at the amylase I locus in cattle. *Animal Production* 16: 209–14.

Statistics Canada. 1982. Mortality, 1979 and 1980. In: *Vital Statistics,* vol. 3. Minister of Supply and Services, Ottawa.

Stearns, S. C. 1992. *The Evolution of Life Histories.* Oxford University Press, Oxford.

Strahler, A. N. 1987. *Science and Earth History: The Evolution/Creation Controversy.* Prometheus Books, Buffalo, NY.

Strickberger, M. W. 1990. *Evolution.* Jones & Bartlett, Boston, MA.

Taylor, C. E. and Condra, C. 1980. *r* selection and *K* selection in *Drosophila pseudoobscura. Evolution* 34: 1183–93.

Tizard, B. 1974. IQ and race. *Nature* 247: 316.

Turner, J. R. G. 1984. Darwin's coffin and Doctor Pangloss: do adaptionist models explain mimicry? In: Shorrocks, B. (ed.) *Evolutionary Ecology, The 23rd Symposium of the British Ecological Society*, pp. 313–61. Blackwell Scientific Publications, Oxford.

Utida, S. 1953. Interspecific competition between two species of bean weevil. *Ecology* 34: 301–7.

    1957. Cyclic fluctuations of population density intrinsic to the host–parasite system. *Ecology* 38: 442–9.

Varley, G. C., Gradwell, G. R. and Hassell, M. P. 1973. *Insect Population Ecology.* Blackwell Scientific Publications, Oxford.

Verhulst, P. F. 1838. Notice sur la loi que la population suit dans son accroissement. *Correspondances Mathématiques et Physiques* 10: 113–21.

Whittaker, R. H. 1970. The biochemical ecology of higher plants. In: Sonheimer, E. and Simeone, J. B. (eds.), *Chemical Ecology*, pp. 43–70. Academic Press, New York.

Whittaker, R. H. and Levin, S. A. (eds.) 1975. *Niche: Theory and Application.* Dowden, Hutchinson & Ross, Stroudsburg, PA.

Whittaker, R. H., Levin, S. A. and Root, R. B. 1973. Niche, habitat, and ecotope. *American Naturalist* 107: 321–38.

Wickman, P.-O. and Wicklund, C. 1983. Territory defence and its seasonal decline in the Speckled Wood Butterfly (*Pararge aegeria*). *Animal Behaviour* 31: 1206–16.

Widemo, F. and Owens, I. P. F. 1995. Lek size, male mating skew and the evolution of lekking. *Nature* 373: 148–51.

Williams, G. C. 1966. *Adaptation and Natural Selection*. Princeton University Press, Princeton, NJ.

Wilson, E. O. 1975. *Sociobiology*. Harvard University Press, Cambridge, MA.

Wilson, E. O. and Bossert, W. H. 1971. *A Primer of Population Biology*. Sinauer Associates, Sunderland, MA.

Wise, D. U. 1998. Creationism's geologic time scale. *American Scientist* 86: 160–73.

Wright, S. 1969. *Evolution and the Genetics of Populations*, vol. 2, *The Theory of Gene Frequencies*. University of Chicago Press, Chicago, IL.

Yoshimura, J. 1997. The evolutionary origins of periodical cicadas during ice ages. *American Naturalist* 149: 112–24.

Index